Ronald Dworkin

THIRD EDITION

Stephen Guest

STANFORD LAW BOOKS

An Imprint of Stanford University Press

Stanford, California

Stanford University Press
Stanford, California
©2013 by the Board of Trustees of the
Leland Stanford Junior University.

The first and second editions of this book were published in 1992 and 1997
by Edinburgh University Press.
Stephen Guest, 1992, 1997

Printed in the United States of America on acid-free, archival-quality paper

Library of Congress Cataloging-in-Publication Data

Guest, Stephen, author.
  Ronald Dworkin / Stephen Guest. – 3rd ed.
     pages cm
  "The first and second editions of this book were published in 1992 and 1997 by
Edinburgh University Press."
  Includes bibliographical references and index.
  ISBN 978-0-8047-7232-7 (cloth : alk. paper) – ISBN 978-0-8047-7233-4 (pbk. :
alk. paper)
  1. Dworkin, Ronald. 2. Law–Philosophy. 3. Jurisprudence. I. Title.
  K230.D92G83 2012
  340'.1–dc23
                                                    2012016359

Typeset by Classic Typography in 10/13 Galliard

Contents

Preface

Although I confidently stated in the Introduction to the second edition of this book in 1997 that there wouldn't be a third edition, here in fact it is. Certainly the subject-matter justifies it. Dworkin has been prolific in the past 16 years, producing four important works, *Sovereign Virtue* (2000), *Justice in Robes* (2006), *Is Democracy Possible Here?* (2006) and, most notably, his significant work *Justice for Hedgehogs* (2011), besides a large number of articles and lectures. It was the publication of *Justice for Hedgehogs* that persuaded me. That work is intended by him to stand with *Law's Empire* (1986), *Sovereign Virtue*, *Freedom's Law* (1996) and *Justice in Robes* to form one large opus containing his theory of ethics, his theory of morality, his theory of politics and his theory of law, in addition to establishing his interpretive method (which is his theory of reasoning on matters of value). And so this third edition is intended bring up to date an account of his work of almost half a century (his first published piece was in 1963). In particular, I hope readers will appreciate the significance in *Justice for Hedgehogs* of his clear endorsement of the Humean principle separating the empirical world from that of value. In a way, all else, especially concerning law, follows.

I'm also motivated in returning to Dworkin by my continuing strong sense that he remains insufficiently challenged. It seems to me that serious writers only "pick" at his various views but don't confront them with the attention they deserve. For example, in spite of so much sense in Hershowitz's recent collection of essays on Dworkin (the best collection, I think), many of the writers still don't fully grasp what I think must have been obvious before even the publication of *Law's Empire* in 1986 but certainly after it, that Dworkin is not engaged in descriptive phenomenology (or, as he calls it "taxonomic jurisprudence"). Dworkin's idea that law is a subset of morality, coupled with his account of the unity of value, is powerful and compelling. It is "liberating" as he rather grandly says in *Justice for Hedgehogs*. In this third edition, I have made more efforts to consider some of the contemporary criticisms. Mostly I find that the criticisms are not actually criticisms at all but misunderstandings or lazy thinking about what Dworkin has actually written. At any rate, where I've thought a criticism carried some reputational weight but misunderstood what Dworkin has said, I've made it my business to bring this to the attention of the reader. My overall aim is to make reading Dworkin more accessible to a wider audience, perhaps those who will get the immediate good sense of the theory and thus approach it in the right frame of mind.

RONALD DWORKIN

Introduction

Lack of appreciation of the potential richness of arguments of value is a widespread modern phenomenon. Morality is thought of as a suspect branch of knowledge, as if evidenced by the common use of scare quotes around the word, as if it needed to be held in pincers. It is interesting to speculate why. Perhaps the reason is that before the coming of age of science, belief in God accompanied confidence in the making of moral judgments, but these days people generally don't believe in God and trust only the observably true claims of science. Ronald Dworkin's theory is about ethical and moral value. Most importantly, Dworkin has in the course of five decades argued, over and again, that there are right answers to questions of value, and spelt out the implications of that fact for the social practice of law, for instance, in his famous theory of rights. Perhaps it is due to the bafflement, not to say, offense, caused by this that he hasn't yet met his great critic. No one has yet effectively attacked his theories of law and politics on the grand scale as Hart did on Bentham, and Dworkin, himself, did on Hart. I believe Dworkin makes an excellent case in his most recent book, *Justice for Hedgehogs*, for saying that arguments about value are, relative to those in science, underdeveloped and misunderstood.

Without a doubt, the ordinary view, expressed through our actions and commitments, is that there are right answers to moral questions. Why should critics single Dworkin out as if he had a unique view about the objectivity of value? Even to say he's wrong is to show the speaker's belief that there are right answers to at least that judgment of intellectual value. I've seen it firsthand for myself over three decades: the "one right answer thesis," as it has become known, is the biggest block to understanding Dworkin and valuable seminar time is wasted on the question whether what Dworkin says *could* be true rather than discussing the question whether what he says *is* true. Dworkin is straightforward on all this. He has continually suggested that we dispense with this skirmishing about morality and instead do it by developing moral and legal arguments to solve questions of ethics, morality and justice. He has now formally expressed all this, since the publication of an important paper in 1996,[1] and he later reinforced his view in *Justice for Hedgehogs*, in his denial of "meta-ethics." Get on with thinking straight about ethical and moral questions—that's his message.

The arguments are relatively simple ones of logic. Someone, the argument goes, who states "there is no value objectivity" must contradict himself; he thereby makes a value judgment he believes to be objectively true. Philosophers who believe in the value of meta-ethics, by contrast, maintain that the meta-ethical statement that there is no value objectivity is essentially different from any directly ethical or moral statement one could make—such as "child torture is wrong." But what is the argument for that separation? No convincing one has thus far been offered. John Gray—who gave our very first paper at our Colloquium in Law and Social Philosophy at UCL in 1999—is a very good example because his thesis there was that not only was there no moral objectivity, but that very fact was a *morally good thing*. The most forceful argument against the denial of the possibility of moral objectivity is that someone who denies moral objectivity must deny the possibility of truth to the statement that child torture is wrong. He must therefore deny the truth of the statement that child torture is wrong, which is to affirm that child torture is morally permissible. These attempts to fiddle around with subjectivity are pointless: the subjectivist can't have his cake and eat it! It's not just that it doesn't make sense to deny morality, it is impossible.

Perhaps the problem is that people are unreflective about the way they themselves ordinarily think and talk; they won't acknowledge their own implicit assumption that moral argument is objective. I know from experience there is a jungle of misunderstanding. Here are a couple of examples. In 2007, Dworkin wrote an article for the *New York Review of Books* ("The Supreme Court Phalanx") in which he criticized a decision of the Supreme Court on the ground that it was unprincipled. The *Review of Books* then published a letter from an academic who did little more than express surprise that Dworkin was critical of the judges in that case since, the academic went on to say, that fact "cast doubt on [Dworkin's] unswerving support for the unelected judiciary." The academic describes himself as giving "a quiet, self-satisfied chuckle" when reading Dworkin's defense of the legislators in that case and he asks rhetorically whether all the Supreme Court decisions that in Dworkin's view are wrong are therefore unprincipled.[2]

I find this level of criticism, transported to the pages of the *New York Review*, baffling. Why would Dworkin's claim that the judges get the law wrong on occasion be worthy of a mention in such a distinguished publication? Why would anyone suppose that the possibility of judges being right wasn't compatible with judges getting it wrong? Obviously, if judges can get it wrong then that implies that they can get it right, too. And why can't a judge be principled but make a mistake? Or if judges are sometimes un-principled, should judges be elected? These are not difficult or deep points, yet people treat these typical positions Dworkin holds as though they were particularly 'Dworkinian' and odd. No wonder Dworkin just replied that it doesn't follow that because the Court has made an unprincipled decision that the institution of the Supreme Court is bad. It just made a bad deci-sion. Perhaps the Supreme Court employed the wrong principles, as lawyers will point out in court, and after a decision, just as frequently as they point out the use the Supreme Court has made of the right principles. Indeed, Dworkin has on many occasions in the *New York Review of Books* both praised and condemned Supreme Court decisions on the grounds that it has, and has not, decided in accordance with principle.[3] This sort of criticism of Dworkin is strikingly banal but typical; its sort has filled law journals for decades.

All this skirmishing makes little sense because Dworkin is—and this is well known—argumentative in the very best sense of spelling out the reasons he has for the many positions he holds. He writes a lot, and his arguments are clearly laid out, original, precise and always display a very high intelligence. His set of exacting arguments for the objectivity of value has been in the easily accessible public domain for many years.

Another difficulty people have in understanding Dworkin is in his merger of practice with theory. Maybe a mystique surrounds the word "philosophy." Dworkin says we can't fully engage in practice without some idea—and ide-ally a good idea—of a theoretical account of what we should or should not be doing; it wouldn't make sense to be engaged in a practice unless we had at least some notion of what were right and wrong ways of going about it. Unlike the right answer thesis, the merger of theory and practice is not how we ordinarily think and so he has spent much of his working life trying to convince us of it. The difficulties people have arise from regarding "theory" and "philosophy" as suspect words, like "value." They need demystifying. They mean the same in this context. They really do freeze people up. Richard Posner is an example. He doesn't want theory—at any rate now, for he had an influential theory of legal reasoning once—only for judges to be "prag-matic."[4] But there is no mystery and there should be no block. Theory and philosophy provide accounts that are only more abstract accounts of what we are used to and so it is difficult to see why such abstraction shouldn't be relevant to what is going on; the more abstract governs the less. I believe that dissolves the unnecessary mystique for all that is left is a more thorough account of the practice. Applied to the case of judges, I can see why the aver-age lawyer would resist philosophical understanding if they thought it had no relevance; often in fact the practices in which they are engaged will be relatively simple (you don't need "philosophy" to help you convey a house). Again, it is a matter of how it is put. Could a judge seriously say that it is of no importance to him whether his decision is fully justified?

Look how these relatively simple points are inflated amongst Dworkin's critics. Richard Posner abandons theory. But to what point? There is nothing left to explain what judges should do when he says they should be "prag-matic." Cass Sunstein has formulated something different. His view is that this theory adds little or nothing to practical reasoning; it is that judges need only concentrate on the case in hand at an "incompletely theorized" level.[5] This is, in fact, Cass Sunstein's *theory* of judicial reasoning which, presum-ably, he would have to coach judges in, so that things don't get out of hand! As Dworkin says, it is like taking a man up Everest to show it is impossible for him to climb it. In the light of both Posner's and Sunstein's criticisms, Dworkin's emphasis on practical reasoning is ironic. Perhaps more than any other jurist, Dworkin wants reasoned practical solutions; it is he, after all, who thinks we shouldn't waste time on questions of meta-value, only on whether particular judgments are, actually, right. To do it at the same time as cutting off access to the fullest possible justification, to him, is an irresponsible devolution of authority.

In an interview in *The Independent* with Angela Lambert in 1993, Dworkin said he wasn't "much good at abstract thinking." I think this remark is very interesting, especially given that Dworkin is an extremely abstract thinker. It was what struck me when I first met him in 1973. He raised the deepest questions. I think in the early days of serious legal philosophy only Ronald Dworkin and John Finnis—who had the Catholic scholastic tradition to guide him on this—firmly understood that legal positivism made sense only on the assumption that it was a moral way of viewing law. Dworkin also had an early sense of the significance of the emergence in the seventies of the philosophy of language and the relevance of Quine, Davidson and particularly Kripke, and early on wrote about the connections between the different forms of interpretation, introducing a level of abstraction that, in *Justice for Hedgehogs*, now for him spreads over the domain of all value.

But Dworkin's self-appraisal as "not good at abstract thinking" still makes sense because he thinks by example and then works backwards into abstraction. In a television interview in the seventies with Brian Magee on the then well-known *Men of Ideas* program, Dworkin said that he studied philosophy before he discovered what a "wonderful subject" law was. His early work was mostly about law. It concerned criticism of U.S. constitutional cases in the *New York Review of Books* and the development of an anti-positivist legal theory. This connection with legal cases provides a good explanation why Dworkin preferred the characterization of law as an "argumentative attitude" rather than a "model of rules." For it is in legal argument that the most consistent, coherent and advanced systematization of real moral argument takes place. Law goes backwards from cases to abstraction; moral philosophy usually goes the other way. Most academic professional moral philosophers are not particularly versed in law. Yet almost any hypothetical example that a moral philosopher thinks up will have occurred in real time at a real place and very careful (first-order) thought will have been put into resolving the problem. What's more, the form of moral knowledge the law embodies aims at coherence of statutes with judicial decisions; that is the way you convince judges to decide in your favor. Showing a moral philosopher only some of the hundreds of thousands of reported cases of the Anglo-American courts of the past three hundred years ought to be sufficient. The philosopher would discover that for every seemingly clear legal or moral rule, some human being, somewhere in the world, will throw up a situation that is new and baffling to solve. Judges and lawyers will consider the moral arguments for an ultimate proposition either way. What the legislature has decided, what previous judges have decided, will supply only part of the reasons each way. Such situations require consideration of other, hypothetical situations to test the principle: the judge's common question, common also in lawyers' offices, "What if . . . ?" Dworkin told me once that he had at times contemplated a book called *Philosophy's Tutor* that would discuss this precise point besides problems of truth and language that legal argument routinely generates.

Some lawyers who have read him and have accepted much of what he says do so because they have quickly grasped the point that legal argument amounts to virtually nothing if no value judgments are required; they get on with developing better accounts of their own fields. Two particularly distinguished lawyers, Seana Shiffrin, in constitutional law, at UCLA,[6] and Stephen Perry, in the law of tort, at Penn,[7] do this, as do a number of significant judges. On record for saying they find Dworkin's work an excellent characterization of what they are about are former Chief Justice Arthur Chaskalson, Justice Kate O'Regan and Justice Albie Sachs, all of South Africa, Lord Hoffmann, formerly of the House of Lords in the U.K., Justice Stephen Breyer of the U.S. Supreme Court, Justice Gopal Sri Ram of Malaysia, and Justice Michael Kirby of Australia.

Among Dworkin's academic readers and critics, I would single out two prominent and well-known critics who have achieved a reputation for the consistency and detail of their criticism, one the political and legal philosopher Jeremy Waldron, the other the political philosopher Jerry Cohen. Each has frequently engaged with Dworkin personally and each has responded directly to arguments that Dworkin has offered. Together they have generated a considerable body of writing. Waldron, for example, has for well over a decade pressed on Dworkin the problem of real world disagreement.[8] His criticism takes two related forms. First, that we can't realistically expect agreement on justice and that Dworkin is therefore wrong to think that our personal convictions—taking all real circumstances into account—could supply the answer about what to do. Waldron appears to think that something outside of justice is necessary (see Chapter 6). Second, since judges are an unelected minority then the judicial review of legislation is undemocratic. I think both criticisms amount to the same thing: that we need somehow to bypass what justice might demand. I can't see how that is possible. In the real world there will always be disagreement. We can't predict whether it will in fact be resolved but it is a matter of fairness or justice whether it will be resolved in the right way. That answer must allow many different ways of resolving disagreement and so that convinces me that judicial review is not necessarily unjust. Waldron fixes a procedure—outside substantive justice—to determine the way forward, and so it naturally appears to follow that legislation by majority is superior to judicial decision. But justice determines the procedure, not the other way round, and the right procedure will be contingent on the circumstances. For example, a dispute over a miner's staked claim will probably be better determined by tossing a coin than by a majority of neighboring miners.[9]

Jerry Cohen has been a critic for even longer than Waldron. He has continually criticized Dworkin's equality of resources on the ground that equality of welfare is closer to justice. Cohen defends the counter-intuitive position that the community must pay for expensive tastes.[10] Against this, Dworkin argues that it can't be egalitarian to ignore the impact of these payments on the choices of others—in economic terms, the lost opportunity costs to others. It is unfair—uncomradely—that I should contribute towards someone's refined tastes (he has taught himself to like fine cigars against the background of knowing their cost). Obviously, if someone was born with expensive requirements that unless satisfied caused that person to develop a serious physical condition, that person has a handicap and it is not a matter of taste; Dworkin has no quarrel with compensation here. I find the argument on this point, like Waldron's on the objectivity of justice, far short of what is required to get a real hook into Dworkin's theory. Criticism of Dworkin from Oxford is, I think, fairly ineffective. Legal philosophy is generally conducted in a different way. Under Joseph Raz, and a number of his students, three of whom are professors of legal philosophy with Raz at Balliol College, Oxford, legal philosophy is a non-normative, non-sociological and "conceptual" subject that, according to Dworkin's successor at Oxford, makes a virtue of being "uninteresting," in the sense that it is not intended to have impact on cases.[11] These philosophers write and talk rather as though they understood themselves to be the direct descendants of the tradition of Bentham, Austin and Hart, and they proclaim a doctrine of "legal positivism," although examination shows that it appears to follow only an apolitical version of that doctrine, barely discernible in Bentham but more discernible in Austin and Hart. Since it takes a proudly apolitical view of law, I can't see it being of help to lawyers, judges or law students in the preparation of arguments. Its declared lack of interest in the practice of law leads me to think that in a generation or two there will be no more legal positivism of the kind taught at Oxford at present.

Perhaps it is his extraordinary perception and moral commitment—these two seem to go together—that impresses me most about Dworkin. I single out both Waldron and Cohen—both brilliant philosophers—as people who perhaps underrate this quality. For him—for anyone—morality can't allow you a perspective outside yourself; you must take responsibility for your views. In Waldron's case, you can't be committed to a position that smoothes disagreement into something that *you* personally don't think is just, taking into account, of course, the circumstances in which disagreement occurs (this last is important). In Cohen's case, you can't, against all your convictions about equality (Cohen's background is Marxist egalitarianism), promote a state subsidy for expensive tastes.

I became a research student of Dworkin in 1973. I was very young and had just come from New Zealand. I arrived at University College, Oxford with all the excitement of someone fresh from the South Pacific. I wanted to study with H.L.A. Hart as I admired the clarity and logic of *The Concept of Law*. But he had just become Principal of Brasenose, and I was enormously disappointed to find a letter in my pigeon-hole saying I'd been assigned to a "Mr. Dworkin." The College porter, Douglas, was a forthright man. "Ha," he said, gloating over my misfortune, "you've got Professor Dworkin. You'll discover." I knew little of Ronnie's work then, but I'd published a paragraph on his "Is Law a System of Rules?" in which I'd forthrightly dismissed his theory, saying it was not as "instructive" as Hart's.[12] I came across Dworkin—shortly before we formally met—at a seminar in which he announced that he believed in "*natural* legal rights." The audience was skeptical. I was fascinated because the idea was so absurd to me. But I rapidly got the sense. All Dworkin meant—and means—is that lawyers engage in genuine debate, doing so by making moral judgments about rights that align with already-settled legal rights.

Supervisions with Ronnie were, to me, brilliant occasions. At our first meeting, I'd brought a hand-written essay. I arrived at his room. He was stretched out horizontally on a sofa, smoking an enormous cigar, lop-sided grin on his face.[13] I sat down upright, in an angular antique chair. He was put out that my essay wasn't typed. I suggested I read the essay to him. He was chuffed by the apparently novel nature of this suggestion. "OK," he said, "That would be very *Oxford*."

One thing I've always admired in Dworkin is his ability to "talk straight," and to say it "like it is." He does not accept implausible claims. He doesn't use jargon, or do large diagrams on the blackboard, or the 101 other academic tricks. A leading U.K. public law scholar once exclaimed to me with irritation when I'd mentioned Dworkin, "I don't *do* Dworkin talk!" The irony is that "Dworkin talk" in public law is nothing other than "rights," "morality," "equality," "freedom," "principles," "rules," "legality," "policy," "integrity," and "discretion," which are jargon-free, normal words of public law discourse.

The greatest mark of Dworkin's work is the humanity present in everything he writes. Equality is at the center, playing more than the role of a redundant qualifier to general principle and having little to do with the "leveling down" form of equality pursued in crude communism. In Dworkin's work, equality concerns decency, and links respect for others with our own self-respect. Coming from the then relatively classless New Zealand of the fifties and sixties, I understood this well, and quickly: I related it to the habit we then had in New Zealand—for all its chauvinistic connotations—of seeing others as blokes. For Dworkin, equality is not opposed to freedom but quite to the contrary celebrates it. That other person must be free, too. On the other hand, other people are part of what defines our duties, and so equality defines the limits of what we may do, as well as what we may own.

I have been lucky. Dworkin first came regularly to the UCL Faculty of Laws, generally becoming more involved from the mid-nineties with the culminating in his appointment, following William Twining, as our Quain professor of jurisprudence. That long period until 2007 when Dworkin left UCL was a golden era for me. Particularly from the mid-nineties, we were all fortunate in having the following excellent philosophers and lawyers from UCL who regularly came and contributed to the Colloquia. From the Philosophy Department, Mike Martin, Veronique Munoz-Darde, Mike Otsuka and Jo Wolff; from Laws, Julie Dickson, Dori Kimel and Riz Mokal; from Politics, Cecile Laborde, Saladin Meckled-Garcia and Colin Tyler; from the Bentham Project, Tony Draper and Philip Schofield. There were regulars from elsewhere: Ross Harrison, James Penner, Janet Radcliffe-Richards, Nicos Stavropoulos and David Wiggins. I was also landed during that period with a set of brilliant PhD students who attended all the sessions and threw themselves in wholeheartedly: Octavio Ferraz, Charlie Grapski, George Letsas, Eva Pils, Tomas Vial and Emmanuel Voyiakis. There were many students, other research students, for example, Alex Brown, Stuart Lakin and Laura Valentini. The standard they achieved was amazingly high and I'm indebted to all of them, as they know.

I have been enormously fortunate in having the best research assistant I could have hoped for. Elettra Bietti prepared the increasingly complex, and difficult to compile Bibliography, adding videos and podcasts to the long list, and she made many corrections to the text. Best, though, were her intelligent and perceptive suggestions concerning the overall coherence and substance; I'm immensely grateful to her for those.

A word, too, about UCL. Dworkin has long and wantonly trampled on the two main doctrines of our College's intellectual founder, Jeremy Bentham. We should not forget, however, that there are significant similarities between Ronald Dworkin and Jeremy Bentham. Both extol democracy, both demand principled action by government, and both think that theoretical enquiry should be motivated by a concern for practical, human outcomes.

The aim of this book is primarily to disseminate Dworkin's thought, particularly in legal theory, and particularly to give a sense of the overall coherence he achieves with other areas of value. My final word is that to appreciate the full subtlety and moral power of Dworkin's theory, you must knuckle down and read his main works. The two great books are *Law's Empire* and *Justice for Hedgehogs*. I warn you that *Justice for Hedgehogs*, while elegantly written and full of examples, is difficult and must be taken step by step. I wonder, given the—to my mind—paucity of criticism of his main theories to date, whether it will be another generation or two before what he has said in that book sinks in.

CHAPTER ONE

A Sketch of Ronald Dworkin

Ronald Dworkin's views are original and strikingly moral. He has a wide reputation as an energetic, original and highly intelligent and informed thinker who has said much of great political and practical importance. He has now for many decades been enormously cited in legal, political, philosophical and economics books and journals, and serious writers who disagree or agree with him are certainly united in thinking his ideas are of great significance.

His recent book, *Justice for Hedgehogs*, provides the most abstract and unified account. It encompasses detailed arguments for his views on method, as well as his views on ethics, morality, politics and law. In short, Dworkin thinks, like Hume, that science and value are different and there are no causal accounts of truth in value, thus making our ordinary view of free will thoroughly plausible. For him, truth represents success independently within either domain of enquiry. Value is best seen as an integral unity—no conflict—of true propositions (just as scientists say of science). His theory of *interpretation* is that our value concepts are inherently controversial and we must make "best sense" of them; in the case of ethical and moral value this means making the best ethical and moral sense. His theory of *ethics* is that we each have a duty to make our own lives valuable. His theory of *morality*, like Kant's, is that we should treat others as having lives that are equally valuable to our own while also observing our duty to make our own lives valuable; he therefore thinks our ethics—our "living well"—allows competition with others where such competition falls short of harming them. His theory of human *dignity* consists of two principles: a right to respect as an equal and a right to ethical independence. His theory of *human rights* is that their violation shows a state's contempt for, rather than a mistake concerning, human dignity, and may justify international retaliation. His theory of *politics* is that governments should respect both principles of dignity; the result is a theory of *democracy*. His theory of *law* is that law consists of the best moral interpretation of existing practices of justifying the coercive power of governments against their subjects; law is therefore a subset of politics which is, in turn, a subset of morality. Since the judicial role properly interpreted is morally integral to democracy there is no principled argument against the judicial review of legislation.

We should join this sketch with some background to his own life and times. Dworkin is an American. He was born in 1931, in Worcester, Massachusetts. His initial interest was in philosophy. He studied for the AB at Harvard College before studying for the BA in Jurisprudence at Oxford University where, at Magdalen College, he was a student of the late Sir Rupert Cross. It was there, as he said to Brian Magee, in Magee's *Men of Ideas* program on British television in the late 1970s, that he discovered his real interest.[1] He then went to Harvard Law School to study law and, after graduating, became a law clerk to the great American judge Learned Hand in the period 1957–58. He became a member of the New York bar and was an associate of the New York law firm of Sullivan and Cromwell from 1958 to 1962, where he dealt mainly with international commercial transactions. In 1962 he became a professor of law at Yale University, becoming holder of the Wesley N. Hohfeld Chair of Jurisprudence in 1968.

In 1969, Dworkin was appointed to the Chair of Jurisprudence at Oxford from which he retired in 1998. Since 1975 he has been the Sommer Professor of Law and Philosophy at New York University where he spends the Fall term of each year in particular co-chairing with Thomas Nagel the well-known Colloquium in Law and Social Philosophy in the law school. In 1998 he became the Quain Professor of Jurisprudence at University College London, where he had been an active teaching and research visiting professor since 1984. His first article was on the topic of judicial discretion, published in the *Journal of Philosophy* in 1963,[2] and there were several other articles, mainly review articles.[3] They are interesting chiefly for two reasons. First, they display the anti-utilitarian strain then beginning to emerge from the wilderness of Anglo-American political philosophy. In particular, it is possible to detect the influence of Rawls's very influential article "Two Concepts of Rules" published in 1955.[4] Second, they display a sophisticated awareness of the nuances of legal and political reasoning.

It was the publication of "The Model of Rules" in the *University of Chicago Law Review* that made his reputation.[5] This article has three characteristic

features of his later writing. It is very well written, having energy and jour-
nalistic clarity, it contains a brilliantly clear summary of the main tenets
of H.L.A. Hart's *The Concept of Law* and above all, it presents a sustained,
original and constructive attack on the thesis contained in that book. The
article, now appearing as Chapter 2 of *Taking Rights Seriously,* has not lost its
initial force and although there are changes of emphasis in his later theory
the emerging thesis is clear and, I believe, mostly unchanged.[6]

It was two years after the publication of this article that, in 1969, Dworkin
succeeded Hart to the Chair of Jurisprudence in Oxford. That Chair had
previously had an American holder, Arthur Goodhart, who had held it for
some years until Hart came to it in 1952. English jurisprudence was then in
the doldrums. As Neil MacCormick, speaking of the time, says in his book
on Hart, "Lawyers had stopped being interested in philosophy, philosophers
in law. Jurisprudence in the universities had become a routine reading and
re-reading of a canon of texts and textbooks."[7] Political theory was also in
the doldrums. The first really rigorous and exciting piece of writing, perhaps
giving a foretaste of the good writing that was to come, was T. D. Weldon's
The Vocabulary of Politics, published in 1953.[8] Things had improved at Oxford
with the publication by Hart of his work *The Concept of Law*. Without doubt,
it was because of Hart that the standard of serious legal philosophy was vastly
raised. Several other publications were of some importance in the field in
the fifties. People were beginning to assimilate Julius Stone's massive and
important three-volume work, published earlier in 1946, entitled *The Province
and Function of Law*. Others were the works, remarkable for their clarity and
breadth of thought, *Law and Social Change in Contemporary Britain* (1951)
by Wolfgang Friedman, followed by his *Legal Theory* (1967). In Britain, influential was Lloyd's *Introduction to Jurisprudence* (1959), which provided a
clear and readable summary of the major schools of jurisprudence and, most
importantly, included a large number of readings from diversely published
works of jurists (although these readings were relatively common in the
United States).

A transitional work was *Oxford Essays in Jurisprudence,* a selection of
papers on jurisprudence, edited by A. G. Guest in 1961.[9] The standard of
writing was very high, although the essays now seem curiously dated. The
tone of the volume was eclectic, consisting of varying analyses of "concepts,"
the writers dealing with topics such as "ownership," "logic in the law" and
"entitlements." With the publication of *The Concept of Law* in 1961, it seemed
that the Oxford jurisprudential die was cast. Rigor, clarity, analysis and close
attention to language were its hallmarks. There was a growing interest in the

subject, too, partly because of the growth in the numbers of students of law at the universities. The United States was not immune from these develop-ments. But the traditions in its law schools, at least for the past thirty or so years, were different. In United States law schools there is considerably more interest shown in the mechanics of legal argument in the courts. Part of the reason for this interest was the great movement in American law schools in the early part of this century towards being "realistic" about what "actually" went on in courts and away from what was perceived to be a "formalistic" tinkering with legal "doctrine." That interest, coupled with the interest, natural to citizens in the United States, in the enormous constitutional power wielded by the Supreme Court to strike down legislation, set a different tone to American jurisprudence. It is not surprising that the term, used by U.S. lawyers, a "hard case," meaning by that an intellectually difficult case, is late in gaining ground here. That term does have, of course, the connotation in the United States of "hard cases make bad law." But it does, too, retain a connection with the case which is "worth appealing," as Karl Llewellyn put it.[10] The idea has long been part of United States law. There is no equivalent in Britain, in my view, to Britain's loss.

When *The Concept of Law* was published in 1961, Dworkin's background was both of Oxford jurisprudence, when there had been big changes, and of the jurisprudential traditions of the United States. The sixties were times also of social transformation. It is not possible here to explore the causes of the particular spirit of liberalism generated in that time. The civil rights movement was already in existence, but there were greater changes impend-ing. One impetus must have been the Vietnam War. Both events were major causes of the strong feeling among thinking people of the time for coherently articulated principles of governmental conduct. That, in turn, provided an impetus towards the reinterpretation and analysis of concepts such as "rights" in a more overtly political sense. Political philosophy of this sort took off and, in 1971, John Rawls finally published his influential *A Theory of Justice,* parts of the manuscript of which had been circulating privately for some time.

This is, briefly, the setting in which we may view Dworkin's early work. The impression various thinkers have made upon his writing is not entirely clear. Rawls and Hart have obviously made a deep impression. The milieu of legal and political theorizing in which Dworkin began writing was largely their creation. Rawls's *A Theory of Justice* is a stunning articulation of political principles, especially given that it broke new ground. The same can be said of Hart in legal philosophy. But Dworkin's grasp of the requirements of political justification is more abstract than Rawls's. For example, although

Dworkin uses Rawls's idea of "reflective equilibrium," he is more direct and explicit than Rawls in employing it as a method of "constructing" moral argument, not "finding" it. Dworkin is also, like Hart, sensitive to the uses of language but not, as Hart was, influenced by the predominantly fifties school of linguistic philosophy.

People say that he has been heavily influenced by Lon Fuller and there are, too, distinct traces of what Dworkin says in the works of the American realist John Dickinson, whose 'The Law Behind Law', published in 1929, draws distinctions similar to the rules and principles distinction that permeated Dworkin's earlier work.[11] Further parallels might be drawn between Dworkin's work and the methods employed in the collection of materials widely used in United States law schools of Hart and Sacks.[12] But even though Fuller was Professor of Jurisprudence at Harvard when Dworkin was studying law there, Dworkin did not even take Jurisprudence as one of his subjects and there was little contact between them. In that period, too, in the late fifties, Hart visited Harvard and the outcome was the well-known Hart-Fuller debate on the status of legal positivism.[13] There are parallels between Fuller's ideas of the "inner morality of law" and the integrity of which Dworkin writes. I regard the close drawing of influences in this way with suspicion. There is quite a different tradition of jurisprudential thinking in the United States which expects theorizing about what happens in difficult or "hard" cases, whether the difficulties are created by vague rules or by evil legal systems.

I don't think it useful to say that Dworkin was particularly "influenced" by any particular jurists. The chief contributors besides Rawls and Hart to the milieu from which Dworkin derives intellectual support have been philosophers who write in the mainstream of philosophy (and, perhaps, economics) rather than jurists. The major philosophers here are Thomas Scanlon, Thomas Nagel and Bernard Williams. I would mention another philosopher, Gareth Evans. Evans was a philosopher who died tragically early, aged 31. He was highly gifted, and proficient in many different fields of philosophy, including epistemology and ethics.[14] In the period 1973–75, he and Dworkin gave a series of seminars in Oxford on the topic of objectivity in law and morality. These seminars were the anvil at which many ideas were forged.[15] Two things about the Evans-Dworkin relationship struck me. One was their refreshingly straightforward empirical approach to the problems. It is interesting that Dworkin described himself in an interview with Angela Lambert in *The Independent* in 1993 as not having a good abstract grasp: that he needs to see things through examples.[16] He is wrong about abstraction, although he is refreshingly free of the "-isms" and jargon of academic pretension, but it is certainly true that he makes the most skilful use of example; it is natural to a lawyer. His latest book *Justice for Hedgehogs* is a *tour de force* of philosophy by example. After Evans and Dworkin had given some sessions, the idea that truth might "exceed its demonstrability" was finally clarified. This idea, as you will see, is vital to understanding Dworkin's view about the objectivity of value. Evans and Dworkin then invited a number of people, on separate occasions, from other disciplines and, after explaining the problem, subjected them to the most exacting cross-examination. The point was to see whether the idea was accepted in other disciplines that propositions could be true without demonstration or proof; clearly that idea is widely accepted except by many philosophers (who, when pushed, appear to think that their skepticism about its truth also meets the test). I remember a young mathematics don, not really knowing what Dworkin and Evans wanted to know, showing clearly that he thought that maths would be impossible if all its propositions had to be proved to be true. Evans forced Dworkin to be clearer. He had an irreverent style which exactly suited this stage of the development of Dworkin's thought. Much of what was said in that period by Dworkin was published in the following ten years. A particular memory I have is when Evans forced Dworkin to say what the connection was between the justification of decisions in hard cases and the ordinary rules that make up the bulk of the law. Dworkin replied that he thought the justification was the same as the justification of the settled rules. Evans—we all did—exclaimed with a noise of contentment. One of the thrills of those early sessions (attended by only a smattering of BCL students wary of "theory" and who tailed off—but also regularly attended by Joseph Raz, John Finnis, John Mackie, and John MacDowall) was to see how Dworkin would crystallize an idea before the audience; at times it was dramatic. I've seen it since, many times.

The force of that memory will seem trite to those familiar with Dworkin's subsequent publications. But this was before the publication, in 1977, of his collection of essays, *Taking Rights Seriously* and, more significantly, in a time when it sounded perverse to say that democratic principles had anything to do with justifying legal decisions. When I encountered Dworkin at the first seminar he was giving in a series on legal rights (again with Gareth Evans), I was fascinated—affronted—to hear him say that he believed in "natural legal rights." To a positivist, more (myself included) Anglo than American then, this sounded so crass—wrong in so many ways. We knew what a "natural" lawyer was. He may have believed in "natural rights" but would more likely have disapproved of the idea of "rights" at all. But *legal* rights—it seemed it could be a positivist assertion; Dworkin's statement could not be fitted into any category which I had encountered. Perhaps the hold of these categories is still strong. Students try to pigeon-hole him as either a positivist or a natural lawyer. For a long time, at a higher academic level, interpretation of Dworkin was marked by an assumption that he must be one or the other, an assumption that should have been rendered unnecessary by the publication of *Law's Empire* in 1986 but wasn't.[17]

Jerry Cohen recently (2009) remarked to me that Dworkin was the most "original" thinker he knew.[18] Nevertheless, there were background influences. He has long had a stable background. His marriage to the daughter of a wealthy New Yorker, Betsy Ross, was long and happy and the economic and emotional stability—and the glamour—of this must have helped enormously.[19] Since Betsy's death, his relationship and recent marriage to Renee Brendel shows the same order of stability and glamour. Dworkin's ability was recognized early on. He became clerk to the famous U.S. justice Judge Learned Hand. After that, Dworkin flew round the world ("mostly to African states," he told me), very young, engaged in international commercial transactions for Sullivan & Cromwell, the big New York firm. Although Dworkin and Hand were of different political temperaments, clearly Hand made a big impression on him, in particular in his articulation of the idea of a "case to be argued" (so different from the English "what is the rule?"). Dworkin is impressed by good judges—and horrified by bad ones—and understands, as philosophers generally do not, the extraordinary richness, range and depth of moral judgment—constituting the rich and highly structured resource of moral knowledge—that the published law reports contain. Thomas Nagel, professor of law and philosophy at New York University law school, has chaired with Dworkin the well-known Colloquium in Legal and Social Philosophy since 1981 (it is still going), the sister form of which runs at University College London, with Dworkin chairing it from 1999 until 2007. In Oxford, there have been regular seminars which he has attended. The names are numerous, but prominent would be Raz, Finnis, Jerry Cohen and the economist Amartya Sen. There was also a well-known series of seminars with Bernard Williams and Derek Parfit.[20]

I think, however, that a search for origins in Dworkin's case is fruitless. His attitude is explicit interest in problems of the moral justification of law, state and morality. He goes directly to the problem; relentless enquiry into what other people say is not his aim. I would emphasize the intensity of his concern for the effect of philosophy. He wants what he says to be understood and acted upon. He has strong convictions and that is not—extraordinarily—quite understood, particularly in the United Kingdom, where it is found idiosyncratic. An example is the criticism, which is frequently made of Dworkin's model for the ideal judge, whom he calls "Hercules," that Hercules is really Dworkin himself. How could it be a criticism? Dworkin will, of course, put into Hercules' mouth what he, Dworkin, thinks Hercules should say. It would be strange if he didn't. Again, a criticism is made that Dworkin's views are those broadly of the liberal left. That is true, but why is that a criticism? Perhaps the arguments favor liberalism. Again, "his idea" that there are right answers to questions concerning value—which is at least an ordinary view—is taken to be a form of arrogance or "just bizarre."[21]

Although you do not find in Dworkin's writings detailed analyses of what other philosophers have said, it is clear that he has a complete mastery of contemporary debates and an impressive breadth of background knowledge ranging through theories of ethics, aesthetics, economics, language and logic. In *Justice for Hedgehogs* it becomes clear that he is at ease with the Greek philosophers, Hobbes, Hume and Kant. He has published a lot, but the best way to make headway with understanding his thoughts is to hear him philosophize in person. Perhaps he has the air of the Continental café philosophers. He has the extraordinary capacity to deliver a complicated but logically structured argument without recourse to any form of notes. His Maccabaean lecture to the British Academy, delivered in 1977, was such a performance. It was well over an hour long and, for you to judge, the resulting lecture is published, practically verbatim, as Chapter 1 of his collection of essays, published in 1985, *A Matter of Principle*.[22] He is often described as "a performer," at least in the U.K. where he is regarded, I think, as a more of an oddity than he is in the United States (I could be wrong about this). In England, a "performer" could be someone who speaks without substance, an actor; I've no doubt, for example, that many people think the ideal university professor is Stephen Fry. Dworkin has charismatic appeal which arises from his intellectual confidence, sometimes mistaken for arrogance. I've observed it many times—he has a great deal of what might be called, for want of better words, raw intelligence; he understands a point immediately and the rapidity with which he can think of a counter-argument, with an example, is uncanny. Anyone coming to hear Dworkin speak does not get a performance in the actor's sense at all; it is hard work to keep up.[23] This sort of talent is common in music—improvisation, spouts of brilliance, direction—and we take that for granted there; not now, I believe, in much of academic life where, wrongly and sadly, dull conformity to government-set norms has become mainstream.

Let me return to the short and compressed characterization of Dworkin's thought I gave earlier. On law, his intention is to cultivate in us an *argumentative* attitude to law. In fact, it is useful for understanding his work to think of him as a lawyer, or a judge, who is busy spelling out all the arguments pertaining to his function. He is different from the ordinary lawyer, however, because he has set himself the task of justifying all the conceivable arguments. He wants to characterize the best possible justification for making some decision that affects people. I accept this aim, as you will see throughout this work. To me, any account of law that relegates the question of justification to minor status misses one of the most important points about understanding law. That's not to deny that accounts of law that underplay or deny the force of moral justification are possible. It is interesting to consider in what sense one would understand a comparative history of evil legal systems. Wouldn't one first have to appreciate what, for comparison, a non-evil legal system was?[24]

I think it helps to keep this picture of legal argument as a central focus of Dworkin's legal theory. It provides a useful angle of comparison with other legal philosophers, some of whom saw themselves as providing only a descriptive account of how social practices just simply happen to be. Dworkin's idea of interpretation is crucial (see Chapter 4). He does not think that we can get very much sense out of just describing "what law is like." Our whole perception of all those rules and institutions, including courts and legislatures, police, and so on—what may loosely be described as "the social practice of law"—must be colored by our judgment. What we must do is sharpen that judgment. We must try to make "the best sense" of these social practices. Dworkin develops the idea of interpretation relatively late in the elaboration of his work on law; it makes clearer a number of his earlier doctrines, in particular his well-known distinction between rules and principles. The basic idea is that you make the best of what you have before you. I find practicing barristers are attracted to this idea. "What argument can be made from this?" they say, presenting a regulation, or a case.

For Dworkin it is a short step from the idea of "making the best sense" of something to morality. His perspective on law is that of justification. We must interpret the law to make the best 'moral' sense of it. In other words, we must always assume when we try to work out what the law requires or permits that it makes *moral* sense. What is the point, he asks, of justifying action in the name of law unless that action has also a moral justification? This is the major concern of Dworkin's moral and political theory and rests upon what we might call his foundational principle: that people should be treated with equal concern and respect. When we are making sense of law, we must assume that its best sense expresses an equal concern for people.

You should be able to see the critical power this theory has for practice. Which of two rival interpretations of a rule of law is better? For Dworkin, the one that more closely accords with the foundational principle. But, contrary to a popular misunderstanding of Dworkin, this does not mean that in order to work out the law you merely make law into whatever is necessary to treat people as equals. This is the thrust of the charge that Dworkin makes the law irredeemably "subjective." Dworkin has detailed answers to this objection and it is very important to see that these answers are not central to his theory. Dworkin thinks that his theory of law is right, which is natural. He offers reasons to support his theory. He looks for criticisms. What he regards as a side issue is the seemingly more abstract and important question of whether any kind of "objective" argument is possible for law. Instead, he asks you to tell him where he has made mistakes in the arguments. Objectivity involves nothing more startling, in his view, than the possibility of seeking the best answers. For him that does not mean thundering knock-down arguments.

In fact, Dworkin is pleasingly candid in his approach to methodology. His approach is intuitive and practical, in a thoroughly lawyerlike way. Of course, intuition alone is not enough, as most of us would agree. But Dworkin provides us with many of his intuitive insights, mixed with attempts to explain them in a structured account. This method bothers some people. Why should we be introduced to another person's intuitions? We either accept them or we do not. We want arguments. However, that is too simple. Arguments cause us to change our intuitions; our intuitions cause us to change our arguments. It is a two-way process which works and describes the actual arguments that we have in daily life. It should not appear so strange.

Dworkin's theory is part of a massive project he has been developing for over thirty years. It is ambitious. The legal part of it is fairly settled now, with the publication in 1986 of *Law's Empire*. But it is part of his idea that moral, legal and political philosophy—and legal argument—form part of a whole unified theory of value; each conviction we hold for one part must be justified in the light of all other convictions we hold. I can introduce his legal theory through the terms with which he has become associated. His theory of *discretion* is simply that judges are legally constrained in the exercise of their power of final decision. Even though existing legal practices do not supply a definitive answer, the judge must nevertheless make a substantive judgment about what decision best *fits* the settled law. So the judge is bound by law and is not permitted to use his power of decision-making in a stronger sense. In the *hard cases*, which are those where the existing legal practices do not supply a definitive answer, the judge cannot rely on *rules* because, by hypothesis, there are no rules. Instead, he must rely on standards of legal argument which Dworkin calls *principles*, paramount among which is the foundational principle that people must be treated as equals (as in the expression "all people are equal before the law"). Principles, unlike rules, do not apply in an "all-or-nothing" sense, but require argument and justification of a more extensive, controversial sort. As a matter of justice, people have *rights* to treatment as equals. That means, for Dworkin, that the foundational principle cannot be compromised. You cannot say: if we end up with most people better off, that would justify our not treating some people as equals. So Dworkin would disallow the pursuit of community goals which overrode these rights to treatment as equals. In other words, to take rights seriously, we must view them as "trumping" those community goals that depart from the basic equality right. We could not interpret our actually existing legal practices so that they accorded with justice as equality in an ideal world. That could not amount to an interpretation of the *law*. But it is true, too, that the best interpretation of the real law could not succeed in showing that all laws were fair, say. A proper interpretation of the law, according to Dworkin, lies in the idea of *integrity*. Through this idea we must personify the law—treat it as having its own integrity—so that it takes on a moral character, one that consistently treats people as equals. Legislative and judicial events of the past relate to decisions of the present by being part of one integral picture: the community's *equal* commitment to its citizens. Above all, law is an argumentative attitude which rises out of a concern with the extent of the coercive power of the law. "Law's empire," Dworkin says, is "defined by attitude." That attitude "is constructive: it aims, in the interpretive spirit, to lay principle over practice to show the best route to a better future, keeping the right faith with the past."[25]

You should see now that, for Dworkin, questions of law are questions of morality about the legal institutions and practices we have. At the same time, his theory is intended to be practical, in the obvious and appealing sense, and it denies any importance to the distinction between the mundane and the abstract.

CONTEMPORARY DWORKIN

Dworkin moved from Oxford in 1998 fairly dissatisfied with the state of jurisprudence there. UCL was much more congenial. The Dean, Jeffrey Jowell, was intellectually receptive and sympathetic not just to philosophy but to the moral foundations of constitutionalism, particularly judicial review. The UCL Philosophy department contained a relatively large number of moral and political philosophers. The UCL Political Science department had just been established and it, too, had capable political philosophers. There was a group of talented PhD students who hopped between the departments. The mood was liberal, evaluative and practical. Oxford Jurisprudence had, in Dworkin's (and our) view, become sterile. In 2004 Dworkin published his "Hart's Postscript and the Character of Political Philosophy." Towards the end of it he wrote the following telling passage:

> A while ago, talking to Professor John Gardner of Oxford University, I said that I thought that legal philosophy should be interesting. He jumped on me. "Don't you see?" he replied. "That's your trouble." I am guilty of the charge. But let me say what I mean by "interesting." I believe that legal philosophy should be of interest to disciplines both more and less abstract than itself. It should be of interest to other departments of philosophy—political philosophy, of course, but other departments as well—and it should be of interest to lawyers and judges.[26]

Dworkin was bothered by the school of legal positivists who surround the distinguished Oxford legal philosopher Joseph Raz. Unlike Dworkin, Raz had many doctoral students and many of them have prominent positions in law and philosophy departments in the Anglo-American world; they are loyal to Raz and to Raz's teacher, H.L.A. Hart. Dworkin thought, and here a substantial number at UCL agreed with him, that Raz's "descriptive, neutral" approach to law would go nowhere. Raz taught that legal philosophy concerned questions of the "nature" of law, not questions of the application of law in particular legal systems; nor was legal philosophy at all connected with political philosophy, or moral questions generally. There was enmity I observed when Raz came to give a paper at the Colloquium in 2000. Dworkin would make what Raz would regard as a sweeping remark; Raz would pick up a copy of one of Dworkin's books and say something like "But at footnote 145 you contradict what you said at" (picking up another book) "pages 45–48 of . . . " At one stage, Dworkin said, "Stop trying to draw blood." We all looked down at our notes! Perhaps, since this book is about Dworkin, he should have the last word. This group of positivists, he said in the *Harvard Law Review* of 2002, was analogous to a group of "scholastic theologians" who fervently defend a "guild-claim"[27] that what they do is (i) not the practice of law nor is it of the law of particular jurisdictions because legal philosophy is about the nature of law, (ii) not about normative political philosophy because legal philosophy is descriptive and conceptual, (iii) nor about sociology or the anthropology of law because these are empirical disciplines:

> It is, in short, a discipline that can be pursued on its own with neither background experience nor training in or even familiarity with any literature or research beyond its own narrow world and few disciples.[28]

Hart has said, and I believe it to be true, that if Dworkin's theory does not succeed in catching on, it will be because people will not accept the idea that there can be right answers to legal questions when there is no means of *showing or demonstrating* what the right answers are.[29] Dworkin's theory of law must also allow for this possibility because, for him, a legal theory must be "interpretive" of a prevailing political and legal culture. If it interprets a culture in which people just do not accept that there is competition of principles, only conflict, then positivism might be the only liberal legal theory that can make sense of—be interpretive of—that culture. Hart's comment is not a serious criticism. Dworkin's theory better describes the Anglo-American legal and political culture. Indeed, the arguments of descriptive "fit" that he provides equal, in my view, his arguments of moral substance. My own experience with many practicing lawyers, and with many students, at least in the United Kingdom, is that his theory provides a good characterization. Nevertheless, some lawyers say the opposite: they say that Dworkin misunderstands the role of judicial deference, that finding out the law takes no moral effort, only the effort of finding the precedents and regulations.

I believe attending a courtroom is a good test. Let us take the English High Court, although any appeal court in the United States will be similar. Two barristers begin the day with various provisions of the Factories Act 1961 before them. In an hour's time they will face each other before a judge. Each will supply an argument, one to support the truth of a proposition that the defendant, in the particular circumstances of the case, had a legal duty to fence dangerous machinery, the other to say that same proposition is false. Each side will have the same cases and will be familiar with their contents. Each knows that the defendant has a right to a fair hearing. Each knows that there is no "answer" waiting in a statute, or in a case, and that the answer lies in the best interpretation of the statutory provisions and the cases. They know that the judge will try to get the answer "right." They know that they and the judge could be mistaken. They believe that what they are doing is not nonsense. They believe, in advancing their arguments, that these are *legal* as well as moral arguments. They don't at all think that when they are making judgments about fairness, or the justice of it, that they are suddenly abandoning the law and going out on their own. They make subjective judgments about what they believe to the objective requirements and permissions of law.

It is difficult to give a general characterization of Dworkin's thought. Richard Posner has wondered whether Dworkin is a "genuine Kantian" or a "utilitarian of the egalitarian school."[30] In the idea that people have rights to treatment with equal concern and respect, he *is* a Kantian. This very abstract principle in Dworkin's thought asserts the importance of people as ends and not means. It asserts too in the idea of equality, Kant's insistence on the universalizable characteristic of moral rules. Neil MacCormick once described him as a "pre-Benthamite," meaning that Dworkin does not share the modern perspective that distinguishes legal fact from legal value, or, in Bentham's terms, does not insist on the separation of "expository" from "censorial" jurisprudence.[31] There are strains of Bentham, however. Contrary to a common belief, Dworkin is not wholly dismissive of utilitarianism. Since his political theory relies extensively on the idea of the interpretation of existing political practices, many of which are broadly recognizable as utilitarian, some of his ideas take a background of utilitarianism for granted. Indeed, his central idea of rights depends for its force on its ability to "trump" background arguments for increasing average utility. But in the ideal world, his abandonment of the idea of welfare as a metric[32] means that Dworkin does not accept utilitarianism, even in the "egalitarian" form in which he thinks it makes most sense. On the other hand, Bentham's insistence on the importance of a public criterion for law is not far from Dworkin's insistence on publicly articulated principles of official decision-making. Further, going back to Bentham's distinction between the exposition of law and its critique, that distinction was founded, not upon a description of "how things in fact are," but upon the utilitarian merit of the distinction: Bentham thought that Jurisprudence, not facts, should determine how the jurist viewed his materials.[33]

What about Mill? Dworkin's use of the idea of the equality of individuals in the construction of a private sphere of resources publicly protected leaves us with what, at first sight, is a Millian conception. On closer inspection, it turns out that Dworkin's idea of individuality is less private than Mill's. The private sphere is "parametered" (his word) by justice which is a matter of the public domain, and a person's life is to be critically measured by his acting within the parameters.[34] Thus Plato's idea of the "just man," as opposed to the "just system," is closer to Dworkin than to Mill.[35] On the other hand, it is a Millian idea that people ought not to be able to have a "second" count in the utilitarian calculus, when that has an effect on other people's lives.[36] That is very close to Mill's idea of other-regarding action. But Mill was, after all, a welfare utilitarian, and since, as we shall see in Chapter 10, Dworkin abandons welfare as a metric of a just distribution, he is clearly not a utilitarian of the Millian sort.

These comparisons are unhelpful. Dworkin does not fit into an orthodox category. His theory of law is radical in seeing legal argument as primarily about rights, yet conservative in seeing such argument as constrained by history. He is libertarian both in valuing ambition and asserting a right to pornography, yet socialist in believing that no person has a right to a greater share of resources than anyone else. In particular, he advocates a tax on resources people accumulate solely through their talent, as opposed to the exercise of their ambition. Although he makes use of modern economic thinking, he abandons the orthodox criterion of measurement by welfare, for a metric of resources. Finally, he is neither a liberal "atomist" nor a "communitarian," thinking that the distinction does not make more than superficial sense. I think such considerations classify him as a unique and original thinker.

It is necessary now to turn from background to the detail of Dworkin's legal and political theories. I have said that his legal theory is distinctive both in its attack on legal positivism, as he interprets it, and his unification of legal argument with political and moral argument. In *Justice for Hedgehogs* he is explicit that law is a subset of political thought which is a subset of moral thought.

Because much of his work derives from his exploration of legal theory, and because he achieved early recognition from his attacks on a well-known legal theory, I examine legal positivism first. I particularly dwell on one version of that theory which he early on called the "plain fact" view of law. So, I believe, the chronological understanding of Dworkin helps. Linked to this discussion is an examination of the alternative ways Dworkin proposes for looking at the difficult or "hard" case in law. I then look at Dworkin's methodology, dealing with his important approach to the idea of understanding certain human practices, in particular creative practices, and his idea of "interpretive" concepts.

I then look at his legal theory which finds its expression in the idea of integrity. I examine the idea, especially as it relates to his theory of adjudication, and in Chapter 6, I examine the link between legal and political obligation, which Dworkin casts in the form of fraternal association, or community.

I spend Chapter 9 a chapter examining his latest and, I think, most important book, *Justice for Hedgehogs*, on the unification of value, particularly ethical and moral value, and the independence of value from science and empirical truth generally. Given its general subject-matter, obviously that book both draws upon and explains other parts of Dworkin's full theory and I have referred throughout to where it has done so. In Chapter 9 I look at those parts of *Hedgehogs* that are new.

Although it is necessary to know a certain amount about his moral and political theory for the purposes of his legal theory, it certainly is not necessary to know it all. I have left discussion of this part of the theory to the later section. I should say, however, that the idea of the equality of "resources" has consequences for some legal cases, particularly the economic analyses of negligence and nuisance, and the central idea of the impartiality of political principles has consequences for cases involving matters of personal morality.

In Chapter 10, I examine the important distinction between resources and welfare in the context of the idea of equality, as well as Dworkin's view that only equality of resources respects the idea of liberty. In Chapter 11, I examine Dworkin's earlier justification for the foundation of the principles of political liberalism. The arguments there are largely drawn from what he said before *Justice for Hedgehogs*, particularly in his Tanner lectures of 1990. There is a change of emphasis to be found in *Justice for Hedgehogs* but I don't think that he has fundamentally changed his ideas. His views on ethics—how we should live our lives—are presented there a little austerely; or at least that is one way of reading what is called from time to time his "challenge" theory.[37] But I don't think that theory is inconsistent with the idea—prominent in *Justice for Hedgehogs*—that one's own responsibility to live our personal lives well would, given morality's derivation from personal ethics, be a component of how we should treat others morally. At any rate, I think it is important to provide, as I have, an independent account of his thinking before the publication of *Justice for Hedgehogs*.

It seemed fitting to bring several interesting things Dworkin says about religion together with the idea he has used significantly in his extensive writing on abortion and euthanasia, that of "secular sacredness." This all appears in the final chapter, Chapter 12.

CHAPTER TWO

Law as Plain Fact

Dworkin's contribution to jurisprudence in the past forty years is marked by his sustained criticism of a particular way of viewing law and legal argument. In particular, he is critical of a widely influential idea, known as legal positivism, which, briefly, asserts that morality is irrelevant to the identification of law. That doctrine began with Thomas Hobbes[1] and developed into contemporary sophisticated forms, those of H.L.A. Hart and Joseph Raz, for example. Dworkin's attack on it is sustained and detailed. One of the marks of his writing is his insistence on the point of legal positivism. Had no one thought of this before? Asking for point, or purpose, is an ancient tradition beginning with Aristotle. Long before legal positivism, Aristotle and Aquinas, to name only the most distinguished, asked practical questions about how we should regard law, and they supplied answers. Were the legal positivists so unclear on the purpose of positivism? It is an interesting question. I believe Bentham, sometimes called the father of legal positivism, thought legal positivism had utilitarian point (see Chapter 1). Other legal positivists are ambiguous, Hart and Kelsen, for example. That ambiguity hovers between the following two strands of thought.

First, there is a sense in which some legal positivists intended simply to "describe" law. Law is simply there, as a complex of social facts. It certainly was the intention of John Austin, his disciple, and, albeit in a highly qualified sense, of the German legal philosopher Hans Kelsen who referred approvingly to the "legal scientist."[2] Hart's brilliant work *The Concept of Law* certainly begins in that way, with its well-known affirmation in the Preface that, among other aims, he intended a "descriptive sociology" of the law.[3] That is one strand of legal positivism. This idea of law is behind our comparative account of repressive legal systems. Such an account can, of course, serve practical purposes, such as those of historians, or dictators, or anthropologists in search of differences between legal systems. The second strand is practical in, I suggest, a more obvious sense: the law must be identifiable by means of clearly identifiable and public criteria to enable the citizen to keep distinct the demands of his conscience and the demands of the state. Hart spoke for this strand of positivism when he said in *The Concept of Law*:

> What surely is most needed in order to make men clear sighted in confronting the official abuse of power, is that they should preserve the sense that the certification of something as legally valid is not conclusive of the question of obedience, and that, however great the aura of majesty or authority which the official system may have, its demands must in the end be submitted to a moral scrutiny.[4]

It is a liberal idea, and not a coincidence that the growth of positivism paralleled the growth of liberalism in the early nineteenth century. The idea is explicit in Bentham's distinction between "expository" and "censorial" jurisprudence,[5] in Austin's claim that "the existence of law is one thing; its merit or demerit is another,"[6] and later in Kelsen's promotion of law as "science" to counteract tyranny.[7] Ronald Dworkin's theory of law is liberal, too. It is infused with the liberal idea that the state must protect personal autonomy in requiring the abstract and liberal "right to be treated with equal concern and respect" to be debated, through controversial conceptions of that idea, as a matter of law. Here Dworkin's theory departs from positivism. He nevertheless demands the "articulate consistency" of public officials.[8] This is in part what he means by decisions being made in accordance with principle; to this extent, his theory shares the public criterion requirement of the positivists.[9]

Positivism's strong moral virtue is to pronounce the limits of state requirements. It tells us where the law stops and ideology begins; in a culture where there is less homogeneity of political opinion and where there are irreconcilable ideological or fundamentalist conflicts of view, positivism will be attractive for liberalism.[10] According to positivism, since there can be little controversy about what the state requires, ideology cannot be smuggled within the name of law. In parts of continental Europe, and in Latin America, this feature of positivism is thought to be its virtue. The culture of a political community is not necessarily submerged by conflict; competing ideas and interests can be a healthy part of a culture. We can unite through understanding diversity of opinion. An existing consensus might be that convictions of certain kinds matter, say, convictions about democracy, or equality, or rights, and that arguments about these issues just happen to be controversial. I think this more sophisticated homogeneity is true of both the United States and the United Kingdom. It is a good thing. It needs to be protected. It allows for the possibility of a more sophisticated way of viewing law. In communities where people accept that their views compete rather than conflict, legal positivism's stark declaration that law starts where ideology ends is unnecessary. In the United States, the homogeneity largely arises through a strong history of democracy and through the strong central force in argument of the publicly known and written constitution. In the United Kingdom, sophisticated homogeneity has, perhaps, grown in more homely ways. There is less by way of a publicly understood set of principles regulating the political constitution of the United Kingdom. On the other hand, the culture is less diversified than the United States and there is a strong tradition of tolerance and informed and articulate argument.

A chronological account of Dworkin's work would take his criticisms of legal positivism as its starting-point since, like Hart, whose theory evolved from his criticism of the command theory of law, Dworkin's general theory evolved from his criticism of legal positivism. But too often the force of his own theory has been obscured or misunderstood either because people say he does not characterize positivism fairly,[11] or because people have not understood—or read—Dworkin's later developed value-laden "interpretive" account of law. I think Dworkin rightly attacks a view of law which he originally called the "plain fact" view; Dworkin views any account of law in terms of empirical, descriptive, propositions, as a "plain fact" or "external" view of law.[12] I think this view provides a popularly accepted form of legal positivism; I also believe that form is explicit in the early part of Hart's *The Concept of Law*. In this chapter I shall explore the attractions and limitations, as Dworkin sees them, of the plain fact view.

This plain fact view of law has an understandably wide appeal. It asserts that the law is identified ultimately either by reference to what is agreed (by a specified group—a "source" of law in some "social fact") or to some other empirical fact. To illustrate, we can consider the English law of murder. It seems undeniable that this includes causing death within a specified period from an act done with the intention either to cause death or grievous bodily harm and in the absence of lawful excusing or justifying circumstances. Lawyers accept that the "plain facts" of the English law of murder say that. No one who knows anything about English law would sensibly deny it; it is a fact of the English legal system. An examination of this view directs our attention to two serious sources of confusion in legal and political philosophy:

first, the idea that legal concepts include *agreed* criteria as to their application (that is, legal concepts are "criterial"). The second is the idea that empirical facts in the world determine the law even more directly, by supposing it is just some other existing empirical fact. Both issues, I believe, are answered solely by Dworkin's dismissal of the idea that empirical facts of any kind—our agreements, or all other things empirically determinable ("morons") could determine matters of value.

What is special—interesting—about the plain fact view of law is not any metaphysical status it has. Instead, its interest lies in its moral and therefore practical appeal. It is not a value-free metaphysical explanation at all of law but a largely implicit proposal for promoting, amongst others, the values of certainty and the independence of the citizen.

THE APPEAL OF PLAIN FACT POSITIVISM

Note that we can describe, in some detached way, what people ought to do without affirming the value by which we measure their behavior. I can say that a chess player "ought" always to move their pawn forwards on the board, meaning only that, on my reading the rules, I see those rules require it. Or, being the only bilingual prisoner of war, I can describe the orders of the prison commander in translation to my fellow prisoners.[13] The possibility of detached descriptions of normative behavior is important for understanding modern jurisprudential debate. It seems plausible to many that a theory of law should describe "the social phenomenon" of law; we can describe law as normative but we don't have to commit to what it requires. This at any rate is how many people understand *The Concept of Law*, including Hart himself. That common view overlooks the possibility that we might undetachedly choose to look at law from a detached viewpoint. We might think that an account would be better if it were "said in the words of those witnessing it"; for example, presenting historical events through other people's interpretations in contemporaneously written diaries. The choice to interpret history that way would presumably not be undetached, because it might have been chosen to serve some value such as theoretical elegance and coherence. But it could also be a straightforward moral choice where, say, eye-witness reports of executions make the moral wrongness of events striking. There is moral judgment involved in the putting to use of the detached eye of the camera.

Legal positivism declares that morality is ultimately irrelevant to the question of what is legally valid. Hart's definition is as follows:

Here we shall take Legal Positivism to mean the simple contention that it is in no sense a necessary truth that laws reproduce or satisfy certain demands of morality, though in fact they have often done so.[14]

In two further well-known statements, he adds that his "rule of recognition" is the test by which the laws of our legal system are identified as law:

The rule of recognition exists only as a complex, but normally concordant, practice of the courts, officials, and private persons in identifying the law by reference to certain criteria. Its existence is a matter of fact.[15]

The question whether a rule of recognition exists and what its content is, i.e. what the criteria of validity in any given legal system are, is regarded throughout this book as an empirical, though complex, question of fact.[16]

Hart gave at least two reasons for establishing the rule of recognition. Prominent in the early part of *The Concept of Law* is his thesis that it would "cure the defect" of social uncertainty in a society without it. Prominent in the later parts is his thesis that "official abuse of authority" would be revealed because citizens would be able to separate the demands of moral conscience from what the state required.

If we treat as law only what is certain, only what makes for a clear distinction between individual moral conscience and the "demands" of the state, then value is ruled out: there are no empirical facts determining value (the "unity of value" thesis). So, when a judge decides on the grounds of fairness, or equity, or justice, because these are judgments that can't be determined by "plain fact," his judgment cannot be a question of applying what the law says. Since value judgments are inherently controversial, such judgments can only be extra-legal (as when, say, the judge uses his discretion over what prison sentence to impose between a minimum and a maximum).[17]

Dworkin points out both methodological strands in Hart—the reliance on a detached and neutral descriptive approach and the promotion of positivism's value in certainty—but rejects them.[18] He thinks these forms of positivism are wrong. He denies the descriptive approach, which he calls "semantic" positivism, because there are no shared meanings. That is why he proposes the alternative "interpretive" understanding. Law is evaluative and we have rival theories about what law is, conducted as an exercise in what makes most moral sense of our practices. In the cases, judges and lawyers have "theoretical" disagreements over what counts as being law ("the grounds of law") and they do more than trivially dispute whether agreed criteria apply.[19]

Dworkin also denies that there is good moral point to legal positivism. He says there is greater moral value in including, rather than excluding, moral arguments within arguments determining questions of legal validity. Further, he says that this does not deny that there is a distinction between the law as it is and the law as it morally ought to be.[20]

THE DIFFERENT SENSES OF DISCRETION

A consequence of positivism is an account of judicial reasoning. In Dworkin's terms, this version is a theory of "strong" discretion, according to which a judge is not bound by law to come to any decision when the question of law is genuinely controversial. Hart, while notably drawing attention to the distinction between the "core" and "penumbra" of the expressions of legal rules, did not deal directly with the question of what the judge was bound to do in the area of his discretion.[21] Austin and Kelsen, on the other hand, argued that judges had legislative powers but both, too, saw these as confined within wider but still legal principles of constraint. Austin thought that the judges were only empowered in accordance with sovereign inten-tion.[22] Kelsen claims there are no "gaps" at all because, he argued, if a judge is authorized to decide a given dispute where there is no "general norm" covering the matter, the judge is acting validly in adding to the existing law an "individual norm." This is so, not because there is a gap in the law but because the judge is empowered to remedy the law when he considers it "legally-politically inadequate."[23]

Dworkin thinks a theory of strong discretion is entailed by these influential theories of positivism whether or not the theorists realize it. He thinks that judicial positivism is a consequence of the plain fact type of positivism,[24] and entails saying that the law ends at the beginning of uncertainty about shared meanings or understandings about the identification of law. For Dworkin, "plain fact" positivism is exclusionary. It requires that anything not identi-fied as plain fact is not properly called "law." I believe both the "plain facts" version and the value version in Hart confirm the exclusionary view.[25]

Dworkin has been cited on numerous occasions for having drawn at-tention to different senses which discretion has in our legal system. His first article[26] was on this topic and it is interesting to see how he has developed the ideas that he discussed there in his later work, in particular, in his "Is Law a System of Rules?" Dworkin's analysis of the idea of discretion shows how distinguishing between these questions matters, because the essential idea for him is for discretion to be centrally seen as judgment. Officials, specifically judges, must exercise appropriate judgment when exercising discretion, and that judgment must be of a public nature responsive to public argument. The appropriateness or not of a particular judgment made in the exercise of discretion is one that can be tested and controlled by legal argument. The upshot of this is, I suggest, that tribunals and other bodies set up to control the use of official discretion must reflect the discretionary judgment of the courts and differ only where the special subject matter of the body requires it to carry out its specific purpose. If we think of discretion as judgment, this conclusion is an easy one: judgments made by officials of the state must be made in accordance with appropriate criteria, and can be wrong. The idea of discretion as license carries no weight.

There are three senses of discretion analyzed by Dworkin, two *weak* senses and one *strong*.[27] The first sense is the one I have already referred to, that of judgment. A sergeant, for example, "may have been left a lot of discretion" when, say, he is instructed to select his five most experienced men. We mean here that although he has not been given instructions any more precise than this, he has to exercise judgment in deciding which of his men have the most experience. An understanding of this sense is crucial to understanding Dworkin, and his example is helpful. It is, of course, possible to say that the choice for the sergeant is difficult, or that it cannot be determined by any special test. It is clear, too, that we can criticize his choice. We can criticize him for a lack of judgment, as well as for disobeying a clear rule, as we would, for example, if he chose not to select his most experienced men, or chose only two men, or even chose only women. This sense of discretion permeates the common law, and examples of it should be familiar to anyone. One of these is encapsulated in the famous example of the judge's discretion in this sense in declaring a skateboard to be a vehicle for the purposes of the statute prohibiting vehicles from the park. It was discretion of this sort that the judges exercised in the right of privacy cases already discussed, as well as in *Donoghue* v. *Stevenson* and, indeed, in most cases coming before the courts.

A full discussion of the importance of discretion is not possible without distinguishing this first weak sense from a "strong" sense. This occurs in the situation, in Dworkin's words, where a person "is simply not bound by the standards set by the authority in question."[28] We now imagine the sergeant simply being ordered to pick any five men for patrol he chooses. Here the particular qualities of the men are not specified and the sergeant has a "strong" discretion in making the choice. The contrast between these two senses is important and has caused a number of difficulties in understanding Dworkin. He is at pains to stress that strong discretion "is not tantamount to license" and that a proper judgment be made, for example, not one that is stupid, malicious or careless. It is just that his decision is not controlled by a standard furnished by the particular authority in the context of which the question of discretion is raised. If the sergeant is bound by standards in this sort of case, too, how can the distinction between weak and strong discretion be as sharp as Dworkin appears to maintain? This characterization of the difference is, I think, unfortunate. To say that the area of strong discretion is that where the "particular" authority has not "furnished" the standard looks very like saying that the judge has strong discretion just because there is no pedigree test identifying the standards he is to apply. And if we are to agree to that we are bound by definition to say that positivists remit us to a theory of strong discretion in hard cases. A positivist might well deny the validity of Dworkin's move because it is circular and may reasonably demand a stronger argument to lead him to suppose that positivists are bound to accept strong discretion in hard cases. For reasons such as these, his argument has received the criticism that in fact the idea of discretion is not amenable to the sharp distinctions he maintains and exists rather as a gradation from a very weak discretion ("are skateboards vehicles?"), through less weak versions ("what is *reasonable* restraint of trade?"), to a strong discretion ("the Minister may, *if he sees fit* . . . ").

This criticism, common though it is, does not help. It is, in part, like collapsing the distinction between youth and maturity by pointing out the gradation between the two. Granted the gradation, what follows? That youth and maturity are the same? Of course not. I think, too, that the distinction between the first weak sense and the strong sense serves a useful purpose in our understanding of the legal process, which I shall attempt to show shortly. If it can be shown to have an independent purpose, then the distinction should provide some non-tautological support to Dworkin's view that positivists can only support a theory of strong judicial discretion. In any case, the positivist is embarrassed when asked what the test is by which legal standards—those binding judges in weak discretion cases—are identified. He can only produce arguments of the conventionalist kind. He constructs increasingly abstract conventions justifying various propositions in hard cases. He will end with the soft conventionalist approach. His "test" will amount to "being in accordance with the best sense which can be made of the standard furnished by the particular authority." This test will be of such a complex and abstract nature that connection with the point of adopting the conventionalist approach will be all but lost.

The judge has a weak discretion where he has to come to a decision about what is "reasonable" in the circumstances, like the sergeant who has the weak discretion to decide who of his men is the most experienced. In these cases, it is clear what the standard furnished by the particular authority is. But such cases are not the most common kind and the more obvious and problematical case is where a judge must make a decision of the analogical sort, for example, where he must decide whether a skateboard is a vehicle or whether a right to privacy of unmarried heterosexual couples extends to homosexual couples. The judge has a weak discretion here, and there just is no standard furnished by the particular authority. It surely cannot be an authoritative legislative enactment or judicial decision which simply declares that the court must apply the intention of the legislature, or enforce the citizen's right to a fair decision. Dworkin can, in other words, stick to his original position. This is that positivism cannot both have a relatively simple pedigree test for law and, in addition, claim that when a judge faces a question such as (Hart's example) whether roller-skates are vehicles in the context of a regulation that prohibits vehicles from a park, he is bound by law. In order to avoid becoming stuck in the quagmire of soft conventionalism, the positivist must deny the existence of weak discretion altogether. He cannot say that there is weak discretion just because that denies that the standards were "furnished by the particular authority."

We can make use here of Dworkin's analogy with art. It is helpful, in an intuitive kind of way, for understanding the distinction between these two crucial senses of "discretion." The analogy with art raises its own problems, but I believe it helps. Let us imagine a musicologist who wishes to compose a symphonic movement to complete Schubert's *Unfinished Symphony*. That project clearly makes sense. Persons other than the authors have completed novels, poems and plays. Whether or not the piece uncompleted by the original artist counts as "true" art or "part of the work," and so on, should not concern us so much as how to go about the task of completion. Can legal argument be creative? Ask some lawyers who are experienced in courtroom legal argument and you will soon find that it is a highly creative business. Are the great legal judgments creative? It is very difficult to argue that they are not. We can resort to denying that "creative" judgments are in accordance with law, as Dworkin says positivists must argue if they are not to become caught in a maze of soft conventionalism. Is it a satisfactory reply to say that all creative judgments are not about law at all? If we don't think that is satisfactory—as I don't—then I suggest that we are drawn to the idea that the musical analogy brings out so well: that it is possible to be both constrained and creative at the same time. It is this idea that the idea of weak discretion is supposed to capture. The combination of creation with constraint makes it possible to see why "discretion" and "law" are not opposite, mutually contradictory ideas. It shows that the question which is frequently posed by administrative lawyers in England, "Is the matter one controlled by law, or is it a matter of discretion?" is misconceived. Nor is it correct that creative constructions of the law are merely a matter of being consistent with precedents.

A SECOND "WEAK" SENSE OF DISCRETION

Dworkin isolates a second weak sense of discretion which refers only to the fact that an official has the authority to make a decision. This sense should be unproblematic but it is frequently confused with the first weak sense. The second sense means only that the official has the authority, as when we say that the sergeant has the discretion as to which experienced men he chooses. It is clearly different from the first sense, because we can say of his decision that, although it stands (he has the discretion to decide), he exercised it badly (his use of discretion showed that he has bad judgment). In other words, we can recognize that a decision can both stand and be a bad one. This phenomenon is, of course, common in law. The High Court's ruling stands, until overturned by a higher court, by virtue of rules that give its decisions that power. There are good practical reasons for that. Law is an eminently practical enterprise. Decisions must be made and carried out even when there is a possibility that they may be wrong. Hence we should have no difficulty in saying: "This is the law, because it is decided so by the House of Lords, but I think it is wrong, because it was based on faulty reasoning." Academic writers do this; and practicing lawyers often argue that previous decisions of courts were wrong in law, and put that to judges in real cases.

The idea can only be made sense of if we recognize the distinction between the court's discretion to decide, willy-nilly, and its discretion, in hard cases, to make a judgment. The distinction creates some difficulties for positivism, too, because the decision of the highest court supposedly provides the test of pedigree. The idea, for positivists, is that when the ultimate courts of appeal decide a matter, that is the law. How can it then make sense to say both that it is the law and that it was wrong in law? There is one answer but it employs Dworkin's distinction rather than shows it to be otiose. This is that the decision is wrong because the court did not consider an authoritative previous ruling. In other words, the decision was a *per incuriam* decision. It is not, however, a particularly satisfying answer, because such decisions are relatively rare (or rarely admitted) and criticism of the legal basis for the decisions of final courts ranges wider than use of the *per incuriam*–type criticism would allow. Lawyers and academic writers do not usually criticize judgments because crucial precedents have been overlooked, but for much more complex reasons, reasons of the sort that are enmeshed in different levels of abstraction and which attempt to make sense of the law as a whole. In other words, for Dworkin, the operative sense of discretion, present in all hard cases, is the first weak sense of discretion—that the lawyer, whether judge, advocate or law student, can't let up on exercising legal judgment whether the case is easy or hard.

A RETURN TO PLAIN FACTS

An appeal to plain fact gives a robust quality to an argument. In the ordinary day-to-day way of seeing things, the truth of the relevant proposition of law is discovered through relatively simple empirical means. However, a practical outcome argument arises from the empirical possibility of identifying law just noted. It would appear to be a virtue of law—if law is identifiable like this—that it can be identified so clearly; no value judgment is required! In other words, there is a practical reason supporting the law's identification in the "plain fact" way. A failure to grasp practical reason's way of justifying the "plain fact" way of looking at law has caused many problems. It is common to condemn legal positivism on the ground that it is lifeless and "amoral," and encourages the "legal scientist" to make a "cold" and "analytical" appraisal of the facts. From the viewpoint of practical reason, however, the "lifeless" appraisal makes sense, for it now may be claimed as a virtue that it is therefore able to be austerely impartial in its ability to co-ordinate and direct our communal life. Nevertheless, the arguments take a different turn; we can abandon the "plain facts" account of law and just center on the practical reasons for adopting a conception of law that distinguishes sharply between law and morality.

Hart's *The Concept of Law* should, I believe, be read as justifying a particular practical way of understanding law. He constructs a model of primary and secondary rules according to which secondary rules of change, adjudication and recognition lift the simple regime of duty-imposing primary rules into the legal arena (from the "pre-legal" world). This model is justified on the basis that, with the addition of the secondary rules, it remedies the "defects" of a society which could not change its rules by conscious decision, did not have a system of courts and had no means of determining which were the rules of the system. Most significant among these defects is that of the "uncertainty" of a simple regime of primary rules alone. People would not know which rules were rules of law. They would not know how to plan their lives in accordance with law. This is an intensely practical reason for making the identification of law as clear—as plain—as possible. To put the point starkly: Hart's theory of validity, the key concept of which is his rule of recognition, is dependent on its curing the defect of uncertainty in the identification of valid law. Further, of paramount concern for Hart, I think, was that if there were no rule of recognition which could clearly identify what was legally valid, the citizen could not be certain of the source and therefore moral quality of its authority. He emphasizes, for example, that the fact that some rule has officially been certified as legally valid should not be conclusive of the question of obedience. This argument, which appears in Chapter 9 of *The Concept of Law,* is crucial to understanding the complexity of Hart's positivism. The argument links historically to the development of legal positivism as a force in early nineteenth-century England. Positivism was a secular doctrine, associated always with the development of liberalism and related doctrines. One of the ideas implicit in it was that people, whether legislators, lawyers or ordinary people, could use the distinction between what the law was and what it ought to be to free the way for critical appraisal, and not wholesale acceptance of judicial decisions and legislative acts. (There was, too, an urge to clarify what "scientifically" the law was.)

The Concept of Law is not explicit in distinguishing these two sorts of argument for its major conclusions. Nevertheless, both arguments are present in the writings of the legal philosophers Austin and Kelsen, the influence of whose work can so clearly be seen in Hart. Kelsen, more clearly than Austin, was explicit in wanting to place law on a firmly scientific basis. It is not surprising, then, that the way he wrote made it sound as though he were just describing law as it was "out there," as an entity to be observed largely in terms of regularity of behavior.[29] Secondly, of course, utilitarians were concerned with matters of practical reasoning. Why be content with the way the world was? The principle by which the greatest happiness of the greatest number should be urged applied itself to the construction of a positivist model of law.[30] They saw that the way forward for this principle was the creation of legislation which could stand objectively "there" independent of the standpoint from which criticism, based on the utilitarian principle, could be made. Thus, Austin could, in a *practical* sense, declare, "The existence of law is one thing; its merit or demerit is another."[31]

Dworkin says that the plain fact theory, at its barest, is a semantic theory of law, because disputes about law will, in the end, amount merely to being about the correct use of law-related language. This criticism must be tested since it trivializes (perhaps rightly) the plain fact theory. It suggests that disputes about law are, in principle, resolvable dictionary-type disputes. Perhaps the problem should be put in another way. We could say that lawyers, when debating some point of law, are trying not just simply to find out what the correct meanings of words are. They are, instead, trying to make sense of the underlying social phenomena that constitute the law. But this is not helpful. In what does the social phenomenon of law consist? How do we get to it? Hart, for example, says in his Preface to *The Concept of Law:*

> Many important distinctions, which are not immediately obvious, between types of social situation or relationships may best be brought to light by an examination of the standard uses of the relevant expressions.[32]

When legal theorists insist on digging out the meanings of legal language in order to cast light on the nature of law, Dworkin accuses them of having succumbed to the semantic "sting." This means that the theorist has wrongly assumed that there is a level of agreement upon the correct criteria with which to use legal language. Any apparent disagreement, then, must be resolvable as a matter of research into the question of whether the participants are using the language correctly. If the sources theory is correct, it means that the disputants are in simple disagreement over something about which the sources cannot be ambiguous. Then there is no real disagreement, only a misunderstanding.

The popular appeal of the plain fact theory is variously grounded in a motivation for clarity, certainty and objectivity. At any rate, if it is wrong, it is better, I think, to make the case against it along the same practical lines. I suggest, then, that Dworkin is right to make the best sense we can of the plain fact theory in moral terms. I suggest that this is what positivism is fundamentally about and the way law is popularly understood in Anglo-American jurisdictions. It is in this light that we can understand best the appeal, particularly for those on the Continent, and, for example, for Kelsen, of law as a "science." The "legal scientist" appraises the "cold" facts of the law. He describes the "legal material" and organizes it. By so doing he produces an uncommitted and non-ideological, "pure" and therefore useful account of the law.

Again, I believe it misunderstands Dworkin's criticism of positivism to suppose only that he is attacking Hart. Dworkin attacks the plain fact view of law because it is meaningless to talk of law as simply "out there." I believe it was always true, and it is well borne out by *Justice for Hedgehogs*: plain fact as law contradicts the Humean principle. Dworkin instead offers an evaluative account—the interpretive account. Further, he thinks the best moral sense that can be made of law requires *not* thinking of law as exhausted by the clear rules but in seeing it in terms of the moral values that support it. And it is his reasons for this view that constitute his primary attack on the account *interpretive* positivism gives of legal reasoning.

THE "HARD CASE"

We should now understand the full significance of the Dworkinian "hard case." It refers to those cases in the law where there is controversy in the value judgments concerning the identification of the law; those matters of law where the issues faced by a judge or a lawyer are contentious and potentially litigable. Specifically, a hard case is a situation in the law that gives rise to genuine argument about the truth of a proposition of law that cannot be resolved by recourse to a set of plain facts determinative of the issue. It is useful to consider again, for a moment, Hart's regulation prohibiting vehicles from the park.[33] Does it include roller-skates? He says that the law is just unspecific about whether roller-skates are included. Rather, the judge settles matters by declaring what the law is, thereby creating a new rule for the future relating to roller-skates. He says that every rule will have a "penumbra" where its meaning is uncertain and that this is simply a consequence of the natural indeterminacy of our language. Nevertheless, we would not have an idea of what the penumbra was unless we first had a firm grasp of the idea of the core.

According to Dworkin, if the law is no longer clearly identifiable by reference to a plain fact criterion—to the rule of recognition—there is no law on the matter. It follows that, in accordance with his duty to come to a decision, the judge must make his decision on grounds other than legal ones. The phrase so often used in this context is that "the judge must exercise his discretion" in order to come to a decision. In Dworkin's view, this is a conclusion that positivists should want. Positivists appear to place very high value on certainty and its corollaries, clarity and public ascertainability. Of course a "strict plain fact" positivist, concerned only with clarifying what "the plain facts" are, is engaged in empirical enquiry, not making a judgment of value. Nevertheless, it is common to find—as in Hart—both the desire to be descriptive of "plain facts" and an affirmation of the value of certainty in the same person. But certainty will not be a virtue where closer attention to the sensitivity of circumstances is warranted. Not every area of human life can be governed by the use of clear rules which announce in advance of a situation how matters should be governed. Laws governing the granting of planning consents, for example, cannot possibly achieve this. Constitutional law, and its offshoot, administrative law, concern matters which, from the ordinary man's point of view, are, for most cases, better understood in terms of general principle than clear rules laying out in precise detail what is required or permitted.

In any case, two sorts of controversy occur with apparently clear rules. The first is where there is some clear indication that recourse must be made to a value judgment by use of words such as "reasonable," or "fair." These require a value judgment and not a relatively simple "reading off" of what the law requires. So a "fair rent" under the Rent Act 1968 could only be determined after the tenant has fulfilled the precise conditions, both substantive and procedural, outlined in that Act. Likewise for the common law; the apparent clarity of the words of the neighbor principle in negligence is an excellent example: "reasonable foreseeability." On the debit side, it is unclear in the sense that we can't "read off" the law in any given instance. However, the flexibility and potential of the law to be able to deal with the justice of each case is greatly enhanced. And it is not as if the ordinary man, concerned with understanding what is required of him, can't make any sense at all of laws worded like these.

The second type of lack of clarity to be discussed here is a less obvious type because the situations in which value judgments are to be made are not spelled out. Dworkin's example of *Riggs* v. *Palmer* is a good one.[34] There the words of the statute seemed plain: beneficiaries were to succeed to the property of the testator if the formal requirements of a valid will were established. However, the beneficiary had murdered the testator. That raises a doubt as to whether the statute intended a beneficiary in such circumstances to succeed to the property. The court resolved this doubt by giving weight to a principle that no one may profit from their own wrong. In this sort of case, what are the consequences for adjudication? The positivist has two possibilities: he can either deny that there is any law in these unclear cases because of the lack of a plain fact (or criterial or pedigree) test, or he can say that there *is* law there but it requires a different method for its identification. These two possibilities may be considered in turn.

JUDICIAL LEGISLATION

If there is no clear law directing a judge to a certain decision, there is no law that constrains the judge. He is constrained, of course, in the sense that there are other laws that carve out the hollow area where there is no law.

Within that area, however, the positivist must claim there are simply no legal constraints. Take, again, the regulation prohibiting vehicles from the park. It is reasonably clear that ten-ton trucks are prohibited, so the judge is constrained from deciding that a truck driver has not broken the law. It is also clear that no one who walks through the park breaks that law. A "gap" can thus be seen between the pedestrian's non-liability and the truck-driver's liability. What constrains the judge in deciding anything between these two points if the plain fact account is the true one? It is helpful to contrast the judge's role in sentencing where there is usually a maximum penalty provided by law (and sometimes a minimum). In the gap left between the maximum and minimum there is little by way of legal constraint. If the decision is a "perverse" one, the sentence may successfully be appealed against, but the judge has enormous leeway inside this sole constraint. It is, therefore, a familiar idea that judges are not constrained by law in some areas of their legitimate decision-making powers. Indeed, for sentencing there is the strong rationale that individual circumstances vary so considerably it would be undesirable in justice to have clear constraints as opposed to very general guidelines.[35] According to the "gap" account, the judge's decision on a question of law is as free as it is in a sentencing case.

Positivism as here interpreted by Dworkin, in both its descriptive and interpretive forms, does not deny that a judge is constrained. It is, rather, that they are not "legal" constraints but "moral," or "social," or "political." To say that in the unclear areas the judges are bound by non-legal constraints is to preserve a distinction that has the (interpretive) merit of making it clear when a judge is making decisions on controversial matters and thus draws our attention to the discretion a judge undoubtedly has. There are good arguments of political merit that justify relatively stringent controls of judicial decision-making. The judge has a constitutional role requiring that he not be swayed by populism. His specific role is to decide the dispute between the litigants on the particular merits. Judges are not elected precisely for this reason. In the words of Lord Scarman:

> The judge, however wise, creative, and imaginative he may be, is "cabin'd, cribb'd, confin'd, bound in" not, as was Macbeth, to his "saucy doubts and fears" but by the evidence and arguments of the litigants. It is this limitation, inherent in the forensic process, which sets bounds to the scope of judicial law reform.[36]

There is a problem here. Let us say that it is a virtue of legal positivism that it makes clear when a judge is applying law and when he is applying social, moral, etc., standards. If so, we have to accept that the judge's characteristic form of adjudicating is directly counter to what many consider an important feature of our democratic procedures—the doctrine of the separation of powers. There are two further problems in the idea that the judge acts as legislator. Judges do not talk and act as though they were performing the same function as legislators and, further, if they are legislating, this means that their legislative decisions are being applied retrospectively. I will consider both ideas in the following section.

JUDICIAL BEHAVIOR

Certainly, judges speak judicially of their being "bound by law." This is apparent from courtroom language and the reports of judgments, even in the most innovative of cases. Take, for instance, Lord Atkin's introduction to his famous statement of the neighbor principle in the law of tort: "Who in law is my neighbor?" It would have sounded odd had he asked instead: "Who in law ought to be my neighbor?"[37] Most people, I find, accept this feature of legal practice. The law is full of it. The lawyers make submissions in court about what the law is. The judges come to decisions about what the law is. Always there is the background matrix of law from which both judges and lawyers draw their arguments. At times, when a judge decides that there is no argument that he can extrapolate from this background matrix, he will make a pronouncement about the appropriateness of his judicial role to decide such a matter. Take the judgments of Lord Kilbrandon and Lord Simon in *D.P.P. v. Lynch*.[38] In their view, the law did not permit the extension of the well-established defense of duress for other crimes to the crime of murder. Consequently, the question was one of whether it should so extend, and that was a question to be determined by the appropriate institution, namely, the legislature. To do otherwise, they thought, and said, would have been to contravene the proper function of the court.

Does it matter if positivism cannot explain judicial language (and related discourse such as that of lawyers, whose roles are parasitic on the judicial function)? Perhaps judges are just mistaken about what they are really doing. This is not so fantastic, because the immediate concerns of judges, in most cases, anyway, relate to judging rather than to providing more abstract accounts of what they do. Some explanations are common. These range from saying, "Judges speak according to the traditions of their calling" to more sinister accounts of judges "covering up" what they really do. Is it only traditional? What is the tradition? Perhaps it is just that judges are rightly conscious of the doctrine of the separation of powers. They endeavored, at one time, anyway, to express their judgments in terms appropriate to that doctrine: they did not make the law, they only declared what it was. Nevertheless, this explanation is a good reason for supposing that not only do they not legislate but the doctrine of the separation of powers is alive!

What of the explanation that judges "cover up," or "pretend" that the law is there, but in "reality" know that there is no law there? That seems over-cynical because judges are not lying about what they are really doing, although that must be what the claim amounts to in its strongest form.

RETROSPECTIVE LEGISLATION

If, according to Dworkin's interpretation of positivism, judges create new law in a hard case, it follows that the parties are made subject to this new law that was not in force when the events occurred. A natural objection is that this is unfair because it surprises the litigants who now find they are subject to laws which could not have been known to them at the time they did the things that gave rise to litigation. The objection is important although only part of the general legal principle of *nulla poena sine lege*, which means there should no penalty except where justified by law. In other words, law should not be applied retrospectively. There is more to the principle of *nulla poena sine lege* than the protection from surprise. The defendant can still complain that even where he was not surprised by official behavior, he should not in any case have been subject to penalty where there was no law to justify it. This is surely the more important principle. It is the cardinal principle of the rule of law that officials act only in accordance with law. For some areas of law the protection of reasonable expectations is unimportant because of the possibility of being reasonably surprised by a legal outcome while recognizing it to be fully justified. These would be cases where the principle of meeting reasonable expectations had little or no impact. Although that principle has significant impact in both criminal law (where it is often flouted, particularly where there is a common law of crime) and property law (where it is most often respected) it is of lesser importance in, for example, the common law of tort where fair compensation of the injured is the main focus.

We have moved from considering a descriptive, "plain fact" account of law to a considerably more flexible understanding of law that allows for evaluative legal argument. It is now necessary to look at the vexed question—for many critics of Dworkin—of the objectivity of it all, in particular, the objectivity of value and whether there are right answers to controversial questions of law.

CHAPTER THREE

The Complexity of Legal Argument

In *Justice for Hedgehogs* Dworkin refers to an orthodox picture of a relationship between law and morality: that each describes a different set of norms. Law belongs to a particular community but ordinary morality, that is, morality which is not subjective, nor relative, nor conventional, does not. He says that this orthodox picture then forces the classic jurisprudential question, that of asking what the relationship is between these two sets of norms. Legal positivism declares the complete independence of the two systems and further declares that the identification of law depends only on historical fact (although a version of positivism — inclusive or soft positivism — claims that these historical facts may incorporate a moral test for law). His own theory, which he calls "interpretivism," as we will see in Chapter 4, on the contrary, denies that law and morality are independent systems and claims that law consists not only of the enacted rules within the community's accepted practices but also of the principles that provide the best moral justification of those rules.[1]

Dworkin says that there is a "fatal flaw" in the two-systems picture. It is that there is no neutral position from which the connections can be judged. Which system is better, or more accurate? That difficulty, he believes, led in the past to the possibility that the problem was purely "conceptual," merely requiring an "analysis" of the doctrinal concept of law. And so positivists tried to claim that we find the "nature" or "essence" of law without making prior legal or moral assumptions and this supposedly showed us that law and morality were distinct. Other lawyers — including some natural lawyers — who claim to be using the same method, he says, come to the opposite result, saying that an analysis of the doctrinal concept revealed that law and morality were not so distinct, and that morality does have a role in legal reasoning. Dworkin says he finds this analysis more curious than the positivist analysis.

We can't solve the circularity of the two-systems picture, he says, through analysis of the doctrinal concept of law. He concludes that it is no wonder that positivists have such difficulty in saying what they are doing, for they fail to grasp the underlying evaluative reasons required for comparing the positivist and natural law accounts. If the best version of positivism is that it best promotes certainty, as suggested in the last chapter, and therefore the protection of reasonable expectations, the obvious question arises why other principles, such as "people should be compensated for involuntarily caused injury," aren't relevant also. Following this line, he believes, we end up with an entirely evaluative set of questions that will allow us to choose what the best theory of law is.

SOFT POSITIVISM: CAN PRINCIPLES BE IDENTIFIED BY THE RULE OF RECOGNITION?

There is a common criticism of Dworkin's view that the weight of the value-laden idea of principles cannot be captured or identified by a factual—or "criterial" or "sources" or "pedigree"—test such as the rule of recognition. These critics, including Hart, say that the rule of recognition can be rejigged to include them, and so the law to be applied can be identified factually in hard cases.[2] In the abstract, the criticism must fail. If law is identifiable factually, through agreed criterial practice or "pedigree," and the mark of hard cases is that they require value judgments (that's why they are controversial) then the distinction between "fact" and "value" collapses.[3] Dworkin's view is that any value-based extension of positivism to *soft* conventionalism, which includes all the possible rules to govern all possible cases, ends up telling judges to decide between them. It requires a rule saying: "Decide in accordance with the best rule to cover the case," and that is clearly a matter of value. The intuitive pull of the distinction between fact and value is strong. Maybe the distinction is not as clear as it seems to most people; but for the controversial hard cases to be decided by reference to a factual test such as the rule of recognition requires, it seems to me, that the is/ought issue should be tackled first. It is clear, at any rate, from *Justice for Hedgehogs* that Dworkin affirms that distinction, referring to it throughout as "the Humean principle."

To suppose the rule of recognition may incorporate principles only to the extent that "they must be taken into account" is very weak. It transfers the question of assessment of the weight of the principle to judicial discretion. The judge is bound, or permitted, to "take the principle into account" but not bound to take it into account in any kind of way. There is no advance in certainty—if that is what positivism is about—because it remains unclear what weight the principle will carry in any particular case. The lawyers on either side of the litigation will be able to use the rule of recognition to inform the judge that he is bound to take the principle "into account" but that is all. If the judge does not consider it, there is cause for complaint, but if he has taken into account and either made it decisive, or given it very little weight, there can be no complaint.

What has happened is that in order for the principle's essentially value-laden element to be incorporated into the factual test of the rule of recognition it was converted into something value-free or "source identifiable": the judge was required simply to make a value judgment without specifying how he was to make that judgment. Is that what the positivists want? That emendation to the rule of recognition does not achieve much, because it only says that judges may be required by law to make value judgments, and we knew of that possibility when we discussed the force of the use of words such as "reasonable" and "fair."[4] Perhaps there is a more complicated possibility. Perhaps we can only understand the clear rules in a "context" or "matrix" of value judgments. This would mean, I think, that instead of connecting principles with the rule of recognition directly, in the way we have just now done, we connect them by saying that principles are somehow "higher order" reasons by which we understand the simpler type rules identified by the rule of recognition. This is the way Dworkin concentrates on the problem (the problem of "inclusive positivism" in Chapter 4 of *Law's Empire*). Thus, to go back to the case of *Riggs v. Palmer,* the rule identified by the rule of recognition is discovered as the result of two stages of legal argument. First, an apparently clear rule is uncovered which would, *prima facie,* allow murderers to benefit under their victims' will. Secondly, the law is surveyed and the principle of "no one may profit from his own wrong" is discovered to be something that the judge must "take into account" according to the rule of recognition. This second stage requires the judge to interpret the initial plain fact meaning in accordance with the "higher order" principle.

This fails to withstand closer analysis, for the master test cannot correctly identify the first stage "rule." Its identity remains controversial. We can, of course, hope to find even higher order reasons which can direct our interpretation of the "no one may profit by his own wrong" principle, but we shall always return to the initial difficulty: Where is the official practice that clearly determines the result? The very highest order principle which we can affirm with certainty must be one directing judges to decide according to "the best interpretation of the existing rules." We cannot deny that such a consensus exists. But to say that destroys positivism rather than saves it. It would not, for example, be right to use Hart's rule of recognition here, because it is unlike anything he postulated (remember: it consisted of empirically identifiable facts of official practice "normally concordant"). The trouble is that if we reformulate "master rule" to mean an identification of the "best" interpretation of the settled rules, we lose certainty everywhere else. That is not what the positivists want.

Of course, we could not simply save positivism, too, by postulating as the master rule all the rules and principles contained in the legal system. Apart from the possibility that this defense involves circularity (for example, the master rule is to be identified by all the rules, principles and so on, which are identified by the master rule), the undeniable appeal of the idea of a relatively simple test for law, as the master rule thesis supports, is completely lost in complexity.[5] If, indeed, the closest we can get to a positivist "master rule" is that "judges must decide according to the best interpretation of the existing rules" then, as Dworkin says, the theory of positivism collapses into an account of law that is completely evaluative. Indeed, because that "master rule" requires the existing conventions to be part of the interpretation, consistency with the bulk of the existing rules is required and so the conventionalism collapses into integrity.[6]

The soft positivist exists in the worst of all possible worlds. He wants morality to be part of law and he doesn't, so he is confused. He wants facts to determine morality but he breaches Hume's law. He tries to provide a descriptive account of what can't be described. He can't claim the advantages of clarity and certainty that the "exclusivist" positivists can. And although he wants judges to engage in moral argument he doesn't want them to think too hard.

Where do we go from here? Acceptance of Dworkin's theory of law as integrity is incompatible with legal positivism viewed as a historical—plain fact—doctrine. It is time to explore a further question. If justification of a moral sort, perhaps in terms of justice and fairness, is properly a major concern of the legal theorist, what other kinds of theory are available? Dworkin considers two theories he calls, respectively, conventionalism and pragmatism.

CONVENTIONALISM

Conventionalism is the interpretive form of positivism. It claims that the best interpretation of legal practice is that it is a matter of respecting legal conventions. What justifies it? Dworkin says that it serves the ideal of "protected expectations" by giving a "fair warning" to people about what the law requires and permits.[7] Its aim, in other words, is to make the law certain for people. That judges cannot appeal to law in conditions of uncertainty—in hard cases—actually supports the ideal of protected expectations; judges can't "then pretend that their decisions flow in some other way from what has already been decided."[8]

Although the protection of expectations is one obvious justification for following a plain facts view of law, it is not the only one. Some writers have suggested that the most important reason is co-ordination, having in mind "prisoners' dilemma"–type situations, where the best solution can only be achieved by acceptance of a common standard, rather than by individual, but perfectly rational, action. Here what may be important for a judge is not strategic consistency with previous decisions, but, at least for some cases, the creation of a new convention for co-ordinative purposes. For example, a judge may be justified under this new rationale in declaring checks to have the same legal status as money[9] or, perhaps, declaring landlords to be the legal owners of tenants' fixtures. Does this modified explanation gain us much? It achieves more flexibility, because judges need not stick to strategic consistency where a problem of co-ordination arises. Dworkin believes we can't stretch the idea too far without disintegrating it. Co-ordination, which is primarily about achieving what individuals cannot achieve on their own, can't be extended to regulation of any group activity whatsoever. What we are instead looking for is the idea of flexibility, and if this is the important idea, as Dworkin says, we should embrace that idea and abandon conventionalism.[10]

Conventionalism requires only that for a convention to exist on some point of law, there is a bare agreement among lawyers. The idea of "bare" agreement constituting the core of legal argument is very thin. Understanding this point is of fundamental importance to understanding Dworkin and it is a theme throughout his work. A dramatic way of putting this point is to note the difference between a proposition's being true by convention and its being true by independent conviction (see pp. 126–28). This explains clearly why there can be fine but important differences of opinion between judges over matters where the end result—the judgment or the decision—is the same.

THE FLEXIBILITY OF PRAGMATISM

If a more sophisticated account is needed, why not abandon conventionalism? It does not provide an adequate account of the actual complexity of our current legal practices. Even when we improve the idea, by introducing the ideas of consistency of strategy and co-ordination, we are left with not much more than an arithmetic of rules. What might we consider in conventionalism's place? Dworkin's answer is that the requirement of greater flexibility that even amended conventionalism would not allow could be met by what he calls pragmatism. This doctrine is put forward as a better theory—one that better explains and justifies our legal practices—than conventionalism. Pragmatism offers the greatest scope for flexibility. It denies that past decisions create any rights which bind the judge. It is, therefore, what Dworkin calls a "skeptical" conception of law. Pragmatism is therefore to be seen as the opposite of conventionalism. According to this theory, judges may now act with the maximum flexibility in deciding what is the best decision and are not bound by any conventions. In practice, however, pragmatism is less radical because judges would need to look to past decisions in order to work out the most pragmatic solution. Thus, the best decision would, in many instances, just be to continue past practice, although, of course, the difference would be that a judge is not bound by any past decision. The theory just described articulates a common view of law ranging from Griffith in his popular book on the United Kingdom judiciary, *The Politics of the Judiciary*.[11] In that book he rather stereotypically criticizes judges for being biased towards "law and order," meaning that, despite what justice demanded, especially in the field of employment law, judges would seek justifications which stood on the side of what had been previously decided.

If judges are to take into account past political decisions, what precisely is the force of those decisions? If the judge is not bound to follow past precedents, then it cannot be correct to say that people have rights created by such precedents. The judge will always have the power to depart from precedent when that is necessary to achieve flexibility and there would be no argument that had the force, as the assertion of a right has, that the need to be flexible must give way to the need to recognize a right. Nevertheless, Dworkin says, the less radical working of pragmatism in practice will mean that judges will act in most cases "as if" people had rights. Would this matter? Is there a significant difference between people's having rights and judges acting "as if" they had rights? Well, yes. If flexibility means that judges can ignore a person's claim to be treated in accordance with precedent then that person cannot have a right. The right exists only as far as its recognition is in accordance with a decision that is the best practical one for the community. Beyond that, it can be abandoned.

Dworkin thinks that pragmatism is better than conventionalism because it allows more flexibility in determining a better society: it allows judges to make all sorts of judgments about sensible and imaginative ways the community might develop. So it has strength over conventionalism which ties decision-making just to the bare conventions. But because pragmatism recognizes previous decisions according "rights" as only instrumental to making society better, it does not, in Dworkin's terms, take rights seriously. On the other hand, pragmatism has a better sense of what would be best for the community and so should be preferred to conventionalism. Pragmatism's idea of community, though, is not sufficiently complex for Dworkin as it fails to account for the idea of a community of principle. Conventionalism justifies community coercion by reference to bare agreement. Pragmatism's more flexible justification shows insufficient commitment to a group's history and how it relates to the future. Integrity, he says, both unites the past and the present by incorporating the fraternal idea of treating all members of the same community as equals. This idea, as we'll see in Chapter 6, is the basis of Dworkin's analysis of the ideas of democracy and judicial review.

ORIGINAL INTENTION

Useful insights into the principle of certainty may be had by examining what has come to be known, particularly in the United States, as the doctrine of original intention. It is a theory of statutory interpretation which requires judges to interpret the law in accordance with the actual wishes, or intentions, of the founders of the Constitution, so far as those wishes may best be historically identified. Obviously, though, since the founders intended judges to apply statutes and case law, interpretation of the law extends beyond a historical search into the founders' minds and into law created in accordance with their intentions. The popular representation of the doctrine has a "folksy" appeal, one that purports to root current legal interpretation in the historical origins of the legal system. This is the doctrine's simple-minded side and it is open to the objections to the plain fact theory. Despite its naivety the doctrine is popularly accepted in this form; the law is regarded as "there" to be "applied," and what is more concrete and certain than historical fact?

There is, however, another common justification for the original intention doctrine: it prevents judges from making novel decisions. If judges stick to their role, they cannot then be guilty of imposing their "own" values on the citizens. But the argument goes nowhere. No historian doubts that each of the founders personally intended that the Constitution should be interpreted in accordance with justice and fairness. But that coincidence of intentions would appear to permit numerous interpretations which would exceed the clear and explicit words of the Constitution; it would permit novel decisions within the doctrine's requirement of neutrality. Further, that judges be as "unoriginal" as possible is not obviously appealing because it suggests an automaton role for the judiciary: they merely "read off" the law. Although that understanding of the judicial role is by no means uncommon, it dilutes the judicial role to something more like the work of a filing clerk.

However, the same idea can be expressed more palatably by saying that judges should be "neutral" in their decisions, meaning that the judges avoid introducing their own personal moral convictions into interpreting the law. Neutrality likens judicial behavior to a neutral country during war; the judge favors neither side. That idea is not convincing in the judicial context. It borrows from the idea of neutrality in areas outside morality, such as the actual behavior of nations, whereby the neutral country does not play any active part in dealings between other states, or even car mechanics, in which the neutral position of the gears means that the engine is disconnected and does nothing. There is no special virtue in "being neutral."[12]

Dworkin thinks the identification of the original intention poses an insurmountable problem. Presumably, where there are gaps in our historical knowledge we may ask counterfactual questions about what the founding fathers, or subsequent judges or legislators, would have thought had they been asked. Take the English Metropolitan Police Act 1839, which makes it an offence to "repair a carriage" on a street in the London metropolitan area.[13] Is it an offence to repair a motor car? The defense could be raised that the legislators in 1839 did not intend to make it an offence, because they could not have known what cars were; they'd not then been invented. Perhaps we could ask hypothetical questions: What would the legislature have thought had it been confronted with the future existence of cars? Admittedly, it requires some suspension of judgment. What if most of the members of the legislative body did not believe such things could be invented? Or what if it were believed that such things could exist, that they were "unnatural" things, and not at all like carriages?

Dworkin calls the "read off" form of the original intention theory "weak historicism." Weak historicism just accepts that the law is "out there"—plain facts again! "Strong" historicism is the view that there are good reasons for accepting the plain fact clauses of the Constitution as exhaustive of the law, one such reason being that acceptance of the view prevents judicial legislation. Dworkin's criticism of stronger historicism is that it makes sense, unlike weak historicism, but, like interpretive positivism, just does not make good sense.

THE RIGHT TO PRIVACY

A useful way of understanding the reasoning and motives of the original intentionalists is to consider the growth of the right to privacy in U.S. constitutional law. It was the growth of this law and its subsequent application in the landmark Supreme Court decision of *Roe* v. *Wade* which established the right to abortion under the U.S. Constitution. There is no "mention" of a right to privacy in the U.S. Constitution. The first reference in published legal discourse was probably in a famous *Harvard Law Review* article, entitled "The Right to Privacy," by Warren and Brandeis.[14] The argument in the article is fundamentally about the possibility of asserting the existence of rights in the law by means of arguments of principle and coherency, even though there is no explicit mention of such rights in the law. The extrapolation of such rights was nevertheless a workable possibility, and they proceeded to demonstrate it by using the right to privacy as an example. The article was largely prompted by personal experience of invasion of privacy. Warren and his wife were Boston socialites and the Boston newspapers had reported a family wedding in some detail. Much of the argument is concerned with pointing both to other areas of the law where analogous protections exist such as in rights to personal security, rights against libel and slander and rights to literary and artistic property, and to the development of new "demands" of society. The development of these demands created a situation where other rights explicitly recognized in the law could be seen in a clearer, because more abstract, light. The idea of the development of the "intensity and complexity" of modern life led the writers to assert that solitude and privacy had become more essential to the individual and a right to privacy existed which, properly understood, was an instance of a more general right "to be left alone." So, they urged that formerly "disconnected" rights, each developed to cope with the particular demands of a particular stage of change in society, should now be seen as instantiations of a general right "to be left alone."

This article's well-known strategy, that of finding more abstract principles upon which to base less abstract propositions of law, is not, however, as radical as is often assumed. Lawyers, not just in the United States, are perfectly familiar with the form of argument and not just in novel cases. Are skateboards prohibited in the park? That depends upon more abstract propositions making sense of words such as "vehicles," their sense in turn presumably relying on abstract propositions making sense of, for example, the rights and duties of the legislature. It is not uncommon for a lawyer to win a case because he can find a more abstract proposition which lifts a dispute beyond what seems an irreconcilable conflict of interpretations — one perhaps where a lazy judge might feel inclined to toss a coin — and shows the opposing lawyer's case in a bad light and his own in a good light. It is, I venture to say, a relatively common phenomenon in the courts. The difference between the Warren and Brandeis thesis about the right to privacy and the concerns of the ordinary lawyer is just that the level of abstraction is higher and therefore encompasses many situations which would not normally fall within the purview of any one litigated case. The thesis aims at establishing a general right of privacy across the board, without concerning itself with the particular ramifications and qualifications in particular cases. Warren and Brandeis are specific about that:

> To determine in advance of experience the exact line at which the dignity and convenience of the individual must yield to the demands of the public welfare or of private justice would be a difficult task; but the more general rules are furnished by the legal analogies already developed in the law of slander and libel, and the law of literary and artistic property.[15]

In *Roberson* v. *Rochester Folding Box Co.,*[16] the plaintiff argued that such a right of privacy existed in New York law. Without her permission, the defendants had used pictures of her in an advertising campaign, and in a New York court she sought damages for the distress it caused her and an injunction to prevent further use of the photographs. Judge Parker, who gave the majority decision, denied the existence of such a right. It did not exist in precedent and had not been asserted by the "great commentators upon the law."[17] He referred to the Warren and Brandeis article but dismissed the idea of any general such right on what appear to be two grounds. First, the right did not "exist" in the precedents nor, in fact, anywhere other than in the Warren and Brandeis article; and second, the right was too wide and would include all sorts of "rights" which could not possibly be confirmed by a court of law. The first argument should now be familiar. It is Dworkin's weak historicism. We can ask the same question as he does. Why would we be disposed to accept the thesis that the only rights that "exist" within the law are those that are specifically mentioned? Why should the determination of an individual's position in the law by a judge be wholly dependent upon whether there is a verbal counterpart in law expressing that right? Put in that way, the theory seems quite arbitrary. But the argument appears in Judge Parker's decision: "There is no precedent . . . to be *found* in the decisions. . . . Mention of such a right is not to be *found* . . . nor . . . does its existence seem to have been *asserted*."[18]

The more important argument is the second one, that recognizing a right of privacy would be too wide. What sort of argument is that? It appears to assume that some escape from the confining of legal argument to explicit declarations of law is possible. One must conclude this because Judge Parker felt that he had to address the question, and he would not have done so had he thought that the non-existence of an explicitly formulated right of privacy ended the matter. One must be realistic, too. No judge believes that legitimate legal argument may not search for more general principles to determine the validity of disputed propositions of law. Judge Parker's pronouncements, when seen in the light of his choice of a narrower principle rather than the wider one advocated by Warren and Brandeis, becomes a characteristic example of legal argument.

The crux of Judge Parker's argument was a *reductio ad absurdum*.[19] If he recognized this right, then absurd rights such as, for example, a right not to be insulted or a right not to be gossiped about would have to be recognized. Therefore, the general right to privacy could not be said to exist. The failure of the plaintiff's case was thus largely due to the judge's unwillingness or inability to draw a distinction between cases of this sort and a right not to have one's picture used commercially without one's permission. Two years later, the Supreme Court of Georgia decided the other way in *Pavesich* v. *New England Life Insurance Co.*[20] The plaintiff's picture was used, without his permission, in a life insurance advertisement, and he succeeded in obtaining an injunction to prevent further use of the picture. Justice Cobb dealt with the *reductio ad absurdum* problem by the obvious device of recognizing that the right of privacy would, naturally, be in competition with other rights, notably the right to freedom of speech. But this, he thought, should not be a barrier to recognizing a general right to privacy: "This right to speak and the right of privacy have been coexistent . . . each exists, and each must be recognized and enforced with due respect for the other."

These two cases illustrate how judges differ. Judge Parker is not as skilful as Justice Cobb in handling abstractions. The reliance on "asserted" or "mentioned" rights is not a good argument in itself, nor is the *reductio* argument, when useful and sensible distinctions can be drawn between a right not to have one's picture used commercially without consent and a right not to be gossiped about. This isn't to say that Justice Cobb's argument is the best available but rather that his understanding of the possibility of arguing for rights in this abstract, or principled, way makes better sense of legal argument in general. Judge Parker was too wary of "non-explicit" rights and afraid of an "analogical stampede."[21] One suspects the unexpressed worry to be that argument will get out of hand the further it moves from explicit and demonstrable rights to less demonstrable legal propositions argued for in more difficult and abstract ways. From the point of view of a judge, that is a practical consideration of some importance, for where arguments are less easy to understand, their merits are less easily discernible and there is the risk of time-consuming and point-less litigation. But the distinction between good and bad arguments cannot be drawn by fiat, by a distinction between explicit and implicit rights, or by refusing to argue for demarcation areas between the applications of abstract principle.

The original intention theory obviously requires more analysis than this. And the failure of the plain fact theory doesn't obviously obliterate the idea of legislative intention. Is there a way of understanding what it is that does not require us to look at a plain fact conception of it?

THE CONCEPT OF LEGISLATIVE INTENTION

To accept this last possibility is to accept a conception of legislative intention that is more sophisticated than that of a crudely descriptive "psychological group fact." Can "legislative intention" mean more than that? Dworkin thinks the question is always one of interpretation; in the end the idea of the histori-cally "true" intention is just the plain facts theory: historical facts being final determiners of value. The crudest form of the "historically true" intention theory is difficult to take seriously. The founders of the U.S. Constitution, all men, all believed not just that abortion was morally impermissible but that flogging was normal punishment. One serious concern is with judicial neutrality—expressed in the U.K. as judges ought not "usurp the function of the legislature." Dworkin's view is that the idea of legislative intention is a metaphor for drawing our attention to the important fact that the legis-lature has a right to legislate. If we ignore that right or give it little weight, we are making a serious mistake about the nature of our legal system. In a law school tutorial, or a court of law, reference to a statute means reference to what has been decided by the legitimate lawmaker.

Let's consider the original intention theory literally. The first question is clearly: Whose intention? Much legislation is debated in small committees created by the legislature in order to discuss technical or other points in greater detail than would otherwise be possible in the larger chamber. Often these committees accept the advice of specialist persons or bodies as to what should be placed in the proposed enactment. The difficulties compound. A legislator could vote for a measure of which he knows barely anything with the intention of acting in accordance with his party's policy. Or he could understand the point of the legislation but vote for it simply because it will have the unintended effect of furthering his own business interests. Matters become clearer if we move from the idea of mental state and look to what convictions legislators have. This allows us to make judgments about what is an appropriate understanding of what the legislation means. Dworkin gives the example of a person wanting to respect his mother's wishes not to be unfair in business even although she was unfair in business dealings herself by today's standards. How should he act? By just resolving to follow her convictions that certain business methods were fair? That would not be a matter of following her intentions because both intentions (be fair; follow my business practices) are equally genuine; nor is it a matter of following her "true" conviction because both convictions are genuine. Instead, he says: "I must decide which of my mother's convictions—the more abstract or the more detailed—is the right one to follow."[22]

These problems arise from assuming that "legislative intention" is a mental state. It is a good example of what Hart called the fallacy of the "growth of theory on the back of definition."[23] If the definition is wrong in the first place—that is, legislative intention is a mental state—no amount of theory to explain away anomalies not at first sight covered by the definition will make the definition right. The idea of a single group psychological state thus cannot explain legislative intention. In fact, psychological state theories of interpretation are appealing to people because they make interpretation depend on ordinary facts; but it can't work for all genres. It works for conversational interpretation but not for historical interpretation. Many lawyers accept the psychological fact account of legislative meaning but it is impossible, because "the legislators" have varied motives; it doesn't make sense—it is impossible to combine them, for example—without some kind of constructive interpretation.

A philosopher who claims to be sympathetic to Dworkin's idea of constructive interpretation, Scott Shapiro, has recently shown, however, that he fails to understand how for Dworkin value really does determine the significance of facts. Shapiro says:

> Dworkin's claim [is] that those who create legal systems necessarily intend for the content of the law to be determined by the principles and policies that portray the particular legal system in its best light.[24]

As we've seen, this is not Dworkin's claim. (And it is an eccentric interpretation of Dworkin to suppose that he thinks that people could exist who "create legal systems" with "necessary" intentions). But Shapiro argues if it were possible to imagine that there were people who did *not* have those intentions this would be a strong argument against Dworkin's theory. Shapiro engages in a "thought experiment" and says he can imagine people who create a legal system who would not so intend as he believes Dworkin would suppose. Thus, Shapiro concludes, Dworkin's theory is wrong; contradictory, because it "defeats the very purpose of law."[25] Shapiro supports this imaginative exercise with the example of the actual intentions of the framers of the U.S. Constitution.

To repeat, Dworkin clearly believes that rightness of an interpretation is a matter of the moral evaluation of actual or imagined facts of legal practice, not a matter of a description of those facts. So if the best account of law arises out of what the "creators of the legal system" intended, that would be because of the moral value in looking at the legal system that way, not because of the existence of those historical-psychological facts. In Dworkin's terms, Shapiro is only providing a possible interpretation of legal practices, and for the reasons Dworkin gives, not a good one.

The nub is that Shapiro doesn't quite grasp how pervasive a role value plays in Dworkin's legal theory. Dworkin thinks that the whole of law—the theory of law and particular laws—is moral from top to bottom. Law is a branch of politics, which is a branch of morality. No social fact determines law; only value can. No fact contradicts any judgment of value. Hume's principle governs completely. That means that social facts have legal meaning only insofar as they are explained or justified, or nested within judgments of moral value.* These justifications when fully expanded will reveal the different levels of abstractions which any justification needs to reach to be coherent.[26]

THE DEATH OF THE PLAIN FACT
ACCOUNT OF HARD CASES

I have described the plain fact theory, warts and all, with a view to seeing both its initial appeal and its serious limitations. One of the problems with presenting it as starkly as I have is that, properly understood, it carries very little persuasive value. How could anyone ever have accepted it? Has Dworkin been jousting with a straw man? Is there really no better form of positivism existing which can resist Dworkin's attacks? The plain fact theory says the

---

*I commend Cohen's "Facts and Principles," *Phil. & Public Affairs* (Summer 2003) 1, for understanding fully the nature of Hume's principle.

law exists "out there" independently of theory. No one should accept that. Nevertheless, there are significant signs in Anglo-American jurisprudence that people have done so and still do. Dworkin rejects it because he does not see the point of it. We can improve the idea by introducing the ideal of protected expectations. However, Dworkin argues, the resulting conventionalism is too inflexible. Abandoning the idea that law could be identified in any conventional way at all in pragmatism, however, produces flexibility at a cost. This is that we are forced to give up taking rights seriously. The major disadvantage with conventionalism is that it cannot cope with the bridging of the gaps between historically identifiable conventions. The postulation of "higher" and more abstract conventions only supplies solutions ambivalent between litigants, unless the idea of the "best" convention is supplied and that, as we saw, is not something that can be applied without controversy. The major disadvantage with pragmatism is that it denies the intimacy of connection between what has gone before in the law and present decision-making. Both theories ignore the fundamental feature of legal argument that we take for granted in all legal argument: that any proposition of law we assert must "cohere" with all other propositions of law.

From his argument that law must have point, Dworkin asserts that penumbral decisions are not linguistically penumbral, nor phenomenologically peripheral, but highly significant. The hard cases bring to the surface the reasons why we should accept the easy cases as easy. The requirements of consistency and coherency in decision-making mean that the best decisions in such cases must be consistent in principle with those reasons.

SOCIOLOGY AND THE "INSTITUTIONAL" ACCOUNT OF LAW

Leslie Green says that the legal positivism is the thesis that the existence and content of law depends not on its merits but on "social facts," or "facticity."[27] Propositions of law owe their truth to empirical conditions such as the existence of human conventions, not to their morality. So Hart employed the familiar distinction between empirical fact and value to establish the truth of his claim that there is no necessary connection between law and morality so that a law could be grossly immoral (as his discussion of the Nazi grudge informer case showed) but nevertheless a valid law. Perhaps this emphasis upon positivism's facticity is unfortunate for not capturing the sense of positivism's origins in the English enlightenment; positivism was a cry for certainty and clarity and coherence. Its roots do not lie in facticity alone, although "seeing the law" as constructed from social facts was the means (so Bentham thought) to certainty.

What is the argument for the "facticity" of law? That there just *are*—as a matter of being descriptively accurate—laws and legal systems? This can hardly do because that would only report common usage and be neutral as to whether non-moral law is deviant from some central sense identified by some value. What is the law there *to be perceived*? What is left? The question must continually be asked: What is the case for saying that law is empirically identifiable? I believe putting the question like this shows that only judgment of value can determine the central case. In Dworkin's terms, it is a reasonable request that he makes when he says we should look for the point of seeing something a particular way.

An example of the "common usage" mistake is in John Gardner's accusation that Dworkin is "really" a legal positivist. Gardner argues that because interpretation requires first identifying the legal practice to be interpreted, the identification of legal practice, even according to Dworkin's own theory, is independent of aim and purpose. He says of Dworkin's theory that "if judges are to have the aim, on behalf of the law, that law be morally justified, there must be possible morally unjustified legal norms for them to have and pursue this aim."[28] But consider these norms that Gardner says he is able to identify as legal, before identifying them as morally justified. How can he *see* them independently of judging them to be legal? If he can, he's begging the question. Of course—and this can't, it seems, be repeated too often—the fact that people *call* unjustified norms, orders, requirements and so on, *law* can't determine the question. People do, but they also don't! Those predisposed to Gardner's belief do; those not predisposed do not because they invest the law with point. As I put it earlier, according to Dworkin the facts are only there through their moral status; they are moral propositions in the interpretive story (or they have no moral status within that story) and Gardner requires a stronger argument than an analysis of language.

None of this denies the possibility of discussing wicked systems *as law*. Wicked legal systems are clearly law and extremely interesting subjects for study; I believe they are interesting for the light they throw on good law but that is a view amongst many. The causes and effects of law, the structural conservative tendency (emphasized by Marx) and its intrusive and invasive tendency, are all without question matters of legitimate interest and deep study. Recognizing this way of looking at law is not precluded by Dworkin's account, yet there is a persistent belief that somehow the philosophical-moral approach to law that Dworkin has advocated over so many years somehow is derisive of sociological approaches to law. Partly, it arises because of the great persistence in Anglo-American jurisprudence concerning the relevance of descriptivity to statements about and of law. Under this banner, years ago, Neil MacCormick admirably began to promote the study of the idea of the "institutional" nature of law, intended to be something much richer and more complex than the sort of sociological characterization of law in terms of the mere "facts of effectiveness" to which both Kelsen and Hart referred. But I believe MacCormick made too much of it as part of his early avowed position of legal positivism—the idea that there was something there, some "facticity" that warranted study on its own but which also spilled over into understanding and justifying the application of statutes and the common law. My view has always been, as I would say to him over the years, that nothing he said about this was incompatible with what Dworkin ever said or meant, although he clearly thought his book *Legal Reasoning and Legal Theory*, published in 1978, was a rival to Dworkin's *Taking Rights Seriously*, published at the same time. First, there are descriptive, sociological and valuable studies of legal systems; indeed, how could anyone deny the fairly obvious fact that law is more than just a matter of rules? Obviously, this insight does not stand in the way of anything Dworkin says about the nature of legal systems and legal argument. Dworkin focuses on the moral understanding of legal practices. Dworkin does not exclude, ignore or belittle the work of sociologists who, on the other side of the Humean divide (by so frequently their proud admission that they are social "scientists"), investigate the social workings of legal systems. MacCormick's aim was always to make us understand the institutions of law in terms of their overall moral sense *as legal institutions*, although I believe he did not until the last ten years of his life begin to recognize this. It was always a point of humour between us that I would always say to him when I met him that I never thought he was a positivist (*Legal Reasoning and Legal Theory* is a theory of "soft" positivism and that makes no sense except as an attack on itself, as I argued earlier) and he would—sort of—agree. All this is borne out by what he says in the final chapter of his final book, in his final paragraph:[29]

> Human artefacts and contrivances, including any rules by which people try to live, or get others to live, have to be understood functionally. What is their point, what is the final cause to which they are oriented? . . . Honest interpretation that is open about the values it presupposes and that is as alert to system-failures as to system successes judged against those values is the best objectivity that is available to the human sciences, jurisprudence included.

But the focus on 'the institutions of law' can be misleading just because of its power. To suppose that Dworkin doesn't think that the study of the institution of law in a sociological, non-normative sense is somehow not important is unfair. He has never said or implied that. His interest is in the moral way we should view law as legal argument and he believes that requires that we provide moral justifications of the legal institutions in whose name those legal arguments are raised. He proposes as the central conception of doctrinal, legal argument, the moral justification of the application of the coercive powers of the community. How the community is arranged, both in terms of the factually existing legal practices, and the morally normative account that fully explains them (the respective roles of the legislature and the judiciary in a modern democratic legal system, for example) is, for Dworkin, part of that moral justification. Indeed, that we look at the legal institution in this way is itself also subject to moral justification. This is what his theory is all about. No part of this denies the non-normative sociological account of those particular legal institutions—prisons in the United States, non-state tribal legal practices, the religious-legal institutions of the Aztecs, for example—which generate interesting patterns of human behavior for such study. There is no divide (between the "analytical" and the "sociological," say) that is anything other than that brought about by Hume's principle, that value and empirical judgments generate fundamentally different kinds of argument. I don't understand why people think this is a mystery. Fred Schauer, for example, thinks that the distinction I just drew between the purely "descriptive" and the morally normative (between "legal positivism" and Dworkin's theory) is what Dworkin thinks is the argument for legal positivism's being wrong. He says, in the course of discussing approvingly what MacCormick says is the "institutional" approach to law:

> If legal positivism, as a descriptive matter, were true, then what Dworkin calls the doctrinal question would depend on the answer to what he calls the sociological question, and not only would the two questions no longer be distinct, but the latter would have a practical and philosophical importance that would be hard to deny. So Dworkin's argument cannot be taken as an argument against positivism. On the contrary, it presupposes the descriptive falsity of a positivist account of the legal system under discussion.[30]

Dworkin's argument against positivism does not depend on a descriptive attack on it. This is what *Law's Empire* is about (and it makes it clear that his earlier attacks on legal positivism were not phenomenological attacks, or "taxonomic" as Dworkin likes to put it). Instead, he contends that legal positivism makes little or no sense except as a moral normative (interpretive) theory and, even then, not a good one. The argument is long and hard, but in *Law's Empire* he at least makes the case that, devoid of criteria of significance (point), the description of legal practices makes little sense. Further, and more important, the case for *morally normative* legal positivism (Hart's positivism in my view) is that it doesn't make as good moral sense as law as integrity.

Briefly, to repeat the argument earlier in this chapter, conventionalism, as he calls it, doesn't provide a sufficiently rich moral account of the community to which laws apply, nor does it explain law with sufficient flexibility because it too narrowly characterises legal rights as an argument for the satisfaction of reasonable expectations. So Schauer, in dramatically concluding that for Dworkin to think that the sociology of law is irrelevant to adjudication is to ignore "law's most salient characteristic," merely trades off an ambiguity in the idea of what social institutions are. They can be understood socio-logically—that is, in empirical terms—or they can be understood through the making of value judgments (and Dworkin proposes integrity via this route). Schauer fails sufficiently to appreciate the impact of Hume's principle because, in short, he argues that because there is a sociological sense of law, Dworkin can't maintain a separate moral (interpretive) sense. I don't see how that follows.[31]

To say this doesn't require me to add the following, although I think it is nevertheless important. First, I find it hard to accept the possibility of a non-normative sociological account of human institutions (and Schauer probably agrees). Second, I think Dworkin's morally interpretive account has considerable descriptive force over positivistic accounts; it comes much closer to how people view legal systems (whether Aztec, non-state, evil or God-anointed) as partly contestable and partly consensual complex com-munal coercive organizations. But we can agree to disagree on that.

A SUMMING UP

Law is a branch of political morality and the difficult question is how to separate it from the rest of political morality. Legislative rights are rights that the community's lawmaking powers be exercised in a particular way (for example, respecting dignity). Legal rights are those that people may enforce on demand in adjudicative institutions (for example, the law of contract gives me a right to enforce repayment of a loan). The political obligation to obey laws is therefore a legal obligation because it can be enforced through the courts. General political theory deals with legislative rights. A theory of law deals with legal rights by treating it as part of general political theory: it seeks an answer to the normative question of the conditions under which people acquire genuine enforceable rights. The latter question requires reference to particular communities and ordinary political facts will figure in the answer. Legal positivism argues that historical acts are exclusively decisive in such questions. Interpretivism argues that principles of political morality also have a part to play. It follows that legal positivism and his own theory of legal rights are rival normative political theories and not, as he says, rival claims about the unpacking of criterial concepts.

Since they are rival political theories, and law is not about plain facts, we need to consider Dworkin's idea of the interpretive concept, one that is thoroughly evaluative in nature, evaluative of human practices. What differentiates Dworkin's own theory of law is that he claims that his theory makes the best *moral* sense of law.

CHAPTER FOUR

The Interpretation of Law

Dworkin says that interpretation is one of the two domains of understanding in human knowledge and that interpretation stands alongside science (his statement doesn't appear to preclude interpretation in science, nor the presence of empirical facts in arguments of value). What is common to interpretation in all fields is the language of intention and purpose, displayed when we talk of the "meaning" of something. And although Dworkin thinks that it is sometimes odd to say that an interpretation is "uniquely correct," he thinks also that it is odd to say that all interpretations are just interesting approaches. There is something more: if we think that an interpretation is the best one then it seems very odd to say that all other interpretations are just as good. Although interpretive judgments are often said not to be true but "more or less reasonable," or "sound or unsound," Dworkin thinks this doesn't help because there is no point in distinguishing "true" from "the most reasonable." Rather what's needed is a criterion of what's best—success in an enterprise—and what's best in science is something obviously different from success in value; both enterprises nevertheless require what's best. They therefore don't differ in their eligibility for truth, only in their criteria for success. Of course, interpretation is "of" something:

> Interpretation is a social phenomenon. We can interpret as we do only because there are practices or traditions of interpretation we can join. . . . We seek value—point—in interpretations and have responsibility to 'promote that value.'[1]

As we now understand unity of value, interpretation goes "all the way down" and so—again the "unity of value"—it is a question of interpretation just how we should interpret things.

While some developments in Dworkin's approach to legal and political philosophy, notably the idea of interpretation, occurred after some of his important theses had become well known his idea of interpretation places his earlier writings in a clearer light. His aim in *Law's Empire* is to show what is wrong with what he calls the "plain fact" approach to law. In *Justice for Hedgehogs* he makes it clear how far he intends interpretation to extend—to nothing less than over all matters of evaluative judgment and constituting that part of knowledge that is not science.

DESCRIPTIONS AND PARADIGMS OF LAW

We can contrast description with "normativity." Describing what we observe—what we "empirically" know—provides an ordinary sense of description. Normative statements, on the other hand, tell us what we ought to do (or condemn, or praise . . . the list is long) according to a standard. Hart famously, in *The Concept of Law*, drew attention to the existence of standards as necessary for understanding rule-governed behavior. Dworkin's idea of interpretation is not intended to dispense with description and normativity. Rather, he says it is in the nature of some concepts that they can only be understood interpretively. They are *evaluative* concepts. The quickest way to understanding them is through the idea of their "point." We can describe some human practice without making any statement about the point or purpose of the practice. Thus a solely descriptive account of playing chess might take a number of forms, for example, such as "pushing chess pieces on a board." It does not tell us what chess is. On the other hand, an adequate account of chess requires some evaluation of its point; it is therefore potentially controversial. If I provided the details of the rules and then said that the point of the game was to win, many people would agree. But I could go further and say that the game was an intellectual one that required only intellectual strategies, not ones such as causing an opponent to lose through upsetting him (wearing a false beard, say). I could say that the point of chess is to develop the players' intellectual powers and that winning was only incidental to that purpose; this would make it clear that it was cheating, for example, to win via false beards.

Dworkin supposes a level of description which secures a reasonable consensus: no-one thinks rugby balls are essential to chess. Rules such as that pawns may only be moved forward on the chessboard may be understood as a matter of description—and so, in Dworkin's term, is *pre-interpretive*—because there is reasonable consensus about the content of the rule. When Dworkin concedes that even this pre-interpretive data is itself subject to interpretation, he makes it clear that, for interpretive concepts, the distinction between description and interpretation relates primarily to the degree of acceptance; we are able to describe a consensus of opinion. This becomes clear from his discussion of paradigms of law.[2] These are the relatively uncontroversial descriptions of standard understandings of law. They are paradigms only because of their largely uncontroverted acceptance; deviations may mistake the paradigm (and so thinking that the world was not flat during the Dark Ages was not a silly mistake). Paradigms are therefore not "conceptually" distinct from interpretations. We can't escape evaluation and so interpretation is an interpretive idea itself. Put in terms of "point," it is a matter open for interpretation whether a practice has point or not. So people might reasonably differ as to whether a game such as chess has any point, or even whether law must have a point. In other words, if description seems to merge in and out of interpretation, the demand for a more concrete way of drawing the distinction can only be met by saying that the demand itself must have a point.

The idea of "paradigms" might strike some as strange. If there is a consensus, a plateau of coinciding views about what constitutes law, then surely this plateau serves to inform us about what is uncontroversially law. But to deny the "reasons behind the law" ignores the crucial fact that consensus is a coincidence of views, each of which provides a separate justification. Again, the view that there are specific, clear rules of law is a result of particular views, not the starting-point of those views. Paradigms have their point because they act as stable plateaus from which sense may be made of the shifting arguments concerning them. In this sense, someone who rejects a paradigm makes a mistake for, as Dworkin says, "paradigms anchor interpretations."[3]

Further, and this follows from what has so far been said, it is possible to stand back from an interpretation and say both that it is the best interpretation and that the result is not a good one; we still draw a distinction between the best something can be and ideals. This is common within the law. Judges will frequently offer an interpretation of law and then say that the law ought not to be how—correctly interpreted—it is. When judges pronounce this, they are actually offering an interpretation of their own judicial limitations. It is useful to compare the two dissenting judges, Lords Simon and Kilbrandon, in the well-known English criminal case where the House of Lords extended the defense of duress to murder. Lord Simon thought judges could make new law but not where the legislature had more "wisdom":

> I am all for recognizing frankly that judges do make law. And I am all for judges exercising this responsibility boldly at the proper time and place—that is, where they can feel confident of having in mind, and correctly weighed, all the implications of their decision and where matters of social policy are not involved which the collective wisdom of Parliament is better suited to resolve.[4]

Lord Kilbrandon's view is stricter; it is not within the rights of judges to make such decisions:

> The grounds upon which the majority propose that the conviction of the appellant be set aside involve changes in the law which are outside the proper functions of your Lordships in their judicial capacity . . . modern society rightly prefers to exercise that function for itself, and this it conveniently does through those who represent it in Parliament.[5]

To conclude, Dworkin provides us with a new focus in law. At first sight, this focus is upon the hard cases, now to be characterized by the examination of areas of law which are controversial in a more fundamental way than the characterization of such areas as peripheral, or penumbral to more important laws. At second sight, a deeper understanding shows us that, because of the consensus nature of legal paradigms, it is possible for all cases to be hard cases, and that the real focus is not on the difference between what is clear or unclear, but upon the quality of the underlying legal argument justifying the application of coercion by the community.

THE POINT OF INTERPRETATION

Dworkin says we must make "the best" of an interpretive concept that it can be. This is very abstract, partly because Dworkin wants to suggest a connection between interpretation in science as well as value. A useful metaphor is that of "placing a thing in its best light"; we know what poor interpretations are ("*Hamlet* is just a play about courtly manners") and that good interpretations are better. If we accept this, then we must concede that to interpret properly means to engage with the appropriate arguments. A common objection to this general approach is that "best" begs the question and that sometimes we should try to place things in the "worst" light. People inclined in this direction seem keen to be skeptical of widely accepted practices. But it misses Dworkin's point; he doesn't claim that every practice must be understood as morally good but that one must see it in the light of the best possible arguments for it; it is a point about explanation, not ideology. Take historical interpretation. There is nothing in the idea of the best interpretation of the rise of Adolf Hitler that compels us to show him as morally good. Painting the best possible picture of him is compatible with showing him to be the worst possible monster. In the requisite sense of "best," the best interpretation of Hitler would not be achieved by the suppression of facts, or only understanding events from his point of view, or by confining interpretation only to historical materials from his staff files:

> I do not mean that every kind of activity we call interpretation aims to make the best of what it interprets—a "scientific" interpretation of the Holocaust would not try to show Hitler's motives in the most attractive light, nor would someone trying to show the sexist effects of a comic strip strain to find a non-sexist reading—but only that this is so in the normal or paradigm cases of creative interpretation.[6]

Dworkin thinks that value exists in "explanatory" interpretation of history, say. Not all history is interpretive, though. It is description when we say, for example, that there are "mass" intentions such as "Americans are moving towards independence," and some history is just straightforward "retrieval."[7] But historical interpretation relies on an historian's "own sense of point and value" and historians seek "to make the past intelligible to the present." Dworkin gives an example of historical interpretive controversy by looking at Herbert Butterfield's polemic against the Whig interpretation of history of Macaulay (according to whom British history showed progression to a more perfect society). On the contrary, he says, Butterfield thought that history took us "away from the world of general ideas" that Macaulay was proclaiming.

I believe that Dworkin's idea that interpretation requires evaluation is sufficiently abstract to gain acceptance (that is, it is virtually non-ideological): it just says explanations are better when the reasons supporting them are serious. Since people have their own views of what constitutes "the best light," the controversy exists at all lower levels, and the upper level itself can, under his theory, be revised. The abstract nature of interpretation is appealing, I suggest, because it abstracts from the substantial arguments about what is the best interpretation. It also shows the plateau of agreement between two participants who nevertheless offer rival interpretations.

INTERPRETING LAW

How does interpretation apply to social practices such as law? Dworkin says that we may understand a social practice in three ways: *pre-interpretively*, *interpretively*, and *post-interpretively*. Take the pre-interpretive understanding first. Imagine a society in which there is a social practice requiring that men must bow to women when passing them in the street. In this society, no attitude is struck towards the value of the rule. No point is ascribed to it. Hart's analysis of rule-following provides an account this behavior.[8] Members of the society just accept this practice. It is not just that men bow out of habit or do it "as a rule." It is rather that there is an actual rule of courtesy that requires it. That there is such a social rule of courtesy means that men regularly bow when meeting women. This behavior is coupled with the consistent criticism of deviations from this pattern. A further necessary feature for Hart is that this criticism is based upon reasons accepted by at least some members of the society that courtesy is so required. When we assert the existence of this social rule, without reference to its point, Dworkin says that this shows a pre-interpretive understanding of the assertion that a social rule about courtesy to women exists.

Analytically, the pre-interpretive and interpretive stages may be distinguished as two ways of understanding the existing social practice, or rule. We can now imagine that, after a while, people begin to ask what the point of the rule is—why men should observe it—and that their answers will differ as to what the practice requires in particular cases. There will therefore be two parts to the introduction of this "interpretive" phase, one where there is an attitude of questioning, and giving of "meaning," to the social rule of courtesy, and a second where the question arises about the extension of this meaning to particular cases. We can test these distinctions by reference to games, such as cricket, in which a description of the rules is distinguishable from a discussion of its point (is it fun? does it test skill? is it competitive?), which in turn is distinguishable from the way particular rules are to be interpreted (does "bowling" include throwing? or underarm bowling?).

The second interpretive phase arises when people question the point of the rule and suggest restrictions or extensions to its scope. Those who think that the rule embodies respect for the "weaker" sex may think that bowing by men is not necessary when a woman is doing a "man's" job, or is lesbian. Someone who thinks that bowing is a mark of respect for people who have the capacity to bear children may not think the rule should extend to a spinster or the wife in a childless couple. The third and post-interpretive phase occurs when there is consensus about the point of the rule and the restrictions or extensions now apply; Dworkin says it is where interpretation "folds back into itself." This will occur when the community decides to settle upon— perhaps but not necessarily by judicial decision—some particular meaning. After a while that meaning becomes, in the sense discussed, pre-interpretive and the process may begin over again.

This move from pre-interpretive to interpretive understanding is a significant one in legal philosophy, as important as Hart's move in *The Concept
of Law* from the "pre-legal" to the "legal" society. For Hart, the analytical,
pre-legal society consisted of the bare rules of obligation alone. It was only
by the addition of the secondary, or power-conferring, rules that he could
characterize the "modern municipal legal system." Seeing Hart's move as
interpretive would undermine his avowed aim of "descriptive sociology"; we
might ask what the point of Hart's characterization of law is. He is reasonably explicit that it could serve values—certainty, progress and efficiency. The
secondary rules would help to prevent "vendettas" (Hart's word) by creating
a court structure, allow for progress through the dynamic of a legislature, and
stabilize life for those subject to law by creating certainty in the identification
of law through the rules of recognition.[9] This line of argument needs care.
Hart's account is perhaps a good description in some jurisdictions (chiefly
Anglo-European) of the pre-interpretive stage, because it is an account
which people would (and do) accept as a fairly accurate description of law
(at the least they think that certainty is a legal value). Dworkin's argument
is interpretive; so how people speak or what they believe is not determinative; he distinguishes, as between the pre-interpretive and the interpretive
stage, between two levels of interpretation and so the term *pre*-interpretive
is misleading. The pre-interpretive stage constitutes the formal structure
against which interpretive substantive judgments must be made. That way
of looking at things is not contradictory as, for example, Stanley Fish has
claimed[10] because the drawing of a distinction between substance and form
(or, as Dworkin calls it, "fit") is itself an interpretive act—we see that most
clearly now from the unity of value thesis—and one that is, I believe, implicit
in Hart's account.

It helps to distinguish here between questions concerning the nature
of law, often regarded as Hart's interest, and professional questions, often
described as the question "of justification,"[11] with which Dworkin is concerned. Hart's answer to the question of nature ("What is law?—the union
of primary and secondary rules") suits the pre-interpretive attitude because
it attempts to describe a consensus of thinking about law (although surely
not in those legal systems where God is regarded as the source of law). Of
course, Dworkin's theory requires an interpretive understanding of the "nature" question but it also requires an interpretive understanding of the laws
of particular legal systems. As he says, his theory is an account of "doctrinal
law."[12] Note that Hart also—and not unsurprisingly—provides for both the
identification of "doctrinal" laws and their administration. You look to what
he calls the "rule of recognition"[13]—the identifying rule—and see whether

it validates any purported rule. If it does, that rule is a valid legal rule in that legal system, and so forms part of its body of legal "doctrine." Hart also envisages courts as part of his "secondary rules of adjudication" designed to achieve "efficiency."

Nothing prevents skepticism in the second and third stages of interpretation. Some people might agree that courtesy implies respect but then argue that respect—properly understood—implies recognition of another's equal value; they might then reasonably conclude that bowing implies deference which contradicts respect thus understood. They now—perhaps with some success—advocate abolition of the bowing rule. This is an example of Dworkin's internal skepticism at work: the best sense you can make of the bowing rule is that it is contradictory—it is not a courtesy rule at all—and should go.

Dworkin says that the interpretation of social practices is like *artistic* interpretation, which interprets the thing—the work of art—created by people but may be separate from their thoughts and intentions. He distinguishes it from *scientific* interpretation, which interprets things not created by people. Nor is it *conversational* interpretation, which interprets what people mean to say rather than what the interpreter proposes. Dworkin says that artistic interpretation is creative: "A participant interpreting a social practice . . . proposes value for the practice by describing some scheme of interests or goals or principles the practice can be taken to serve or express or exemplify."[14] This contrast between creative interpretation and scientific and conversational interpretation is instructive. The important difference is that neither of the latter two sorts of interpretation requires proposing human interests or goals or principles. That is clear in the case of scientific interpretation, and one should note that some positivists—Kelsen, for example—appear to endorse a scientific conception of interpretation. The case of conversational interpretation is more difficult because the "thing" to be interpreted is not clearly independent of the purposes and practices of language. In order to interpret what a person means we have to make sense of the human purpose behind the attempt at communicating meaning. But it is unlike artistic interpretation because the interpreter is not so free to place his own construction upon what the speaker said. The criterion of what the speaker meant, in conversational interpretation, is what he actually intended his words to mean. Denying this point would deny the distinction between the artistic use of language and its ordinary day-to-day use in communicating.

Dworkin nevertheless says that all interpretation may be drawn under the umbrella of constructive interpretation. All interpretation strives "to make an object the best it can be, as an instance of some assumed enterprise."[15] For conversational interpretation he uses the principle of charity, according to which we make the best of a person's communication to understand what he said, and for scientific interpretation we use the standards of theory construction such as simplicity, elegance and verifiability.

MAKING THE BEST MORAL SENSE OF LAW

How does interpretation apply to law? The rules of law constitute the social practices which are the "thing" to be interpreted in the constructive or artistic way. What does it mean to say that we must show the legal practices in their best light? Dworkin thinks the central point of law is that it provides the moral justification for state coercion; he claims it is our shared concept of law—a pre-interpretive understanding—that views law as constraining and licensing governmental coercion:

> Law insists that force not be used or withheld, no matter how useful that would be to ends in view, no matter how beneficial or noble these ends, except as licensed or required by individual rights and responsibilities flowing from past political decisions about when collective force is *justified*.[16]

Is this a reasonable thing to say? Dworkin has certainly described a common view of law. In any case, if we do see law as a form of justification, it seems reasonable that moral justification is preferable to any other.

There are some obvious objections. It is question-begging, we might say. Also, perhaps, the definition endorses itself as a peculiarly bourgeois idea: that invoking law promotes the state, also in some question-begging way. The committed anarchist will find no joy here. We can't be suspicious of the assertion that law must be cast in its best moral light from some ground such as that law and morality are "conceptually" distinct; that also is question-begging. There is a certain straightforward sense in which we should think of law in the light of our own morally evaluative judgment; Dworkin's unity of value thesis, if true, provides support just for the value to be gained from looking at law this way. And very important is that the anarchist should consider whether his own view is an attempt to cast law in its best moral light; presumably he thinks there is moral value in anarchy.

CONCEPTS AND CONCEPTIONS

Dworkin makes frequent use of a distinction between *concepts* and *conceptions*. Concepts embrace a discrete set of ideas that are employed in all interpretations; a lowest common denominator of meaning, common in dictionaries. A conception, on the other hand, will take up some controversy that, according to Dworkin, is "latent" in the concept. The seminal analysis of the distinction between concepts and conceptions is to be found in an article by Gallie, entitled "Essentially Contested Concepts," and his idea was taken up by many political philosophers, notably Rawls in *A Theory of Justice*.[17] Gallie argues that some concepts, such as art, democracy, social justice and "the Christian life" are, by their nature, ideas which can only be understood as involving controversial argument. He lists a number of conditions which are part descriptions of any "essentially contested" concept and these entail, I think, the idea that such concepts are understood through different conceptions. These are that the concept must be "applausive" (i.e., critical), "internally complex," and "variously describable"; it must also admit of "considerable modification in the light of changing circumstances" and that "to use an essentially contested concept means to use it against other uses and to recognize that one's own use of it has to be maintained against these other uses."[18] And, in order to distinguish such concepts from "radically confused" concepts, Gallie says that users of such concepts must recognize the "authority" of an "original exemplar" of the concept, and the competition among users must enable "the original exemplar's achievement to be sustained and/or developed in optimum fashion."[19]

We know, for example, what democracy is in some obvious sense: we don't confuse democracy with mountains. There are ideas that we understand to be thought of as "democratic" ideas, such as free elections, the equality and freedom of people, the rule of law but, although there are other ideas we would probably agree upon, we might only agree on democracy's being, broadly, government by consent. People have different conceptions about the force and scope of consent. The kind of consent required, for example: consent as evidenced by proportional representation, or by the system of the single non-transferable vote, or block voting for trade unions? Take the idea of equality, as expressed by "one person, one vote." A conception of that idea was once that it could not include women. Others view democracy as a system of procedural, majority rule only while others view it in a substantive way, as essentially about the protection of minority interests and rights. Others view democracy as a constraint on decision-making at all levels rather than any particular scheme of government. Others have found democracy in the idea of the one-party state. These ideas can be debated on the common ground that democracy is about government "by consent," and on even wider grounds concerning equality and freedom.

CONCEPTS AND INTERPRETIVE DISAGREEMENT

An important thesis in *Justice for Hedgehogs* is that moral reasoning is conceptual interpretation of our practices in using moral concepts; here interpretation dispenses with the normal use of a difference between author and interpretation. When we disagree about morality, we disagree not about what an author said but about ideas that are part of our common understanding and shared practices. In introducing this idea, Dworkin (calling upon an earlier taxonomy he drew up in *Justice in Robes* and drawing together remarks he had made elsewhere) distinguishes between different kinds of concepts. Most important for understanding legal positivism are what he calls "criterial" concepts which refer to our sharing a concept when we use the same criteria for identifying instances of that concept; a triangle is a criterial concept because we identify instances in the same way: a figure with only three straight sides. In most cases, but not all, he says, our use of the same criteria means that our focus upon an instance of a concept is precise.[20]

Not all concepts are criterial; there are concepts — known as "natural kind" concepts — where agreement is not the test. Take the concept of lionhood. Here we may use different criteria for identifying lions but nevertheless have no trouble understanding that we are talking about the same thing. Our differences would not necessarily mark a mistake of language, as when we discover that one of us is talking about the bank of a river and the other about the Bank of England. These are not cases, either, where we are each being a bit vague. Rather, we use such natural kind concepts referring to something whose identity is fixed in the natural world; we suppose ourselves to be referring to the same thing even though we use different criteria. Note that while criterial and natural kind concepts are independent of each other they may still have in common the use of a decisive test (what a central case of baldness is, for example, or — very likely — the DNA constituting lionhood). In each case, this will mean that "genuine" disagreement is ruled out "once all the other pertinent facts are agreed." In my view, when Dworkin originally talked about thinking of law as consisting of "plain facts," echoing a common understanding of "straight talk" and certainty, he was referring to both "criterial" and "natural kind" concepts — those where the object of discussion is regarded as determinable. Once we see what concept we are talking about, we must be in agreement because there are either already agreed criteria, or we agree that there is some determining characteristic (although we might not be sure what it is).

Interpretive concepts are different, constituting a "family of concepts we share in spite of not agreeing about a decisive test." We agree, but only through appreciating that their application is constituted by their best understanding. Also pertinent to understanding interpretation are paradigms. These, he says, are shared understandings of "particular characterizations" that "permit us to argue." The agreement is different from criterial and natural kind concepts because there is not a decisive test: paradigms are consistent with difference; even debunking, he says, is consistent with agreement. Dworkin says that distinctions between criterial, natural kind and interpretive concepts are not clearly indicated by usage; he thinks, for example, that people on the whole wrongly think the meaning of democracy is criterial. He also thinks that interpretive concepts are important because it is through them that people must see that their disagreements are genuine, and that their interpretation guides their judgment. It follows from the fact that moral concepts are interpretive that they can't be analyzed neutrally. Engaging in what the best sense is of a particular moral concept rules out a non-committed, detached and neutral account. Even to adopt—if one could—a detached position on the actual use of such a concept would be to engage in moral argument (as Dworkin's arguments concerning skepticism show). It follows, he says, that meta-ethics is a misconceived project.

Dworkin considers the possibility that at some abstract level where there is agreement about certain moral statements, moral concepts are criterial. He gives as an example Rawls's statement that people accept that justice is about non-arbitrary distinctions in the assigning of rights. Nevertheless, Dworkin thinks this is still non-criterial because many people accept that it is God who determines justice and so justice is not characterized in everyone's view as constituting non-arbitrary distinctions. In that case, are any of our moral concepts criterial? No, he says. Is there agreement in morality at least that in the establishing of a moral proposition there is criterial agreement (reflecting the most abstract moral requirement) "that something should, or should not, be done"? Again he disagrees because moral judgments are not always concerned with commending some course of action. Are moral concepts the natural-kind sort where they possess a "distinct property" (like being particles of some sort, say) which we discern through a special faculty of intuition? He says this could only be true if there were agreement on which particles came within the concept; there would be agreement on instances then and not the criteria. But Dworkin thinks that we don't agree on what comes under the concept. He says our agreement is pretty minimal; we agree on paradigms sufficiently to say that we share our moral concepts but there is little beyond that minimal agreement. So, Dworkin concludes, moral concepts must be interpretive.

HART'S THEORY AS A NON-DESCRIPTIVE INTERPRETIVE THEORY

It is instructive to apply the distinction between concepts and conceptions to Hart's *The Concept of Law*. I have already suggested that Hart's book is an interpretation rather than a neutral description of law. That interpretation is close to what Dworkin calls "conventionalism," the point of which is to serve the ideal of protected expectations which I examined in Chapter 3. Dworkin has told me that he now regrets not having begun his chapter entitled "Conventionalism" in *Law's Empire* with a general statement that he regarded Hart's theory of law as best understood as a conventionalist theory. To employ the terminology, *The Concept of Law* is Hart's "conception" of the concept of law.[21] Dworkin provides a justification that is an important part of his approach to interpretive questions. In short, it is that we have a responsibility to "construct" answers to this sort of question, and that it is a reneging of responsibility to stand off and assume that there just *is* an answer "out there" which, maybe, is in the powers of someone else, or even nobody, to resolve.[22]

This is not "abstract philosophy" removed from the realities of the courtroom. Take the landmark torts case in the U.K. of 1932, *Donoghue* v. *Stevenson*.[23] In this case, the House of Lords devised a new relationship of liability between the ultimate manufacturer, a maker of fizzy drinks, and the ultimate consumer, a woman who became ill after eating a decomposed snail in one of the manufacturer's drinks. Lord Atkin argued that the manufacturer was liable because of a general duty in tort law upon those whose acts could reasonably be seen to affect others (known as the "neighbor" principle of tortious liability). Lord Buckmaster's view was that liability in this sort of case was limited to categories already existing in tort: since there were none to cover the case and there was no contractual relationship between the parties, the woman's case had to fail.

I believe the language of concept and conception well describes their differences: each had a different conception of the same concept of tortious liability. They agreed on the concept but disagreed in their conceptions of it. They shared the idea that tortious liability was the basis for common law compensation for involuntary wrongs and the idea that liability arose from a relationship between the parties. But Lord Atkin's conception of the concept of tortious liability was wider than Lord Buckmaster's. And we might agree with the many commentators that Lord Atkin's conception was the better one because it integrated otherwise seemingly discrete heads of liability through the neighbor principle.

We needn't only take famous cases. Even in mundane day-to-day cases of legal argument the distinction between concept and conceptions is apparent. Take a typical case involving the interpretation of some section of a safety regulation. The concept—that discrete set of ideas around which agreement collects—is the employer's duty to fence dangerous machinery. The employer's lawyer argues for the conception of that duty which absolves the factory owner from an employee's negligence. The inspector's lawyer argues for the opposite conception under which employers have duties to guard even against negligence. Even if we don't accept that "best" means "morally best," given everything else about the legal system the distinction between concepts and conceptions is useful in understanding the above differences.

THE CONCEPT OF LAW AS INTEGRITY

What, for Dworkin, is the concept, as opposed to the correct conception, of law? I have already mentioned the central idea of justification. When we talk of law, the "discrete collection of ideas" which we "uncontroversially accept" concerns the justification of the use of state power. Thus, he says, "legal argument takes place on a plateau of rough consensus that if law exists it provides a justification for the use of collective power against individual citizens or groups."[24] Dworkin's theory must, therefore, be responsive to real legal arguments. Further, his theory attempts to justify *law*, not how ideally the world should be. The moral judgments are a subset of what is politically required and so the best interpretation of the legal materials must draw upon the best moral theory of the legal system.

The meld between the legal materials and moral theory is achieved in the idea of integrity. It is a principle requiring that law cohere in a way that is distinct from justice, according to which the right state of affairs exists in society, and distinct from fairness, a conception of equality according to which "each point of view must be allowed a voice in the process of deliberation."[25] Integrity means that law should always be created, or interpreted, to form an integral whole. This injunction expresses the virtue of integrity, which is distinct from, but, according to Dworkin, on the same plane as, the twin virtues of justice and fairness. Dworkin characterizes justice and fairness in general terms as follows:

Justice . . . is a matter of the right outcome of the political system: the right distribution of goods, opportunities, and other resources. Fairness is a matter of the right structure for that system, the structure that distributes influence over political decisions in the right way.[26]

The problem is when justice and fairness compete with each other; Dworkin wants to be able to find a principled relationship between them rather than merely compromise. To flesh all these abstractions out, let us suppose that the most just society would outlaw abortion. Let us also suppose that the fairest society gives each person a voice in the process of decision. Imagine a society in which a majority of people want, and vote for, legalized abortion in specified circumstances. Obviously, if we accept both these suppositions, we are bound to conclude that there is a conflict. Imagine the following situation. The legislature adopts a compromise between justice and fairness by granting rights of abortion to women in proportion to the number of pro-abortion legislative votes. Let us say that there was a two-thirds majority vote against and one-third for abortion. A statute now allocates permissions for abortions at the rate of one to every three requests, with some fair request system, perhaps a lottery. We do not know as a matter of demonstration whether abortion is just or not, but we do know that there will be some justice done because either justice permits abortions in the specified circumstances or it does not. Justice is then apportioned according to the fairness of allowing "each point of view its voice in the process."

The question is whether this is an appropriate response to this serious question. It amounts to a compromise between justice and fairness and such compromises have been tried before. Dworkin uses the example of the U.S. Constitution which originally compromised slavery by counting three-fifths of a state's slaves in determining the state's representation in Congress.[27] In the United States such legislative requirements are known as "checkerboard" statutes because they produce a symmetrical result—contrasting and general. Dworkin uses our intuitive response to this sort of compromise by suggesting the virtue of integrity. He compares his argument with the discovery of the planet Neptune, whose existence was confirmed, not by direct observation, but by its gravitational effects on neighboring planets. We notice the virtue of integrity by noting its pull on justice and fairness, he says, and it is this virtue that allows for a principled adjustment rather than raw compromise between justice and fairness. The idea of integrity appears first in *Law's Empire* and is the fundamental virtue in Dworkin's legal philosophy. I believe the idea is present throughout Dworkin's earlier work particularly in his account of justification in hard cases. There the general scheme for arguing for decisions was to argue in terms of value, in particular by arguing and asserting matters of principle.[28]

A WORD ON "COHERENCE"

The requirement of coherence in the law is more than just *consistency* or, as Dworkin prefers to call it, "bare consistency." Bare consistency just amounts to the absence of logical contradiction between two statements of law. Coherence must, rather, be consistency "in principle," that is, it must "express a single and comprehensive vision of justice."[29] While generally we must produce arguments consistent with previous decisions and statutes, and with arguments that have been used in the past, it is not only consistency that is at work.[30] Bare consistency, for example, is an impossible requirement because we all accept, as properly characteristic of legal argument, that some previous decisions are mistaken. We cope with mistakes by justifying their unique position with arguments that are much richer than bare consistency can permit. We might, for example, be prepared to put forward an argument for overturning a line of cases, not because they are inconsistent with another line of cases. There may be no such line. Or, if there are, under bare consistency, the argument for retaining them is just as good as for abandoning them by declaring them mistakes. Coherence captures the logical tone of consistency but permits other judgments of right and wrong. The incoherent account a child gives of his afternoon's activities goes further than inconsistency. For his account to be coherent it must "make sense," not just be consistent. On the other hand, coherence describes a situation at a highly abstracted level, where we are reduced to saying that things must make sense, or "hang together" without being much more specific. Coherence is only fully understandable in the context of particular cases, but is not enough on its own. Take the sorts of arguments that were used in *Donoghue* v. *Stevenson*, the decomposed snail case. Lord Atkin, I suggested, was trying to make coherent the idea of liability for negligence, by finding an abstract way of expressing various forms of existing liability in contract and tort. He thought, as many others have since thought, that the principled way was through the neighbor principle. His argument, I suggest, had the virtue of coherence. It makes sense, or "hangs together," because it provides a way of arguing from the facts of that particular set of circumstances, to all sorts of other circumstances, by means of a principle—the neighbor principle. It does this while clearly showing why the previous cases were justly decided and why it would be wrong to restrict liability in negligence only to certain categories of case (as Lord Buckmaster did). In Dworkin's terms, there is a deeper value that justifies the more abstract way of viewing the different cases and understanding it allows the categories to be explained and then changed (or "fold back into themselves").

Dworkin sees the special virtue of the "single vision of justice" as representing the ideal of community or, as he prefers to call it, the ideal of "fraternity." This ideal provides the best justification for the personification of the state which "speaks" with integrity's "one voice." I shall turn to his idea of community, which is his liberal and individualist response to the conservative "communitarians," in Chapter 6. In short, his view is that one's being an *individual* gives rise to certain public virtues, among which is the duty the state has (and the duty the individual has to uphold) to ensure that people are treated as equals.

NUANCES IN IDEAL WORLDS

The connection between integrity and the ideal of equality is crucial to Dworkin. It is through the single vision of the law, he says, that the state treats its citizens as equals. It is not just that of consistency in dealing which is, as Hart has pointed out,[31] "compatible with great iniquity," but incorporates the idea of treating people as equals. Integrity is the principal virtue of legal argument and it is a moral virtue in the political sphere. Thus, legal and moral argument cannot be separated. Legal argument must, according to Dworkin, characteristically refer to the right each person has to be treated as an equal. To illustrate, Dworkin takes us through a number of worlds. In what he calls the "ideal ideal" world, there is no need for the virtue of integrity. Imagine the perfect world where everyone behaves as they should. The perfectly just legislative decision is made in the abortion case, referred to above, and everyone votes for it. In any case, the legislation is not needed as everybody does what is morally right. Here, the legislators are not torn between the issue of substantive justice and the issue of fairness. Everyone concurs, and rightly. Since the state, by hypothesis, treats everyone as equals, there is no need, in the ideal world, for the separate virtue of integrity. This is so because it is a corrective concept, one which is only necessary when there is a tension between justice and fairness. Another way of putting it is to say that Dworkin's use of the idea of integrity is designed to construct an ideal judicial system, where principled trade-offs are perfectly made by judges. The judges have a correct conception of justice with which they work, but they are permitted to trade it against other factors arising in the real world.

This argument establishes, I think, the unique nature of integrity. Its function is to constrain states in the real world, where decisions are often unjust but fair. Since its function, its special virtue, is to constrain, it is, too, an ideal but one that exists in the "ideal *real*" world. In other words, in the "real real" world, the one you and I live in, legislators, and lawyers and judges, must aim at the ideal of making all laws form a coherent whole, one that makes the state speak to all citizens equally. It means that integrity represents a striving, in the real world, for a justice which, Dworkin says, "abstracts" from institutions. "Pure" integrity, he says, "declares how the community's practices must be reformed to serve more coherently and comprehensively a vision of social justice it has partly adopted, but it does not declare which officer has which office in that grand project."[32]

CHAPTER FIVE

The Evaluative Coherence of Legal Argument

Dworkin says the law must be coherent and it must treat all members of the community as equals; in particular, lawyers of all castes (law students through to the highest appellate judges) should attempt to integrate their decisions and arguments within the body of existing law but do this in the best moral way. There are two quick ways into this idea. First, if you had to choose between two possible meanings of a regulation, would you choose that one that made more moral sense or less moral sense?[1] Second, you would look at Dworkin's well-known model of the ideal judge, a judge who is super-intelligent and exceedingly hard-working, whom he calls "Hercules." As he is an ideal judge it is banal to deny he exists, although that has been a woefully common criticism of Dworkin's theory. In any case, things can exist in ideal worlds and we should not suppose that the only form of existence is in the real world; indeed, it is an interesting question just what the "real world" is. The "free market" is an ideal, and its existence is shown by the way we judge market imperfections in the real world. Monopolies exist in the real world and they distort the market; so they are imperfections by reference to a standard that doesn't exist in the real world. The difficulty people have with Hercules is that he is so different from the formidably clear idea of Bentham's "command of the sovereign" and Hart's similarly clear test of the "rule of recognition." By using Hercules, Dworkin provides only a scheme for legal argument. He cannot provide a set of premises from which conclusions might be drawn by means of deduction—as both commands and the rule of recognition allow—because that formalistic account, he believes, is wrong.[2] In the following idea, however, we can see how Hercules provides us with an idea of how to go about identifying the law:

> If a judge accepts the settled practices of his legal system—if he accepts, that is, the autonomy provided by its distinct constitutive and regulative rules—then he must, according to the doctrine of political responsibility, accept some general political theory that justifies these practices.[3]

We need to construct a theory of the "settled" practices and then draw from that theory an argument justifying further legal propositions. Legal argument will then, in most hard cases, develop as the result of a tension between two dimensions of argument, one that argues towards a "fit" with settled law, the other that argues towards "substantive" issues of political morality. While the twin abstract injunctions in Dworkin "to make the best sense" of law, and "to treat people as equals," propel his legal and political philosophy, it is the distinction between "fit" and "substance" that forms the cutting edge, for him, of legal argument.

We shouldn't place weight upon the distinctions between reasoning, "theory" and "philosophy" here. Scott Shapiro, for example, thinks that Dworkin places too much weight on the intellectual capabilities, and therefore trustworthiness, of judges. What Dworkin expects from judges, he says, "is so abstract and uses techniques unfamiliar to most nonphilosophers, the normal institutional checks are bound to be ineffective."[4] His fear is that too much by way of moral decision will be left to them. Shapiro says that practicing lawyers become "irritated" when discussion of jurisprudence is remote from the concerns of legal practice and Dworkin's theory is particularly remote. Of Dworkin's argument that legal practice should be placed in its "best moral light," he says:

> Dworkin never considers in any meaningful way whether such a methodology is appropriate for participants with normal cognitive and moral capacities. On the contrary, Dworkinian interpretation presupposes a tremendous trust in the philosophical abilities of group members and in their good will for carrying out such rigorous intellectual exercises.[5]

But for its scope of subject-matter, philosophy is only acute thinking. It is more abstract than, we might say, day-to-day practical thinking but often only because it doesn't limit itself to orthodox conclusions (like the conclusions of great judges, I think). What is the objection to this way of thinking other than that it is too difficult for some people? Does Shapiro really think that good judges are incapable of going back a few stages into the abstract and drawing connections? My own experience of legal practice is that judges do engage like this and the law reports provide plenty of examples. Civil rights cases in the United States on the most abstract interpretations of equality and freedom? This is not to deny there are poor judges and judgments, for there is clear institutional recognition of this obvious fact in the form, for example, of courts of appeal. Judges aren't so bad. In the U.K. they could do with more time and research facilities. I suspect Shapiro thinks of philosophy as a professional subject, largely undirected by practical thought and perhaps confined to members of departments of philosophy. We should be a lot more relaxed than that, and we shouldn't assume that because a philosopher might rephrase or re-interpret in other language what a judge has decided, that what the judge has achieved is less abstract, less thoughtful or less acute than what philosophical discussion might achieve.

If we can't trust judges over legislators, we can make judges administrators, or triers solely of fact. This was Jeremy Bentham's enthusiastic solution. Perhaps it is time our systems of legal education, the training of judges and recruitment to the legal profession should be reformed. I'd be prepared to go along that line although I'd need to be convinced that things were in such a state as Shapiro makes out. Nevertheless, I think his only concern against Dworkin on the trustworthiness of judges arises from an unduly narrow view of what philosophical reasoning is.

"SUBSTANCE" AND "FIT" AND THE CHAIN NOVEL

Dworkin's analogy between legal argument and the writing of a chain novel is useful. Several novelists get together with a proposal that they each write a single chapter of a book to be jointly authored. One begins, another writes the second chapter, and so on. There will be certain constraints of "fit" upon the second author and these constraints will tend to increase on the subsequent authors, although (convincing) changes of direction will be possible. Constraints will be such things as the names of the characters (Christine in the first chapter cannot without explanation have the name "Thug" in the second chapter, for example), language (it would be crazy if the first chapter were in English but the second in Sanskrit) and plot (imagine if there were no logical explanations for alterations in place and time, and for the actions of any of the characters). These suggestions do not exhaust the many possibilities of "fit," and it is important to appreciate that, for Dworkin, the question of "fit" is itself open to interpretation. Lack of appreciation of that simple point is almost total amongst Dworkin's critics.[6] A striking example is Stanley Fish, who doubted whether there were genuine pre-interpretive modes of legal and artistic argument and so was able to say that there were no genuine lines of "fit." Dworkin's argument in reply was just a repeat of his claim about paradigms: our agreement on some evaluative point suggests the argument is exhausted for the time being—but not final—and so the agreement may be treated for the purposes of further argument as settled (as something which further interpretation may later confront). Obviously, the acceptance of the genre of novel, for the chain novel, is itself open to interpretation. There is nothing to stop the second writer deciding that the first chapter is the first part, not of a novel, but of a political document. It would be odd, but not unintelligible, because presumably there was some agreement about the genre which got the novelists going.[7]

We might ask whether, if there are no requirements of fit ultimately distinct from interpretation, everything becomes too subjective. Fish thinks that subjectivity dissolves into discrete communities of people in agreement who can only talk past those outside "the club." This argument doesn't get us far; arguments *within* these clubs—the "Shakespeare club," the "post-modernist scholars," the Ku Klux Klan—will be just as subjective and the idea of a "group of interpreters" fails to advance the argument. For example, Shakespeare interpreters hold diametrically different interpretations between themselves about characters in the plays. Further, language is rich enough to enable everyone—not just those in discrete clubs to join in. There is no obvious reason why agreement can't be secured between communities through translation.[8] It is still an important question whether the distinction between "fit" and "substance" is useful but I'd defend Dworkin on this, particularly in the light of the unity of value thesis of *Justice for Hedgehogs*. Our judgments about interpretive matters, such as literature, and law, are complex; they contain many elements of constraint. Overall judgments we make are the result of various sorts of judgments, some of which are independent judgments acting as a constraint on others. That seems to me to be a sensible way of arguing—advancing bit by bit, from the sure position to the less sure. Dworkin is bound to hold this view, because any kind of constraint on the sorts of judgments we make cannot be of a plain fact, "out there" kind. The constraints must themselves issue from judgment. In his words:

> It is a familiar part of our cognitive experience that some of our beliefs and convictions operate as checks in deciding how far we can or should accept or give effect to others, and the check is effective even when the constraining beliefs and attitudes are controversial.[9]

Let us turn directly now to the question of "substance" while continuing to recognize that "fit" amounts to general acceptance of a particular and revisable interpretation. In the chain novel example, there may be a number of different ways in which the novel could develop, each of which fits equally well with the constraints accepted as existing in the first (and subsequent) chapters. In these cases, the chain novelists will have to make a different sort of judgment about how the novel should develop. This judgment will be one about the novel's substance. Which development would make the novel better as a novel, for example? The answer to this question is, again, an interpretive one. The novelist may decide that it would make a better novel if a character's diffidence is emphasized rather than diminished, say, where this trait is shown to be particularly human in the face of important events. She might, for example, decide that it would be a lesser novel if diffidence were shown to be cowardly, or only to be a good quality for a poker player. Although such decisions would each "fit" with the character's diffidence in the earlier chapters, a substantive judgment about the novel's direction and worth would have to be made about the character's development.

You must bear in mind the controversial nature, or "essential contestability," of all of these claims. There is no getting away from it because the characterization of the arguments can only be achieved in this schematic way. None of the following arguments is denied as possible by the scheme of literary creation described here although, of course, we would want to examine the arguments for each claim closely. "It is not a novel but a political tract," "'diffidence' is a feminine trait and should not be ascribed to a man," "it is unimportant to emphasize human qualities in the novel," "*all* novels are political statements"; the list is endless.

The point is that under Dworkin's abstract portrayal of interpretation, all these statements are possible ones. It does not follow as, I think, many people think, that each one is as good as the other. Some examples might help on this point. Let us take Dworkin's literary analogy and broaden it to encompass art and music. What if Dickens, in the second chapter of *David Copperfield*, had begun to call David "Goliath" and had transported the Murdstones (now called the Plantagenets) to Abu Dhabi, where Mrs. Murdstone, resurrected from the dead, ran a fish-processing business? Isn't it unlikely, if not absurd, in the absence of some link, to say that this second chapter is a chapter of *David Copperfield*? Even in this reworking there are some recognizable links ("Goliath" is recognizable as the former "David"; the "Murdstones" are common to both chapters). If there were *no* links, no "fit," wouldn't we think that Dickens had begun a new story?

Or take art. It is by virtue of lack of "fit" that we can say that my abstract painting of "red blobs against a green background with white triangles" is not a representation of the Mona Lisa. There is just nothing to connect them. Calling it the "Mona Lisa," or painting it with the intention of its being a representation, will not do the trick either. Again, however, there is no plain fact of the matter that says it is *not* such a representation; that, too, we must remember. Maybe the blobs and triangles, the blended shades of green, in my painting, capture just the right mood—or feel—of the Mona Lisa. But the connection will be tenuous if not downright implausible, and the strain will be to find the link of fit, the link that makes the argument possible, albeit tenuous.

What about music? Let us take a musicologist who completes the Schubert *Unfinished Symphony*, of which Schubert only wrote two complete movements. The new movement is four hours in length, and consists of a 1,000-strong choir of Fijian men plus twenty bass guitarists and an amplified Australian didgeridoo. It is in twelve-tone. The effect from a distance is impressive. It is music of a kind. However, the links with the first and second movements of the Schubert symphony are non-existent. Again, we must be wary. We must not be arrogant. Of course, it may be that the substance of the music captures something "inherent" in the Schubert piece. Nevertheless, the pull of the requirement of connection by way of "fit" is too strong for the argument to be very convincing.

The literary analogies irritate some perhaps who suppose that literature and art generally must be the antithesis of law. Dworkin has been accused of being a "culture vulture," for example, because of his use of the analogy.[10] The crude attitude is this: What have literature, and so on, to do with law? The answer is that if both art and law are interpretive activities then an examination of the role of interpretation in literature is highly relevant. What is so different about the interpretation of law that makes the literary analogy misleading? One common answer is that "law is a practical subject concerned with decision-making." Should that make a difference? Why, for example, should any interpretive activity not be concerned with decision-making? Neil MacCormick told me that the society I imagine would corrupt art. It is simply not clear to me that it would, if we accept, as I think we should, that judges of art are not objectively right merely by virtue of the fact that they were invested with that authority to judge. It would be corrupting if the Booker Prize winners were thought to have written the best books only because the Booker Prize Panel decided that way. Likewise for law; it would be corrupting if we thought that judges always offered the best interpretations since it would stifle creativity in the same way. It would also make nonsense of the reason for appealing a decision.[11] I'm inclined to believe that it is the positivist frame of mind—there certainly is one—that draws this distinction between law and art too abruptly. Something more is needed to cross the bridge between general acceptance of some point of view and the substantive principles that justify that point of view; this is brought out in the way that a lawyer will justify novel propositions of the common law.

THE COMMON LAW AND "GRAVITATIONAL FORCE": ANALOGY AND INTEGRITY

How does Hercules decide the common law? In "Hard Cases," Dworkin proposed the thesis that previous decisions exerted a "gravitational force" of fairness, so that Hercules would be bound to consider previous cases as to whether he had, in fairness, to decide in accordance with them, to the extent, anyway, that those previous decisions exerted "force." This thesis must now be seen in the light of Dworkin's account of integrity, which he calls the "first virtue" of law. Previous decisions exert gravitational force directly through integrity; it requires the account of the previous case that forces the best argument for showing that the law treats all its subjects in the relevant aspects alike.

Integrity makes good sense of arguments by analogy. Such arguments, when used by judges, cannot be arguments of deductive logic because those would not exclude irrelevant considerations such as the litigants' names. Arguments by analogy require value judgments because, as Hart in a similar context pointed out, "logic does not classify particulars." It is only by appeal to arguments of moral weight that we can make sense of arguments which purport to dismiss characteristics of precedents as "ir-relevant." Joseph Raz and Neil MacCormick both stress the importance of analogical arguments in the law. Raz, for example, says that "Dworkin's theory of adjudication is the most extreme case of total faith in analogical arguments."[12] MacCormick, throughout his work *Legal Reasoning and Legal Theory,* shows in patient detail the extent to which judges rely on such arguments.[13] Both jurists emphasize the constraining role of analogy, allowing the judge only to come to a conclusion which does not, in Raz's terms, introduce "new discordant and conflicting purposes or values in the law."[14] Both Raz's and MacCormick's analyses of analogy are compatible with Dworkin's view.

PRINCIPLES AND POLICIES

Dworkin's well-known distinction between *principles* and *policies* serves several purposes. It is intended to characterize distinctions which lawyers actually use in describing what judges should do. I think he captures that discourse successfully. It is also intended to attack certain assumptions within popular utilitarianism. Primarily, however, principle and policy are terms of art for him and formal definitions are to be found in Chapters 2 and 4 of *Taking Rights Seriously*. Remember that for him a legal right is a form of political right (in line with his view that law is a subset of political morality). He does not change his view in *Law's Empire*, nor in *Justice for Hedgehogs*.[15] Roughly, principles describe rights, and policies describe goals:[16]

> A "principle" [is] a standard that is to be observed, not because it will advance or secure an economic, political, or social situation deemed desirable, but because it is a requirement of justice or fairness or some other dimension of morality.[17]

In *Justice for Hedgehogs* Dworkin says that it is better to study personal ethics in terms of our responsibility rather than what we have a right to demand; on the other hand, he says that it is better to see political morality in terms of rights.[18] And so principles describe rights which aim at establishing an individuated political state of affairs. So, he says:

> A political right is an individuated political aim. An individual has a right to some opportunity or resource or liberty if it counts in favor of a political decision that the decision is likely to advance or protect the state of affairs in which he enjoys the right, even when no other political aim is served and some political aim is disserved thereby, and counts against that decision that it will retard or endanger that state of affairs, even when some other political aim is thereby served.[19]

Policies, on the other hand, describe goals which aim at establishing an unindividuated political state of affairs:

> A "policy" [is] that kind of standard that sets out a goal to be reached, generally an improvement in some economic, political, or social feature of the community.[20]

We speak of making something a "matter of principle" and mean that we should act in some way rather than another, whatever the consequences are, because fairness, or justice, or some other matter of morality demands it.[21] Lawyers have no difficulty at all in speaking in this way about legal rights nor, indeed, do most people. There is nothing significant in the fact that "rights talk" receives more public articulation in the United States, other than that Americans in general are less apathetic towards the ideas. "Policy" is more ambiguous and is at times used loosely, sometimes even just to mean that the judge has run out of good arguments and is striking out on his own. When this happens, often as not the judge is being honest about guessing what policy the legislature was getting at (which is consistent with legislative intention), or is deciding on some vague sense of "what the public might want" (which is often also no more than deciding what the legislature intends). More often, though, it is used in the way Dworkin says it is, that is, it is a reference to the consequences that would follow from deciding in favor of one of the parties. The usual example is where the judge decides one way because to decide otherwise would "open the floodgates of litigation." All law students are familiar with that sort of reasoning.

Sometimes judges talk quite loosely about "policy" when they mean "principle" in Dworkin's sense. In the *Spartan Steel* case, referred to by Dworkin in *Taking Rights Seriously,* Lord Denning does just this:

> At bottom I think the question of recovering economic loss is one of policy. Whenever the courts draw a line to mark out the bounds of *duty,* they do it as a matter of policy so as to limit the responsibility of the defendant. Whenever the courts set bounds to the *damages* recoverable . . . they do it as a matter of policy so as to limit the liability of the defendant.[22]

He says he decides on policy grounds but on inspection they seem perfectly principled and, in fact, in favor of the integrity of law: for he says that if other bodies, in all relevant respects the same, were excused liability, then so should the defendant; this is an argument of fairness, not policy.[23] In other words, the quoted passage above added nothing of substance to his judgment. A complicating factor is that disagreements with Dworkin's idea of policy often take issue with the content of a policy rather than its form. Dworkin is clear that the distinction is one of form and not content. For one person a political state of affairs could be a matter of principle and for another it could be a matter of policy and so the distinction is independent of a number of differences of political opinion. Two people can disagree about a particular political decision, say, one to allow police to detain suspects indefinitely, one doing so on the ground of principle, the other on policy. One argues that, in the long run, such a policy will not work and, in fact, may be counter-productive. The other can argue that the policy is wrong because it is in principle wrong not to provide for trial. The distinction defines the setting in which rival conceptions of what is politically justified may be argued. But the idea of a principled argument has implications for understanding how it is unaffected by arguments of policy. This is borne out by Dworkin's well-known statement that rights "trump" utilitarian goals.[24] It is important to dispose of one problem that might appear to rise from catastrophic cases such as civil disturbance, or war, where the suspension of rights seems justified in the pursuit of a goal of returning to situations of normality. Martial law, in other words, clearly makes sense and is well-catalogued in our moral, political and legal thinking. Martial law is only justified in wartime, when war is "raging."[25]

The argument then goes that if rights can be abolished for the sake of goals, where is the distinction left? But the criticism is superficial. There is no logical problem in saying that there is a special category of emergency, where all sorts of acts are justified. Martial law is a good case, but there are others like, for example, laws on quarantine. The correct argument is that in the name of rights you can suspend them so that they may be returned when the emergency is over. In fact, it is when "emergency laws" are made indefinite and not for a fixed period of "suspension" that we begin to suspect that a stage has been reached in political life where rights are considered by the government as unimportant. It is important, therefore, to see that catastrophic situations do not provide counter-examples to the distinction between rights and goals; on the contrary, such situations tend to prove that distinction rather than weaken it.

RIGHTS AND UTILITARIANISM

I think the connection between rights and utilitarianism is relatively clear in Dworkin. He is anti-utilitarian in a sense which, in fact, gains wide acceptance. The most well-known sense of utilitarianism trades wrongs done to individuals with improvements to general welfare. There are standard examples: the innocent man who is punished—and the fact of his innocence successfully hidden—in order to avert general law-breaking, or the justification for euthanasia on the unmarried, depressed and fatally ill orphan tramp on a desert island. A common intuition about these examples is that there is more to the moral choice than the totting up of the overall welfare (the conviction of an innocent person versus widespread civil disorder; one killing versus general unhappiness and cost). We can see that the intrinsic wrongness in these cases is something more than an assumption that the consequences would always be bad if these acts were carried out.[26] We can also see that the violation is direct and has something to do with the people involved; that is simply part of the fact that they are people. We can call it an attack on a right to humanity or dignity.

The point is that this widely understood version of utilitarianism lacks a conception of a person other than as temporary "container" of welfare; for Dworkin, clearly, treating people with equal concern and respect requires much more than this.

Dworkin's attack on utilitarianism is an attack on this version. But in Chapter 12 of *Taking Rights Seriously* he is prepared to accept a version of utilitarianism which incorporates a reasonably robust egalitarian premise. It requires, though, thinking of an agglomeration of choices consistent with the right of each to be treated with equal concern and respect—a democratically worked combination of voting, for example. Dworkin's discussion of the reverse discrimination principles and his "right to pornography" discussion particularly bear out this interpretation of utilitarianism.[27] In *Taking Rights Seriously,* he announces:

> Utilitarian arguments of policy . . . seem not to oppose but on the contrary to embody the fundamental right of equal concern and respect, because they treat the wishes of each member of the community on a par with the wishes of any other.[28]

But Dworkin's attack on straightforward utilitarianism is the orthodox one that utilitarianism fails to take rights seriously because any claim of right can be submerged by appeal to the overall consequences; in other words, it is that—outside of emergencies—claims of right are not defeated by a simple appeal to a marginal increase of welfare. He says that what is important "is the commitment to a scheme of government that makes an appeal to the right decisive in particular cases."[29] For example, the Dworkinian understanding allows the right not to be detained indefinitely without trial to defeat the argument that a policy of giving such powers to the police will have the effect of reducing violence by some margin. In his words, arguments of right will "trump" arguments of policy, meaning that in cases of conflict, rights have a priority.

These ideas form a major thesis in *Taking Rights Seriously.* In his later writings, he appears to relate claims of rights to what he calls "background" justifications for communal goals. Prominent among these "background" justifications, of which there are a number, are utilitarian theories.[30] The idea of rights "trumping" goals assumes, therefore, a wider significance than is first to be understood from *Taking Rights Seriously.* It is now not obviously anti-utilitarian in strain. I think the reason is simple. Dworkin's development of the idea of interpretation requires him to see rights arguments as interpretive of the practices of justifications for communal goals. So the assertion of rights attaches to the background justification—itself, of course, subject to interpretation—of a particular community.

There is a subtle difficulty here. An interpretation of practices concerned with justifying communal goals won't be an ideal endorsement. Hart does not appreciate this in criticizing Dworkin for being unable to give an account of rights in either brutal totalitarian regimes, where no interpretation could yield a background justification for communal goals, or a society where people are perfect, like angels. Dworkin only needs to reply that these communities are not ones with the appropriate background justifications for rights.[31]

Dworkin denies that rights are "timeless" and "fixed by human nature." They are a relative idea, relative to the background justification. They "figure in complex packages of political theory":

> I am anxious to show how rights fit into different packages, so that I want to see, for example, which rights should be accepted as trumps over utility if utility is accepted, as many people think it should be accepted, as the proper background justification. . . . But it does not follow from this investigation that I must endorse . . . the package of utilitarianism together with the rights that utilitarianism requires as the best package that can be constructed. I do not. Though rights are relative to packages, one package might still be chosen over others as better, and I doubt that in the end any package based on any familiar form of utilitarianism will turn out to be best.[32]

In *Justice for Hedgehogs*, Dworkin confirms all this and widens the scope of the argument. He says that rights must be a claim in favor of an individual's interest that is sufficiently strong to overcome an "otherwise adequate" or "proper" political decision: "Political rights are trumps over otherwise adequate justifications for political action."[33] It is wrong to think that rights can only trump government decisions in favor of the general good. Rights can be invoked against a tyrant because the principles of dignity (respect for the objective equal worth of people and their personal responsibility for forming their own lives) state the principle of legitimacy. It follows that "all political rights are derivative from that fundamental one." So what a tyrant does contrary to that principle is trumped by its own force.

Dworkin also helpfully draws out the idea of political "trumping" from personal ethics:

> This trump sense of a right is the political equivalent of the most familiar sense in which the idea is used in personal morality. I might say, "I know you could do more good for more people if you broke your promise to me. But I have a right that you keep it nevertheless."[34]

THE DIFFERENT KINDS OF RIGHTS

Dworkin produces a useful taxonomy of the forms of right-based arguments in his article "Hard Cases." The different forms of rights he describes cross political theories and the use and emphasis laid on each will reflect each kind of political theory. He distinguishes, for example, between *absolute* rights, ones that withstand no competition (as in theories that posit, for example, an absolute right to life), and rights that are less than absolute. The important point is, remember, that the idea of a right is defined by its ability to withstand competition against non-urgent goals (for example, "any of the ordinary routine goals of political administration"[35]). We may distinguish between *background* rights and *institutional* rights. Background rights are those rights which argue towards some state of affairs without referring to the right some institution has to make a decision. An example would be where someone proposes that we have a right, when there isn't one in the legislation or constitution. A philosophical Robin Hood might argue that we have a background right to another person's property, say, if we "need" more. That statement can be understood without reference to any legislation or constitutional principle in the Anglo-American jurisdiction. We can disagree with the content of the statement, but at least we understand its sense.

However, some people will disagree that even more plausible seeming statements of such rights make sense: they will claim they are political rhetoric aimed only at saying what rights people *ought* to have. This was the substance of Bentham's criticisms of the rights proclaimed by the defenders of the French Revolution, that they were "nonsense on stilts." But it cannot be nonsense to say—whether or not you disagree—that, for example, a fetus has a right to life, or that people have the right not to be detained by the state indefinitely without trial. It is difficult to see the advance in saying such statements ought to be rewritten as "a fetus ought to have the right to life." If rewritten this way, the argument remains the same: it urges a state of affairs based on a claim to dignity. I doubt, too, that argument alters the distinction of type between background and institutional arguments. The point is that there are at least two different sorts of argument, each independent of arguments concerning unindividuated goals ("policy" arguments) which urge a political state of affairs. One is drawn from institutions, the other not. Arguments which deny the existence of rights independent from institutions but allow for arguments urging changes in those institutions, clearly employ the distinction Dworkin recommends. If the arguments are directed at the particular conception of rights Dworkin employs, they are relevant only to Dworkin's attempt at distinguishing rights from policies, not to the distinction between background- and institutional-type arguments.

Dworkin draws a further distinction between *abstract* and *concrete* rights. Abstract rights are grand statements of rights such as "people have a right to free speech" or to "dignity" and so on, which are "abstract" because they do not spell out the impact which they are intended to have on any actual social situation, or how such rights are supposed to be weighed against other rights. On the other hand, concrete rights are more or less definite about such matters as, for example, when we say that people have a right to publish defense plans classified as secret provided that this publication will not create an immediate physical danger to troops. This right is a "concretization" of the abstract right to free speech.

THE INTERPRETIVE CHARACTER OF THE COMMON LAW

Dworkin's theory of law is interpretive, as we have seen. It is not, therefore, fully responsive to descriptive criticisms which take the form "This is not actually how judges behave." There are cases when judges make policy in Dworkin's prohibited sense. On the other hand, both judges and lawyers criticize "policy" decisions as not being lawyerlike. It is what is characteristic of judicial practice that is important. If lawyers criticize reasoning by policy, this must be taken into account, too. Only in that way will we get to a proper account of what judges characteristically do. It is "descriptively" true to say that, in the United Kingdom, the House of Lords and the Court of Appeal have justified decisions on grounds that Dworkin thinks are wrong. It is equally true that lawyers have condemned such actual or envisaged decisions. Random examples are Lord Parker's warning against the usurpation of the legislative function by the judiciary (itself a theoretical, interpretive statement about the judicial role), in *Fisher* v. *Bell*,[36] Lord Simon's similar warning in *D.P.P.* v. *Lynch*,[37] the House of Lords' statement that it is for Parliament and not the courts to create new exceptions to the hearsay rule,[38] and Lord Scarman's statement in *McLoughlin* v. *O'Brian*[39] that it is for the legislature, not the judiciary, to decide matters of policy.

Public attitudes towards the role of judges is also significant. There was considerable public criticism of the United Kingdom judges in the well-known case of *Shaw* v. *D.P.P.* (the "ladies directory" case) because judges there created a new criminal offence. People thought that was solely a question for Parliament to decide.[40] The extensive criticisms of *Shaw* v. *D.P.P* are thoroughly consistent with Dworkin's suggestion. Many of the cases which are used to show that policy decisions are characteristic of the legal system are those in which Lord Denning was involved and his position in the judicial world has to be treated with care. He was a great judge. Many of his decisions are Herculean in the best sense: imaginative, innovatory and just. His judicial career was of the Dworkinian sort because his judgments revealed the creative possibilities of the judicial role. Many lawyers were suspicious, feeling that he was under-emphasizing, or even ignoring, the role of rights of only a particular sort, those which create certainty by giving rise to reasonable expectations. And at times Lord Denning frankly legislated. We should not let this fact blind us to the innovatory sorts of genuine legal judgments he made. I think Lord Denning legislated when he tried, famously, to create a married woman's "equity" by virtue only of her status as a wife in order to bind third parties so that she could remain in the house. He was overruled by the House of Lords and there Lord Upjohn said: "I am of opinion with all respect to the Master of the Rolls statement of her rights . . . her mere equity not amounting to an equitable interest nor being ancillary to or dependent upon an equitable interest does not bind purchasers."[41] Of course, that Lord Upjohn said this does not mean that the Court of Appeal legislated since that is an interpretive matter. This case is useful as an example of a case famous for a common interpretation that Lord Denning was departing from law, although moved by a considerable feeling for the justice of the result he produced. This case can be contrasted with Lord Denning's equally famous judgment which confirmed the principle of "promissory estoppel," *Central London Property Trust, Ltd.* v. *High Trees House, Ltd.*[42] More commentators are prepared to say about that case that it was a highly imaginative and bold decision *and* in accordance with legal principle. There are many other such judgments in Lord Denning's career. My point is that in making judgments about his role in cases, we do employ a distinction between imaginative, creative decisions that are outside the judicial role and those that are within it.

United Kingdom law is scattered with other examples where creative decisions by Lord Denning appear on either side of the border between adjudicative and legislative function. For example, in *Lim* v. *Camden Health Authorit*[43] Lord Scarman, in the House of Lords, made the following remark:

> Lord Denning M.R. in the Court of Appeal declared that a radical reappraisal of the law is needed. I agree. But I part company with him on ways and means. Lord Denning M.R. believes it can be done by the judges, whereas I would suggest to your Lordships that such a reappraisal calls for social, financial, economic and administrative decisions which only the legislature can take.[44]

THE RIGHT TO DAMAGES FOR EMOTIONAL DISTRESS

In *Law's Empire*, Dworkin analyses the House of Lords case of *McLoughlin* v. *O'Brian*.[45] It is useful because it contrasts his arguments of "fit" and "substance" and shows what he means by a "policy argument." It was a car accident case. The hospital was not far away and Mrs. McLoughlin arrived a short time later to find her daughter dead and her husband and other children seriously injured. It was a shocking scene and she suffered severe psychological trauma. She sued the driver of the other car. It was a hard case because there was no precedent for awarding damages where the shocked person was not at the scene of the accident.[46] Dworkin suggests six possible interpretations of the common law in this case.

1. *Success (for the victim) only where there is physical injury?*

No, he says, because this does not "fit" the law where damages are available for nervous shock.

2. *Success only where the injury, whether physical or emotional, is the direct consequence of the accident?*

No, again because it does not fit the law where it is clear that damages can be awarded for indirectly caused loss.

3. *Success only where the emotional injury occurs at the accident, not later?*

No, because this is contrary to substance. The judge should not act arbitrarily. Given the circumstances of this case it is a distinction that lacks any moral substance. To all intents and purposes, Mrs. McLoughlin was in exactly the same position as someone who was at the scene of the accident. That is not to say that there could be moral differences drawn, as where, for example, there was no family relationship, or where a long time had elapsed, and so on.[47] But drawing distinctions only on grounds that are morally relevant is not only just what lawyers do all the time but what lawyers think they do as part of identifying the law ("the law supports the defendant *because* otherwise it would draw a *morally* irrelevant distinction.") Positivism has to explain the law much more awkwardly even if it can do it: "there is no law on whether Mrs. McLoughlin should succeed, but morality steps in and tells us that there it would be morally irrelevant to draw this distinction and so, by analogy, by fairness, the judge should decide in favor of her." Speaking from my personal experience, that positivist mind-set often makes a hash of it.[48]

4. *Success only if the decision in favor of Mrs. McLoughlin is economically efficient?*

No, says Dworkin, because that is a matter of policy and does not respect "the ambition integrity assumes, the ambition to be a community of principle."[49] Mrs. McLoughlin would not, in other words, be accorded her right to be treated as an equal with everyone else. There is a complication here, though. People might have a right to a redistribution of economic resources on other grounds than overall economic efficiency. I leave discussion of this for Chapters 8 and 10. Dworkin develops such an idea—which first appears in obscure fashion in his article "Hard Cases"[50]—in Chapter 8 of *Law's Empire*, a difficult chapter.

5. *Success only where the injury is foreseeable?*

Dworkin thinks this is the best since no unfair financial burden need be placed on any person by it, given the competitive and therefore relatively cheap availability of insurance.

6. *Success for foreseeable injury, except where an unfair financial burden is placed on the person who causes the accident.* ("Unfair" meaning "disproportionate to the moral blame for causing the accident")

"Which story," he asks, "shows the community in a better light, all things considered, from the standpoint of political morality?" One story would be in accordance with a principle of "collective sympathy," in this case towards individuals suddenly required to pay large amounts for accidents they cause. It is this principle, he says, which supports safety regulations, public insurance schemes and so on. The other story is the more draconian one that people at fault should pay for the foreseeable consequences. Given the prevalence of liability insurance, Dworkin thinks that interpretation 5 is the correct interpretation.

LAW AS ARGUMENT AND THE IMPLICATIONS FOR LEGAL EDUCATION

It is helpful to think of Dworkin's theory of law as concerned fundamentally with a cast of mind, that of the argumentative lawyer. In the final chapter of *Law's Empire*, he rather grandly says:

> Law is not exhausted by any catalogue of rules or principles, each with its own dominion over some discrete theater of behavior. Nor by any roster of officials and their powers each have over part of our lives. Law's empire is defined by attitude, not territory or power or process.[51]

The lawyer thrives in that area of publicly argued standards which should appeal to judges and other lawyers. His field is that of the multitudinous arguments and standards that he has to make coherent sense of in the context of law. Significantly, it is the field which the law student studies. I think that Dworkin's theory is of relevance to the appreciation of legal education. Legal positivism does not explain it well since it lacks a complex enough theory of hard cases. The point should be particularly grasped for English legal education.[52] It should go without saying that law students (and the legal systems of which they become a working part) would be better off if they gained a more abstract awareness. At the top end of the profession, too, there is at times a pressing need for a more clearly articulated theoretical structure when the sense of what counts as a correct argument becomes fuzzy; for example, whether higher courts are permitted to employ policy arguments and, if so, which ones. Often these cases show—in my opinion—diffidence towards constructive legal theorizing. A good example is the current debate whether judges should be "deferent" to Parliament. The way the question is commonly phrased makes the point. There is a general assumption that because judges aren't elected, are public schoolboys, were educated at Oxford, are largely men, then their decisions are presumably illegitimate; never mind that the like argument—if we are to stay at this level—could be applied *pari passu* to both the House of Commons and the House of Lords. Hence, in that revealing English term "deference," the judges must always "defer" to what Parliament wants. However, the judiciary can't be illegitimate *because* judges aren't representative; they are part of democracy the way many unelected officials are, right down to the humble unelected voter, who has official status albeit a minor and practically powerless one. And judges aren't "below" Parliament as the curtsying metaphor of deference implies; their democratic job is to interpret the law and uphold the rule of law, a crucial democratic principle. Deference is no part of it unless we think of the top-down quality of "command," "sovereign," and all that panoply of horror that Bentham visited upon us, in fact with the very best of interpretive intentions.[53]

It is the idea of the *point* of integrity that links the discussion here of legal education with the subject of the next chapter. For, according to Dworkin, legal argument must aim at the coherence demanded by integrity for a special reason. It is that integrity should reflect a commitment by the community to treating all of its citizens as equals. For him, legal argument is fundamentally concerned with public argument. We turn, then, to consider the relationship between the idea of integrity and community.

CHAPTER SIX

Integrity and Community

Dworkin means his idea of integrity to be something over and above consistency, the idea of treating like cases alike, or, as he says, mere "elegance." Integrity requires consistency but also compliance with respect for human dignity in ways, already discussed, that constrain governmental decisions about the community's future. Dworkinian integrity arises naturally from the idea of personal integrity. The community is to be regarded as having a personality that is subject to the same sort of moral criticism that we make of a person who has not acted with integrity. It is therefore necessary to examine the crucial personification that Dworkin makes of the community.

Daily, we make judgments about communities (and governments and states) in respect of what we perceive their duties to be, whether to reduce unemployment, curb crime, keep the streets clean. We criticize governments for abusing human rights, and states for ignoring international law and committing war crimes. Two points are relevant to such criticisms. The first is familiar: the personification of the community can suppress individual rights and responsibilities and so we might wonder whether this is wise. The second is whether we can and should require the community, thus personified, to act with the same sort of integrity required of individuals.

Ordinarily, we have little difficulty in ascribing moral responsibility to groups. We talk freely and correctly of the responsibility of corporations, for example, and we mean this to be something over and above the ascription of responsibility to executive members of corporations. If we criticize individual members of a corporation, we may do so in a couple of ways. We will assume controlling members did the act in question—taking unjustified risks, say. In this sense, we make them responsible. But our criticism will focus on what has been done in the name of the corporation. We'll sue the corporation and this supports only a secondary responsibility on the part of the corporate officials. When the matter is criminal, we may prosecute a corporation by identifying certain officials as the "mind and brains" of the endeavor and they will be criminally liable as individuals.[1] Another way to criticize corporate members is to say that what they have done is outside the authority of the corporation. Criticisms of the parliamentary member who does not attend debates, or the council worker who skives, may be either criticisms directed towards the failings of the individual, or a mixture both of that and a criticism about how the offices themselves are run.

Most of these sorts of criticism assume corporate-type responsibility. The idea of group responsibility is in our language and common stock of moral thinking. It plays a significant role in our legal system, permitting a more complex allocation of rights and responsibilities than would otherwise be possible. Does ascribing responsibility to corporations make them "faceless" and absolve their members of responsibility? The members of a corporation are connected to corporate responsibility by a complex web of rights and powers. It is an indirect but nevertheless vital relationship, and it is not as though the "veil of the corporation" can't be lifted. The alternative of abolishing the idea of corporate-type entity altogether seems to go too far the other way.

Perhaps it is not so clear whether corporate-type entities should be required to act with the same sorts of virtues as individuals; there are such obvious differences between individuals and sometimes vast constructions of relationships. This is a question the answer to which we need to find in Dworkin's account of integrity.

MORAL INTEGRITY AND EVIL LEGAL SYSTEMS

A more fruitful possibility is the second question I asked, namely, can the idea of integrity be helpfully applied to the community? What is personal integrity? It is interesting and important to note that the idea is not one which, in the usual case, directly concerns particular actions. If it is used in this way it takes the form of praising the action because it was that of a person who "has integrity." Most often we use the idea by invoking the idea of trust, as for example, we will assure ourselves that Richard was a "man of integrity" and we could trust him to be truthful. The idea of "acting according to principle" is highly relevant here. Richard will be a man who takes his decision according to what he considers the correct moral view of any matter. Saying that a person acts according to principle is part of saying that a person has integrity and conversely, and more frequently, we say that an "unprincipled" person "lacks integrity." There is a further element, too, of reliability. You can trust someone who acts on principle to be consistent in his judgments, but only to the extent that principle demands this, so that integrity is not the same thing as blind loyalty, with which integrity is sometimes confused.

How do these two ideas of moral principle and consistency fit within the metaphor of the community's integrity? The idea of equality is important. The community must act according to moral principle and it should, as far as principle demands, be consistent in its dealings with citizens. The metaphor of personification works thus far. However, equality is fundamental to Dworkin. Does it make sense to envisage genuine integrity in the Nazi SS commander in spite of the racism inherent to "the SS virtues"?[2] Hart's well-known criticism of Lon Fuller's equally well-known eight principles of the "inner morality" of law helps. Fuller claimed these principles, which loosely describe requirements of procedural justice, would ensure that a legal system would satisfy morality's demands to the extent that a legal system which adhered to all of the principles would explain the all-important idea of "fidelity to law." In other words, such a legal system would command obedience with moral justification. Fuller's key idea is that evil aims lack a "logic" and "coherence" that moral aims have. Thus, paying attention to the "coherence" of the laws ensures their morality. The argument is unfortunate because it does appear to claim too much. Hart's criticism is that we could, equally, have eight principles of the "inner morality" of the poisoner's art ("use tasteless, odorless poison," or "use poisons that are fully eliminated from the victim's body," etc.). Or we can improvise further: we can talk of the principles of the inner morality of Nazism, for example, or the principles of the inner "morality" of chess. The point is that the idea of principles in themselves, with the attendant explanation at a general level of what is to be achieved (e.g., elimination of non-Aryan races) plus consistency, is insufficient to establish the moral nature of such practices.

It is unfortunate that Hart's criticism obscured Fuller's main point, which concerned fidelity to law. It is reasonable for him to say that claims made in the name of law are morally serious. In this light, the idea of an "inner morality" of poisoning is grotesque. To understand the position of evil legal systems, Dworkin draws a distinction between the *grounds* of law and the moral *force* of law. The grounds of law are obtained by looking from the point of view of a participator. In this way we could predict how a judge in Nazi Germany might decide a case. For example, take a hard case under the Nuremberg laws, say, to do with the confiscation of Jewish property.[3] We could take account of widely believed theories of racial superiority to provide detailed arguments about which way the case should be decided.[4]

But it is part of Dworkin's theory that to make these sorts of prediction is not to endorse the result, since a full theory of law here would require, in addition to an account of the grounds of law, the moral force of law. It is easy to fall into traps here. There have been criticisms, most notably by Hart, which have taken the line that Dworkin had merely added a gloss to positivism by adding "principles" and "underlying theories" by the use of which hard cases in any legal system, however evil, could be decided. Thus Hart takes the view that since Dworkin regards legal rights as a special sort of moral right, any rights arising should have a weak *prima facie* moral force which would be overridden by a strong background morality. So Hart says:

> If all that can be said of the theory or set of principles underlying the system of explicit law is that it is morally the least odious of morally unacceptable principles that fit the explicit evil law this can provide no justification at all. To claim that it does would be like claiming that killing an innocent man without torturing him is morally justified to some degree because killing with torture would be morally worse.[5]

Dworkin's answer is that most structures of community power will have some moral force, because, he says, "the central power of the community has been administered through an articulate constitutional structure the citizens have been encouraged to obey and treat as a source of rights and duties."[6] It must follow, he says, that the decision whether a statute gives rise to a moral right is a moral question, for "we need the idea of a legal right, which someone might have in virtue of a bad law, in order to express the conflict between two grounds of political rights that might sometimes conflict."[7]

Dworkin's solution to the live problem of evil legal systems is of importance to practicing lawyers. What should lawyers and judges do if they find themselves caught up in such a system? Dworkin has posed the problem as an interpretive one. Lawyers are to treat the problem as one in which they are expected to make moral judgments in interpreting the law. How would lawyers do this? The Nazi legal system is not a good example as it is too extreme. The least of the problems there is what the grounds and force of the Nuremberg laws were.

Nevertheless, we can refer to less evil systems. These might have a number of good points and the judges and officials who administer its laws do so conscientiously and independently. There may be clear procedural constraints.

An example is the former apartheid legal system of South Africa. Here, Dworkin says, judges and lawyers may be in a position to make interpretive judgments that work. It is wrong to suppose that the grounds and the force of law are unconnected. If there are contradictions in the grounds, say, between racially discriminatory statutes and principles long declared in the courts, the judges should interpret those statutes to resolve the contradictions; this makes much better sense of Fuller's point about consistency, for example. Given the idea of interpretation, the judges do not have to accept the "face value" of discriminatory statutes. Their task is, instead, to make sense of the statute in the full matrix of rights and duties in that legal system. And even an interpretation where there is no escape from interpreting a statute as morally repugnant, just the fact that the very best moral sense that can be made of it is that it is morally repugnant, is itself a declaration against that statute and an isolating judgment about the legislature that produced it.[8] In any case, to go back to the Nazi legal system, there were vast areas of law at the time in Germany that were untainted by the immorality of the time; most of the property law, for example. Such laws created moral and political rights of expectations that courts could quite properly enforce. These considerations show a more discriminating way to understand evil legal systems: for the question is not conceptual but a question of what enforceable rights people have within a state.[9]

COMMUNITY AND LEGITIMACY

Dworkin thinks that communities are essential to our dignity: on the one hand, for example, anarchy is an attack on dignity. On the other hand, coercive government is a threat to dignity and so we must ask the question whether there is a conception of government that is consistent with individual dignity. Legitimacy arises from the idea of political association and, according to Dworkin, has two dimensions—the justification of acquisition of the power of government and the justification of the exercise of that power. Legitimacy is therefore different from justice because governments may be legitimate without achieving justice if they act in good faith to treat each member with equal concern and respect. Dworkin also says that legitimacy may exist to some lesser degree: "particular policies may stain the state's legitimacy without destroying it altogether. Its legitimacy then becomes a matter of degree: how deep or dark is that stain?"[10]

In *Law's Empire*, Dworkin explores what he calls "the puzzle of legitimacy," the problem of identifying our individual political obligations to the community. Since it is a question concerning our duty to obey law, it is also a question about integrity. In general, his answer lies in the idea of our *associational*, or as he earlier emphasized, our *fraternal* relations to others in the community. Further, Dworkin needs to consider the idea of political tolerance. Many of his views are clearly expressed in his essay "Liberal Community,"[11] which is a clear statement of how far he thinks the community may determine or influence a person's private life. He develops his views in the context of attacking the eighties group of political philosophers known as the "communitarians" who envisaged, and hoped for, much more emphasis on the value of the "communal life." I shall consider his arguments in this article since they encapsulate much of what he later says in *Justice for Hedgehogs*.

Dworkin places great emphasis on the right we have to live our lives "according to our own lights" and we have seen that this general principle receives some later refinement in *Justice for Hedgehogs* as the second component of dignity. The essential idea is well argued in "Liberal Community." Dworkin's treatment of the idea of legitimacy follows a familiar path. He considers and rejects one popular response to why people have an obligation to obey government, or the political structures. The idea is that people have "tacitly consented" to this, as though they had contracted with other members of their community that certain powers would be exercised in political administration by others on their behalf. Political legitimacy is based, therefore, on the fact that people have consented to the way that they are governed. As is commonly pointed out, there often isn't any consent at all. People are born into communities and do not choose them. Although "tacit" consent is not consent, there is clearly intuitive appeal to the idea. It is surely reasonable that if political institutions are just or if there is a significant element of "fair play," or if members of the community receive many benefits—consent should have been forthcoming. There is some contortion because it requires imagining as facts something that did not happen—what is often called "counter-factual" consent—but the principle of consent seems nevertheless apt.

Dworkin rejects both justice and fair play as the grounds for political legitimacy.[12] Justice, he says, is too wide a ground to explain the idea of citizenship, because it extends beyond communal requirements. It is too "conceptually universalistic," he says, to be personal enough to make sense of the particular duties of citizenship which a person owes to his own community. Fair play, too, is insufficient because it is not clear how you can incur an obligation merely because you received a benefit. We don't have an obligation to another merely because they gave us a gift; why should one benefit demand another benefit in return? Dworkin gives the example of a philosopher who delivers interesting and valuable lectures from the back of a truck and asks whether we have a duty to give him money. In any case, he says, it is not clear how it would fair that a citizen who obtains benefits in one political community should suffer corresponding detriments when there are better benefits to be obtained under another political community.[13] Since the citizen does not have the chance to test another political system, the argument seems to collapse into saying that the citizen has to obey only because he happens to have been born into one particular political community and not another.

Dworkin says that there is a more sophisticated way to approach the fair play argument. If we concentrate on the idea of fairness alone, we may be able to say that the citizen should obey government because it treats him in a way that is actually fair "according to the standards of justice and fairness on which it is constructed." Dworkin doesn't, however, think this is sufficient: a government could be fair to you—for example, not discriminate against you—but not in a way that guarantees you benefits; if you don't receive benefits then, according to the argument of fair play, there is no require-ment to suffer detriments. The underlying difficulty in both the justice and fair play arguments for political obligation in Dworkin's view is that they both depend on an idea, drawn from the idea of consent, that for political obligation to be established, the citizen must "join in" in some way. Dworkin thinks that communal obligations, of which political obligations are a part, are far deeper than the mere idea of "joining in" or choice will allow. They are, instead, "associative" obligations:

> They are an important part of the moral landscape: for most people, responsibili-ties to family and lovers and friends and union or office colleagues are the most important, the most consequential obligations of all.[14]

It is an interpretive idea, parasitic upon existing communal practices. The central point is that there are many obligations that arise simply out of the existence of certain types of relations, such as the relationship between a parent and a child, and out of the association of friendship. The obligations in such relationships often and characteristically transcend choice, although the obligations, like the obligations of the fair play argument, are reciprocal:

> It is an important part of our own ethical responsibility, and therefore part of our moral responsibility to others, that we accept for ourselves and require of them the particular associative obligation—political obligation—that we are now considering.[15]

Dworkin thinks that political obligation arises from what he calls its "fraternal" nature: such obligations consist of special obligations to the group, they are personal in that they run directly from each member to each other member, they involve a concern for the well-being of others and the group's practices must show an equal concern for all members. This last requirement is important since it will furnish the moral light in which to cast group or communal practices of obligation. He says, however, that the equality condition does not rule out all hierarchical communities as it might first seem. What is important is that the hierarchies should not be class-based and so an army will be a fraternal organization if it meets the conditions of equality but caste systems that count some members as inherently less worthy than others will not.

The communities or groups in which fraternal obligations arise are not constituted by genetic or geographical or historical or psychological facts. The idea is the result of interpretation—a moral judgment made about actual practices.[16] Dworkin says that arguments about the obligations of people in political communities in this fraternal way are more sophisticated. Communities are more complex and comprise closer relationships than a description of them in terms just of geography and history ("crude nationalism") and a more moral commitment than any idea that communities display "fair play" or justice between their governments and their citizens. Dworkin thinks that associational obligation arises because there is a requirement for a special structure of protection without which here is a threat to dignity through the coercive power of government. Those connections between people that focus on such features as ethnicity, religion or color and which often give rise to a call for "self-determination" don't, in his view, constitute genuine associational features and such "tribal" associations are a "powerful source of evil."

A proper community, one in which it is fraternal association that provides the justification for political obligation, places weight on concern for well-being and equality. Dworkin calls such a community a *community of principle*. Such a community fulfils the four conditions of having special obligations to the group, being personal, showing concern for the well-being of others and showing an equal concern for all. The community of principle, he says, makes the responsibilities of citizenship special because each citizen must respect the principles of fairness and justice that are embedded in the political arrangements in his particular community.[17] The community of principle, therefore, provides a better defense of political legitimacy as well as a defense of our own political culture.

FOUR CONCEPTIONS OF COMMUNITY

Dworkin's conception of community is important for his conception of legal argument. If, through his idea of interpretation, he is to link moral with legal argument, the idea of communal obligation towards the institutions of law must be sufficiently rich and complex to make the task possible. The connection, for Dworkin, between the rights of individuals and the law lies in the justification of tolerance.

Dworkin considers four arguments which attack the liberal idea that communities should be tolerant towards unorthodox minority behavior. To varying degrees, these ideas all share the same emphasis on the importance of the community. The first is that a community, as a matter of justice, is permitted to act on its own behalf through the mechanism of majority rule, and intervene to prevent, as far as that is possible, minority conduct of which it disapproves. The argument does not depend upon any idea of the wrongness of the unorthodox conduct. Rather, it depends on the justice or fairness in the majority being permitted to "have its own way." Dworkin is critical of the idea; it contradicts, he says, what we believe justice and fairness require in a democratic community. Democracy does not allow "winner take all stakes" in economic matters—for example, democracy is allied to the free market and opposes the centrally planned economy in which the economic environment is assigned to government. So if in a democracy we are free to make private economic decisions, why should we not be free to make decisions about, say, our private sexual lives? The argument from justice or fairness to the community's majority is therefore insufficient to permit intolerance towards a minority:

> If we insist that the value of the resources people hold must be fixed by the inter-action of individual choices rather than by the collective decisions of a majority, then we have already decided that the majority has no right to decide what kinds of lives everyone must lead.[18]

The second argument against tolerance speaks to the concern that a community should have for the well-being of its members. A proper community should care for the members which compose it and tolerance of wrong conduct ignores the well-being of an individual. No one suggests that a community should ignore the physical illness of its members. Communities should implement programs of disease prevention—clean water, effective sewerage, adequate housing and so on. So why should the community not show similar concern for the moral well-being of its members, prohibiting sexually unorthodox behavior or pornography?

Dworkin rejects the analogy between physical and moral health saying we cannot "cure" morally unorthodox behavior. When the community steps in to prevent a person from having homosexual relations, it doesn't make sense to say that the community is trying to encourage the homosexual to do what he "really wants" to do ("volitional paternalism") but instead is trying to make the homosexual live the "right way" ("critical paternalism"). What then, asks Dworkin, is living in the "right way"? Dworkin says that it is a necessary condition of having a valuable life that you live in a way that you can endorse; one must, he says, be able to "take responsibility" for one's life. What is the possibility of making the homosexual endorse the new way the community forces him to lead his life? He continues as a homosexual, now miserable because he is not permitted to live it in the way that he himself believes is the right way, for him, to live. Dworkin says that if the community found a way of "brainwashing" the homosexual into thinking that he was endorsing his new "orthodox" life, the whole argument for ensuring morally correct sexual conduct would be self-defeating. It would simply mean that the community had admitted that it could not obtain a genuine endorsement and, therefore, a life of genuine—authentic—value.

Dworkin thinks that a third communitarian argument against toleration has more substance. It is that people have various sorts of needs—for example, a common language and culture[19]—which can only be supplied by a community that has a fairly high degree of homogeneity and so tolerance of unorthodox behavior could threaten the necessary homogeneity, and thus threaten people's needs. Dworkin thinks the argument has more substance because it is sensitive to the idea that there might be a necessary bond between the community and the individual. Nevertheless, although the argument holds generally for material needs such as economic wealth, Dworkin says he does not see why a "moral homogeneity" is required as well. Nor does he see why community intolerance on, say, unorthodox sexual matters would help supply intellectual needs, such as those of having a common language and culture.

Dworkin then provides a response to this argument against toleration through an attack on Michael Sandel's argument that it is only through the community that people are supplied with a sense of "self-identity."[20] Sandel's argument is deeper than the argument that in order to see myself as a New Zealander there has to be a New Zealand in existence, since that is merely a tautology. The analogy works well with religion: a Muslim might not be able to distance himself, say, from his being Muslim. Having a religion—taking one's religion seriously—describes an understanding of one's own way of being that is integrally linked with being a member of a group that sustains and supports one's religious being. Tolerance then shows a bad side for it breaks down the homogeneity required to give people, in this religious sense, a means of self-identity. Dworkin thinks that if the self-identity thesis is just a matter of saying what people are like in general—as a matter of phenomenology—it is wrong, for we can fairly easily identify ourselves independently of any particular community we in fact identify with. It overstates the case to say that Muslims cannot identify themselves as people independently of their religion. To accept this is not to deny that Islam is important to them, or to deny that Islam is what they have committed their whole lives to. Those individuals who would lose all sense of who they are if they were detached from whatever community, are more likely to be pathological cases. Dworkin thinks that Sandel's point is not unimportant, just that it is not about self-identity. Further, he thinks that even if such a degree of undetachability of self-identity from community was true for everyone, it would be very implausible to suppose that it applies to sexually orthodox conduct. How could people lose their self-identity if they learned that their community tolerated homosexual conduct, for example? Dworkin then argues that even if you grant that people could lose their self-identity in such cases, it would most clearly only work in communities of a particular sort, and not necessarily all political communities. Even granted the strongest version of the self-identity thesis, it could still not follow, in Dworkin's view, that a person could not "reassemble" himself in the light of further understanding about what it was to be identified with a political community. After all, we shouldn't rule out the possibility of identifying ourselves—proudly, perhaps—as members of a tolerant community. Why should people not be able to reassemble their sense of identity, built around a somewhat different and more tolerant set of conditions, when their faith in the morality they associate with their family or community is for some reason shaken? Certainly, says Dworkin, our experience on these matters may differ. It is not too difficult to imagine circumstances of mental breakdown and trauma as the result of isolation from a familiar pattern of social conventions. But there is not sufficient evidence to suppose that the link between a sense of individuality and attachment to community, especially in sexual matters, is as strong as the communitarian argument would seem to require.

These arguments provide a good laboratory for understanding Dworkin. I find these arguments full of clarity and rigor. Like many of his arguments, they are lawyerlike. They build on reasons and are straightforward. I know from experience, however, that it is a way of arguing that leaves some in a state of despair. They say that Dworkin is being unfair. Sandel and the other communitarians *must* be saying something more than this. No one can make mistakes of the magnitude Dworkin suggests. And, in any case, Sandel's argument has a sort of appeal, it has to be said. Or, conversely, Dworkin is fighting a "straw man" because the original thesis is so bad it is not worth attacking.[21] Let us examine the claim. It is true that Sandel is saying something of significance and Dworkin doesn't belittle it. He does, however, point out successfully and politely that it sounds better than it really is and that the idea of self-identity is a red-herring. No one of course loses their self-identity unless they have very serious personality defects. But if all that Sandel means is that people are committed to, and feel strongly about, the wrongness of tolerating homosexuality in their community, then the argument is not that strong. Dworkin's arguments against the communitarians' plea for intolerance, on the ground of the need for self-identity with the community, shows that the identification of the individual with group morals at best applies to a non-political group of sexually neurotic individuals.[22] Sandel would be on much surer ground, in my view, if he claimed that prejudiced people still deserve respect in spite of their views and that this might permit (say) regulation of public displays of homosexual conduct. The argument for intolerance can't be as simple as that "many people in the community don't want homosexual conduct." Dworkin exposes the flaw.

It is the fourth, and final, argument of the communitarians that Dworkin considers to have the most content. It says that people are related to, or are to be identified with, their political communities in such a way that the life of the community is part of their own life. I think the health analogy I used to explain the second communitarian argument may be used here, too. The argument there was that, simply, the community should take an interest in the health of any one of its members. Here it is that a person should care about the community's health because that affects her own health. That person's health is part of the health of the community. It is not that the community must take a paternal interest in her health but rather that she must take an interest in the community because that is integrally connected with her own well-being. This is a richer account of the idea of community, in Dworkin's view, because the life of the member of the community and the community are viewed as an integral whole. Perhaps tolerance of unorthodox sexual conduct undermines the integration of a person's life within the life of the community. Dworkin thinks this idea mistakes the character of communal life for it supposes that it is just the life of a very complex and large person. This richer account of community which rightly includes the idea of integrity "succumbs to anthropomorphism; it supposes that a communal life is the life of an outsize person."[23] A community cannot, for example, have a sex life.

This quick criticism needs closer attention. Integration isn't the idea that a community is solely composed of its members. It has a life of its own.[24] That must follow from the idea of group responsibility. It also makes no strange claims such that communities are somehow more genuine entities than individuals, or as people like to say, "ontologically" or "metaphysically" "prior" to them. Dworkin borrows Rawls's idea of the difference between the members of an orchestra and the orchestra to give integration more shape. People can see the orchestra in these agency terms. The flautist can take pride in the orchestra's achievement independently of the pride he can take in his own performance, which contributes to the orchestra's achievement. His own well-being is tied up with the orchestra's well-being.

What, then, asks Dworkin, are the conditions which give rise to this relationship of agency, whereby the well-being of a member of a community is integrally related to the well-being of the community? It must lie in actually existing social practices of agency, he says. I cannot merely become an agent by a simple declaration. Such social practices must recognize certain acts as acts of the particular community—say, the orchestra—rather than those of the community. That must include only acts that have been done self-consciously towards that end. Further, there will be restrictions in relation to the scope of the individual members' roles and the "dimensions" of the community. The business manager of the Berlin Philharmonic cannot, for example, take "musical" pride in a particular performance, although he might take "business" pride in a successful tour. And, further, it follows from this argument that the communal life will be a restricted one. The orchestra's life is a musical one. The orchestra has no other life. It is not, as Dworkin says, prone to headaches, or problems with friendships, nor does it have a sex life, although individual musicians will. So what are the characteristics of the political community? The communal acts of the United States are constituted by practices of officials:

> The formal political acts of a political community—the acts of its government through its legislative, executive, and judicial institutions—meet all the conditions of collective agency. . . . Though the acts of particular people—votes of members of Congress, for example, and commands of generals—constitute these collective acts, this is only because these officials act self-consciously under a constitutional structure that transforms their individual behavior into national decisions.[25]

What else? Do we have a collective national sex life? Our practices do not include any such life. And the fact that we do not choose to become the citizens of a particular community, unlike the members of a symphony orchestra, seems, further, to restrict any such idea.

COMMUNITY AND DEMOCRACY

Dworkin is clear that majority rule is not valuable in itself. Clearly in some cases—an overcrowded lifeboat, for example—a majority vote would be wrong and a lottery much better. He asks if democracy means majority rule then why should we care about it so much? We do treat democracy as a value and if we thought there was nothing intrinsically good about it this "would make much of our political life silly."[26] Democracy requires "background ideals" to guide us and so, naturally, Dworkin thinks that we need to understand our concepts of political virtue as interpretive concepts. A community that accepts the twin principles of dignity (equality and personal freedom) must, he says, accept them in its political structures. Again, each person must be treated as of equal objective value and each person must be treated as responsible for identifying and pursuing success in their own life: "A conception of democracy is a conception of how that challenge is best met through political structures and practices."[27]

Dworkin's legal theory, therefore, raises the question of the justification of the entire political system. For him, it is a democratic justification. What does democracy justify in the way of law? Democracy, at least in the United States, is popularly understood as majority rule. Yet that idea, on further examination, is not clearly able to explain even some of the most familiar institutions and structural provisions of democracy. Powerful officials, such as judges or secretaries of state, are not elected; even the existence of entrenched legislative provisions which protect familiar institutions of democracy such as universal suffrage seem to contradict the idea of majority rule. The problem exists in the U.K. but is there only dimly understood; it is however clearly acknowledged in the United States. The U.S. Constitution provides explicit disabling provisions, pronounced in the form of fundamental rights, such as the right to conscience and freedom of speech, to equal protection, and to due process. Judges may declare statutes in contravention of these provisions to be outside the Constitution and therefore of no legal effect. This is an enormous power and it is exercised to overturn legislation passed by even overwhelming majority votes in state legislatures. Are judges, right at the heart of the legal process, routinely and characteristically doing something that is inconsistent with democracy? But democracy appears to be the fundamental moral principle that gives the required moral force to legal argument; the "one person, one vote" principle clearly embodies an abstract and appealing combination of equality and liberty.

It is well known that the United Kingdom lacks a strong rights-supportive culture in comparison with the United States.[28] Nevertheless, Dworkin thinks both countries are at fault and that both U.S. and U.K. constitutional lawyers have favored procedural rather than substantive defenses of democratic constitutionalism in both legal systems. For example, he is critical of Ely's well-known democratic defense of certain of the disabling provisions of the United States Constitution.[29] Ely argued that disabling provisions of the Constitution such as the right to free speech are democratic because although at times contrary to what a majority of people want, recognition of minority speech is necessary to participation in the democratic process. Ely acknowledges he is unable to account for certain rights, such as freedom of religion, because these provisions don't appear to protect democratic procedure. There is a problem, too, with the view, widely accepted, that the Constitution protects private choice in matters of personal morality. Under Ely's account, it would seem to be within the Constitution for a state, for example, to outlaw homosexual conduct, because to do so would not upset the democratic structure; gays would still be able to vote and form views based on the uncensored exchange of ideas but would lose out because they form a minority.

Dworkin thinks the Ely-type account fundamentally misconceives what democracy is about. He distinguishes between two conceptions of collective action, each of which might be considered as a candidate for democracy.[30] *Statistical* collective action simply "counts heads" and provides a statistical readout of what people want. On this account, a majority rule system is justified. Majority rule is the functional expression of what the individual wants, read over a collection of individuals. Simply, statistics are gathered. But, employing either Rawls's idea of the symphony orchestra, or the idea of collective German responsibility towards the Jews, we can distinguish another form of group action, that of *communal* collective action. Dworkin says the communal sense of democracy is better. He says that it allows us a better reading of Abraham Lincoln's famous statement that democracy is "government of the people, by the people and for the people" and gives us a better understanding of Rousseau's idea of the "general will."[31] We should distinguish, he says, between two types of communal collective action, the *integrated* and the *monolithic*. The integrated type places weight on the importance of the individual while denying that collective action is statistical only. The monolithic view of community is a more "Hegelian" conception which gives the community a more independent role. Dworkin rejects it because it denies the importance of the individual and also because it provides a better interpretation of actually existing democracies.

Democracy is of fundamental importance because of the distribution of political power and the consequent implication for coercive interference with private lives. If, as many of us think, democracy is based upon equality and fairness, Dworkin says that it is an important question whether treating people as equals means giving them equal political power. What does "equal political power" mean? He looks at this in two ways. We could compare citizens *horizontally*, ignoring for the time being the question of political authority, and try to make them equal *vis-à-vis* one another. We could also, he says, compare citizens *vertically* with the officials of a political system. Dworkin draws yet another set of distinctions.[32] Political power could be measured by *impact*, which is the difference we are able to make on our own by voting one way or the other. Under this conception, a member of the legislature has a considerably larger impact than all of his constituents, even those who voted him into power, and so a vertical equality of power will not be possible.

We can distinguish this power of impact from political power being measured by *influence*, by which Dworkin means the ability to make a difference by leading or inducing others to believe or vote or choose. In a proper working representative democracy, he says, "rough vertical equality of influence is achieved." The idea is that, if things are working properly, each citizen has the same chance to influence the relevant political representative, who will see himself as bound to take all views into account in his decision on which way to vote in the legislative chamber. Each citizen has the power, in other words, to influence the politician, although each citizen will not have the same power of impact as that politician.

Equality of impact works for the horizontal comparison of the powers of citizens but only at the expense of abandoning democracy. First, we could make all citizens equal in their political power by giving them virtually no power at all, which would be perfectly compatible with many forms of totalitarianism. But second, says Dworkin, "it does nothing to justify a central assumption we make about democracy, which is that democracy requires not only widespread suffrage but freedom of speech and association, and other political rights and liberties, as well."[33] For example, the idea of censoring a person's views only makes sense when we understand the relevant equality to be equality of influence. A censored person can, of course, still have equal impact, provided his vote has not been taken from him.

Particularly interesting is that Dworkin does not believe in equality of political power. Equality of political power as impact does not make sense and, he says, equality of influence would mean restricting people's convictions and ambitions in a way that would deny them the moral worth they should be accorded in a democracy. The view is striking because, at least as far as horizontal political equality is concerned, there is appeal in the idea of making citizens equal in the amount of political influence they can bring to bear. Dworkin prefers to explain this intuition in other ways. For example, we can just simply say it is unjust that Rockefeller has so much more money than other people. As a result, he has a disproportionate political influence which arises, not because he has exceeded an equal amount of political influence allotted to him, but because it is disproportionate to the maximum amount of political influence he could have had under a just distribution of resources. That way of putting it allows for an unequal political influence.

The central emphasis in Dworkin is always that democracy embodies the fundamental right to dignity. Because they are of equal and objective value, individuals may (and must on occasions) exercise their personal convictions both privately and publicly. In a democracy, a person must not be prevented, under some assumed constraint of equality of influence, from pursuing an ambition of "taking pride in the community" and taking part in the "communal goal of political activity." While this means in principle people may contribute as much money as they would wish to political campaigns, in practice, because of the unjust distribution of resources, there need to be limits. And further, since corporations aren't real persons—they don't vote, for example—under Dworkin's theory, corporations would not be capable of "taking pride in the community," nor would they have the appropriate sort of "integrated interest" in the "communal goal of political activity." The principles of human dignity therefore do not permit corporate donations to political campaigns; speaking of Justice Kennedy's argument in the *Citizens United* v. *Federal Election Commission* in the U.S. Supreme Court decision of 2010 that guarantees that big corporations can spend unlimited funds on political advertising, Dworkin says:

> The nerve of his argument—that corporations must be treated like real people under the First Amendment—is in my view preposterous. Corporations are legal fictions. They have no opinions of their own to contribute and no rights to participate with equal voice or vote in politics.[34]

PRINCIPLES OF DEMOCRACY

Dworkin unsurprisingly concludes that we need more than a "statistical" governing in a genuine democracy.[35] Arguments for democracy must be sensitive to the relationship between individuals and the community and the principles of dignity. People must be treated as of equal objective value, and they must be kept in a position that respects the authenticity of their lives. Rather than thinking of democracy as a stock-market-type institution in which individual traders push up the price of currency, we need "background institutions and assumptions that elicit and nourish the needed pair of democratic attitudes: collective responsibility and individual judgment."[36] The argument for democracy will, in the light of these principles of dignity and these democratic attitudes, yield three main principles, which Dworkin calls those of *participation, stake* and *independence.*

The principle of participation, he says, is part of the idea of collective agency. We are not a member of some community or organization unless we have some role to play. And, in a democracy, we only have a democratic role if we are treated as an equal in that role. So, he says, this latter reason shows why an orchestra is not a democracy, because the conductor is assumed to have special merits. It follows from the involvement of the foundational principle, too, that the participation of any member of a democratic community ought not to be limited by assumptions about worth, talent or ability. Dworkin does not think the principle of participation is the basis of our structures of universal suffrage and representation. It is, rather, that it shows historical reasons for their adoption. It is not inconsistent with the principle to treat people as equals by giving them a weighted vote, as in the creation of special voting districts for deprived areas.

The principle of stake requires that there be some sort of reciprocity between those in power and citizens. People should have some sort of stake in their community if their community is properly to be regarded, unlike a statistical community, as "theirs." If this were not the case, we would be in the absurd position whereby German Jews would have been responsible, as members of the German community, for that community's crimes against them. Those Jews had no stake in that community. It is in his discussion of the principle of stake that Dworkin makes an important concession to the problem of founding the obligations of the citizen to the community in the real world. The integrated conception of community suggests that citizens do not have communal obligations where they do not have a full stake in the community. At least the statistical conception can stand off from this requirement and allow other, perhaps non-democratic because arithmetic, principles to govern the obligations of citizens. Dworkin concedes that the integrated conception is like a "black hole," into which all other ideals are sucked. His answer is to modify the principle of stake to require not that the community must have achieved what equality requires, but that its leaders are motivated by that.[37] It means a "good faith" requirement, according to which if the leaders act in good faith and assume that people should be treated as equals, all citizens have a stake in that community. An example would be, I suppose, almost any European or North American state: things are by no means perfect, but governments by and large seem genuinely both to proclaim and carry out to a significant extent a belief that people are of equal value.

All his earlier work on democracy coheres with Dworkin's second principle of dignity as described in *Justice for Hedgehogs*, for that principle embodies the importance of moral independence, affirming that a democratic government must not dictate what its citizens should think about politics and ethics:

> Just as it is preposterous for a German Jew to accept collective responsibility for Nazi atrocities, it is preposterous that I should think of myself as sharing integrated collective responsibility within a group that denies my capacity to judge for myself.[38]

From this principle, Dworkin derives structural guarantees of freedom of speech, association and religion on the basis that people must be allowed to take responsibility for their own personalities and convictions. He also says that the principle prevents the enforcement of morality, although he thinks that it can be defended as a matter of justice, too, independently of arguments about the structure of democracy. It is not strong enough, in his view, to say that the principle of independence only protects a person's judgment, so that it is being observed when a homosexual is allowed to vote, although not allowed to have sexual partners of his choice. There is no point to a person's judgment being untouched when he cannot shape his own ethical life in his actions:

> That is why people who object to moralistic legislation say that they want to 'make up their own minds', not have the majority do it for them, even when the legislation leaves them free to think what they like so long as they do what it says.[39]

Dworkin thinks that the structural constraints on majority rule which Ely justified, on the basis that they were necessary for democracy, are better justified under an integrative account of democracy. For example, Ely's account, one which statistically simply counts heads, allows for freedom of speech only on the ground that the public needs the most informed opinion. But Dworkin says that the integrative account can emphasize the speaker side of free speech; equality of respect for the speaker may require that he, the speaker, must be able to speak his mind: "It is, after all, the speaker's right to speak not the audience's right to hear that the First Amendment protects directly." More important, he claims that the integrative account can justify constitutional constraints that Ely admitted could not be justified under his own theory. Dworkin says that freedom of religion is supported by the principle of independence, so that citizens decide for themselves matters of personal conviction and conscience. The protection of the system of criminal procedure is more complicated, he thinks, but is nevertheless part of the principle of stake. The due process requirements ensure, he says, that a criminal suspect belongs "in a community of responsibility" for as long as possible and the presumption of innocence is a "presumption of continued membership" in the community.[40]

The principle of participation supports political liberties such as free speech. The principle of stake is behind the equal protection clause, because it should show whether the government's decision reflects a good faith in equal concern for its citizens or, rather, prejudice and partisanship. Further, the principle of independence governs the idea of a "right to privacy," by ensuring that people are able to make their own moral judgments about the kind of lives they wish to lead. Dworkin concludes that there is an integrative relationship between a political community and its individual citizens, comprising the application of the three principles of participation, stake and independence. Consequently, the communal conception of democracy allows us to understand the disabling provisions of the Constitution "not as compromising democracy but as an important part of the democratic story." That relationship is not, however, as intimate as the monolithic Hegelian form of community would require. The communal life Dworkin envisages for it is restricted to formal political decision-making on questions of justice.

Nevertheless, Dworkin says that integrated citizens, who will make critical judgments about the worth of their own lives, should rightly regard their own lives to be diminished by injustices within the community. That more complex connection between individual and community, now familiar to us through Dworkin's confident separation of ethics from morality and his integration of morality into politics in *Justice for Hedgehogs*, amounts to a more complex and meaningful form of personal life:

> That fusion of political morality and critical self-interest seems to me the true nerve of civic republicanism, the important way in which individual citizens should merge their interests and personality into political community.[41]

JUDICIAL REVIEW OF LEGISLATION

Again, democracy is an interpretive concept and so what is part of it is an evaluative question. We need therefore to consider the common claim that the judicial review of legislation is undemocratic and therefore illegitimate.

Dworkin thinks this claim is confused. Democracy doesn't determine the history of a country but, rather, assumes it, and so local practices will figure in questions such as whether judicial review can be "corrective" of democracy or even whether it is required at all. There is nothing *a priori* concerning these questions. His view, as we know, is that a democracy is not constituted by a majoritarian model of government but by a model which he calls in *Justice for Hedgehogs* a "partnership" model which clearly arises from the ideas of "fraternal" and "associational" obligation. It is a procedural matter how legislation is organized and it is determined through particular historical practices. Different countries, all democracies, do things differently; it is recognition of this that makes us distinguish procedural justice from substantive justice. A contemporary critic of judicial review is Jeremy Waldron. He thinks that judicial review contradicts democracy because it allows a minority—judges—to overturn the wishes of a majority—legislation.[42] Dworkin says that Waldron has a "majoritarian" view of democracy because on the "partnership" view (*Justice for Hedgehogs'* term for the earlier "communal" view) the majority view must be a legitimate majority and Waldron can't assume that judicial review couldn't make the majority view legitimate by striking down majority legislation that denied minority rights to dignity. Dworkin therefore thinks there is a problem with supposing, as Waldron does, that majority rule is inherently principled, although he admits that Waldron's view is popular, if "surprising." Dworkin says majoritarian rule is, in itself, "plainly" not a principle of fairness. First, a majority decision is not fair unless it refers to the right community. China can't legislate voting rights to New Zealanders and then by majority vote, legislate for New Zealand. Second, and in any case, majority decisions are not always fair. Dworkin gives the example of a decision made in a lifeboat about who should go overboard to save the rest from drowning. He says that, in these special circumstances, far from being fair, a majoritarian decision would be wrong—it would be bullying—and drawing lots, for example, may be fairer. Dworkin's general point arises from his unity of value thesis. No point is fixed, from which one can stand back and adjudicate between two views of what substantive justice requires. Justice is neither criterial nor Archimedean. One can't say, "You three people disagree, so we'll decide by majority rule," because that assumes the inherent rightness of this third point of view. Any "third" point of view is also evaluative. Even a requirement of unanimity could only mean, in reality, unanimity *in principle*, and that is only another way of requiring that the decision be right. Dworkin concludes there is no value in the "arithmetic equality" of the majoritarian conception: "Political equality requires that political power be distributed so as to confirm the political community's equal concern and respect for all its members."[43]

He has more to say, however. He thinks that the "partnership" conception says that judicial review only "may" be democratic and that local historical circumstances have to be in place. Judicial review will only be democratic if there is no discrimination of birth or wealth in place, and—Dworkin says this is "crucial"—judicial review plausibly improves the community's legitimacy. The fact that judges are not elected is a "red-herring." Instead, the question is whether judicial review contributes to legitimacy, and whether it does will vary from community to community, and nothing is guaranteed in advance. Other methods might be superior. He suggests an improvement in the U.K., for example, would be a reformed Upper House with elected members "without comic titles or dress," making former Commons members ineligible and having longer terms. An improvement in the United States, he says, would be shorter terms for Supreme Court justices.

One point needs to be cleared up, which is that it must be wrong to say, as Waldron says, that courts are "majoritarian" institutions ("The Supreme Court is a majoritarian institution; the problem is the very small number of participants in its majoritarian decision-making").[44] First, for Waldron's statement to be interesting it must refer to the whole of the branch of the unelected judiciary, not just selected courts. A High Court in the U.K. certainly decides by a majority of two to one where three judges are sitting; but there are many courts. There is not a majority overall of judges. Obviously not, because judges don't sit in a central court (like a legislative chamber) and vote. But Waldron could well feel this strengthens his case for criticism: it is bad if they decide by majority but even worse if they don't even do that. However, second and much more important, to stress the procedural means by which court judgment becomes a decision is a lamentably poor characterization of what judges do. The judiciary is not a representative body. It shouldn't be (I don't mean that judges shouldn't come from a cross-section of the community). It has the particular function of deciding what the law is. If the legislature strays from the law by violating constitutional rights, it is wise to have some form of institutional check. One such possibility (there is no "necessity") is an unelected judiciary, which it seems sensible to say, should be educated in the law and wise to the temptations of partisanship. If judges are to check those majority decisions that depart too far from the moral principles that give the legislature its moral power to decide, they must of course do so by applying those very same principles. It is therefore difficult, at least for me, to see what the argument is against it if there is sufficient consensus for it. That judges are not elected is a complete irrelevance. Many offices within a democracy are unelected including, of course, probably the most important office in a democracy, that of the voter.

We need now to look at the objectivity of moral and legal argument. Dworkin has refined and developed his views on objectivity in value. But in the next chapter, I shall look at how he developed his idea of "the one right answer thesis" chronologically. It all came from his consideration of hard cases. Many, if not most, of the difficulties in understanding him rest upon the fetishistic hold of the plain fact theory in, I regret to say, its primary and primitive sense, as something "objectively" "out there."

CHAPTER SEVEN

Objectivity in Law and Morality

The problem of objectivity is what many people find as the major stumbling-block to understanding Dworkin's theory. It comes as a surprise to people that Dworkin thinks there are right answers to evaluative, and therefore moral, questions. Nevertheless, most people think there are right answers to such questions. People disagree whether abortion is morally permissible, for example, and their disagreement is just about what is right. Those who think it wrong and those who think it right at least agree that there is a "right or wrong" about it. In what follows, unlike the pattern of the rest of the book, I have traced Dworkin's arguments in chronological order. Not only do we get a fuller understanding but there is pedagogic interest in the way his present thesis—that truth in law is dependent on nothing more mysterious (or less mysterious) than correct legal argument—was developed from two early ideas. The first lies in his attack on Devlin's idea that public opinion was a criterion of morality and the second lies in his idea that there were practical reasons why the positivists would choose provability—or demonstrability as he used to call it—as a criterion of truth in law (e.g., accordance with a rule of recognition).

LORD DEVLIN AND TAKING A MORAL POSITION

Dworkin's first arguments about the objectivity of moral reasoning arose in his criticism of Lord Devlin's thesis that, in certain instances, the state has the right to use the criminal law to enforce matters of morality. The state could gauge what was a matter of morality by using the ordinary juryman's view (that of the man in the "Clapham omnibus") based on his deep feelings of "intolerance, indignation and disgust." Devlin had put forward this thesis in his famous lecture of 1958.[1] Unlike most of Devlin's critics, Dworkin sees merit in the general thesis because of the direct connection it makes between democracy and morality. The idea of a consensus permitting different moral views is genial to democracy in which each individual should enjoy equality of respect; the Clapham man's vision contains an implicit egalitarian premise that the ordinary man's views *count* in determining our moral environment. Dworkin analyses the assumptions that Devlin makes about the nature of morality. Dworkin thinks that the idea of a "public morality" is more complex than the description of a juryman's feeling at a particular time can allow, and that Devlin is wrong to suppose that an accurate gauge of it could be gleaned from crude expressions of public feeling.[2] Instead, public feeling, or juryman outrage, is subject to a rational "sieve" which sorts out mere expressions of feeling from expressions of a genuine "moral position."

We must, for example, produce reasons for our views.[3] They do not have to be particularly abstract or philosophical but the expectation is that we should at least understand that there are reasons for what we claim. ("I hate gays." "Why?" "Oh, no reason.") And prejudiced views are not moral views. The person who says, "I hate gays because they are sissies" fails to express a genuinely moral position. Naturally, this is not to say that what counts as a prejudiced point of view will never be controversial; you and I may disagree whether our different views on positive discrimination, for example, are based on prejudice. The common view that "everyone is prejudiced" is not at all helpful, either, for that just means that we all have different views, some right and some wrong. Mistakes of fact, too, do not qualify as moral reasons. To use Hart's well-known example, it was wrong of the Emperor Justinian to have said that homosexuality was morally bad because it caused earthquakes, for there is just no evidence to show any connection between homosexuality and earthquakes. Emperor Justinian's view did not constitute a moral position: there is no factual evidence upon which his view could conceivably have been based. (I assume he meant that being gay incurred the wrath of God, who caused earthquakes, but if so, there are still problems with the view.)

Mere repetition of a view is insufficient to establish a moral position, too. The person who says that homosexual conduct is wrong because "a friend told him so" supplies an insufficient reason since we expect the genuine expression of a moral view to be one which a person endorses himself to be true. That is not to deny that we can learn from others, or that there might be a special category of religious reasons of an authoritative sort. Emotional reactions also are insufficient. "That action makes me sick" is not a sufficient reason since we expect a reason why, and in any case we think that one good way of attacking a moral position as confused is by simply saying that the argument for it is emotive. We tend to think here with persistent emotive statements that the speaker is obsessive, or has a phobia. It is easy to imagine other sorts of disqualifying reasons once we get the idea. The rules of logic must hold some sway, and there are all sorts of subjects about which we just can't have moral views. You just cannot have moral views about gold, for example, and you can't consider tempests irresponsible.

Dworkin's chief point is that a community consensus on morality runs deeper than a surface description of what people in fact, at a certain time and in a certain mood, think or feel. Any sensible conception of consensus exists at the level of reason or conviction and crosses surface differences. To those who are suspicious of any attempt to oppose "the common man's view" with "reason," it will come as a surprise to learn that Dworkin is not opposed to the ideas both that there is a community morality (democracy, for example) and that the community's morality should count. "What is shocking and wrong" about Lord Devlin's thesis, says Dworkin, "is not his idea that the community's morality counts, but his idea of what counts as the community's morality."[4]

CONVENTION AND CONSENSUS AS BASES FOR MORALITY

From his criticism of Devlin, it becomes clear that the difference between a convention and a public *consensus* is important for Dworkin. In his view, morality is not constituted by public conventions which say conduct is morally required or permitted by the test of what most people think. Otherwise slavery would have been right once, or we would be driven to weak justifications of the wrongness of, say, rape of the form "well, everybody thinks it is wrong." A consensus instead means a coincidence of the same convictions. In our community there is a coincidence of independently held convictions that rape is morally wrong. But that fact of consensus is not the reason for thinking rape wrong since we think it is wrong for quite independent reasons, such as assault, dominance, distress, pain . . . the list is long. If rape were wrong by convention, there would be a parroting mistake of the sort I discussed in the previous section. Yet another way of putting it is to say the last reason one would give for saying that rape is wrong would be that everyone thought it to be wrong. That would be a disastrous way to teach children if it were the only way they were taught morality, for example.

Of course, some conventions provide a reason for behaving in a particular way as, for example, the convention that you take your hat off in church; this, however, turns out to be only the conviction that you should not offend others and you follow the convention in order not to do so. It is not that you follow the rule simply because other people consider that you should.[5] There is, true, a misleading and unimportant sense in which morality is defined by convention, as where we say, "Theirs was a morality of slavery." The triviality, and danger, of the use of the word "morality" in that phrase becomes clear when we use phrases such as "the morality of the Nazi party was immoral." The relevant distinction here was drawn neatly by Bentham and Austin between "positive" and "critical" morality; positive morality being social conventions created by man (and hence possibly evil) and critical morality the standards by which those social conventions are judged. Hart later used the distinction in *Law, Liberty and Morality* against Lord Devlin's equation of public consensus with morality in order to show that public consensus in itself might harbor prejudice, lack of logic, repetition of views and so on.

This distinction is present throughout Dworkin's writings. In *Taking Rights Seriously*, he criticizes the conventional rule of recognition theory, in his second attack on the model of rules ("The Model of Rules II"). The paper in which he does this, in my view, is one of the best of his early papers and is often overlooked; it was originally published in the *Yale Law Journal*.[6] The argument in its basic form merely repeats the argument above in relation to the judicial duty to decide according to the law. Dworkin first argues that that duty cannot be exhaustively defined by the rule of recognition because judges have duties to decide according to law when the rule of recognition has run out in hard cases. Secondly, the judicial duty cannot even be partly defined by the rule of recognition because that would be to confuse positive with critical morality. He uses the example of the vegetarian who declares, in a way which is familiar and intelligible in moral conversation, that everyone has a duty not to eat meat, meaning not that there is such a convention but that there are independent reasons why we should be vegetarian.

To the critic who says that Dworkin's argument is correct about the nature of moral argument but not about the arguments needed to establish the legal, judicial duty, I think he is right to reply that legal positivism cannot be invoked in its own support. Further reasons, he says, are necessary to show why the duties incumbent on a judge are not moral duties; the straightforward assertion that judicial duties are fully defined by convention is insufficient. It follows that the rule of recognition "mistakes part of the domain of the law for the whole" because it misses out the identification of the judicial duty in hard cases. Further, it makes the usual confusion a consensus of official (and other) views about what constitutes law with the existence of conventions for identifying law. In other words, that the officials of a community recognize criteria for the identification of law should be understood as meaning that they accept independent and critical reasons for recognition and that coincidence in thought shows just that—consensus—rather than the acceptance of a convention. The objectivity of morality for Dworkin, then, does not depend on an external world—"out there"—of moral reality in the form of conventions.

REFLECTIVE EQUILIBRIUM AND THE DUTY TO CREATE

Dworkin's dismissal of the "out thereness" of the plain fact theory has a moral edge. He wants moral responsibility to attach to people, not to entities existing outside us, maybe unknown to us. In one of his most interesting essays, "The Original Position" in the *Chicago Law Review* in 1973,[7] he makes significant analyses of two of Rawls's most fundamental theses, the starting-points of moral reasoning by way of "reflective equilibrium" and, when political questions are asked, the "original position." "Reflective equilibrium" is the name that Rawls gives to the methodology of moral reasoning. It envisages an equilibrium being attained between moral intuitions, or convictions, and abstract positions on general questions of morality (moral theories) that we hold. The "equilibrium" between the two should be reached by our comparing our intuitions with our structured moral beliefs. Sometimes our intuitions embarrass our theories, as when our intuition that just wars are morally permissible embarrasses our theory that innocent life must never be taken. The process of reflective equilibrium thereby supplies justification to our moral psychology. Either the theory is modified or developed in a way that can explain the intuition (say, for example, innocent life must not intentionally be taken, with some attendant theories about what constitutes innocent life and what intention means), or the intuition begins to lose its impact and finally disappears given the coherence of the theory.

Of course, the abstract positions on general moral questions that we hold will make sense of the particular intuitions we have. The process is ongoing. We modify, or even eventually abandon, intuitions in the light of our generalizations and acquire new intuitions both in the light of theory and new experiences. Arguments we have with others about moral issues should develop in the same way. We test intuitions we hold against general positions we hold. We embarrass others by pointing to inconsistencies between their intuitions and their general positions.[8] Dworkin's view is that Rawls's description of the method of reflective equilibrium is ambiguous between two models of moral reasoning (which I shall shortly compare). I think Dworkin's view is that Rawls's idea is insufficiently prescriptive and runs the danger of appearing to be a successful moral psychology, showing admirably the development of a person's moral beliefs but not clearly why any person should engage in it.

We shall recognize the first model because it is an "out there" view. Dworkin calls it the "natural" model, because it supposes that reflective equilibrium is fundamentally concerned to expose an already existing set of moral truths. It has the following consequence for moral thought. When there appears to be an irreconcilable clash between moral intuitions and moral theory, there is no immediate cause for concern. We assume, under this model, that the solution, the reconciliation, is possible but that we do not ourselves possess the knowledge or mental acumen to make that reconciliation. The solution outstrips us, but that does not matter. The second model, the one Dworkin favors, is the "constructive" model. According to this, there is a duty upon us to make the reconciliation, and to construct the answer. There is no "out there" to absolve us from that responsibility and, of course, from *Justice for Hedgehogs* we should now appreciate that Dworkin thinks that it is the unity of value thesis, combined with our personal moral responsibility to attempt reconciliation of apparently conflicting values in terms of other, perhaps more abstract values we endorse, that supports this view.

Dworkin regards moral reasoning as something we should engage in to make coherent the different judgments on which we act. People must not renege on this responsibility by simply assuming, as the natural model assumes, that moral intuitions can have a "correctness" that can outstrip their explanatory powers. They are not permitted to say, when faced with *prima facie* conflicting intuitions (say, about just wars or prohibiting abortion), that some reconciling explanation exists although it has not been, and may not be, discovered by men. This is a strongly secular thesis, demanding that we act on principle rather than faith, placing responsibility firmly on the individual. Reflective equilibrium is to be understood in terms of ingesting and reworking basic moral intuitions and being prepared to act according to a plan understood to be as coherent as a person can possibly get. He may not get it right, but the duty is upon him to try nevertheless.

In *Justice for Hedgehogs* Dworkin specifically returns to Rawlsian reflective equilibrium; he says his own method is "more ambitious and more hazardous" because Rawls allowed "subordination, compromise, and balancing amongst different values" (for example, insisting on the "lexical priority" of liberty to equality). Dworkin says instead that each value in his own (similar) method must be assessed in the light of others and should be driven by "truth"; in particular, he thinks that Rawls's account is of a range of values much smaller than his own.[9] The idea of the construction of moral judgments is important for another reason. In a society of relative agreement, the idea of community is connected with the idea of public articulation about principles of justice. This is an idea that Dworkin develops in his theory of integrity.

"TIES" AND INDETERMINACY

In some earlier articles and lectures Dworkin had allowed the possibility of a "tie," that is, a situation where a judge may be faced with arguments that are equally balanced on either side. This is a middle position, one where there is a genuine indeterminacy—where there is no right answer to the proposition being debated. Dworkin considers the question in Chapter 13 of *Taking Rights Seriously*, entitled "Can Rights be Controversial?" where he says that it is possible to imagine an enterprise or practice whose "ground rules" recognize the possibility of a tie; he denies there that such ground rules are part of the foundations of legal argument in the Anglo-American system. This chapter has been taken by some to mean that Dworkin was making a descriptive claim about "the Anglo-American legal enterprise," and that he has failed to appreciate that there "really" are ties, as though the question were one which was easily settled. This article, and these remarks, stand consistently with Dworkin's later developed idea of interpretation. Judgments about the objectivity of law are interpretive judgments and so judging there to be ties in the law cannot be ruled out. Dworkin's view is that legal argument, like moral argument, requires decision, and always demands the best decision, that being the one that applies the true proposition. The recourse to ties may (although not necessarily) be a failure in responsibility to make the best decision. It could represent "copping out," where the judge who says "This is all so difficult and I'm just going to toss a coin" would be an example. It is one kind of decision, and decision itself either way will have some benefits if only to settle the matter, but in a court case it would be highly irresponsible not to consider the merits of the arguments of each side and decide in accordance with the balance of reasons. None of this excludes the possibility of discourses, or areas of value, or "domains" as Dworkin now speaks, where it is appropriate for propositions to have "tie" value, perhaps particularly in literature, where some interpretations are right just because they recognize that scenes, phrases and so on are fundamentally ambiguous, sometimes intentionally so.[10] Dworkin says we should appreciate that there is no "default" position, when we are uncertain about whether a proposition is true or not, that it is indeterminate. Whether a proposition lacks truth value must be the result of an interpretive judgment. Merely being uncertain about whether something is true, or false, or indeterminate, is just a psychological state that doesn't affect the truth value one bit.[11]

I recall Dworkin using the following example on several occasions during the seminars that he and Gareth Evans gave in Oxford during 1973–74 on objectivity in law and morality. A company runs a competition to advertise its breakfast cereal. A number of questions are set, matching heads to bodies of famous rock stars. There is also a "tie-breaker" question that does not admit of a demonstrable right answer as, obviously, the questions about the rock stars do, which asks competitors to say in a jingle of a set number of words what the virtues of the particular brand of cereal are. Five competitors obtain right answers to the head and body matching and, unlike some competitors who have also obtained right answers here, have written their jingles within the word limit. The task is then left to the competition judge to decide between them, on the basis of the tie-breaker, which one should receive the prize on the basis of the jingle. In other words, the judge has to decide which of the five entries is the "best" one. There are no precedents, nothing. Yet, would it seem right if the judge were random in his selection? Don't we expect some judgment? What does the judge do? Both Evans and Dworkin thought it couldn't be ruled out that some answers would be better than others; further, that it would be odd if the best answer weren't the right answer. Dworkin was more explicit about responsibility in the situation and his position here receives much emphasis in *Justice for Hedgehogs*; the judge has a responsibility to search out to the best of his abilities reasons that favor one side rather than another. Before dismissing the competition as a game, Dworkin thought the judge must attempt to understand the reasons that competitors have to suppose that one entry might be better than another and, if necessary, go back and look at the entries with the mission of deciding which was the best. Nothing much follows from cornflake jingles. But where a decision must be made, say, between two people about who is to carry the financial responsibility after a major road accident, there is a feeling of urgency. For law, Dworkin's position lies between the twin extremes of a pre-existing moral reality and a total subjectivity of values. The truth of propositions of morality springs from the importance of morality, from the commitment we should have when asserting propositions about how, morally, we should act. If moral propositions, and hence legal propositions, have to be "objective" then it is in this sense we have to understand them: "A true interpretive claim is true because the reasons for accepting it are better than the reasons for accepting any rival interpretive claim."[12]

This may seem to some to be irredeemably subjective; however, the argument does not force that conclusion. The requirement that moral intuitions or convictions be made coherent is one check, and that check is clearly one that is testable against other people's working out of coherent positions against their own intuitions and convictions. Objectivity is marked by reasons for and against. A requirement of publicity still obtains (and perhaps that is the force of the question, "Where does the proposition *come from?*") although that requirement is one of public reasons in general, and needn't refer to an independent metaphysical reality.

THE "CRITICAL" AND "SKEPTICAL" VIEWS

Dworkin attracts many skeptical responses, mainly due to the perceived "subjective" nature of his views. His arguments amount to nothing, it is said, because rational argument about these matters is not possible. But skepticism comes in a number of different forms and it is important to be clear about these. Consider, for example, the situation in a typical court. To understand skepticism we need an "ordinary" view to be skeptical about. The lawyers for each litigant, and the judge, as well as many others, are all participants in an argumentative institution. By that I mean that everybody concerned accepts that the institution has some sort of "meaning," and that the part each person plays in it makes some sort of sense. Common and related responses are as follows: (i) Some say that being engaged in the legally argumentative mode assumes courts to be applying "conflicting" rules in a "smoothing" and perhaps unconscious way, thus endorsing hidden bad values; (ii) Others say that the assertion that "everyone accepts" the meaning of law, morally endorses it in some insidious way, perhaps endorsing capitalist or masculine values, or perhaps just endorsing a generally conservative way of directing the community; (iii) Others say that the ordinary view doesn't allow for the "insider mole" who is working away at changing things, for example, by working in a law school. Understanding these three responses is helped by the idea of the "insider" and the "outsider" to an institution. This metaphor is used widely in different ways. It is present in Hart, whose distinction between internal and external points of view marked a step in the development of legal philosophy.[13]

What are Dworkin's positions on these matters? He clearly thinks that the concept of law, those "discrete ideas about which agreement collects," is an interpretive and therefore "insider's" view concerning the moral justification of a particular community's use of coercion.[14] First, the idea that the institution of law suffers from internal conflicts must itself be an interpretive position; it can't be true by fiat. And the idea also sits perfectly well with a non-skeptical position. A practicing lawyer has no difficulty in understanding that, if there are conflicts, he is under a duty to try to resolve them (he does it by distinguishing cases, or over-ruling, or "confining a case to its facts," for example). A much stronger form of skepticism, however, looks from the outside, and decides that law, as an institution, is inherently flawed and conflicting. Insiders, according to this skepticism, will not be able to make sense of it for reasons arising from the nature of law itself. This difficult—and perhaps ultimately obscure—view becomes clearer if we think of it in the light of the sense in which Marxism viewed law and its embodiment in a capitalist conception of property as exploitative. But this version of skepticism, too, is interpretive: it is global internal skepticism. It says all law is flawed because it is capitalist and thus exploitative. The sooner it goes the better. The third "insider mole" response is interpretive, too. The mole's task depends on the ordinary view but attacks it in the same way as either the first or second forms of skepticism, that is, either partially or globally.

Dworkin makes use of the metaphor of the "outsider" and the "insider" to describe two kinds of skepticism. He distinguishes between *external* skepticism and *internal* skepticism. External skepticism of moral values, or the *Archimedean* view (because Archimedes calculated he could lift the Earth if he were sufficiently external to it and had both a long pole and a fulcrum), denies that there is any special metaphysical realm of which moral judgments are a description and by virtue of which values are either true or false. It is a form of skepticism that is "disengaged," because it places the skeptic in a position in which he does not have to argue for any particular moral (or value) judgment he makes. It is, instead, a matter of mere "opinion" for him. The external skeptic both requires there to be something "out there" to make moral judgments true and then denies that there is anything "out there" to make them true and so establishes her skepticism. It is supposedly not an interpretive position but a "metaphysical" one.

This view receives further comment in *Justice for Hedgehogs*. If the "metaphysical skeptic" claim rests on the idea that "out-thereness"[15] is needed to make a moral judgment true, that must be an interpretive judgment about what makes moral judgments true. Just as a utilitarian might say "assuming utilitarianism to be true, since the greatest happiness principle favors prohibiting early-term abortion, the judgment that early-term abortions are morally prohibited must be true," an "Archimedean" might say "assuming out-thereness to be true, the judgment that early-term abortions are morally prohibited cannot be true." And if the Archimedean thinks it is not false, then it follows that she is making a moral judgment that early-term abortions are morally permissible. How can the Archimedean escape this? She wants there to be no morality because there is no scientific evidence for it; she doesn't act like that, of course, in her ordinary life, but with her philosophical hat on, there is no morality. She can't get to that position by laying down conditions for what counts as morally right; she can't escape logic (if something is not prohibited, then it is clearly permitted). Moral judgment does not require something in addition by way of a description of something existing "objectively" in order for it to have substance; and the external skeptic fails to be "external" for just that reason; scientific objectivity is irrelevant. The assertion that, for example, torturing babies is wrong does not require an extra judgment about the objectivity of the assertion. "We use the language of objectivity," says Dworkin, "not to give our ordinary moral or interpretive claims a bizarre metaphysical base, but to *repeat* them, perhaps in a more precise way, to emphasize or qualify their *content*."[16]

Dworkin does, on the other hand, allow internal skepticism, which is engaged. So a person who says that there is no morality because God is dead, engages with moral propositions by denying their force; he makes a deeper philosophical moral assumption—that there would be morality if God were alive—which he accepts and from which he derives his skepticism. All this works for other fields of value such as interpretive claims in literature and other artistic fields. An interpreter is skeptical in this sense in judging that an intelligible interpretation of *Hamlet* was not possible because the play completely lacks coherence. The skeptic is here prepared to grapple with the substance of the arguments about which she is being skeptical; she requires coherency for interpretation to take off and there is just no coherence here (as the Archimedean requires "out-thereness" and there is just no "out-thereness" there). There is nothing stopping the skeptic taking a broader skeptical view, say, that literary criticism itself is pointless because it tries to make order out of something that is necessarily conflicting, or that it deals only in fantasy, or serves no useful or important purpose in human affairs. Dworkin calls this last kind of internal skepticism "global" internal skepticism, because its skepticism is "global" about literary criticism. Internal skepticism may also arise in relation to a social institution such as law. A person might take the view that, on any interpretation, adjudication fails to make sense because its various rules and principles are too fundamentally conflicting to be resolved or made coherent in any way.

THE DISAPPEARANCE OF EXTERNALISM

What follows is a refinement of Dworkin's views over three decades on what is often called "the one right answer" thesis. Later, in Chapter 9 on *Justice for Hedgehogs*, I deal with the different dimensions of that problem as it developed originally from criticisms that his promotion of the idea that argument in hard—controversial—cases was argument about what the law was. I think everything I report Dworkin saying there is completely compatible with what he says in *Justice for Hedgehogs* (some of which was aired earlier in his 1996 paper "Objectivity and Truth: You'd Better Believe It").[17] If, as independence seems to require, value can only derive from value, Dworkin does not think this matters. He says it is merely a restatement that value exists in an independent domain from science. Science also derives from science and, indeed, it is even common to think that this is one of science's virtues. The problem is we don't yet have the confidence we should have with arguments of value that we do in fact have with science; our modes of arguing value are comparatively under-developed. It is not surprising, given the successes of science in the last two hundred or so years, that scientific method has dominated the way we think about truth. Moral philosophers— and others—who suppose that scientific accounts of truth are required for value have too often, in Dworkin's terms, wrongly encouraged "a colonial philosophy setting up embassies and garrisons of science within value discourse to govern it properly."[18]

Unity of value would not make sense if judgments of value could not be true or false. Justification would not be an issue and moral judgments would be relegated to matters of mere taste. However, as Dworkin points out, it is normal for us to act and talk as though there were moral truth. In the ordinary way, we consider the act of torturing babies "just for the hell of it" as morally wrong quite independently of what others believe, and we wouldn't have any hesitation in forcing our judgment on the torturer. We normally think that the wrongness of child torture can be justified independently from a report of our "feelings" about the matter. On the other hand, there is no scientific evidence for the truth of such moral beliefs. What people in fact believe, what past histories tell us, and feelings are, we understand, often irrelevant and often unclear guides. So widespread skepticism about whether there are moral truths is unsurprising.

Nevertheless, Dworkin claims that there is no threatening skeptical position against the objectivity of value. Either such skepticism is contradictory, or it is merely a roundabout way of making a moral judgment. However, he is keen to point out that there is a genuinely skeptical position that does not threaten the objectivity of value, because it derives from value itself; for that reason—it is internal to value—Dworkin calls it *internal* skepticism. His example is the view that morality is not universally applicable because of cultural difference. This, he says, states a moral view (which he thinks is wrong, incidentally) because it claims that a statement of morality is false if its applicability crosses cultures. Dworkin has always been clear that he has no deep quarrel—one that challenges the coherence of the idea—with internal moral skepticism, because, he says, such skepticism expresses a coherent hypothetical moral view. He concentrates his energy, however, on the *external* skeptics. Their claim is that either there is no moral objectivity because (i) it is an error to suppose that there are things in the world (Dworkin calls them "morons") according to which moral judgments could be objective (*error skeptics*), or (ii) because ordinary moral judgment can be re-described in a way that shows they have a different and subjective status (*status skeptics*). Both the error and status skeptics are external to morality, Dworkin says. They each believe they look at morality "from the outside" in a detached and disengaged way and, from this external perspective, make a value-free judgment about it. Dworkin deals with these positions in turn.

Error skepticism, according to Dworkin, is self-defeating because it relies on the claims that moral judgments can be true only if they are proved by empirically determinable facts and that there are no such facts. He then says that this is only an internally skeptical position. Take abortion. The external error skeptic says abortion is neither morally wrong nor wrong. Dworkin concedes that there are no "morons" in the world that make either of these statements true. But, he says, if there is nothing to make abortion right or wrong, it can only follow, according to the external error skeptic's claim, that abortion is morally permissible. It further follows that the "external error skeptic" contradicts her claim that first-order moral judgments lack objectivity (and that our ordinary talk about morality is defective).

Status skepticism, on the other hand, is the main kind of skepticism amongst professional philosophers. Such skepticism uses a well-known distinction between *first-order* and *second-order* moral claims. First-order claims are ordinary moral judgments; second-order claims are about such judgments, just like the difference between doing arithmetic as in "2 + 2 = 4" and talking about arithmetic as in "arithmetic is taught in schools." First-order claims of morality can't be true or false according to status external skepticism because a second-order claim about them is that they are not descriptive of anything but are only "expressions" (of feelings or emotions, say).

Summing up, error skepticism says ordinary moral claims are "misconceived" (there are no "morons" out there) and status skepticism says such claims are "misunderstood" because they should be understood in a more accurate way. Status skepticism, according to Dworkin, is the popular form because it at least allows us—unlike "error skepticism"—to keep our convictions such as that abortion is wrong.

But in spite of its popularity amongst philosophers, he says, status skepticism is also self-defeating; no meaning is added by such claims as "abortion is *objectively* wrong" or "abortion is wrong *is true*" or "it is an *external fact* that abortion is wrong." Rather, these expressions only express emphasis; they are just a more graphic way of saying that abortion is wrong. Since the status skeptic denies them, just like the error skeptic, these denials must also be first-order moral claims. Dworkin employs no special logic or sleight of hand to establish this straightforward argument. Why, again, are these moral claims different from philosophical claims? If the status skeptic claims that these moral expressions are part of our semantics, his claim is disproved by our semantic practices because people who claim that torturing babies is wrong clearly mean something different from "this is what they feel"; it is instead the reason for that feeling. And they certainly don't mean it is true for them but not true for others.

Some philosophers argue that our moral beliefs are 'really' desires for a state of affairs we would be willing to bring about, because beliefs don't motivate; since desires can't be true or false then, they argue, there is no moral objectivity. But Dworkin denies that beliefs don't motivate. For a start, that I have a desire at the least will on many occasions imply a belief I have (my desire that the killing stop implies I believe that murder is wrong) and in any case it is possible to believe something is morally right but have the desire to do exactly the opposite. Dworkin gives as an example Richard III's desire to do what he knew to be wrong: "I'm determined to prove a villain."[19]

Yet another form of status skepticism asserts that second-order statements aren't re-writes of first-order statements but exist in a completely different philosophical discourse. Dworkin takes Richard Rorty as an exemplar of this sort of argument. It works quite well for explaining fiction. Lady Macbeth makes true statements from within the play but in another discourse, because she is fictional, her statements can't be objectively true. Rorty applies this argument more generally. He says, for example, that we can play a mountains "language-game," which is independent of whether mountains actually exist, and so we can do the same with a morality language-game. The philosophical language-game is independent of whether morality is objective. Another such line is taken by the "projectivists" who appear to say that we can be committed to morality and act according to its dictates, but that these are only commitments that are "projected" onto the world, and thus without attendant objectivity. In these cases, Dworkin says the language-game strategy fails because it does not supply an argument showing why the alternative language is not a restatement of the original first-order claim. Unlike fiction, we cannot show that there are different language games whose difference prevents us from asserting that moral judgment is true beyond its own respective game. By contrast we know very well why *Macbeth* is fiction. (Dworkin says he can't see that Rorty's use of capital letters—"The World as It Is In Itself"—will do the trick).

Dworkin achieves something significant here; he reinterprets Hume not as moral skeptic but quite the opposite, as someone who supported the independence of value from science. The Humean principle, as Dworkin calls it, tells us that we can have confidence in looking to value to justify our moral judgments and therefore not be skeptical of morality at all. The independence of value is important for his book; it requires that values are interconnected and mutually supporting. And what Dworkin has also done is demolish the idea of second-order theorizing about morality. That domain is captured by morality (tying it to science, or to language, is just irrelevant) and so Dworkin is free to develop a full account of morality based entirely on evaluative judgments. This cuts so much deadwood from the so-called metaphysics of morality or moralizing. For too long, debate about the credibility of morality itself has existed under the shadow of reality determined by science and this has been to the disadvantage of morality. The realists amongst moral philosophers try to show the interaction between "morons" and ourselves, and fail, while the anti-realists, who believe in mind-dependent morality, exist under the same shadow, for they have to say, bearing the realist camp in mind, that morality is somehow made up, coming entirely from within. This is, as Dworkin says, "an entirely bizarre assignment. How can they be values if we can just make them up?"[20] Morality cannot be just a matter of taste, mattering only to the person whose taste it is.

Where do Dworkin's arguments on skepticism get us? The crucial point is, I think, that Dworkin disapproves of the casting off of one very important moral responsibility by the simplistic assertion that there is nothing "objective" in the world by virtue of which moral judgments are only "opinion." Our moral responsibility is to make our views publicly accountable. The problem with the metaphysical approach is that it appears to deny any possibility for responsible argument. It thus denies the need for a public stance other than, perhaps, a declaration of what a person is going to do. We should be able to hold the skeptic to account for his "opinion." In any case, as a matter of sociology, in the practical world of law, not only are there few global internal skeptics (Marx perhaps), but a belief in external skepticism makes absolutely no difference to legal argument:

> The skeptical challenge, sensed as the challenge of external skepticism, has a powerful hold on lawyers. They say, of any thesis about the best account of legal practice in some department of the law, "That's your opinion," which is true but to no point. Or they ask, "How do you know?" or "Where does that claim come from?" demanding not a case they can accept or oppose but a thundering knock-down metaphysical demonstration no one can resist who has the wit to understand. And when they see that no argument of that power is in prospect, they grumble that jurisprudence is subjective only. Then, finally, they return to their knitting—making, accepting, resisting, rejecting arguments in the normal way, consulting, revising, deploying convictions pertinent to deciding which of competing accounts of legal practice provides the best justification of that practice. My advice is straightforward: this preliminary dance of skepticism is silly and wasteful; it neither adds to nor subtracts from the business at hand. The only skepticism worth anything is skepticism of the internal kind, and this must be earned by arguments of the same contested character as the arguments it opposes, not claimed in advance by some pretense at hard-hitting empirical metaphysics.[21]

We can, of course, be skeptical about all this by denying the possibility of genuine argument about legal and moral issues. Is there really such a genuine subjective doubter?

"KNOCK-DOWN" ARGUMENTS

People like arguments that demonstrate, or prove, or otherwise provide a convincing "knock-down" effect. A theory that legal argument in pivotal cases does not consist of such arguments thus appears weak. Nevertheless, theories cannot be wrong because people just want them to be wrong and so we shall examine the claim that there can be no right answers unless they can be proved right. Some people object to the idea that there can be true propositions of law but will accept that there can be "best" or "better" answers. A consideration of this view is instructive because it throws some light on the hold that the demonstrability thesis has on people. It is very common, too, for people to say of a non-demonstrably true proposition that it is not true "but only a matter of opinion." But there is nothing to be gained by saying that although a proposition is the best statement of the law it cannot be true. Why not say that the true statement of law is one that expresses "the best" view of it? What advance on clarity has otherwise been made? Further, we must not confuse "doing our best" to produce a correct, true statement of the law with producing the correct statement, because, of course, we could be wrong. This common confusion shows, I think, the real problem people have with undemonstrable truth. How can we know, how can we be certain, that the proposition is true, or "the best"? People want certainty when none is possible. It does not follow that there can be no correct or true propositions. The judge who does his best may get the law wrong, but his best endeavor is nevertheless an endeavor to state the correct proposition of law.

The fact that something is "only my opinion" does not release it from the arena of truth. It used to be people's "opinion" that the world was flat, but that opinion turned out, it now seems, to have been false. We form opinions all the time which turn out to be true or false. In fact, the function of the phrase "in my opinion" is often used precisely in the recognition of the fact that the speaker recognizes that he may be wrong and that therefore the opinion is capable of being wrong or right. A much better question to be concerned with here is whether the concept of truth shared by lawyers is a good or sensible one. Given that they do employ the concept of truth, that concept might be confused or wrong, in the same way that it seems reasonable to say that people were once confused and wrong in thinking the world was flat.

There are two important matters to consider. First, is a concept of truth that exceeds demonstrability a good one for people to use generally? We might answer that question by considering, for example, other areas of discourse to see whether there is a general use for it. Second, if it is good for general use, are there special reasons why it should not be sensible for lawyers to employ it? Note that we can make short work of the assertion that truth cannot possibly exceed demonstration, for that assertion cannot itself be demonstrated to be true. Consider the following statement of the demonstrability thesis:

Only propositions that can be demonstrated, or proved, to be true, are capable of being true or false.

We can't demonstrate this to be true. Pro-demonstrabilistas embarrass themselves by asserting it. I think much of the nonsense that is spoken about Dworkin's "one right answer" thesis ends here. I've seen so much time wasted by angry people at Dworkin's seminars where they start (ignoring the substance of what he has to say, for example on rights) and finish with: "But that can only be your subjective point of view, Professor Dworkin, because you can't prove it." The argument is embarrassing. The interesting question is what leads them to accept the demonstrability thesis. Does it have something to commend it? More important, is it within our power to adopt it or some other criterion or definition of truth? We can, after all, adopt definitions (or postulates, axioms, guides, stipulations and so on) to guide our reasoning in other fields, such as geometry or economics or wartime codes. Such postulates are chosen not because they are true but for other reasons. "The cat is on the mat" may be an unpractical, unworkable code, because too easily broken, for "the missile is on target." If practical considerations are therefore the clue to the justification of at least some kinds of postulates, are practical considerations relevant to the adoption of the demonstrability thesis in law, regarding it now as a postulate? My view is that the case to be made for the adoption of the demonstrability thesis in law turns out to be no more than the case for positivism. It is, presumably, that laws should only be seen as "existing," that is, being true or false, or valid or invalid, when their existence, truth or validity can be demonstrated by reference to actual official practice so that, for example, the "defect of uncertainty" may be cured, or so that reasonable expectations may be fulfilled.

The arguments against this view, however, approach the problem of what is a sensible conception of law and legal argument, and not arguments that depend upon some fixed, immutable idea of truth "out there." In other words, the appeal to the demonstrability thesis, as if it were an independent argument, is misleading.

NOT "NO RIGHT ANSWER" BY DEFAULT

In the domains of value, Dworkin does not say there is always a right answer. Rather, it is not the case that there is no right answer. So he thinks there are right answers on all sorts of matters (he thinks, as do you and I, that it is right that we do not torture children) but on others there are not, for example, on the question of whether claret is "nobler" than white burgundy. Nevertheless it follows from the above (and he says it), that he thinks that the question of whether there is a right answer in an evaluative domain is itself an evaluative question. Many philosophers take the view that in such domains it follows by default from the indeterminacy—the inability to "knock down" as the Archimedean thesis requires—that there cannot be a right answer to that matter.

Take the question of whether abortion is wicked or not. Here there is controversy and people may simply be uncertain as to the answer in some clearly defined circumstances. However, it does not follow from our actual psychological state of uncertainty that there is no right or wrong of the matter. This is not to say all indeterminate judgments lack a truth value. If neither Picasso nor Beethoven was a greater artist than the other then that means that comparisons (of that sort) between them are indeterminate. But that is quite different from saying: I am uncertain whether Picasso or Beethoven is greater, therefore we cannot assign a truth value to any statement that claims one to be better than the other. Claims that a matter is indeterminate require something more than a report of a psychological state (whether a state of uncertainty in me or a state of uncertainty arising from the fact that two or more people have different views) and, it turns out, the argument has to be one of the same order, and as demanding, as an argument for saying that a particular value claim is determinate. In other words, there is again no Archimedean point from which value judgments, determinate or indeterminate, can be assessed for their truth. As we have seen, Dworkin thinks there can be good arguments for internal skepticism in literary interpretation. Nevertheless, he also suggests that it is healthy to discern conflict since seeing conflict is often a more constructive diagnosis that leads us to seek "deeper divergent understandings."

We should return to law. Positivism, Dworkin says, takes the default line on questions of legal controversy. In hard cases, where judges, lawyers and law students are uncertain about what the law is, positivism says that it follows that there is no truth of the matter and so purported legal claims here can be neither true nor false. So when judges decide, they are making new law. Since the default argument is false, and we have every reason to suppose that the sorts of reasons advanced by lawyers and so on of the ordinary legal sort are those which determine whether legal claims are true or not, it is highly plausible to say that the criteria of truth are not contained in some Archimedean universe. This conclusion removes a great deal of the misunderstanding that has bedeviled purportedly skeptical accounts of what legal reasoning is about. Dworkin's injunction is that any other kinds of approaches are time-wasting because they are beside the point.

A SHORT SUMMING UP

It is clear that Dworkin is not a total subjectivist, inserting his "own values" into other people's lives. That is a crude but very popular view about anyone who expresses views forcefully. It is clear, too, that he is far from claiming there is "a right answer" to all moral questions buried somewhere if only we could find it. Is the middle road, built, as I have suggested, on reason and commitment, possible? You must ask yourself two questions in order to consider the feasibility—and desirability—of this middle position. First, should moral judgments be subject to (although perhaps not necessarily the product of) any form of rational sifting or are they essentially arbitrary assertions? Secondly, when you yourself make a genuine—heartfelt—moral judgment do you really believe that what you assert is anything other than true?

We should now be acquainted with Dworkin's views on the interpretive nature of social practices, his views on the fundamental simple-mindedness of legal positivism and the superiority, flexibility and complexity of integrity. We are also armed with his views on the objectivity of certain kinds of controversial propositions. It is next necessary to examine the relationship between the fundamental idea for him of the equal objective worth of human beings and the idea of integrity. We have seen, too, the way Dworkin develops the connection between the idea of community and the treatment of the citizens who compose it through the idea of integrity. What does "treating people as equals" really mean? It is this very abstract idea of "treating people as equals," one of Dworkin's most fundamental ideas, which I shall now examine.

CHAPTER EIGHT

Treating People as Equals

When discussing Dworkin's idea of making "the best sense" of law, I said that one of the abstract principles driving his political philosophy was that a government should treat its citizens "as equals." It is necessary always to go to this ruling principle in interpreting Dworkin. Since it is so abstract it is difficult, I believe, to dissent from it; rather, the interesting arguments depend on what equality means in particular cases. In brief summary, Dworkin is against discrimination on the basis that some human beings are less worthy than others, and for democracy because that distributes political power in a way consistent with equality. Further, he says that the distribution of the community's resources must concern only economic resources; first, because an assumption about available resources lies behind any judgment about the comparative worth of human lives, and second, because securing resources to people recognizes their liberty to use them. For him, equality is therefore inseparable from liberty. Since a person's right to liberty is constrained—or, his word, "parametered"—it means that people living ethically different lives can, within a scheme of just resource distribution, approve the political scheme from their own perspective. But this short summary is a taste only and we must turn first to the content, at the most abstract level, of the idea of treating people as equals. The problems in this idea, and Dworkin's treatment of it, will occupy us for the remainder of this book.

THE APPEAL OF EQUALITY

Do we need to justify the injunction that people should be treated as equals? There are two important reasons why we should. The first is that the idea of equality is bandied about in political debate in a loose and unexamined way. Equality is thought to be the enemy of liberty. Those, for example, who advocate "equality" often advocate the reduction or restriction of private medicine or private education, on the ground that benefits will be spread more equally by a publicly ordered distribution. The popular criticism is that such a public distribution denies people the choice to make their own decisions on medical and educational matters. The argument, that a person's liberty to choose what he does is part of what makes him a person, has a powerful hold on us. On the other hand, the apparent counter-argument of the egalitarian—why should one person's liberty be obtained at the cost to another's?—also has a powerful hold. This apparently irresolvable conflict between equality and personal freedom has the effect of making people take sides. It is possible to discern a connection between the political left and equality, whether it is moderate as welfare liberalism or extreme as communism, and the political right and personal freedom, where there are also moderate and extreme versions. The seeming conflict is unfortunate because it is by no means clear, even on a superficial analysis, that freedom and equality are incompatible. Dworkin goes further than anyone else in saying that both are inseparable notions. To him, each idea emphasizes an important aspect of the other. It is critical, therefore, that one is not swayed by popular understandings of these terms.

The second reason is that the idea of equality, as Bernard Williams[1] points out, seems either too strong or too weak to be able to do much work. The strong sense is that used when, as the French revolutionaries declared in article 1 of the Declaration of Rights, it is held that "men are born and remain equal." The statement seems patently false in respect of ability, wealth, status, good looks, height and even weight. Noting this feature, Jeremy Bentham remarked at the time in his well-known contemporary work *Anarchical Fallacies* that it would follow that lunatics could lock up sane people, and idiots would have a right to govern![2]

To make more sense than this we should turn to a weaker sense of equality which says that human beings are equal *qua* human beings, that is, in Williams' terms, they are equal in sharing a "common humanity." This rescues the strong sense from absurdity although it also means that we are not given a clear lead as to how to treat humans as humans. We are, rather, merely being reminded of the fact that all people are equally human. The chief problem in the idea of equality concerns, of course, the filling out of how people should be treated as "ends." Respecting a person means seeing that person from the "human point of view." So we distinguish, for example, between the person and the particular status, or "title," he has and we say that there is a failure of justice when people no longer distinguish the title from the "man who has the title." The hierarchical society which ignores the distinction is poorer because the view becomes accepted that titles, and status, are foreordained, or inevitable. Further, in such societies, an important problem is that people lower in the hierarchy endorse their own lowly status as acceptable, in the same way as those above will endorse their previous lowly status before as in the proper order of things. Everyone accepts "their lot" as inevitable.

Of course, all sorts of goods in society are limited and so it will, necessarily, be the case that a hierarchy, although not necessarily a preordained hierarchy, will form. How, then, to give equality any bite here? Williams thinks the idea lies in a properly understood equality of opportunity and thus draws the connection between equality of opportunity and equality of persons. His argument depends first on distinguishing people from their status and seeing people from "the human point of view," and second upon seeing that people may, as a result of their environment, in which they are denied goods, not have a real possibility of attaining status further up the hierarchy. We have, in Williams's words, to be able to abstract people from their "curable" environments.

Some philosophers think equality provides no substantive justification for treating people in any way. Take the views of Joseph Raz, which are representative.[3] He distinguishes three senses of weak equality. First, equality as what he calls merely a "closure" principle, which marks off a general rule as applying only to those instances that come within it, as for example, in the statement "Every human being is equally entitled to education." This, he says, states nothing more than that human beings are entitled to education, with the reminder that it is only the quality of humanhood that is relevant. The work of the phrase, in other words, is done—or "closed"—by the idea of being human. A second sense is more fruitful. This is where claims to equality refer to an actually existing inequality of distribution, such as, for example: "Human beings have a right to those things that others have but they themselves do not have." This sense, Raz thinks, has more promise. It comes closer to expressing the sentiments of the signatories to the French Declaration of Rights. Raz points out, as have many others, this principle can be satisfied by a leveling down rather than a leveling up.[4] Really, stripped of its rhetoric, the principle is saying no more, and of course no less, than that humans have a common humanity. The third sense is one that Raz refers to as "rhetorical" equality. According to this sense, reference is made to equality with good rhetorical effect ("we are all equal—as human beings") but without a substantial intellectual foundation. He is not against this rhetorical use if it works to bring about a better community but thinks that it is, nevertheless, an intellectual fudge. In his view, again shared by many others, the statement that "all human beings are entitled to equal respect" could just as well be rendered as "being human is a ground for respect."

I don't think these criticisms are weighty. You are, of course, saying something that makes great moral sense when you say that people are to be treated equally as human beings because it draws attention away from their irrelevant features and to what makes them human. (Shylock: "If you prick us, do we not bleed? If you tickle us, do we not laugh?"). If you say merely "human beings deserve respect" you are saying something less because it would be consistent with "well, this human being deserves less respect than those others." The French revolutionaries meant something by "equality": it was wrong for the French aristocracy to have so very much more than others just by virtue only of luck. These attributes, they were saying, are irrelevant to our being equally human.

Useful is Dworkin's distinction between treating people *as equals* and giving people *equal treatment*. The primary idea, he says, is that of treating people "as equals," and the idea of "equal treatment" only derives from the former. Giving equal treatment to human beings would mean giving as much by way of resources, say, to a handicapped person as to someone who was not handicapped. It would not, in other words, be sensitive to the differences between people and a confusion of the two ideas leads people to reject equality as a moral ideal. If the injunction that we should accord primacy to treating people as equals is deemed to be the most abstract injunction in political philosophy, we will be led, Dworkin says, to saying that handicapped people do not have a right to equal treatment but, rather, a right to unequal treatment. The handicapped person, according to the primary abstract principle, must be entitled to more unequal resources to compensate. If I have two children, and one is dying from a disease that is making the other uncomfortable, I do not show equal concern if I flip a coin to decide which should have the remaining dose of a drug. This example shows that the right to treatment as an equal is fundamental, and the right to equal treatment, derivative. In some circumstances the right as an equal will entail a right to equal treatment, but not, by any means, in all circumstances.[5] I think that the success of equality-cynical arguments comes from drawing too marked a separation between "equality" arguments (which permit us to drop equality in favor of "closure" principles) and "humanity" arguments which are thought to be sufficient in themselves. But I believe with Dworkin that there is equality within humanity: you can't treat people with respect unless you see them as in some important sense equal to yourself, as having equal objective moral worth to yourself. Leveling down is consistent with treating people with lack of respect—it is just arithmetic after all and so detached from morality. This is not to say that leveling down could be required by equality, say, where it is better that a "whites only" golf club be closed.

EQUALITY AND UTILITARIANISM

Dworkin has an interesting view of the relationship between rights to equality and utilitarianism. He links them through a direct appeal to what is intuitively understood by the utilitarian maxim that governments should aim to maximize the average welfare of their citizens. He says it owes its "great appeal" to the inherent egalitarian premise that no person is to be accorded more weighting in the greatest happiness calculation than anyone else:

> Utilitarian arguments of policy, therefore, seem not to oppose but on the contrary to embody the fundamental right of equal concern and respect, because they treat the wishes of each member of the community on a par with the wishes of any other.[6]

The idea of equality is here drawn from the non-specificity of persons in utilitarianism. John Rawls famously remarked that utilitarianism was "no respecter of persons," which is to point to a malign side of the doctrine. The best-known criticism of the doctrine draws upon this malign characteristic by pointing out that a utilitarian calculation, say, one involving large imbalances in wealth, could justify great misery among a few people in order to achieve a marginal gain in overall happiness for a large majority of people. Dworkin, on the other hand, points to a benign side to utilitarianism. He emphasizes that the greatest happiness is for the greatest number and thus people are distinguished equally by the fact that they are numbers or points or receptacles of pain and pleasure. This is consistent with the principle that people should be treated impartially; that seems clear from the utilitarian idea that no person is to count for more, nor less, than one.

It is difficult not to agree with Dworkin on this point historically, since the growth of utilitarianism accompanied a parallel growth in liberal and egalitarian reforms. And the force of the argument that there is an equality premise contained in the utilitarian calculation is strong. Briefly and crudely, the empty, numerical aspect of utilitarianism emphasizes the importance of equality; the maximizing aspect emphasizes the importance of our well-being.

Dworkin's argument is striking in being at odds with many interpretations of the doctrine. For him, the appeal of utilitarianism lies in its condemnation of the view that any form of life is inherently more valuable than any other. So, for example, if a community has only enough resources to give medicine to some of its members, the sickest must be treated first. Or, if more members of a community want a new swimming pool than would prefer a theatre, the swimming pool comes first. But no person should be preferred because he is inherently worthier of more concern (is "graded higher") and the wishes of the theatre-lovers are not to be preferred because theatre is a more worthwhile interest than sport. Teasing this "no person to count more than one" premise out, Dworkin distinguishes between a person's personal and impersonal—or "external"—preferences. A person's personal preferences are those which concern his own life. His impersonal, external, preferences concern how he thinks other people should live. Dworkin says that the satisfaction of impersonal preferences would corrupt utilitarianism because it violates the utilitarian requirement that the worth of a preference be left from the overall calculation. If impersonal preferences count, then there is "double-counting": someone preferring how another person should live may negate that other's preference. In the real world it will often be impossible to separate personal and impersonal preferences because often both will be expressed in a single statement. Take, for example, the white law school candidate who prefers all-white law schools because (i) it raises his chance of admission and (ii) he doesn't like black professionals. He does not approve of blacks doing professional jobs. There is also a problem concerning the substantive argument against double-counting because a person might vote not for themselves but for the good of others. What is the wrong? Is it that he will effectively cancel out the vote of a person who wishes to live the life of which he disapproves? This doesn't seem like double-counting.

At the end of his article "Equality of Welfare," Dworkin reconsiders the idea of egalitarian utilitarianism and says why it could not "purport to supply all of a plausible general political or moral theory." The egalitarian utilitarian would have to explain why it is not as good to aim at maximum average misery as maximum average happiness, for example, or why there is anything to regret in a natural disaster that kills thousands though it improves the situation of a few.[7] Dworkin says this because egalitarian utilitarianism aims at the maximization of welfare based on a number principle ("no person to count for more nor less than one") and does not value welfare as a good in itself. It is just a reference to one of the empty senses of equality as defined by Raz. Dworkin thinks that the explanation for what is wrong with these two situations lies in further political principles, amongst them one which holds that those who aim at the failure or misery of others do not show the others the concern to which human beings, at least, are entitled.[8] He thinks that the best grounds we have for instituting the well-known fundamental rights in a liberal society, the sorts of rights usually collected under the title of a "Bill of Rights," are that they are learned by experience to counteract the effect of double-counting which, in the real world, can hardly fail to occur. In his view, the rights to freedom of expression and to free choice in personal and sexual relations should be defended because the political process will not usually be able to make the necessary discriminations in order to eliminate the different views about the worth of these activities.

It is also interesting to note the contingent, historical nature of this case for fundamental rights. It follows that there is no substance in the charge often made against liberals that it is inconsistent to endorse a general right to freedom of speech but not a general right to freedom of property. The arguments for maintaining a right to freedom of speech because of the antecedent likelihood of corruption will be of a different historical character from the arguments for instituting a fundamental right to property. Some limitations by a community on rights to property do not obviously show a denial of a right to equal concern and respect.[9] The striking interpretation Dworkin offers of utilitarianism is reconcilable with the idea of rights as trumps because, crudely, if equality is the more fundamental principle, it should trump any consequences that flow from it; in my view, the possibility of trumping shows that egalitarian utilitarianism is not really utilitarian. However, Dworkin thinks, with obvious evidence on his side, that the Anglo-American communities he discusses have traditions motivated by some form of utilitarianism, yet he is clearly not a utilitarian for none of his work would make sense if he were. His dalliance with utilitarianism is sensible, though, in the real world. There we must make interpretive sense of our existing practices and, if those practices are utilitarian, the best sense has to be given to them. It is interesting to note that he draws a strong connection between egalitarian utilitarianism and representative democracy. In Chapter 6, for example, I considered his view that, in the real world, citizens had a stake in the community where the government acted in good faith in assuming that citizens should be treated as equals. In his essay "Liberalism,"[10] Dworkin asserts, for example, that claims for the protection of freedom of speech or sexual preference are democratic in the face of what even a large majority of people want. This suggests to me that his view is that the political and utilitarian culture of these communities requires interpretation as egalitarian utilitarianism. In other words, he thinks that we can have a moral stake in our communities in the real world where politicians act on good faith within a tradition that some form of utilitarianism is the proper test of justice.

EQUALITY VERSUS UTILITARIAN ECONOMICS: THE CHICAGO SCHOOL

Dworkin's attack on the so-called Chicago school of law and economics, of which Posner proposed the most articulate form, is an attack based, as we would expect, on his endorsement of the abstract principle of equality, and is directed against a highly unconstrained form of utilitarianism. It takes some elaboration of the economic market to see clearly what the law and economics movement claims. Probably the fastest way to it is through the concept of paretonism, named after a twentieth-century economist, Pareto. Paretonism is a criterion of measurement of an increase in welfare primarily in terms of the relationship between two parties. Situation A is *pareto-superior* to situation B, if in situation A at least one of the parties has more welfare—is "better off"—and neither of the parties has less than in situation B. A *pareto-optimal* situation envisages the end of a possible chain of pareto-superior changes where there could be no further situation where one party would be better off without the other being worse off. It should be seen that the criterion implies a distributional constraint: no one loses. In economist talk, a pareto-superior situation is "morally attractive" because there is no "loser." In the real world things are very different. There are market "imperfections." A perfect market transaction is one where the parties bargain, exercising their freedom as a "rational maximizer" would do to mutual advantage; the market is not "distorted" by a monopoly, for example; the parties have "perfect knowledge" and there are no "transaction costs." This rough definition is widely accepted as a basic platform of understanding. But in the real world, there are in fact very few pareto-superior situations because there almost always will be a third party left worse off, for example, a local trader who is undercut by the transaction between A and B. To cope with the practicalities of the real world, the economic lawyers of the Chicago school use an alternative way of viewing the market. That school employs a different criterion commonly known as the Kaldor-Hicks criterion. This measures wealth increases rather than welfare. Further, it does take into account whether any person is left worse off. The criterion only requires that the wealth created is more than sufficient to compensate in wealth the worse off person; there is no requirement for any compensation. Kaldor-Hicks is ordinary accountancy in the form of cost-benefit analysis.

An example would be a factory that moves to another town with cheaper rents and labor. The town it moves from loses but the new factory and the town it moved to gain sufficient profits for it in principle to be able to compensate the losers with money. Since that is so, there has been an overall economic benefit. Simply, the cost-benefit criterion is paretonism with welfare replaced by wealth, and with the distributional element (no one worse off) removed. The simple formulation shows the limited ethical attractiveness of Kaldor-Hicks over paretonism, although it is, of course, a useful way of measuring the overall effects of wealth movements. Amazingly, Posner adopts this criterion as the measure of how a judge should decide a legal case. In an effort to side-step the fairly obvious shabbiness of his idea—judging as an accountant, no less—he attempts to rein in the autonomy component of paretonism with the idea that the parties have given their previous consent to such an accountancy outcome, what economists call *ex ante* consent. He says that parties to litigation accept, or consent in advance, to the outcome of the court case, because they have consented in advance to allocation of rights according to the wealth-maximizing principles:

> The notion of consent used here is what economists call *ex ante* compensation. I contend . . . that if you buy a lottery ticket and lose the lottery . . . you have consented to the loss.[11]

Dworkin must be right in saying that the idea of consent, which is intended by Posner to import the idea of a genuine exercise of autonomy, is confused with fairness. Posner seems to envisage actual consent, saying that his own arguments improve on the kind of fictional consent of Rawls's original position because the consent under wealth maximization is concerned with actual people making choices under what he calls "natural" ignorance. There is no actual consent in the case of litigation and so the argument must rest on either self-interest, which clearly fails, or fairness. The analogy with the lottery is a most unfortunate piece of advocacy on Posner's part, too, because it is a partisan appeal to what he thinks the business of litigation is. It is especially interesting given both his training as a lawyer and status of judge. If the question is one of fairness, therefore, Posner's argument for the justice of wealth maximization is a circular one. He cannot import fairness into the model which he intends to use to show us that wealth maximization is fair.

Some lawyer economists use a different tactic; they say that losers suffer "demoralization costs," including recognition that an outcome is unfair or "morally unattractive" and that these should be compensated. But you can't just "buy off" an unfair result; a genuine grievance is likely to remain. In any case it cannot get round the problem because the efficiency criterion doesn't require the losers to be compensated. I recommend Dworkin's two articles "Is Wealth a Value?" and "Why Efficiency?" for a careful and considered attack on Posner's theory and on Calabresi's part defense of court wealth maximizing on the ground that the best solution is one which trades efficiency against justice.[12]

Posnerian economic analysis of law took off in the eighties. It is common now to analyze cases this way in law schools, although judges rarely do. It is just utilitarianism of a sort particularly vulnerable to criticisms based upon the importance of being fair to litigants by applying the law in a way that is sensitive to consistency and equality—Dworkinian integrity, in other words. Its downfall arises from its lack of a principle of distribution other than wealth maximization. Posnerian economics are cruder than egalitarian utilitarianism as interpreted by Dworkin, because that requires egalitarian constraint: "no person to count more, nor less than any other" in a sense more substantial than mere "closure" or "numbers." The damning thing about Posnerian law and economics is its abandonment of paretonism; there no person is worse off, unlike under the Kaldor-Hicks cost-benefit analysis. In other words, says Dworkin, Posner "cannot claim a genuine Pareto justification for common law decisions, in either hard or easy cases. His relaxed version of paretonism is only utilitarianism with all the warts."[13]

REVERSE DISCRIMINATION

We have seen how the important idea of integrity, for Dworkin, links to the idea of equality through the intermediary of fraternity and community. The state must treat its citizens as equals because that is the idea that gives full-bloodedness to the idea of a community where every member is of equal moral status. The idea of treating people as equals requires that in the ideal world the state must speak equally, and justly, to all. Dworkin has, on many occasions, applied the Herculean technique to various areas of both United States and United Kingdom law. Examples are cases relating to the abolition of slavery,[14] reverse discrimination,[15] free speech,[16] criminal procedure,[17] right to privacy,[18] abortion and euthanasia.[19] It would make this book too long, and destroy its purpose, if I tried to do justice to the subtlety of his arguments in all these cases. I have already discussed part of his analysis of the cases on the right to privacy.[20] A number of his analyses read like clear and thoughtful judicial decisions. I shall examine one of these analyses, the problem of "reverse" or "affirmative" discrimination. This problem can be stated simply and it shows very clearly how Dworkin sees political and moral argument as integral to legal argument. Although largely he treats the issue as predominantly constitutional, it has wider importance. In U.S. constitutional law the question whether legislation offends equality is a clearly *legal* question. Since it amounts to an argument for the moral point that a policy of reverse discrimination does not necessarily offend equality, Dworkin's point speaks more widely.

First, we must understand the legal setting. The Fourteenth Amendment of the U.S. Constitution provides that no state shall deny any person the equal protection of its laws. A reverse or affirmative discrimination program gives preferential treatment to a minority group. The aim is to raise the status of the group in the community and thereby reduce overall community prejudice to it. The question is whether the Fourteenth Amendment prohibits such programs, where permitted by state law. The question is not whether such programs would actually work to reduce community prejudice, for that question is an empirical one. Obviously, if a program of reverse discrimination in fact would not reduce prejudice it could not be justified. Instead, the question is whether such programs are justified in principle. In other words, is it a violation of the equal protection amendment just to have such programs, irrespective of whether they work or not? My experience is that many people do not separate these two questions with any clarity. They think that there is nothing left to the question of equality if the programs can be shown not to work. But this is a silly way of dismissing the question, for programs of different kinds might be devised that did work, and the mere fact that they did so would not be a sufficient justification. If a person is genuinely denied his right to the equal protection of the laws, then the question of whether, because of the denial of his right, some good community goal is advanced is irrelevant. The question is, instead, to be settled as a matter of *rights* to equal protection of the laws.

Note how the question is both a legal and a moral one. In deciding whether reverse discrimination is legally justified, we have to enter a debate about what equality requires, and this is a moral question. In the discussion that follows, bear in mind the positivist view of law. A common criticism of Dworkin is that the "inherent vagueness" of legal terms such as "equal protection of the laws" proves his theory wrong. The criticism is that such terms cannot be "filled out" by any argument of a sufficiently controlled kind to merit being described as "legal." Let us see. The state law of Texas, as it stood in 1945, provided that only whites could attend the University of Texas Law School. After prolonged litigation, in 1949 the Supreme Court struck down this law as contrary to the Fourteenth Amendment.[21] Most participants to the debate on reverse discrimination accept this decision. The Texas law was a law motivated by racial prejudice and denied blacks, simply because they were black, the same chances that whites had to become lawyers. Of particular importance, at this stage in the development of this argument, was the fact that in Texas, the law school of the state university had a unique standing in preparing candidates for admission to the bar. Given this standing, it was impossible in fact for separate black educational facilities to be equal. This policy of admissions is invariably assumed, or argued, to be a necessary element in an "affirmative action" program which will improve the position of minority groups in the legal (or medical, etc.) professions. It is necessary to point this out to show why the later case of *Brown* v. *The Board of Education* still had something to decide.[22] We should compare this case with the following. State law permits a law school entry program that allocates a number of places to minority groups. They have to have sufficiently good academic records to enable them to take the course, but apart from that, their entry is unaffected by the average grade required for entry to the course by those not members of the minority groups. It follows that there will be some applicants, not from minority groups, who fail to be admitted, even although their average grades are higher, perhaps considerably so, than that of the average grade of the minority intake. Is denying these applicants a law school place denying them their rights of equal protection of the laws? In other words, does the decision on the Texas University Law School apply squarely to their case?

What does "equality" mean? If a person is entitled to "equal protection of the laws" it is reasonable to suppose that means that laws must embody the principle that people have a right to be treated as equals under the law. The principle must be that laws must not be prejudicial. Or, another way of putting it, the laws must not be constituted so as to put people at a disadvantage for some irrelevant, arbitrary, and therefore insulting reason such as that their skin is colored black. This seems a fairly uncontroversial understanding of the Fourteenth Amendment. Employing Dworkin's argument, a reading of it casts it in its best moral light. How does it apply to the reverse discrimination program? Is the majority applicant with higher grades denied an opportunity to attend law school on a prejudiced and insulting ground? It is difficult to say this, given it is part of a policy designed to reduce racial prejudice; it is only that the majority applicant is at a disadvantage as a result of the policy. But for any policy, surely, there will always be someone who is disadvantaged. The point is that he is not disadvantaged because of prejudice. Is the majority applicant denied his right to equal concern and respect by being denied a law school place? He has been considered along with everyone else. His grades are found to be below the cut-off point for majority applicants, which is what the discrimination program institutes. Is the implication here that he is inferior? No, the policy affirms the equality of both the majority and minority groups. Less worthy of respect? No, the policy affirms equality of respect. Less worthy of concern than minority applicants? No, because the policy does not deny that applicants from the majority group should be admitted.

This argument is appealing. There is an absurdity in applying a case of clear racial prejudice in Texas to prevent, as a matter of principle, a program designed to reduce racial prejudice. Other policies do not cause these difficulties about discrimination. Take, for example, a highway which has to be constructed across the path of a number of houses, which have to be demolished. The owners are disappointed, they are disadvantaged, they lose out, but they are not insulted or denied an equality of respect. In one way, the property owners have a stronger case than the loser in the reverse discrimination case because they have, at least, rights to their own property, whereas in the normal case, no one has a right to a law school place. Even then, that right is one that, at best, gives a right to compensation, not to a right which would see the highway scheme abandoned. (We need to assume a highway scheme of a properly administered sort. Fourteenth Amendment problems would arise were there state laws requiring that highways be routed through black areas just to avoid inconvenience to whites, say).

Dworkin appears to allow the following, however. Say it was a commercially wise decision, as it may have been, to produce only white lawyers in Texas immediately after World War II. Or, that alumni gifts to the University of Texas would fall dramatically if blacks were admitted and the consequences of that could outweigh any damage done to blacks because of continuing discrimination. These commercial policies could be approved by unprejudiced, personal votes. Obviously, in the end, these conclusions will depend, somewhere down the line, on prejudiced thinking. It is possible that a majority of personal votes could support a policy of this discriminatory sort. Contrasting "ideal" arguments against utilitarian arguments, Dworkin says that the University of Texas could not produce an "ideal" argument for its discrimination, one that would justify discrimination by arguing that it would lead to a more just society. On the other hand, reverse discrimination programs can, since their purpose is to reduce prejudice of minority groups. This account is revealing. It shows, I think, the interpretive character of

Dworkin's account of rights "as trumps." To say that the best form of utilitarianism is uncorrupted utilitarianism, because it takes into account what I have called the "numbers" view of fairness, is not to approve utilitarianism. Rights act as a constraint on community practices where those practices include justifications for decisions aimed at improving community goals.

The account is important for understanding how a community might legislate on the question of sexual practices, including the consumption of pornography. A majority might wish, voting personally, for a particular kind of community "cleanliness" or "moral environment." At what point is the line between personal and impersonal preferences crossed? We might want to draw that line along the distinction—also rough—between public and private behavior, taking the robust line that only a perversely sensitive person could object to minority sexual activity taking place out of sight. This was, for example, the line the Williams Committee took in 1979.[23] Or, following the Millian tradition, we might try some definition of "harm," perhaps to include, as Raz does, the idea of restriction of autonomy.[24]

In *Law's Empire* there is a more fully worked out justification of the idea of reverse discrimination, although it is consistent with the arguments so far described. Dworkin does not explicitly mention the idea of personal and impersonal preferences. He prefers, instead, the idea that there are certain "banned" sources of prejudice (which, I think, must be understood as including the idea of impersonal preferences). Simply, we must try to reduce the role of potentially prejudicial decisions. That is the ruling idea. It is to be preferred, he says, to the idea that discriminations based on certain racial characteristics, such as being black, must always be "suspect," for historical reasons. And it is to be preferred, too, to the idea that, in most cases, such categories of classification are simply to be banned. Why is prejudice the ruling idea? True to form, Dworkin thinks that banning categories of classification cannot be properly understood unless the principle that they are wrong because they are prejudiced is made clear. We can (and do), he says, properly introduce classifications which distinguish between people by their characteristics, even though these are inherent characteristics over which they have no control. He says that "if race were a banned category . . . then intelligence, geographical background, and physical ability would have to be banned categories as well."[25]

The idea that it is prejudice at work here will, of course, supply us with a list of categories which we will regard as suspect. History tells us that where some form of racial discrimination exists there is very likely to be prejudice at its basis. Since it is prejudice driving condemnation of discriminatory classification, where prejudice is absent, so is the condemnation. In other words, any set of "suspect classifications" may be rebutted where it can be shown to be genuinely based on people's unprejudiced preferences, or shown that the justification is unprejudiced. The result is that, in a reverse discrimination case, Dworkin argues that the argument that classification on the basis of race is in itself wrong (the "banned categories" view) is untenable because the only principled argument in support of it would be that "people must never be treated differently in virtue of properties beyond their control."[26] It follows that if there is no prejudiced reason behind introducing the reverse discrimination program from which unfortunate majority applicants suffered adverse consequences, the appeal to prejudice (as opposed to some other argument[27]) lacks any power at all. Again, to use Dworkin's term in his earlier writings on reverse discrimination, where is the "insult"?

A BRIEF SUMMARY

We have examined, by way of general introduction, the idea of equality and settled upon a so far relatively unanalyzed conception of "common humanity" as the main thrust of that idea. We have examined, too, Dworkin's important distinction between the ideas of "treating people as equals" and "according people equal treatment." The idea of treating people as equals is at the root of his criticism of the Posnerite school of the economic analysis of law. This criticism is made in the context of communal practices of justifying political action by reference to the maximization of community goals. So Dworkin's argument is an interpretive one, interpretive of that context. His answer is that unconstrained pursuit of a community goal, such as wealth maximization, does not make good sense. Likewise, in his particular application of the idea of constrained utilitarianism to the problem of reverse discrimination, he argues that prejudiced voting is not permitted as it constitutes an unfair "double count." On the other hand, if a background political justification is striving for communal goals, as it appears reasonable to say is actually the case in the United States and the United Kingdom, those goals that are not founded on prejudice, or contempt for others, are justified. Further, equality of respect requires respect for the autonomy of individuals to make procreative choices and choices about when and how to die, even where intrinsic, sacred issues are at stake, simply because the state has no right to use coercive powers on matters of conscience.

CHAPTER NINE

Justice for Hedgehogs

In *Justice for Hedgehogs* Dworkin boldly affirms the independence of arguments of value from arguments concerning matters of scientific fact. Value arguments, he maintains, remain wholly and securely within their own domain of value. Mostly, but not at all exclusively, he is concerned with moral value. He claims it is wrong to assume that external forces could create conflict between moral values, as Isaiah Berlin and others have urged. Rather, he says, we should be more confident in justifying our judgments of value by reference to the more abstract values we hold. He also says that we have a personal responsibility for making our judgments coherent. "Value judgments are true, when they are true . . . in view of the substantive case that can be made for them."[1]

These ideas together form what he calls the "unity of value" thesis, the "big thing" that the hedgehog knows in Archilochus's comparison of the fox and hedgehog famously used by Berlin ("The fox knows many things but the hedgehog knows one big thing"). Take the well-known supposed conflict between freedom and equality in the distribution of resources. If we think that people are of equal value as human beings but also that people should be free to keep what they have worked for, we must try to see in what ways equality and freedom need to be qualified to respect both values. We cannot simply discard either value if it is inconvenient, say, by denying people equality of bargaining power but affirming maximum freedom for the market: "You cannot determine what liberty requires without also deciding what distribution of property and opportunity shows equal concern for all."[2]

Dworkin's claim is that matters of fact do not determine our ultimate judgments of value; he is not saying that the value judgments we make are not connected at all with judgments of fact. Value judgments most often invest some fact with value, as where we say that intentionally killing in some circumstances constitutes murder. Dworkin makes his general point that facts do not determine moral beliefs with a striking example. Imagine that scientists show that a sudden short existence of—let us say—a huge magnetic field in a particular area coincides with changes in the moral beliefs of all those living in that area. People who had a strong conviction that abortion is morally wrong before the magnetic field occurred, have an equally strong conviction after it occurs that abortion is morally permissible. He says that this example shows it would make no difference at all to the way we justified our change in moral belief. We wouldn't say "I think now, because of the magnetic field, that abortion is permissible." Rather, we would give the moral reasons that we now think support our changed convictions; perhaps we now believe that the mother has a superior moral right, or that we think that lack, or relative lack, of sentience in the fetus makes a difference, or perhaps we have some other reason. "The only reason you could have to think that truth has caused your moral opinion is an independent belief that your conviction is true."[3]

The first part of *Justice for Hedgehogs* is a ringing endorsement of Hume's distinction between fact and value and it claims for value both independence and objectivity. The second half takes up the challenge of justifying our moral judgments and is broadly an endorsement of Kant on morality with a plausible addition (or extrapolation): that "living well" might responsibly include an integrated balance—a trade-off even—between personal ethics and morality. Dworkin's life work has been to convince us of the importance—*Taking Rights Seriously* and *A Matter of Principle*—and the pervasiveness and coherence of value—*Law's Empire* and *Sovereign Virtue*. To him, it is not just that we can't rewrite our moral convictions into expressions, desires or appearances, but that it is morally ridiculous to think we could: it is something that we should not want to do. Skeptical attempts fail to secure the significance and seriousness of moral conviction; instead, they belittle it. As he says, if there is nothing there to be skeptical about, there would be nothing bizarre about my believing abortion to be absolutely wrong but encouraging a friend to have one.

PERSONAL ETHICS AND DIGNITY: THE IMPORTANCE OF AN AUTHENTIC LIFE

One of the striking points about *Justice for Hedgehogs* is Dworkin's use of a distinction between personal "ethics" (how we should live) and "morality" (how we should act towards others). He thinks morality derived from our sense of ourselves and what we think is right for ourselves is the basis on which we work out what is right in our conduct towards others. He therefore looks for an ethical, not moral, standard to guide our interpretation of moral concepts. An obvious obstacle to the idea is, however, that our personal responsibility to do what's best for ourselves seems to clash with what we should do for others. Dworkin is remarkably original in his attitude to this: he thinks it is too "austere" a way of looking at it because it denies what he calls our "authenticity," that is, our personal responsibility to make our lives our own, endorsed by us, and us alone. He says that if we are to live genuinely authentic lives, and thus live our lives responsibly, we need to conceive our personality and life in a way that can "break out of distinctly moral considerations." The austere—Kantian—view that our personal life consists of continually doing what is morally right—that is, that our personal life is always a reflection back on how we treat others—is, he says, "sad." It makes morality seem like an "arduous and unpleasant mountain we must constantly cross."[4]

Dworkin therefore proposes a different way of understanding the categorical nature of morality. It doesn't just promote our personal desire; that is too "implausible." Rather, we need to find what personal goals would fit and justify our sense of having obligations. He says that both Hobbes and Hume claimed ethical bases for moral principles. However, Hobbes's moral principles, deriving from a "social contract" and based only on the need for individuals to "survive"—a matter of "self-defense"—is not, Dworkin says, a sufficient condition for living well. An ethical life can't be based on what we need in order to defend ourselves. Humean "sensibilities" are, he says, "more agreeable," but sensitivity alone cannot answer problems about the way we should live; our ethical life couldn't consist of our just following our feelings. Nor, he says, can Hume's utilitarian principle help, because while it would mean treating everyone's interests equally, this "can hardly serve as a strategy for living well oneself."

Opposing the conventional view, Dworkin distinguishes between having a good life and living well. A good life is not just having what one wants, but living according to our critical interests.[5] Nevertheless, he says, it is "wildly implausible" to suppose that living a morally good life is the same as living well. In fact, a decent view of our moral responsibilities could easily lead to a life not lived well:

> It is hard to believe that someone who has suffered terrible misfortunes has had a better life than he would have had if he had acted immorally and then prospered in every way, creatively, emotionally and materially, in a long and peaceful life.[6]

We can understand the satisfaction of our drives, tastes and preferences but it is considerably more difficult to understand our desire to live a critically good life—a life of pleasure is not enough. We want, Dworkin says, to live responsibly. He suggests an analogy of art with life; we value our lives for their "adverbial value," the value of the "performance" rather than the "impact" they have on others:

> On any plausible view of what is truly wonderful in almost any human life, impact hardly comes into the story at all.[7]

Further, striving for a good life is not the same as minimizing the risks of a bad one. Lives are better for "spontaneity, style, authenticity and daring" and the setting of difficult or impossible tasks. But these can go crashingly wrong: living well is not the same thing as maximizing the chances of the best possible life. On the other hand, he says that we can have a bad life in spite of living well. It is not just that our life can be bad because we made bad choices but because of matters of luck and the circumstances in which we find ourselves. We may, for example, be prejudiced against, or be born disabled, or we may die at a tragically young age. We can also have a good life in spite of our living badly. Dworkin gives the example of the Medici prince who lives a life of achievement and refinement but does so through killing and betrayal. The distinction between "living well" and "living a good life" makes sense of the phenomenon of "moral luck." We can feel regret for something that was not our fault, as would the bus driver who drives without fault but twenty schoolchildren die as a result of the bus crashing. It makes sense to say that the bus driver "lived well" but had a "less good life" because of the accident. The distinction also makes sense of whether what happens after your death affects the goodness of your life: it doesn't affect how well you lived but it affects the goodness of your life.

It would be a mistake, says Dworkin, for us not to care about how we personally live. Judging people to be equal is much more of a principle of morality than it is of ethics; it tells us that no one's life is "more important" than anyone else's. The principle that we should show respect for ourselves is clearly ethical because it describes the attitude we should have to our own lives. Is it, then, important to "live well"? It is different from enjoyment, although enjoyment is linked to what we believe is "living well"; "pleasure," too, is not pure feeling independent of belief about what gives rise to it because it is "fused with ethical flavor"—even the enjoyment of doing what we know we shouldn't.

Authenticity, he thinks, is "the other side of self-respect," for it requires accepting responsibility for our actions both towards others and ourselves. I can't treat an act as mine unless I accept responsibility for it (I can't hive off my responsibility for something I've done by saying my parents are to blame, for example). I should also be prepared to acknowledge limits both to what I ask of others and to what I ask of myself. I can't demand that others fund ridiculously expensive projects I have in mind (such as major help in building a vast monument to my personal god); nor should I suppose that because I made some relatively minor mistake in my life I should suffer a life of hair shirts and dire poverty. Authenticity demands, Dworkin says, that we strive for independence but this idea is not the same as the commonly understood value of "autonomy"; that idea does not adequately bring out the way we have to balance the ethical and moral determinants and do so while being bound to some extent by an "ethical culture." His example is that it is not possible to live a life of medieval chivalry in Brooklyn in the present age.[8] The idea of independence must capture the internal ground between those inescapable influences on us and our being dominated: "We cannot escape influence but we must resist domination." So autonomy is not a "range of choices" as, for example, Joseph Raz has argued.[9] Rather, Dworkin says:

> Authenticity is damaged when a person is made to accept someone else's judgment in place of his own about the values or goals his life should display.[10]

FROM DIGNITY TO MORALITY; THE OBJECTIVE EQUAL VALUE OF OTHER LIVES

Dworkin wants to integrate ethics and morality. He wishes to respond to the question of why we should be moral. If there is something special about our own life and this integrates with the lives of others, then the reason for think-ing our own life important—which is surely not that difficult to establish—is a reason for treating others on the footing that their lives are important also. Is there some special importance about your own life? Obviously you are responsible for it—that is what authenticity is all about—but this is different. Do you have a reason to care whether another's life fails, or only your own? That is, does care for your own life's success reflect something "of universal importance?" Objective value is independent of subjective matters of taste, pure preference and so on. So what is the case for objective importance? First, note that the importance of our lives seems to be universal. For example, it fits well with a common view that we should care for people in the third world whom we have never met nor ever expect to. Consider the case for the opposite view. Is it only my life which has special importance because I alone have a special responsibility for it? No, because curators have special responsibility for works of art, which themselves have independent objective value. Dworkin points out that it is a sadly popular view that in some cases if you have special characteristics—you are American, or Sunni, or Jewish, or a talented musician, for example—this gives your life "special importance."

However, he says, while these things might be parameters of success for you, that doesn't mean they are of an objective value that makes your life special and different from the lives of others. He gives Richard Hare's example of the Nazi who thought it would be "objectively right" for others to kill him if he turned out to be Jewish.[11] Dworkin thinks that view wouldn't survive full integration with a larger scheme of value; he asks how an anti-Semitic view would be able provide a sensible explanation in the face of the question "how, exactly, could objective importance be thought to depend on nasal structure?" Religion is a special source of such ideas: the justification of slaughter on the ground its members have "special importance." Why should that be a ground, for that sort of god would care nothing about converting others to worship him?

Here Dworkin draws a distinction between "recognition" and "appraisal" respect.[12] "Recognition" respect refers to the respect due a person merely because they are a person. "Appraisal" respect allows us, independently of this respect, to make a judgment about a person's worth. A good example of both recognition and appraisal respect working in a common idea is where people say, "I disapprove of his saying it (*appraisal*) but I recognize his right (*recognition*) to say it." Dworkin says dignity requires recognition respect. If you think that recognition respect is important then it must follow that you think appraisal respect is important. Human beings have dignity precisely because they can choose, and make their own lives; they therefore can make something of their lives—have worthwhile lives—equally as they may have worthless lives. Hare's Nazi must at least think that, when it turns out that he is in fact Jewish, the fact that he's made something of his life—had a career, been disciplined, etc.—should count for something: "Few people could honestly accept that counterfactual release of ethical responsibility."[13]

Dworkin concludes that the first principle of dignity is a recognition that all lives are of equal objective value; he calls it "Kant's principle." It means that your reason for thinking it is important how your life goes is your reason for supposing it is important how everyone's life goes: "… you see the objective importance of your life mirrored in the objective importance of everyone else's."[14] But if there is "equal objective importance" in the lives of others, then it looks as though you have to work equally to improve the lives of others as you do your own life, which appears to be the utilitarian view, and that would mean that it would be virtually impossible to improve your own life. Authenticity, which Dworkin says is the second principle of dignity, makes us responsible for our own lives, but the view that all lives have "equal objective value" may deny that possibility.

The answer lies in an interpretive integrated account of the apparent tension between the two principles. Dignity should be understood from the perspective of each of its two components—equality and freedom. Each reflects the other and no compromise is required: "We need to find attractive interpretations of the two principles that seem right in themselves—that seem to capture what self-respect and authenticity really do require—and that do not conflict with, but rather reinforce, each other."[15]

HOW WE SHOULD TREAT OTHERS

Dworkin says there are two kinds of conflict. First, there is the conflict between our own and other people's interests, and second, there is the conflict between our courses of action when we can help, but only help some people. Here he thinks that what he calls Kant's golden rule of universalization is helpful because it is consistent with the idea that ethics and morality form an integral whole: "We must show full respect for the equal objective importance of every person's life but also full respect for our own responsibility to make something valuable of our own life."[16] We should take the conflicts in turn.

The first situation of conflict between others and ourselves arises only if we suppose the ultra-demanding interpretation that we must have equal concern for others' well-being. Dworkin says that failing to make sacrifices is consistent with regarding human life as of equal importance. Somewhere a line has to be drawn. For example, if I win a lottery I don't have to give the money away to a good cause. So how do we draw the line? Dworkin thinks that the risk to a stranger's interests cannot be measured in terms subjective only to the stranger. If, for example, a person is building a gigantic temple of great importance to him and needs a great deal of assistance, we can't have a duty to help him. Rather we need an objective test. This, he suggests, would register a deprivation of "the ordinary opportunities people have to pursue whatever ambitions they choose." But where the risk to the stranger is greater than the risk to me, my responsibility will be greater, for example, where it would be relatively easy for me to rescue a child from a paddling pool. Again, we might ask whether the test of risk is subjective. Should the builder of a gigantic temple divert money from his project to prevent someone from starving? Here we can argue that certain sorts of "subjective" projects do not reflect proper respect for other people; Dworkin actually goes further than this and suggests that particularly selfish or fanatical projects that ignore the suffering of others show a lack of self-respect. It is here that an element of objectivity about relative cost enters: there can clearly be an imbalance between the demands of selfish and fanatical people and the costs of those requiring help.

Dworkin also thinks that a crucial aspect of determining our duties is the degree to which we face others, something measured by proximity. I have a duty to pay a boatman $50 to rescue a drowning man I can see, today, on the beach. But I can have no duty to give him $50 to rescue someone on a later day, because "the morality of rescue hinges on an interpretive question and . . . we must take natural human instincts and behavior into account in answering that question."[17] He says that moral "principle of confrontation" is at work in determining community expenditure on catastrophes. Often much more effort and money is put into rescuing people rather than into the prevention of such eventualities. Sometimes, however, great suffering may make confrontation irrelevant. Dworkin's view is that it is an appropriate human impulse to give help where circumstances confront us. We must give to the charity that will help the catastrophe now, not give to the charity which will accumulate the money for a century before helping.

DO NUMBERS COUNT?

The second situation of conflict is that between people who need help but where help can only be afforded to some. Take the example where one person has a lifebelt and, not far away, are two people also with a lifebelt. Each lifebelt is the same distance from you in your boat, each lifebelt is surrounded by sharks. You can save the one person, or the two people, each with little relative risk, but you can't get to both lifebelts. Dworkin says he doesn't accept the general view that you should make your decision by reference only to numbers. He says that would be right from an impersonal viewpoint (of "welfare consequentialism") because that would improve well-being overall. On the other hand, if we went from a "rights-based" viewpoint, we should have to give each person an equal chance and so the final decision could be decided by a lottery (that is, given that only one lifebelt can be approached, either two or one would be saved).

Dworkin thinks that neither approach would be right. First, consequentialist approaches are wrong and second, no one has a right to automatic aid. A potential rescuee "has a right only if, under the circumstances, ignoring his need would show disrespect for the objective importance of his life."[18] Further, he says you may make moral judgments about which life to save (if all swimmers are strangers, you could choose to save the brilliant musician, for example) but not where the "ground of preference" is ruled out contrary to "respect for humanity," that is, some form of contempt, say racial prejudice (the swimmer is black, for example):

> You can offer a reason why it is particularly important that a musician or a peacemaker survives without supposing that it is objectively more important that their lives flourish than anyone else's.[19]

Dworkin also says there might be arguments of fairness where it might, for example, be better to save one young man rather than two older ones. On the other hand, it wouldn't be right to choose one swimmer just out of whim (with the aim, say, of showing that one can counter convention):

> The principle that it is better to save more rather than fewer human lives, without regard to whose lives they are, is a plausible even if not inevitable understanding of what the right respect for life's importance requires.[20]

The distinction between "recognition respect" and "appraisal respect" is enormously helpful here. Of course people's lives can be worthless in Dworkin's view because we can fail to take responsibility for our lives and fail to make our lives authentic ("we cannot release ourselves from our responsibility to live well"). Someone who drifts into drug addiction and dies early has had in his, and many people's eyes, a worthless life; we nevertheless still must regard this person as someone who has a life of equal objective value; they are still one of us, as a human being.[21]

COMPETITION BETWEEN OURSELVES AND OTHERS

Imagine two scenarios. First, there are two of you in the Arizona desert, and you are both bitten by rattlesnakes. You both see a vial of antidote but you get it first, and he dies. Second, it is the same as before but he gets the vial first and, before he drinks it, you shoot him and take the antidote yourself. Dworkin says that "impersonal consequentialism" morally permits both scenarios, other things being equal. (If he is young and you are old it would probably be different.) Nevertheless, most people feel there is an intuitive difference between omissions and acts. For example, speaking of the third world, it would be much better to fail to contribute to Oxfam, say, than to travel to a third-world country and produce the same effect by shooting a number of people.

We can compare the two principles of dignity against these two cases, although Dworkin says we should distinguish "bare competition harm"— whereby someone is harmed—in the sense that they lost out in a fair competition with another—from "deliberate harm." Deliberate harm is serious. Since responsibility requires that we be in sole charge of what happens to our bodies, it constitutes a violation of what we need for our responsibility for our own lives to be effective, and so it violates the effectiveness of other people's responsibility for their own lives. Dworkin believes it is this connection between dignity and bodily control that justifies the distinction between omissions and acts. Nevertheless, consent—the ability to give of which is a mark of dignity, he says—may allow bodily control by another: "It is no violation of dignity for one football player to tackle another or for a doctor to kill a dying patient at the latter's urgent and reflective request."[22]

Dworkin thinks that where harm to others is caused unintentionally, the best way to approach the question of responsibility arises through considering how risks to injury might be managed. It seems that the freer I am of liability the less I have to compensate others for accidents, but I'm then more likely to incur loss from accidents that harm me. Dworkin says that suggests a negligence principle which states we should only be liable when we don't exercise "reasonable" care towards others. What care should I take? Clearly I don't have to take absolutely all steps to avoid harm to others. Dworkin suggests a more refined version of Judge Learned Hand's famous test of reasonableness.[23] The gist of that and Dworkin's refined version is that we should only be liable for accidents we could have prevented without damaging our interests more than the accident damaged the interests of the victim. It envisages maintaining an equilibrium (in Hand's case, an economic equilibrium) between the parties. Dworkin's exact version is as follows:

> People each achieve the maximum control when everyone accepts, in principle, that he should bear liability responsibility for damage he has inadvertently caused to others when that damage could have been prevented had he take precautions that would not have impaired his opportunities and resources as much as the damage he was likely to cause would likely impair the opportunities and resources of others.[24]

Dworkin then asks a question concerning the extent to which we may harm others. For example, what principle should prevent us from removing the liver of a person close to death, without their consent, to benefit a young patient, say? How different is this from rescuing one of two people drowning when only one can be saved?

One popular answer—which Dworkin largely rejects—is to be found in the "doctrine of double effect"; this says that it is permissible to "let someone die" where, in the circumstance, allowing it is not the "means to an end" of killing. You are not just letting the old man die because you want to kill him; rather, you are letting him die because you want his liver. Another example is the famous "trolley problem" of Judith Jarvis Thompson.[25] According to this it is morally permissible to switch a runaway trolley onto a track that has one person strapped to it rather than onto a track that has five people strapped to it, but you are not permitted to throw a large person onto the track to stop the trolley.

Dworkin says that it seems intuitively odd that we should baulk at throwing the large person onto the tracks but not in sending the trolley to the single person. In each case the outcome "seems better" because five people are spared. He makes the example more difficult by making the principles govern *ex ante* decisions. Imagine a "spare parts lottery."[26] A group of people agrees that if more than five of them need an organ transplant and the needed organs can be transplanted from a single body, the healthy people may draw a lottery as to which one of them will be killed. Each member increases his life expectancy by this means. While there are clearly gruesome sides to this proposal, the choice is not obviously a bad one. The question arises whether it would be wrong to treat people as if the lottery were in place by implied consent, in other words, by treating the spare parts scheme as fair by virtue of hypothetical consent. Dworkin dismisses the claim of consequentialists who say that such a scheme would ruin our cultural taboo against killing people; he calls it mere "whistling in the dark speculation." Other philosophers, including those who endorse the "double-effect" doctrine, have claimed that it is always wrong to "aim at death" and they use the trolley cases to support their claim. In answer to the double-effecters, Dworkin says that it would not seem to matter if someone aimed at death if their motive was good—to prevent a murder, for example. Merely to say it is wrong to aim at death just restates the problem without justifying it. The "principle of double effect" offers no answer, for it makes intention relevant without saying why.

Dworkin thinks that to say why requires, instead, the "second principle of dignity"—that of the responsibility for making one's own life. Dignity is not compromised by competition harm, and so this explains the double-effect cases because dignity is only compromised when it requires that I alone make the decision. The victim's dignity is not compromised merely because one life is saved and another thereby doomed. For example, you are allowed to drive in my neighborhood thus contributing to the risk of your causing a car accident, but you are not allowed to kidnap my children for an hour to force me to give funds to Oxfam. In the first case, you merely engage in creating a justifiable risk of harm, but in the second case you intentionally make a decision to harm another. Another example is that we may bomb a munitions factory in a just war knowing civilians will die but we may not intentionally bomb citizens in order to terrify them into surrendering: "Aiming at death is worse than just knowingly causing it because aiming at death is a crime against dignity.[27] The essential point in all this is that you can't kill someone with the conviction that it would be better they died. If you rescue someone by killing someone else then that is wrong but rescuing someone knowing someone else is going to die anyway is morally permissible. The difference is in the intention with which a person acts.

There is a limit to what our intuitions can take and Dworkin is of course well aware of this. Intuition is a guide, but argument is what is needed to explain (including explain away) our intuitions. But he considers an extended trolley case in which throwing a switch sends the trolley away from five people tied to the track and towards one tied to the track. This time, however, if the latter were not tied to the track, the trolley would loop round and get the five tied to the track from behind. Dworkin says that "philosophy students" generally think it makes a difference whether the switching is done with the intention of diverting the trolley from the five or single-mindedly sending it toward the one. Although Dworkin thinks it is a highly artificial example, it nevertheless tends to confirm his claim that the test is whether we are knowingly aiming at a death: "In any case, however, neither reaction would be so evidently wrong as to disqualify the distinction because it fails in this hyperartificial case."[28] Of the spare parts lottery case he says first, that we can't suppose it is justifiable because hypothetical contracts are not contracts, and second, that in any case it would not be justifiable if you had consented because there are some things our dignity doesn't allow us to consent to. "That is why we shouldn't sell ourselves into slavery—we might have longer lives but we would live in indignity."[29]

Dworkin also has some remarks to make about the idea that sometimes in problematic situations we should "let nature take its course." He says there is a difference between the competition between the two drowning swimmers for both swimmers will die if the rescuer does nothing, that is, lets "nature take its course," and the simpler trolley case where the single tied-down person will not be killed if the rescuer does nothing. What does "nature take its course" mean? That the rescuer pretend he's not there? Why should he pretend? If we are both shipwrecked and there is one life jacket why should we "let nature take its course" and do nothing?

THE MORALITY BEHIND CONVENTIONS

Dworkin says we can make "some people special" through "datable and voluntary acts" like promises. And we also have such relationships through associations such as family, or by being a member of some political association, as most of us are. It follows, he says, that social facts—"contingent conventions"—can affect our duties, as parent, child, colleague, and citizen, perhaps in the form of what local laws have been enacted. The question, then, is how conventions—which are only facts—shape our duties? How do we derive what we ought to do from a mere fact? And so he asks, "Doesn't Hume's principle condemn the entire phenomenon of obligation as an enormous mistake?"

Some philosophers propose general moral principles to explain conventional obligations. David Lewis, for example, has argued that it is a moral right to have one's expectations protected and so some prominent conventions are explained this way.[30] Dworkin thinks this claim is incomplete, for it is not clear that all our expectations give rise to rights. Others, for example John Rawls in his *Theory of Justice*, have claimed that conventions of government can be explained through our duty to respect just and useful institutions. Dworkin's reply to this is that it isn't clear we have a duty to respect such institutions— where they are the institutions of other states, for example. Others, such as Nozick in his *Anarchy, State and Utopia*, say that since we take the benefit of our conventional arrangements we must take the burdens of them, that is, that we shouldn't be "free-riders." To this, in turn, Dworkin replies it wouldn't explain many conventional role-obligations such as parenting. In any case, the anti free-riding principle better supports the institution of promising, and even then there are purely gratuitous promises—ones carrying no burden—that create duties. And if Nozick's free-riding principle is intended to apply to the general institution of promising as opposed to particular promises, it is difficult to see that there is, as such, a general requirement to contribute to an institution that benefits me. A good example is that of buskers: we have no duty to give money to buskers because they play to us (although of course we may have other grounds to do so). On the contrary, our obligations to fulfill our promises arise because a promise has been made.

How, then, can a promise create an obligation, given the Humean principle? Dworkin says that this is only a problem if you think that promises create an independent ground of moral responsibility. Instead, he says, promises *fix the scope of* a more general duty not to harm others by encouraging the promisees to expect that we will act in one way and then failing to act in that way. More generally, the moral force of promises arises out of an even more general duty not to fail to respect our own and another's dignity. Promises, Dworkin says, clarify but don't create duties. The duty to carry out your promise arises because you promise, yes, but by way of a determination of the scope of a duty already generally in place.

The study of promising requires considering the stages at which the two principles of dignity—equality and freedom—are at work. Lying to another "corrupts" the basis of our relationship—we place the other at a lower level; we offend the principle of equal objective value of people. We also harm the other by impairing their ability to exercise responsibility for their own lives; they are harmed by being denied the truth. It is also self-harming, Dworkin says, because it compromises self-respect.

Imagine my encouraging you to attend a conference with me and then my changing my mind when I've seen the list of speakers. Do I have an obligation to attend? There are two questions. First, have I harmed you? Second, if I have, had I a responsibility not to? Dworkin says I've harmed you if you went and it was boring and useless for you. It is more difficult, however, if you went but, as it happens, you found it enjoyable and, in fact, you didn't mind that I didn't come. Dworkin says that in this second case, I've harmed you but to a lesser extent, and in two ways. First, I created the risk of harm to you, which is "a kind of harm"; second, I harmed you in the sense in which a lie harms because I changed the basis of the beliefs on which you may have acted. Then the question is whether I had a moral responsibility. Yes, says Dworkin, because I "singled you out" and that "must have some moral consequence." Perhaps there is circularity in saying that a promise requires that you convince me that you will carry out the promise, because (one could argue) I would only be convinced if you already had a promissory obligation. Dworkin denies there is circularity if you suppose that promising, instead of creating an obligation, is just a convenient device for making explicit your responsibility to another person; it eliminates uncertainty:

> The conventions of promising provide me with a much more efficient device for doing the same thing. They provide a vocabulary through which someone can immediately ratchet up his encouragement to the level . . . so that other

facts that might in different circumstances argue against responsibility become close to irrelevant.[31]

None of this is "magic," he says, because the conventions "are parasitic on underlying and independent moral facts."[32] Certain stylized ways of abusing people (e.g., "fatty") have the same logic: they clarify non-conventional ways of harming people. Also, no degree of encouragement about how you will responsibly act can eliminate what in the end you ought responsibly to do. For example, "I don't promise" doesn't, of course, excuse you, and saying "I promise" where it is ill-judged doesn't create an obligation. Further, promises aren't independent of a background of responsibility not to harm others. Dworkin gives the example where he writes to a completely random person and promises them that he'll walk from Land's End to John O'Groats in a few weeks' time. This does not create any duty for him to do so; this promising is not a "self-contained practice that generates obligations automatically." Rather, it is that:

> The point of promising is to set the bar very high for successful excuses for disappointing deliberately encouraged expectations.[33]

It means that the bar has, correspondingly, to be set high for counting something as a promise, and so the onus will usually be on the promisee to prove that there was a promise and an ambiguity will usually be construed in favor of the promisor. In other words, promising is a matter of integration with our "other and more general convictions about not harming."

THE IDEA OF HUMAN RIGHTS

Another important area which Dworkin examines is human rights. Clearly, what people mean when they refer to them is something different (although obviously related) from ordinary moral and political rights. They have an urgency and an international dimension that most rights do not have. What they are, and their force, cry out for explanation in the world generally and particularly in this present day. One strategy of explanation derives from the "Westphalian conception of sovereignty": human rights trump national sovereignty conceived as the principle that states must not interfere with the internal affairs of another nation. This was the principle decided at the signing of the Treaty of Westphalia which ended the Thirty Years' War in 1648.

If we accepted this principle, it would also be necessary to decide which political rights were sufficient to justify sanctions. Further, severe sanctions

5

have to be authorized under international law and, even then, such sanctions would have to be designed to do more good than harm. However, Dworkin thinks that the trumps-over-sovereignty idea sets "too high a bar":

> It would nevertheless be wrong for the community of nations, even if licensed by international law and likely to be successful, to march into any nation to establish equal pay for women or more adequate primary schools or to invade Florida to shut down its gas chambers or establish gay marriage there.[34]

It is only "barbarism" that justifies overriding the Westphalian principle, he thinks, yet determining what counts as barbarism is notoriously difficult. Dworkin suggests another way of doing it. He thinks that the most basic human right is a right to an attitude by governments to the individual "as a human being whose dignity fundamentally matters." Because it is a very abstract principle it serves to cross most disagreements about what constitutes respect in any particular case. The major difference, therefore, between human rights and other political rights is the distinction between mistake and contempt. Presumably, a government might mistakenly suppose that the death sentence is necessary to maintain civil order within a democracy but still believe, on a reasonable interpretation, that the dignity of its citizens is of fundamental importance. The death sentence would not be a breach of a human right, although it may be a violation of a political or legal right (e.g., under the U.S. Constitution). On certain matters, such as the institution of torture or genocide, the matter speaks for itself—torture and genocide clearly show contempt for equality of respect. Dignity of course consists for Dworkin of both the principle of equality and the principle of personal responsibility. And so the second principle of dignity is of fundamental importance too. A government which enforces religion on certain of its citizens denies those citizens a fundamental right to make their own decisions about matters of conscience and importance. Torture, he says, is "the most profound outrage" and it violates the right to dignity in both its aspects. Are human rights universal? The answer to this is both yes and no. First, that people have a fundamental right to dignity must be a universal claim, but second, what counts as dignity will have to be "sensitive" to "different economic conditions and political and cultural profiles and histories."

Unsurprisingly, Dworkin says that whether human rights are breached is not a matter merely of a government's expressed statement of its good faith but is an interpretive question. And human rights instruments "invite interpretive questions" about whether "a nation's record" shows good faith towards dignity.

THE MEANING OF LIBERTY

The meaning of liberty is of course for Dworkin an interpretive question. How should we approach this idea? On the assumption that government is coercive, traditionally, philosophers have considered two main questions. First, by whom should I be coerced, and second, how much should I be coerced? Those questions have thrown up two answers. The answer to the first uses the idea of *positive* liberty: people must be permitted to play a role in their own coercive government. In other words, government must be *self*-government. The answer to the second uses the idea of *negative* liberty: people must be free over a "substantial range" of their decisions. Dworkin says that there are possible puzzles here, for how can a group have self-government for everyone? And how can a legitimate government not have coercive power over a range of personal decisions? He says, however, that the second principle of dignity—personal responsibility—explains why both are forms of liberty. Personal responsibility has two dimensions. Not only should a person be free to participate in collective decisions, he should be free from collective decisions "in matters that his personal responsibility demands he decide for himself." So liberty has two dimensions: (i) positive freedom in the conception of self-government so that people must participate in "the right way," and (ii) negative freedom describing those choices exempt from collective decisions, choices which are a necessary part of personal responsibility. Further, because of the unity of value thesis, they will only conflict on bad interpretations of them. Isaiah Berlin thought in a democracy there would be inevitable conflict because democracy could only be promoted by suppressing individual freedom.[35] Dworkin thinks Berlin's problem partly arose—only partly, because Berlin also did not believe in the unity of value—with his conception of negative liberty. Berlin treated "total freedom" and "negative liberty" as the same and, says Dworkin, that view can't be defended by saying that what liberty is, is as a matter of plain fact. It is not a criterial concept because people who debate the meaning of liberty use different criteria in determining its meaning. If liberty as total freedom is the correct interpretive view, then of course democracy conflicts with liberty. He says, however, that we shouldn't interpret liberty that way; a government does not compromise liberty when, for example, it prevents citizens killing each other. The punishment of the offender is not an affront to his dignity. On the contrary, Dworkin says, government would fail to protect your dignity if it didn't prevent murder.

On the other hand, it demeans your dignity if it claims that a large majority can dictate your religious observance. Liberty must take a stand on what are matters of ethical foundation such as our personal choices in religion, and personal intimacy, and beliefs in political and moral ideals; people have a right to independence in these matters so far as it doesn't interfere with rights to independence of others. Laws can also violate ethical independence in other ways, as when governments make restrictions motivated by a belief in the superiority of some views, for example, censorship and mandated flag salutes. Some laws violate ethical independence in both ways, for example, prohibitions on same-sex intercourse or marriage constrain "foundational" choices as well as being motivated by a belief in the superiority of certain ways of living well, or political censorship. But, Dworkin says, there is no violation of ethical independence where the matter is not foundational, or the government does not assume any "ethical" justification. The government can rely on moral, as opposed to ethical, arguments to conserve resources, impose taxes, impose traffic fines and so on and such laws may nevertheless have serious consequences for individuals. It is certainly true that preventing murder and theft makes it more difficult to live as a Samurai or Robin Hood, and taxation makes it more difficult to have a life of collecting Renaissance masterpieces:

> Properly motivated laws of my community are part of the background against which I make my ethical choices. My own ethical responsibility for making those choices is not diminished by that background.[36]

Dworkin thinks that the literature on paternalism underrates the importance of the distinction. "Making people wear seatbelts" doesn't undermine our ethical independence or our authenticity. We are not denied any foundational choices if we think that our life will be better if we court danger, as those with "seatbelt convictions" might think. The real cases of ethical paternalism are constituted by cases such as the Inquisition. In fact, he says, at present ethical paternalism is not particularly in vogue and restrictions are more often justified by reference to fairness. For example, if the majority doesn't want pornography then it is fair to ban it because the majority has the right to live the way it sees fit.

Why, then, if the majority can institute planning laws, is it prohibited from creating laws that protect a particular religious way of life that suits it? Dworkin's answer is just a repeat of the importance of personal responsibility: "The second principle of dignity makes ethics special. It limits the acceptable range of collective decision."[37] Dworkin uses a swimming analogy in which the lanes are defined, each swimmer getting the space to get on with his own life. Another swimmer may cross a lane to help but not harm. Morality defines the lanes and ethics governs what we do to swim well, and so morality and ethics cooperate and don't compete.

What arguments are available to resolve differences of opinion about liberal rights to due process and free speech? He says the right to due process flows from the government's duty to respect the first principle of dignity of treating "each person's life as of distinct, objective and equal importance." Two examples would be the protection of the innocent, since punishing an innocent person is a particular form of "moral harm,"[38] and the right to free speech. A set of arguments widely used to protect positive liberty by enhancing democracy are those including the protection of a right to information and a right to participate in government. Dworkin thinks these arguments don't go far enough. He thinks there are other arguments that arise from the right to ethical independence different from a right to positive liberty. These would be, for example, the protection of a person's right to pornography, since that is not necessary for positive liberty. As an example, he looks at the banning of hate speech which shows, he thinks, the relationship between positive and negative liberty. Think of the Ku Klux Klan clan leader who is prevented from rallying others to his political opinions and at the same time ⬚⬚⬚⬚⬚ ⬚⬚⬚⬚ed from his "foundational" right to "bear public witness" to his ⬚⬚⬚⬚⬚⬚⬚⬚ ⬚ ⬚⬚d is his ethical independence because the hate leg⬚ y fear of violence—or moral harm to others— :stable" views. Dworkin emphasizes that these isingly—policy arguments for free speech such ges truth and knowledge) and Oliver Wendel :nhances the efficiency of the market) but are it to dignity.

⬚⬚ONSIBILITY

ral judgments are not determined by scientific ich facts cannot, therefore, determine our moral full-scale attack against those who argue that ow that it is already determined what human rances—will in fact do, they therefore lack free- they think they possess it) and, further, cannot nsible for their actions. In professional philo- against "determinists" who regard themselves as "incompatibilists," those who think that full judgmental responsibility is not compatible with all our judgments being caused by scientific occurrences.[39] Dworkin says that non-compatibilism is not an intellectually stable position because it asks us to believe what we cannot believe. He acknowledges that what we think "ordinarily" cannot be an argument in its favor (we quite "ordinarily" thought once that the world was flat) and more argument is necessary in order to establish that our ordinary belief that we have free will is right. I wonder whether Dworkin need concede this much, quite apart from his extensive arguments against value skepticism. How about the following? Our ordinary views about value objectivity and free will can't be mistaken, because our ordinary lives would not make any sense at all without them. We need objective sense in our lives to live it; it makes no sense to suppose that we are doing things all the time, things that affect others and ourselves in serious ways, over which we have absolutely no control. Our ordinary lives would be nothing if our values were really matters of taste alone, and moral responsibility a sham.

Dworkin gives the following example to show how untouched the worth of our lives is by knowledge of scientific facts. Just imagine the following scenario. A gifted neuroscientist is able to make such accurate predictions of what an artist will paint that he can exactly map the sequence of brush strokes, the precise use of color, and so on. Indeed, with the help of a powerful computer and robot, he produces a painting that is identical to the masterpiece the oblivious artist shortly afterwards finally finishes. (The artist has been working in his studio for many years; it is the flowering of his genius). The question is whether the value of that work of art diminishes in any way when we learn the artist was going to do all this anyway. The artist acts against the background of his own conscious understanding of what he is doing; that conscious understanding is sufficient in itself to resist any account that his work was of no value because his work wasn't "really" creative. Although we would applaud the scientific feat, Dworkin says it would have no relevance to the question of the value of the artist's work. The artistic endeavor is measured against what is important: that the artist strove to produce his painting in a remarkable combination of talent and conviction.

Dworkin says we must look to ethical, rather than moral, principles to define the relationship between cause and responsibility; we should begin in our own "ordinary ideas" about our own responsibility. He says we in fact distinguish between "mind-control" cases, where people are under the control of another, and "mental deficiency" cases, where people are in control but shouldn't be held responsible because they lack some capacity. Dworkin thinks that this "responsibility system" has wide appeal and that it is necessary to explain it in light of the incompatibilist possibility. If his argument that physical—scientific—events and causes have no impact whatsoever on our moral judgments, or on our moral responsibility, then we need to consider what kinds of moral judgments determine our responsibility. He considers two alternative accounts. The *causal* principle, he says, "places our mental life in the context of the natural world"—it claims that physical causes directly eliminate our responsibility. In strong contrast, he says, "the *capacity* principle locates responsibility within the brackets of an ordinary life lived from a personal perspective."[40]

It is easy to see one relation between cause and moral responsibility. If, say, the frontal lobe of someone's brain is missing we know that he is likely to be incapacitated. But, Dworkin says, we shouldn't say a person is excused from murder *just because* his frontal lobe was missing when he killed; that account, he says, would not fully state his excuse. Rather, it is that he is excused if the moral requirement that he have a particular capacity—before he may be held to have responsibility—is not there; an excuse, say, in the form that he lacked the capacity to know what he was doing or, if he knew, that he couldn't judge whether it was wrong. This is an important and subtle distinction that Dworkin makes; it is between a moral principle of responsibility that refers all questions of responsibility to whether a person could "causally control" his action, and one in which the determining factor is that he had the "moral capacity" to control his action. To suppose that the presence or absence of physical causes fully explains our personal responsibility doesn't integrate with all the rest of our beliefs about responsibility. Instead, it appears to rest our lack of responsibility on, in Dworkin's terms, "a haphazard piece of quantum whimsy."

In many cases, there are facts that influence our behavior, even though we are still clearly subject to moral censure. An obvious example is an unsuccessful attempt to do something that was in fact impossible to achieve (there was no money in the pocket we attempted to pick, say). We have no problem with ascribing blame in such circumstances, but the causal control principle would suggest we would be blameless. Moreover, we don't have control over many of our beliefs because they are controlled by how the world in fact is. It would make no sense to say that we are freer because we can believe anything we like (that is the way to madness). And some of us cannot act otherwise than the psychological facts of our personalities allow; we have natural dispositions to behave in sometimes striking ways. In an important sense, Mother Theresa "can't help" but be selfless, and Hitler had a disposition to evil—but such facts don't withhold us from judging these two people. Even further, we don't assume lack of responsibility in cases where people have mental problems, or where they are simply immature, as with young children. Those with mental problems and children are often just as capable as others of initiating action. The problem is instead that of identifying the extent to which incapacity has distorted their judgment. We might presume lack of capacity in such cases, but it does not inexorably follow that they lack capacity and therefore responsibility; we need to make a moral judgment.

The capacity principle allows us to make these fine-tuning adjustments to responsibility rather than the imposition by the causal principle of a blanket response to these questions. Since the matter is an interpretive one—it is a question of value—in choosing between the two accounts of responsibility we should choose the one that makes the most sense. In short, the causal control principle makes little sense of how we actually think.

SUMMING UP

People live well when they sense a good life for themselves and pursue it with dignity: that means respect for the dignity of others and the lives *they* pursue. "Living well" and "having a good life" are different: we can live well and not have a good life (e.g., catastrophes occur; grave injustice, etc.). Some effective ethical conviction is essential to responsibility in living. Style is not enough; appraisal is important. Good lives are not trivial. Someone's life does not "achieve the needed importance" just because he thinks it does. It is difficult to say what gives weight as well as dignity to a life, and a "great and durable achievement" is only possible for "very few." Most good lives are good for "much more transitory effects," such as skill, raising family, making the lives of others better. A life can be bad through poverty. Having the resources to live may be at times merely parameters that enable the development of a worthwhile life; at other times they may be seriously limiting. Those due entirely to the community's particular economic stage are parameters (for example, where the community is particularly poor) but those economic restrictions due to injustice are limitations. Whether a life of relative poverty is less good depends, therefore, on whether there has been injustice. Grave injustice makes it difficult for the rich to lead a good life. For the untalented rich, the impact of injustice on their lives counts against the value of a life led with other people's money. A malign culture teaches the poor that a good life is a wealthy one, along with its power. "Nothing better illustrates the tragedy of the unexamined life: there are no winners in this macabre dance of greed and delusion."[41]

Justice for Hedgehogs is an extended treatment of Dworkin's views developed in a remarkably consistent way over many years. There are two marks to the book. First, it is a full statement of his method in philosophy and so bears importantly on his work in legal theory as far as objectivity and the relevance of morality. It is a fully worked out affirmation both of what arguments in value consist of—reliance in the end on our personal judgment and conviction—and the objectivity of it all, namely, that nothing in law is subjective. Second, it takes up the insight of its first part that all talk of moral and ethical value consists of moralizing, not what has been called "second-order" or "meta" morality and ethics. And so it is not surprising that it consists of the provision of answers to common moral questions about dignity, rights, equality, freedom, liberty, harm, promising, consequentialism and justice. Perhaps *Justice for Hedgehogs* will explain to many why they feel that Dworkin's arguments appear to have the arrogance of someone who thinks he is right. He does, in expressing his first-order views, and these critics expect something else. Surely straightforward analysis shows that it can't be arrogant to do this, nor even odd. People who think that a view is arrogant because it expresses the belief of the person whose view it is, themselves express a view and so, by their own argument, are arrogant as well. Perhaps that sounds defensive. I think not. For about thirty years, the prevailing intellectual culture, at least outside mainstream philosophy departments, has been one that overplays the force of subjectivity. Its effects have been, in intellectual argument, to suppose that judgments—about everything that is unscientific—are the expression of mere tastes. It is an unthought-out—sloppy—view since we so very clearly, each of us, distinguish between judgments that tomato sauce tastes good *to us* and that's an end of it, but the September 11 acts were immoral—evil—and that is true not just to us but true for everyone, whatever they think.

CHAPTER TEN

Equality of What?

Dworkin, more than any other contemporary political philosopher, has taken on the pivotal issue in liberal-democratic thinking of the nature of equality and has forcefully developed that idea to produce a strikingly original theory of the distribution of resources. His approach is pragmatic. He assumes that we should treat people as equals and then views the problem as one of distribution. How should a government, as far as is practically possible, reorder society so that people are treated as equals? What, in other words, should it attempt to make them equal in?

Dworkin's theory of the just distribution of resources, or wealth, was raised in two extremely difficult but important papers he published in 1981.[1] He has since refined and expanded his views. I would commend his dense but brilliant article, "The Place of Liberty," published in 1987.[2] These three papers are republished in *Sovereign Virtue*. In some senses, however, he is quite straightforward. Assuming his arguments that people should be treated as equals is right, he asks, what resources should people be entitled to, in the ideal community? The obvious answer—inescapable in my view—is that, since we are of "equal objective value," in principle, every person in that society would be entitled to an equal amount of the total resources available to that community. Dworkin's concern is to show the inter-relationship of the twin liberal ideals of equality and liberty. We should remind ourselves how both these ideals are contained in his account of dignity: (i) each person is of equal objective value and (ii) each person has responsibility for the development of his own life. How do we preserve individual liberty in requiring that each individual be treated equally—as a human being? Dworkin's conclusions are highly original because he attempts a reconciliation of equality and liberty and most people are used to thinking that theories of liberalism make sense only on the assumption that equality and liberty are polar opposites. At first sight, his theory of equality of resources is a mixture of socialist equalizing and *laissez-faire* economics. On the contrary, Dworkin's strong defense of equality is at the same time a strong defense of liberty. From *Justice for Hedgehogs*, we can also confidently say that their joint defense is a defense of individual dignity.

One of the strongest messages from *Justice for Hedgehogs* is Dworkin's belief that political philosophy has to work to counter the deep—"shameful"—injustice in the real world. His starting point is, of course, dignity: coercive government is legitimate only when it shows equal concern and respect for individual responsibility. *Laissez-faire* is not an option. Giving economic forces completely free rein can't be right because a government can't be neutral in the real world; it would be a policy favoring only some groups of people. Everything a government does in some way affects the economy, and the community cannot be sensibly thought of as a "race" for people with special skills. Nor is aiming for an "aggregate" of welfare or well-being or wealth satisfactory because, although allowing for sharing "the purpose of the enterprise" shows treatment in some sense as equals, these favor whatever the commodity is rather than the person. Some will lose out dramatically. Nor could making people equal in their welfare be right (if it were possible). People disagree about what makes them happy, and what happiness is, and will differ widely in what their opportunities and capacities are for attaining happiness. It follows that making people equal in these ways would lead to the imposition of a collective judgment about what lives were good and "annihilate personal responsibility." People would be made equal in spite of the choices they'd made.

Dworkin says we need, instead, to satisfy the two principles of dignity and choose a metric of equality that is shorn of assumptions about welfare—in other words, resources. We must then distinguish between personal resources (physical and mental qualities) and impersonal resources ("wealth measured as abstractly as possible"). Dworkin says only impersonal wealth can be measured without welfare assumptions—it can be distributed through economic transactions and redistributed through taxation, government programs, etc. Dworkin says the community should aim at making people equal in their impersonal wealth:

> A community that respects personal ethical responsibility must concentrate on a fair distribution of means when it fixes its political settlement. It must leave the choice of ends to its citizens one by one.[3]

We shall examine in detail, first, how Dworkin makes his case for equality of resources and why he thinks it is preferable to equality of "welfare." The answer to this question informs us as to how equality of resources differs from utilitarianism. Secondly, we must look more closely at the principles of the market baseline, in particular what Dworkin calls the principle of abstraction. Thirdly, we must look at Dworkin's application of this ideal theory to the real world that you and I live in and look, particularly, at his important idea of the "liberty deficit." Finally, and most importantly for this current study, we must see how Dworkin relates the ideal of equality of resources to legal argument.

REASONABLE REGRET

Here is the problem. The idea that everybody should be equal in welfare is initially attractive but, on closer inspection, incurably problematic. If people are to be treated as equals, what should they be made equal in? Happiness? Wealth? Pleasure? Success in a chosen field (say, building a hugely expensive monument to their religion)? Beauty? Health? Luck? Plots of land? Just "whatever they want"? Some things are unattainable by some people; others are not attainable by anyone. That is part of why some people claim equality to be a myth. But some of these things are attainable, like success or happiness, and the means to attaining them are possible. A government cannot just endow people with success or happiness but it can provide the means — or "endow the potential" — through the distribution of wealth. Reading literature helps to distinguish these ideas. Gatsby was wealthy but not happy. What, at any rate he believed, would have made him happy was marrying Daisy. Pleasure and happiness, while run together in Bentham, are clearly distinct; many people live happily but there is not a great deal of pleasure in their lives (the ascetic monk who is happy being "at one" with his god) and, the other way round, people can have unhappy lives infused with many pleasures (Gatsby again).

"Welfare" is a collective name for most of those things in the above list that are attainable by people and thought good by people. It is now a term of art used by economists and philosophers to describe various states of well-being or happiness or pleasure and so on. The question of the principles we should use in making people as nearly equal in welfare as possible thus makes some sense. In general, it means that a government would have to ask what constituted welfare for different people and then distribute resources so that people were, as best as could practicably be secured, equal in that welfare.

Dworkin considers three ways in which we might consider the idea of welfare. We might think of it as the achievement of success—fulfillment of a personal goal—in some area, whether it is to do with our own or other people's lives. Or we might consider it the attainment of some sort of conscious state, such as pleasant feelings, as the early utilitarians thought it to be. Or, we might think welfare to be some form of either of these two possibilities, but add the rider that the judgment of a person's success or his attainment of a particular conscious state is one to be judged objectively, say, in face of a denial by that person of his level of welfare. Dworkin's most detailed discussion of the problem focuses on the question of the equalizing of success in personal preferences. How do we make judgments about people's lives? Dworkin thinks we can, and that the crucial idea is what he calls the "critical" value of a person's life. He thinks it is a shallow measurement of a person's life that it be judged in terms of the mere satisfaction of personal preferences. Such a life, he says, would be a matter of "relative success" only. Through the idea of the "critically valuable life," Dworkin dispenses with much of modern utilitarian thinking and welfare economics on the ground that it is too concerned with lives of relative success. He says, "The language of preferences (or wants or desires)—seems too crude to express the special, comprehensive judgment of the value of a life as a whole."⁴ Relative success—attainment of desire—is what many people think is wrong with hedonism.

How, though, do we measure overall success of a life? A government needs to have a hold on this idea before engaging people in making them equal in overall success. Dworkin tries several tacks. Just asking a person what value their life is to them does not always seem to yield the right result. What of the "miserable poet" who thinks life is not worth living because he has not produced a great poem? He thinks, but we don't necessarily, that his life is a failure. However, this sort of judgment will not, he says, work for the ordinary case. Take two people, Jack and Jill, who live similar, ordinary sorts of lives and are successful although not highly talented. The relevant difference between them is that Jack thinks his life is valuable while Jill thinks her life is humdrum; she wants more. If overall, critical success is to be measured by their relative subjective judgments of value, then more resources have to be given to Jill because her life, in her view, is not as successful overall, measured against Jack's. Dworkin thinks this result is counter-intuitive because it lacks objectivity. To inject objectivity, Dworkin suggests the idea of "reasonable regret." Jack and Jill should judge their lives by asking themselves whether there is something that they could reasonably have had which would have made their lives overall more successful. "The more that people can reasonably regret not having done something with their lives, the less overall success their lives have had."[5] Dworkin suggests that they should try comparing their own lives against what would have been their ideal life given the right circumstances, or against a life devoid of value. Nevertheless, the counter-intuitive result that Jack and Jill come up with different evaluations of their lives judged overall does not go away.

Could we really make people equal on the criterion of their subjective judgment of overall success alone? Take Jack's point of view. He says he regrets not having more resources in order to take up motor racing. Shouldn't there be a brake on how much he may have to take up motor-racing? It would seem odd if he could simply refer to his aspiration in order to have more resources justifiably transferred to him. Jack and Jill, like most people, both regret that they have had fewer rather than more resources. How do we determine what is "reasonably" more? How could Jill compute what she could reasonably have more of in relation to Jack in order to be equal in having a life of overall success? That is only possible, says Dworkin, by making use of some scheme of fair distribution of resources in which the judgment of overall success is not included: "Reasonable regret cannot itself figure in the distributional assumptions against which the decision whether some regret is reasonable is to be made."[6] In other words, what is reasonable can't be determined by a subjectivist welfarist judgment: that would be circular.

Dworkin's argument is an original version of the otherwise familiar anti-utilitarian argument that welfare is not subjectively measurable between people.[7] If Jack's claim about what he reasonably needs to have a successful life has to be costed against Jill's claim, clearly a metric between them is necessary. What metric is available? According to the view that human beings are of equal moral worth, there is no reason in favor of giving any person less or more wealth/resources than any other. Resources are necessary (but not sufficient) for achieving lives of success and a particular attraction of concentration on equality of resources is that it creates a neat synthesis of equality and liberty.

Jerry Cohen has been a constant critic of Dworkin's theory of equality of resources. Cohen doesn't like any idea that the free market should intrude into the question of what is a just distribution of wealth. (I should say that he is quite Marxist in approach and certainly Marxist in background.) He approves the well-known "egalitarian ethos" and, naturally, the moral good sense of the Marxist slogan "from each according to his ability, to each according to his need," and so he proposes that the egalitarian duty is to improve a person's needs "for fulfilment in life," by which he means improving a person's "potential for welfare."[8] It is difficult to see exactly what this means. Although Cohen thinks of himself as a "welfarist," the idea of "potential for welfare" is fudgy. Just "giving a person welfare" isn't right in itself because our state of moral being has, largely, to be dependent on what we make of our life and so a direct concern with welfare is paternalistic. But if Cohen's belief is really not paternalistic, he must think that the material conditions with which a person can make his own life are important. And so it would appear to follow that potential for welfare is not welfare at all; the welfare needs are really resource needs (along with an ethos of non-discrimination also required by equality). Or perhaps Cohen thinks that the resources available are not so important and that what is really important is the "caring" that the welfare ethos brings about, in other words, that while resources are necessary what is important is that there is a "caring" ethos that is created by thinking of justice as a matter of caring equally for the welfare of others. The problem with this interpretation is that if the resources are distributed very unequally then the "caring ethos" is not worth much. We have to get real. However much you care that another person be happy, if they or you haven't got the resources to do anything about it, the caring fades to nothing.

But of course it is easy to appreciate Cohen's distaste for market determinations of what is just. The free market demonstrably yields often grotesque injustice, and the communal spirit of the egalitarian ethos is attractive. In the ideal world, where there are limitless resources, and we all respect the egalitarian ethos, there doesn't seem much of a problem with the idea, especially if we concede that we may make interpretive judgments about what people are lacking, and then either help or not hinder them in obtaining what they want. But what sort of world is that? Applying the principle to the real world[9] is not even of intuitive help other than to say that we should *care*. Simply, there are limits to what is available to satisfy the demands of care. Cohen doesn't front up to the obvious problem. How, for example, could Cohen's account make sense of the day-to-day distributive decisions concerning the use of expensive equipment that the NHS is required to make? The drugs can't go to the patient who suffers the most—the one with the least welfare—because its expense will mean (like the diamond mountain) that some other patient runs the risk of suffering more; for example, she may have to wait longer for dialysis. If so, this would violate equality. Or how could Cohen make sense of our important right to justice according to law? That right must be defined against the background of the rights of others not to be denied access to the courts (otherwise the time spent on each case would be too long). It is very difficult, very problematic to see how direct reference to comparative measurement and the inevitable price mechanism is avoidable, or why.[10]

THE ECONOMICS OF EQUALITY OF RESOURCES

The Jack and Jill sort of debate—a comparison of what makes them happy—is often carried on in discussions on the value of utilitarianism, particularly on the question of the incommensurability of values. Nevertheless, it should not be confused with the debate over the merits of utilitarianism. Dworkin, it should be remembered from Chapter 9, has a unique conception of utilitarianism, that of egalitarian utilitarianism. According to Dworkin, orthodox or "teleological" utilitarianism regards welfare as a good in itself and so, although he doesn't endorse this form, he sees sense in its maximization,[11] but "egalitarian" utilitarianism is a conception of equality that emphasizes making people equal in welfare.

This "egalitarian" utilitarianism poses the more interesting questions for Dworkin. He says there are a number of difficulties with it. One is that it is ambivalent between preferring maximum average happiness and maximum average misery. Why? Because the utilitarian part is concerned with welfare and the egalitarian part is concerned with making people equal. So there is no principle within this form of welfarism for separating the situation where everyone is equal in a low degree of welfare but where there is more welfare overall.[12] Most people would balk at the idea that we should increase population merely in order to obtain more overall welfare at the expense of lowering everybody's standard of living. "Teleological" utilitarianism can get round that problem by saying that levels of welfare are intrinsically important, irrespective of distribution. Nevertheless, the most important objection, for Dworkin, is just that egalitarian utilitarianism is vulnerable to the charges already laid against the possibility of equalizing people in welfare, whether it is some form of success or enjoyment. This cannot be achieved without an independent criterion of distribution and, of course, without knowledge of the availability of the means to this welfare. We have to know at least that there are some resources available. In a very poor country, it might not be possible even to consider equalization of welfare; basically, there might not be sufficient food to go round. Equality of resources is Dworkin's conception of treating people as equals in the distribution of resources. It is, of course, an ideal conception and is concerned with the articulation of the principles according to which our political institutions should be organized.[13] The ruling idea is that a person's resources should be measured by what it costs others for him to have them, always of course on the assumption of the equal moral value of each person:

> Under equality of resources . . . people decide what sorts of lives to pursue against a background of information about the actual cost their choices impose on other people and hence on the total stock of resources that may fairly be used by them.[14]

This is the familiar "opportunity cost" of economics but it is explicitly linked to fairness. Each person's treatment as an equal in equality of resources must be measured in terms of the cost to the resources of other people. It is natural, therefore, for Dworkin to say that equality of resources presupposes an economic market of some sort. Dworkin exposes a number of important problems in the idea of the ideal market, problems which speak to the rift between right- and left-wing contemporary political debates on the relative importance of liberty and equality.

THE AUCTION

What follows is to some extent technical. The principle that people are *prima facie* entitled to equal resources has been established, although the implications in practice of this principle still need to be drawn out. Dworkin proposes an imaginary auction as a model whereby equality of resources might be achieved. Immigrants to an uninhabited and economically rich island take part in this auction. According to the model and consistent with their being treated as equals, the immigrants arrive at the island in full knowledge of the nature of the auction and of the economic riches of the island, and capable of making genuine, individual, non-coerced, "authentic" choices. No immigrant has come to the island with extra resources. Accordingly, each immigrant is given an equal number of some form of currency (Dworkin suggests clam shells) and each bids for various goods, including plots of land, on the island. Even the size of the various goods, or the plots of land, will be determined by the bidding. The bidding continues until a stage is reached where no one "envies" any other person's bundle of goods. Dworkin introduces *the envy test* as follows: "No division of resources is an equal division if, once the division is complete, any immigrant would prefer someone else's bundle of resources to his own bundle."[15] This envy test is an economic, not a psychological test, of widespread use in economic thinking. It is a shorthand way of testing a situation to see what the rational self-maximizer would have achieved.[16]

The principle that people are of equal objective value is at work here. It explains the envy test, because no person is to remain envious of another's goods. Further, it governs the assumption that people come to the auction as equals, so that no one person begins from a superior position of resources or superior knowledge. According to Dworkin, the equality principle also creates the conditions for the conduct of the auction. Imagine that the division of the goods on the island is the result of a pre-division by some person. That person, say, divides the land up into plots the size of football pitches. The auction is held and, as a result, no person envies any other for the bundle of goods that she holds. The result would be that the plots of land contained in the bundles are weighted in favor of the football-size plots as opposed to any others that could have been made. That is why, he says, there should be a requirement built into the auction that the size of the divisions should themselves be open to auction. The auction would be similarly weighted if the auctioneer had traded the island's resources for a large number of equal bundles of—to use Dworkin's examples—pre-phylloxera claret and plovers' eggs. The envy test would be met, but there would be an inherent weighting of the auction towards the particular tastes of the auctioneer. The auction begins without any of these sorts of assumption; there are no initial divisions of lots or trading of goods.

It is important to see the relevance of attribute of taste and the presence of luck. The goods available on the island may not appeal to the taste of everyone and it may be a matter of luck what tastes could be satisfied. If there were only pre-phylloxera claret and plovers' eggs available on the island, the person who liked such things would be lucky; the person who did not would not be able to claim that the division of the resources under the auction was unfair. The auction concerns the equalizing of resources, not the equalizing of welfare, because as Dworkin has argued, that does not have a metric.

Luck is relevant to the popularity of tastes, too. If few people share the same taste, the price for them may be low because not many people will bid to satisfy them; on the other hand, the price can be high if there is no popular demand that enables economies of scale in production. Again, under equality of resources, these considerations do not affect the fairness of division by the auction. It is not a matter of fairness that some people have tastes that are cheaply satisfied and others have expensive tastes. In short, a distribution could not be challenged as unequal on the ground of the contingent facts of the goods available and the varieties of taste.

THE HYPOTHETICAL INSURANCE MARKET

The envy test is important. It checks that people are being treated as equals because it disallows as an equal division of resources any division which leaves a person preferring another bundle to his own. You can't envy what another person has if you could have bid, just like that other person, to have it. Crucial for the development of the economics of equality of resources is Dworkin's distinction between *option* luck and *brute* luck. Option luck is the sort of luck we might have in gambling, or in playing the stock market, whereby we take a deliberate risk in relation to something. Brute luck, on the other hand, is merely a matter of how risks fall, such as the bad luck we would have if a meteorite fell on us. Dworkin thinks that option luck is consistent with equality of resources, and indeed, it is a fundamental idea in his development of the idea of personal liberty. People are free to take risks and reap the consequences. The gambler who wins made a deliberate choice to take a risk and the true cost of that risk is to be measured against what it costs those who have chosen a safer life. The price of that safer life is forgoing any chance of gains. The gambler who loses has at least been in the position to take a risk, with consequent possible gains. He has thus paid the price, losing, for having had the chance to gamble.

Dworkin concludes that there is no general reason why risk-taking should be limited, although he thinks that there could be qualifications such as those based on paternalistic reasons (saving a person from themselves by restricting their choices in ways that they themselves would approve), or reasons of political morality (for example, you should not take a gamble with slavery). He argues that we should modify the envy test to include option luck by supposing that we can't envy those who have taken risks and been rewarded—these are risks we could all have taken.[17] Dworkin does not, however, think that brute bad luck is consistent with equality of resources. It is simply because we can't help brute luck; it is not an option for us. We can't help it if we are struck by a meteorite, or struck down with cancer, or we are born without any limbs. This, however, is not an insurmountable problem, since it can be dealt with through insurance which can convert brute luck into option luck.

Brute bad luck is serious. A person who suffers a great disability from birth cannot work and earn money. Worse, he is dependent on the resources of others in the community. If we are to take the equal moral value of people seriously—that is, we are to take their dignity seriously—then we must regard the seriously disabled person as equally entitled to a share of resources as ourselves. They are born with a deficit, in other words, and the moral requirement of equality requires compensation to bring that person up, in resources, to the same level of resources as any other, in the ideal community. In the simplest case, we can buy insurance to protect our property against theft, for example. We pay a premium which gives us compensation if our property is stolen. That price is the amount an insurer would be prepared to accept in order to bear that risk. He works it out taking into account the risk of theft, the possible payouts and the market for insuring against such a risk. The cost of the insurance is measured by actuarial calculation against the loss of resources of the insurer if a theft occurs. This simple idea is the key to an elaboration of a hypothetical insurance market carried out by Dworkin to justify compensating brute bad luck. The problem with much brute luck is that it occurs before anyone is near the position of being able to take out insurance to convert it into option luck. In fact, there is usually a cruel Catch 22. Those people who have had really bad luck because they were born, say, with spina bifida disease, would not be insured because there is no insurable risk and, even if there were, they would be too young to afford the premium.

Nevertheless, it is relatively easy to calculate the risks of the occurrence of handicaps. It is only a matter of statistics. Therefore, where people could not have insured, we can hypothesize what insurance people would have bought had they known of the risks. Such a hypothetical insurance market, Dworkin says, provides us with a workable baseline from which to work out a premium. This baseline is workable even though people may differ in what they are prepared to risk and in what they are prepared to pay. People would, he says, make roughly the same assessment of the value of insurance against handicaps such as blindness, or the loss of limbs, that affect a spectrum of different sorts of lives. He does not think that it would be necessary to "personalize" insurance for each individual. The possibility for this kind of compensation for handicaps is there in principle, according to Dworkin. At any rate, he does not think that it would be possible to find an alternative that would have fewer practical difficulties. Clearly he thinks that the great merit of the hypothetical insurance form of compensation is that it is principled; it measures the cost of the system against the background of equality of resources:

> There is no reason to think, certainly in advance, that a practice of compensating the handicapped on the basis of such speculation would be worse, in principle, than the alternatives, and it would have the merit of aiming in the direction of the theoretical solution most congenial to equality of resources.[18]

Back to the immigrants. It will thus be by means of a compulsory insurance levied upon the immigrants that those of them who come to the island with handicaps, or who later develop handicaps, will be compensated for their brute bad luck. This will then place them in the situation of having the same resources—or as near to the same resources as money can compensate—as those of the immigrants who are not handicapped. The cost will, of course, be the combined premiums. It follows that the resources owned by each immigrant will be equal but less than they would have been in the community before the hypothetical insurance system was installed, although, of course, no person will be in an unequal position through brute bad luck. That is morally justified according to the most abstract principle that the state must be organized to respect the rights each person has to be treated as an equal.

In order to compensate handicaps in people it is not necessary, Dworkin says, to have some idea of what constitutes "normal" powers. The difficulties inherent in that idea (for example, by what criteria would one determine that disabled people were not "normal" and so deserving of compensation?) are not necessary in the hypothetical insurance system. There the market determines which handicaps—the instances of brute bad luck—people would be prepared to insure against because their preferences will be tied to the cost. That market will, therefore, determine an upper limit on the handicaps that are compensatable. This is because a person's resources should be measured by what it costs others for him to have them. The upper limits will be determined by factors such as the risks people would be prepared to take, and the premiums they would be prepared to pay, and the total resources available. Rather unexcitingly, but realistically, it would become a matter almost entirely of the sort of actuarial calculation that takes place in insurance offices each day.

Similar sorts of argument are available for those who lose out relatively in the labor market through lack of intelligence and skills. Here, too, Dworkin thinks that a hypothetical insurance market could set a premium which measures, in terms of costs to others, how much a person should be compensated for his lack of employment talents. We assume the immigrants know what their workplace talents are but do not know the resources available to pay them and thus their likely income levels. They then insure themselves against not having the job they believe their talents would warrant. The rarer the job—one that few people have the ability to do (but for which there is a genuinely competitive market)—the insurance premium for not having that job would be fantastically high; the premium would almost match the possible payout. Further down the scale of skills, it will become much more sensible to insure, for, says Dworkin, "many more than twice as many people have the abilities necessary to earn the amount earned in the fiftieth percentile than in the ninety-ninth percentile of a normal income distribution."[19]

By these means we should be able to calculate the amounts per person by which a talent-led economy falls short of an ideal distribution. Could we devise a redistributive tax scheme under which those with less than average talents are compensated? How would we pay for it? A flat-rate tax, at the level of the average under-employment premium, would be unfair, says Dworkin, because rich people would pay the same as poor people. He therefore concludes that, with a number of refinements, premiums could be graduated to match earnings. This could even be economically efficient. The declining marginal utility of money (you achieve proportionally less in increases in welfare the more money you have) would affect the amount people would be prepared to pay for insurance against not having high-paying jobs. There would be likely to be cheaper premiums at the lower end as the result of there being many more people in the market there and insurance firms could make more profit (there would also be greater competition). Reductions in cost could also be achieved by, first, placing the onus on people asking for the more expensive insurance to show that they were not mistaken or dishonest about their talents and, second, through co-insurance, the requirement that people pay a proportion of the difference between what their talents can produce and the level of employment they have insured against not having.

It is useful to be reminded what Dworkin is doing here. He assumes that each person in the community is, as a human being, of equal objective value. He assumes also that each person has the responsibility to make the best out of their lives. These two principles—clearly those of dignity as we can now see from *Justice for Hedgehogs*—imply an economic market. We should be treated as equals in the market and we should be free to trade as we wish. Since making people equal in welfare would be unfair because there would be no criterion to temper subjective assessments of welfare, people must be made equal in resources. However, brute bad luck in the form of disabilities such as lack of skill or being physically disabled, means that some people will end up having less than equal resources. Dworkin justifies a scheme of redistribution whereby those worse off are compensated on the basis that people would take out insurance not to be worse off and the cost of this insurance is the combined sum of the premiums that an insurance market would be able, hypothetically, to collect. In practice those premiums would be paid for in the form of a progressive tax.

What about brute good luck? If the idea of equality requires that people do not earn less solely through lack of talent, it seems that the principle demands that the more talented you are, the more tax you should pay. Having a talent is no more a matter of your own choice than having lack of talent. It is, in some senses (and it is often described this way), a gift. We noted that in the hypothetical insurance market a highly talented person need not take out an insurance premium, because his talents are sufficient to do without insurance. This suggests that the hypothetical insurance tax scheme cannot fix levels high enough to make the less talented as well off as the very talented. That will mean a failure in the envy test: people will still envy the talent-earning capacities of the most talented. Dworkin's answer to this is just that the envy test cannot be expected to eliminate differences between people in the way they are actually born to be. He compares two worlds. First, the world in which people know of their disadvantages in relation to the talents and ambitions of others and suffer from it. Second, there is the world in which people do not know of their disadvantages in this way but have an equal opportunity to insure against the disadvantages. Dworkin says the second world is to be preferred, and that his hypothetical insurance argument intends to reproduce the consequences of the second world, as far as it can, in the real world:

> It answers those who would do better in the first world (who include . . . many of those who would have more money at their disposal in the second) by the simple proposition that the second is a world that, on grounds independent of how things happen to work out for them given their tastes and ambitions, is more nearly equal in resources.[20]

Nevertheless, Dworkin has not argued that wealth differences should be eliminated. He says doing so would distort true opportunity costs and thereby affect everybody. First, we cannot argue for a community in which we all have the top income; the total resources could not sustain that outcome. The closest we could get to that is to say that no one should have that income, and that each of our lesser incomes moves relatively closer to that top income. But that would have the effect that, for example, J. K. Rowling might have refused to write any more books, and so people's choices to read about Harry Potter would be affected. Such an outcome would be, Dworkin says, "choice insensitive" and that contradicts the point of the hypothetical insurance market which was to make people's choices relevant to the setting of the tax level. That, says Dworkin, "is exactly why the immigrants chose an auction, sensitive to what people in fact wanted for their lives, as their primary engine for achieving equality."[21]

Dworkin thinks that the dislike of wealth differences is a response to the present society in which we live, in which wealth is admired for its own sake. Dworkin is not a right-wing libertarian. He is much more socialist-egalitarian than is commonly recognized although he believes, unlike many socialists, that freedom to live one's own life according to one's own particular lights is fundamental. He thinks that a community that had equality of resources, run along his lines, in which wealth differences exist but which reflect different ambitions and tastes, would not give rise to the same attitudes and motivations that distort much of the way we live now.

LIBERTY AND EQUALITY[22]

Crucial to Dworkin's conception of equality as equality of resources is his view that we must distinguish the person from his particular circumstances (of disability or talent). What does this mean? It helps to go back to the idea that people should be treated as equals and to the idea of the "common humanity" of people as proposed by Bernard Williams and discussed in Chapter 8. People are alike in their being "human" so that physically handicapped or talentless people must be treated as "equals," that is, as equal in humanity as the non-handicapped and talented.

On the other hand, people differ in their ambitions and tastes and these differences go right across the spectrum of talent and handicap. People are creative. They can further their ambitions and cultivate and develop tastes. But to treat people as equals only requires that they be given the capacities, by way of equality of resources, to do these things. In other words, Dworkin assigns tastes and ambitions to the person and the person's mental and physical powers to his circumstances:

> The distinction required by equality of resources is the distinction between those beliefs and attitudes that define what a successful life would be like, which the ideal assigns to the person, and those features of body or mind or personality that provide means or impediments to that success, which the ideal assigns to the person's circumstances.[23]

In other words, equality of resources stops short of compensating people for their particular tastes and ambitions but requires compensation for lack of talent and physical incapacity. It stops short because of liberty. Dworkin's project is, as we have seen, to locate liberty in the idea of equality, and that project requires separating out that bit of equality that treats people as part of "common humanity"—having "equal objective moral worth"—from the attributes of a person that are capable of development and fulfillment. It would be a wrong part of the equalizing process to make people equal in the achievement of their ambitions (equality of overall success); as Dworkin argued, that is what is wrong with equality of welfare. To repeat: equality of resources is the correct principle of distribution within a political scheme pledged to treating people as equals because "common humanity" requires that people be put in a position equal with others in order to be free to conduct their lives in a way they wish.[24]

A NOTE ON CONVICTIONS

It is necessary now to turn more specifically to what happens once there has been an initial distribution of resources at the auction. Dworkin amends the envy test to apply, not to the bundle of resources that a person has the moment the auction is finished, but to the bundle of resources that the person has over his whole life. Dworkin's theory is not, as he is at pains to emphasize, a "starting-gate" theory. The general principles that determine equality of resources in the first place determine distribution right through-out a person's life. It means that no person should ever be permitted to reap benefits attributable to his luck-endowed talent alone. Of course, he may reap benefits attributable to his ambition—to his hard work—alone. That is fair. In Dworkin's terms, a distribution of resources is faulty when it becomes "endowment sensitive" rather than "ambition sensitive." Is this a justifiable distinction in the distribution of wealth? Dworkin says it is fair and the answer can be found in the envy test. A person who, solely through his talents, achieves a greater share of a community's resources will be envied by other members of the community because he has received an extra share through (brute) luck alone; but no one will envy his acquired benefits that are the result of hard work or the exercise of imagination—it is always open to anyone to have formed those ambitions and done the hard work.

In his later Tanner Lectures,[25] Dworkin considers the criticism that his theory requires too much of a distinction between personality, such as ambition, and the circumstances that a person finds himself in. Is there a relevant difference? He says that our convictions about what we should do in life—our ambitions—should not be regarded as "obstacles" in the way of our leading a good life. The point is that if our views about what constituted a good life were to be placed in the same category as matters of mere luck—disability or talent—and discounted, then that would be an unjustifiable restraint of liberty. My views express what I believe to be truths about the way my life should be led. It would perhaps be perverse to suppose that my views limit my choices. True, my views limit my choice in one way. I do not choose what I do not choose to do! That is nothing to do with the "metaphysics" of choice, Dworkin says, but is simply an expression of "the logic of ethical life."

Let us try this argument yet again. Why is talent not part of personality? Could we be *ourselves* without it? Our convictions express our view about the right way to lead our lives. Imagine my convictions to include the belief that the best life for me would be playing the violin to the best of my talents. What would it mean to say that I am not to be compensated for these convictions? To lead my life in accordance with my convictions I need more resources than Dworkinian equality of resources allows (depending amongst other things on how good my talent is, a place at a conservatoire, a Guarnerius). So here is an objection: my personality, in the convictions I hold, are part of the circumstances in which I live. I must, if I am to be compensated for my circumstances, be compensated, too, for my convictions. Dworkin denies this. He says that our views about what constitutes the good life cannot be regarded as handicaps (unless we thought them wrong, in which case they would not be our views). Perhaps Dworkin is persuasive after all. He is saying that one's convictions are not a matter of luck. But, then, Dworkin says: "I can decide not to do what I believe to be best for me, but I cannot decide not to believe that it would be best." That sounds as though it were a matter of luck! Further on in the Tanner Lectures, he seems to offer a separate argument that "convictions are part of us not part of our situation." It seems reasonable to ask in reply: Why should not talents be part of us?

It may be useful here to return to the striking claim that handicaps and talents are a matter of luck. Our convictions are not a matter of brute luck, but circumstances are, so circumstances must be adjusted in accordance with the abstract principle of equality to compensate the handicapped and tax the fruits of talent. We have no problem with the idea of a person who, through bad luck, suffers some genuine handicap.[26] That we can easily agree, from the abstract principle of equality, requires a different allocation of resources from the total available. Luck does the intuitive trick. Why should a person be worse off than anybody else through brute bad luck? If we stick to the logic of this approach, we must be struck by the argument: Why should a person command more of the total resources available merely because by luck he happens to be more talented than other people? That must offend the abstract principle of equality. I find this argument highly compelling although I'm in a tiny minority. Many people are convinced that the only reason they have less money than others is that they have not worked as hard. I think this is a sad mistake to make. The idea that someone has "earned" a vast sum of money—someone like Warren Buffett, or Bill Gates—because they have worked proportionately harder is not a healthy thought. It directs attention not just away from the fact that some people are lucky in that their genetic make-up allows them more productive work in the economic market, but that some people are lucky in other ways—they occupy natural monopolies, for example (e.g., merchant banking). I'm afraid there is such a thing as inborn talent—it is certainly not the case that in each of us is a Shakespeare, an Itzhak Perlman, a Picasso or a Churchill. We are all human and so we all partake of this; we should rejoice in the partaking, not be envious or disbelieving.

METHODOLOGY: THE BRIDGE ARGUMENT AND THE MARKET BASELINE

The auction presupposes liberty in the idea of bargaining in order to equalize resources. It follows, Dworkin says, that liberties are not to bargained for in the auction or the subsequent market transactions. In other words, liberty is fundamental to the market and cannot be itself a tradable commodity. Liberty has a more fundamental position than a tradable commodity. That is why, he says, it is wrong to suppose that several famous debates, some fought in the U.S. Supreme Court, were merely debates over the correct compromise between liberty and equality, as though liberty were no more than what people happened to regard as in their interest. Rather, liberty must be in place before the arguments about equalizing can make sense. That, in Dworkin's view, accords sense to certain fundamental liberties while denying that there is a general and overriding right to liberty. However, this is already too cryptic and we are leaping ahead. What, first, are the constraints based on liberty which Dworkin says must be added to the market baseline? The overriding idea, against which every aspect of the market must be tested, is, of course, Dworkin's foundational principle that people must be treated as equals. Dworkin calls this the *bridge* argument linking his foundational requirement to all that goes on in the market. In other words, we must select the baseline constraints for the market that best give effect to this foundational principle.

One constraint is straightforward. There must be a constraint of liberty to protect personal security (the *security* principle). Dworkin leaves development of this idea for future discussion and obviously thinks that there are market-independent reasons—consistent, of course, with treating people as equals—for constraining liberty in order to protect personal security. There are market reasons, too. It is not a real contract if we are coerced or manipulated into agreeing to its terms. Given this liberty-protecting principle, Dworkin introduces the existence of the wide principle of *abstraction*, which inserts liberty into the market baseline as one of its major assumptions, and includes the idea of *correction*:

> [This principle] establishes a strong presumption in favor of freedom of choice. It insists that an ideal distribution is possible only when people are legally free to act as they wish except as far as constraints on their freedom are necessary to protect security of person and property, or to correct certain imperfections in markets.[27]

The principle of "correction" is a practical principle behind the application of the principle of abstraction to situations in the real world. We cannot assume in the real world that the market will always achieve results that are consistent with treating people as equals. The market will need correction at certain points. For example, where there are extra costs—such as pollution to third parties—this principle permits regulation to mimic an ideal market outcome in the real world where these costs (called "externalities" by economists) can frustrate people's ambitions and projects. It may be used, too, where such ambitions and projects require co-ordination rather than bargaining, in those situations where the intention is to make things run smoothly, for example, where choosing what side of the road people should drive on.

The major point of the abstraction principle is that it serves liberty by setting the conditions for discovering what a person's freedom truly costs other people. That is why, in Dworkin's view, it is so much part of the idea of equality. If people are not free to make discriminating choices right from the start, the real cost to others will be hidden; as economists say, "true opportunity costs" will be suppressed. Imagine, for example, that, before the auction, the auctioneer divided the land on the island up into football field-sized lots, or traded all the goods on the island for champagne and cigars. This would show a failure of flexibility, making the array of goods very much less sensitive to the plans and preferences of the immigrants. Their freedom is reduced. Dworkin says that this principle of abstraction bears importantly on the question of whether, if a majority wants a religious or sexual orthodoxy, there should be an enforcement of that orthodoxy. He thinks that the principle generally supports the liberal view that the state should be neutral between people's moral views, even when there is a majority preference.

Why? Because the idea of opportunity cost is neutral between the kinds of lives people wish to lead for themselves (the second principle of dignity). Just as a person will find it prohibitively expensive to spend his life amassing the works of Picasso, so will a person who wants to surround himself with a sexual or religious culture like his own. Of course, in a community where there is a predominant culture it is likely that living an unorthodox life will be more expensive because those wishing to share that life will be relatively few. That is the other side of the coin, for it would be unrealistic—going too far—for a minority to be assured of a social culture which is congenial to them; that is asking too much. If equality of resources were committed to producing a culture in which lives were supposed to be, as Dworkin says, "equally easy to live," then the driving force would be equality of welfare, and that fails because there is no metric of cost.

Two other principles are of great importance for Dworkin. These are the principles of *authenticity* and *independence* (see Chapter 9), both of which spell out more precisely requirements of the principle of "abstraction"—the presumption in favor of freedom of choice. Any person who comes to the market must be able to make genuine, "authentic" choices. Obviously, if he has been duped, by lies, or misleading advertising (enhanced in the case of youth), the lifestyle he chooses will not be the one he would have chosen had he been fully free. In his state of lack of full realization, his choice will not be properly costed against the choices of others in the market. He will suffer a liberty deficit and so the market baseline will have to include protection against inauthenticity, such as preventing fraud and misrepresentation in inducing contracts and fixing a minimum age of contractor. Dworkin develops this in the direction of freedom of speech. Freedom of speech is linked to the formation and development of personality. Only in a culture where ideas are tested against others, and *a fortiori* where people have a right to express their views and attempt to persuade others, will the appropriate conditions for the development of the "authentic" personality be achieved. Indeed, Dworkin thinks that this is such an important aspect of the ascertainment of true opportunity costs—and thus the equalizing process—that only in matters of personal security should the right to free flow of opinions be abridged, for example, as in the "clear and present danger" test of the U.S. Constitution.

The principle of independence (see Chapter 9) is best understood through the bridge argument. The bridge argument, if you remember, requires that all principles governing the market baseline must be consistent with the foundational principle that people should be treated as equals. Simply, the independence principle requires that markets reflecting prejudice or contempt for people are faulty. Imagine that white immigrants, who form the majority, are prejudiced against blacks and buy up large tracts of land for the express purpose of keeping blacks out of white areas. Dworkin says that there is nothing in the principle of abstraction that would prevent this; nevertheless, it is forbidden by the foundational principle that people should be treated as equals. The principle of independence can be relevant in two ways. First, like the principle of abstraction it must be incorporated into the market baseline because it distorts opportunity costs; obviously, if people are discriminated against, the true opportunity costs (to them) are hidden. In other words, the auctioneer must disallow bids based upon prejudice. Second, even markets operating on an unprejudiced baseline will need to be corrected after prejudiced bids have been discounted. In the real world, the principle of independence will have to operate alongside the principle of correction. Sometimes, the market will have to be bypassed just in order to achieve the result that would have been achieved had prejudice not infected the transaction. It is important to appreciate that Dworkin does not think the elimination of prejudice is a matter of the *ad hoc* patching up of a corrupted bargain. It is more fundamental: it conflicts with the right to dignity itself.

It will not hurt to summarize Dworkin's theory yet again. We equalize people in resources by a market device, using the envy test, in order to measure what people wish to do by what that will cost others, who are equally people. We distinguish people independently of those aspects of them attributable to brute luck, such as handicaps and talent, leaving them only distinguishable on their convictions and ambitions. In judging what the cost to others will be of what they have, we assume that each such person should have physical security and the conditions for free development of personality, and be free from prejudice. We assume that the overriding principle is that people should be treated as equals, and so that in the real world the market can be corrected in accordance with that principle. Most important to realize is Dworkin's connection between moral requirements of equality and liberty and the so-called free market. This latter is a moral market—it is regarded on the far right for example as one of the virtues of the capitalist free enterprise system—and so it is ensnared by morality. If we take liberty seriously then we should be free to bargain with others; it is a common human desire. If we think that we should come to the market more or less as equals (for there is a vast difference between plundering and bargaining) then we are bound to regard the market as subject to correction by regulation. This maintains the abstract nature of transactions between the parties—thus enabling knowledge of the true costs and so preserving the liberty of bargaining—as well their independence as equal moral beings. These principles underscore all transactions, so there is always a bridge between actual transactions and the more fundamental principles of a decent community. Politicians who refer to the virtues of the "free market" don't understand what these virtues are. Mostly it is merely rhetoric that underhandedly reinforces exploitation by business or, in Dworkin's terms, the hiding of the true opportunity costs and impact on the community.[28]

A THEORY OF IMPROVEMENT

Of course, the theory so far advanced describes a utopia. For that reason, many people would like to say that it is useless. Why talk about an imaginary world? That is just philosophers' dreamings. What about the "world of social reality"?[29] This is a common and silly response. We can't understand the world of "reality"—the "real" free market, say—unless we understand what to measure it against. In order to have some idea of the "harsh realities" of the world we must develop some idea of what it would be like not to be harsh. If, in the "real" world, life is unjust, we must have some idea of what would count as a just decision. Dworkin's theory is no more ideal than any theory of market economics. We understand the imperfections of the market dominated by monopolies only because we have in mind some ideal market in which there are no monopolies. It is no answer to an economist who is giving advice about why and how monopolies should be controlled to say that his project is misconceived because, actually, there *are* monopolies. He knows there are. That preliminary aside, however, it can be of exasperatingly little help to say of a real world institution that it needs radical overhauling in comparison to some imaginary model. Something less abstract is required. Dworkin is aware of this problem. He needs some means by which he can attach his critical model to a program of reform in the world in which we actually live. He attempts this through the idea of an "equity deficit" which represents the difference between the circumstances of a person in the ideal world and his circumstances in the real world.

Dworkin says there will be two sorts of equity deficits in the real world. First, resource deficits, by which people will have fewer resources than they would have been entitled to under an ideal egalitarian distribution. Second, there will be what he calls *liberty deficits*. These will arise because of some failure, again in the real world, of the baseline principle of abstraction. Dworkin says it is possible for a person to be worse off in liberty, but not worse off in resources. Say the sale of marble is prohibited if it is intended to be used to produce satirical sculpture. That prohibition is not justified by the principle of abstraction which assumes freedom to do what people want with resources so that true opportunity cost is known. In any case the value of the marble to the satirist sculptor may not be the same as it is to the person who wishes to construct a marble bath. The sculptor has, let us say, a desperate wish to make satirical points and has a political commitment not shared with the bath maker. That difference in value cannot be measured in money terms. Nor can it be measured in welfare terms if we are to accept, like Dworkin, that equalizing people in welfare fails, partly because it has no metric. We must therefore, according to Dworkin, measure our improvement of society by measuring the reduction of both resource and liberty deficits. Could we devise some general test of reduction? What about a "resource" form of utilitarianism? This will not work, says Dworkin. Just an increase in community resources when there is no worsening in any person's liberty deficit would still allow for some people being worse off. That cannot be permitted within Dworkin's scheme because it would be contrary to the foundational principle that people should be treated as equals.[30]

What about a "dominating" test, namely, one that reduces equity deficits of some people without increasing the equity deficits of others? This is a subtle test. Note how it differs from the Pareto test of improvement in welfare. There could be an improvement as far as equality is concerned without an improvement in welfare; a good example would be the elimination of a "whites-only" golf club. Indeed, an improvement in equality might mean the reduction of welfare for, say, some rich people (no golf, or having to mix with non-whites, perhaps):

> Even though they limit freedom, they leave no one worse off, with respect to the value of that freedom, than he would be in an ideal situation. So dominating improvements in equality are much easier to achieve, and are therefore of much greater practical importance, than Pareto improvements.[31]

We can go further, says Dworkin. Some non-dominating improvements (in other words, reductions in equity deficits which result in the increasing of equity deficits for others) will sometimes be permissible. If, for example, there were no new liberty deficits, and the resource deficits of the worst-off were improved then, he says, that might be justified at the cost of some resource deficits being increased. Dworkin produces a rule-of-thumb-type guide to the kinds of political decisions that might be made. However, he does not think that a "general and comprehensive" formula is possible and prefers a fresh inspection of each non-dominating claim. It bears some similarities to the Rawlsian "difference" principle, according to which any improvement in the worst-off is a gain in justice but, as Dworkin says, is "more guarded." It is clearly different in the sense that Dworkin's rule of thumb is based squarely on a foundational principle, that of treating people as equals:

> Non-dominating gains are justified where no one's deficit loss is greater than the largest deficit gain to a member of the most disadvantaged class.

The intuitive expression of this is that in the real world where some people have more than they ought, we should tax them and give the surplus to those who have less than they ought. However, we must note the extremely important rider Dworkin adds here. It is that no program of improvement in his view is justified if it introduces, as he says, "new and significant" liberty constraints. Why? The argument is startlingly simple. It is just that liberty and resource deficits are incommensurable. It is not possible to measure, in terms of improvements towards equality, the loss of, say, free speech, in terms of an increase of rice for the very poor.

However, we do live in the real world and we are considering, not the ideal world, but only how we might move towards it. Why, then, don't we just restrict freedom in the name of bringing us closer to the ideal world where there is maximum freedom? Dworkin says we cannot. Any person who has some liberty taken away in the cause of improving equality will be "victimized." Not every loss of liberty will be a case of victimization, however, because no person is entitled to more liberty than the ideal distribution would allow. However, beneath that level it seems right to say that people will be victimized, because any person suffering from a liberty deficit suffers a loss of freedom, so rendering political decision-making less authentic. Consider our satirical sculptor. Or the man who wishes to make political speeches. If they are prevented from pursuing their desired activities they are unable to work towards a world where decisions about resources are made in conditions of freedom, that is, in accordance with the principle of abstraction. Decisions will be less authentic, according to Dworkin's justification of free speech in terms of the baseline principle of authenticity. The implications for the real world are difficult, as we would expect. Dworkin considers three cases in which the principle of victimization would be helpful.

The first is restricting campaign expenditure by political candidates. In the United States, Congress limited the amount any one person could lawfully spend to advance the interests of a particular political candidate.[32] In *Buckley* v. *Valeo,* this statute was declared unconstitutional by the Supreme Court on the ground that it violated freedom of speech under the First Amendment.[33] Under an ideal egalitarian distribution, Dworkin thinks that such a restriction would be unjustified. In Chapter 6, I discussed his view that the freedom to be able to influence political thinking is a significant freedom of a properly democratic community. In the ideal society, where there is genuine equality of resources, no person would be able to amass such an amount of resources as to have a disproportionate political impact. In the real world, unjust differences of income permit some political candidates to make a disproportionate impact. In Dworkin's view, the financial constraints placed upon political candidates were justified. Since they did not impose restrictions on freedom that were less than would have been permitted under an ideal egalitarian distribution they were not, therefore, instances of victimization. The constraints come closer to mimicking the just society although in that society there would be no constraints. And why in that society shouldn't a person devote his money and time to political causes, rather than, say, to sport, or to buying a second house, or having a large family?

The argument works most easily for this case of political constraint because it concerns solely a financial constraint. Dworkin tests the argument against two other areas of concern: restrictions on freedom to use private medicine and restrictions on freedom of contract. If private medicine were abolished, as political parties do, from time to time, promise, this would reduce the freedom of rich people to choose their doctors and times of treatment. The test Dworkin proposes—the victimization test—is whether the freedoms so reduced would take these people's freedoms below what they would have under an ideal distribution.

Dworkin thinks that there are a number of answers to this question and that this fact in itself speaks to the practicality of the victimization test. Two possible sorts of ideal distribution might be possible in the real world. First, a comprehensive private system combined with government insurance for what the average person would be prepared to insure. Second, something like the British system, whereby there is the National Health Service combined with the availability of private medicine. If we assume that the National Health Service would not be improved by abolishing private medicine, then we could compare the National Health Service alone with either of these two possible ideal distributions. Then we could ask whether, compared with these, we would obtain better care, or faster service for less than life-threatening illnesses, or more choice for particular doctors. If the answer is yes to each of these three questions then we would have to conclude that the government was victimizing people by outlawing private medicine and leaving only the

National Health Service as it presently stands. Dworkin gives the example as an illustration of a way he sees his theory of improvement might work. It is not intended to exclude other possibilities. He says that the government might abolish private medicine in favor of a more close-to-ideal version of the NHS, or it might limit queue-jumping.

Dworkin also considers restrictions on freedom of contract, such as those imposed by New York State in the early years of the nineteenth century on bakers' employees' hours and conditions of work (for example, bakers were forbidden to work for more than sixty hours each week). These legal restrictions were declared unconstitutional by the Supreme Court in the well-known case of *Lochner*.[34] His answer is that at first sight it seems right that freedom of contract should not be restricted, because it victimizes the employees. They had the freedom not to enter into the contracts. On the other hand, Dworkin doesn't think the decision was right. It did not in his view adequately consider matters, also matters of fundamental importance such as the question of security—health and safety, for example—or whether these were genuinely authentic choices facing the employees—did they have equality of bargaining power or were they in reality faced with no other choice? Dworkin also thought *Lochner* was insufficiently respectful to the policy behind the New York legislation; he thought the Supreme Court should not have assumed that the legislature would fail to compensate those who became unemployed because of its legislation.

CONCLUSION

The question "Equality of what?" is answered by equality of resources. We saw, however, that the practical application of this idea was complicated by the unfortunate intrusion of luck in people's circumstances. That requirement led to the irrelevance of certain types of circumstance in calculating equality of resources, for example. It remains for Dworkin to explain why people should be treated as free and equal human beings. He requires, in other words, an extended account of the fundamental principles of liberalism, and I now turn to that topic.

CHAPTER ELEVEN

The Basis of Liberalism

We have considered in detail Dworkin's important ideal of the political scheme of equality of resources. It is guided by his foundational—humanistic—principle that people should be treated as equals. But we have also seen that there is a need for a fully developed division between people's public and private responsibilities. That distinction is worked out by Dworkin in a number of different contexts. It is inherent in his rejection, in the ideal world, of utilitarianism, even of the egalitarian sort. It is inherent, too, in the argument for a participative political equality of influence, as opposed to an equality of *impact*. Dworkin further develops the idea of the division in a direct and simple attack on the contractarian account of liberalism in his Tanner Lectures. It is necessary, first, to understand what is the substance of recent debates on the justifications for liberalism, and second, to understand the nature and significance of the contractarian approach.

WHAT IS LIBERALISM?

Liberalism is more than a set of discrete beliefs about rights to personal freedom, or to the treatment of people as equals, or to the unhampered exercise of one's personal morality. It refers to these things, of course, and is easily summed up as primarily about benign tolerance. Liberalism also aspires to be more rigorous than this and to form a justified doctrine of beliefs which has coherence and, therefore, the force to oppose anti-liberal arguments and attitudes. Liberalism has a unique problem which arises, I think, from its central requirement of tolerance. This requires that the true liberal must accept much of what other people do at the same time as disapproving of it. The contradictory tone of this is one of the major reasons why people find it morally difficult to accept (there are, of course, other reasons—self-interest, for example). That contradictory tone is inherent in the idea: "I disapprove of what you do but I'll strongly support your right to do it" or in "We have the right to do wrong." Justifying liberalism intellectually is not easy and, when justifications are needed in urgent practical occasions, they are particularly difficult to sell. It involves the liberal in the seeming doublethink of feeling the importance of, say, individual freedom, and then appreciating but permitting its abuse. Political life is full of such problems. It is often tempting for a government to appeal directly to wide support ("public opinion") for banning activities when such activities should be tolerated because of the possible effects of prejudice. Because of this the political case for tolerance will almost always be at its weakest when intellectually it is at its strongest. When tolerance triumphs politically, too, it is more likely than not to be supported by the unsatisfying utilitarian argument: "If the government got into the habit of doing this, it would be a bad thing."

Liberalism's problem, therefore, is that it appears hypocritical. It tries morally to justify the state's permitting immoral conduct. Before seeing what solution Dworkin proposes, it helps to give a short review of ways in which answers have been sought to the problem. A depressingly widespread justification for liberalism is that it follows logically from the perceived impossibility of the objectivity of moral reasoning. (I have mentioned the pervasiveness and harmfulness of this idea in the Introduction.) The argument goes: "Our moral views are our own personal matters of opinion only. We are all therefore entitled to our own views and have no right to enforce them on other people. It further follows that the state must be tolerant toward everyone's views." But this justification is wrong since it depends on a mistake about the impossibility of moral objectivity. Briefly, it does not make any sense to say both that there is no right or wrong about moral matters and to say that tolerance is morally right. There is another view, too, although it is constituted by a set of more or less informal attitudes rather than by an intellectual thesis. This is the woolly idea that liberalism means that you should refrain from being critical of what other people do in the exercise of their freedoms. A weak version of the idea makes for a certain sort of blandness in dealing with other people ("you see no wrong because they have a right to do what they are doing") and is surprisingly common. A stronger version—certainly present amongst many people in the sixties—is that you must not only tolerate what other people do but you must also approve of it. You have to see it as actually good. This "hippie" liberalism takes tolerance to its extremes, extending beyond the simple endorsement of the exercise of freedom, to the acts resulting from that freedom. There are obvious problems with the attitude, the main one being that it is naively optimistic—it hopes for too much. It shares, too, the blandness of its weaker version. A fairly clear strain of liberalism—associated with Mill—wants to keep alive personal moral criticism of both others and ourselves and hippie liberalism does not allow this. Hippie liberalism does, though, escape the crude assumptions about the subjectivity of moral opinions, and its amiable and attractive side includes the injunction that we should take an active and open interest in the activities of others. Nevertheless, its stronger version suggests that liberalism need not be detached from a consideration of the right sorts of lives people should lead. Usual criticisms of liberalism include the charge that it is "anti-perfectionist," meaning that it permits people to live, as a matter of right, morally "imperfect" lives, without any control or criticism. It is thus thought to be a morally impoverished theory.

One group that lays this charge consists of the "communitarian" critics of liberalism. They say that liberalism's case for tolerance relies too heavily on "the priority of the individual and his rights over society."[1] Individuals are not, they say, "atomistic" beings who can be judged as independent of the moral strands that bind them to the rest of the community. The community has sufficient central focus in people's moral lives to require communal duties of an anti-liberal nature. In short, the good moral life of the individual cannot logically be separated from the good of the community.[2] The arguments are too detailed and diffuse to be dealt with here. The one overriding thing that is not clear, however, is that liberalism depends on any idea that community values are not important or that individuals can only be seen as "atomic" units.[3] It is also not clear that the important goals of a community, and the moral reasons for its existence, are inconsistent with the foundational idea that people have rights. In *The Morality of Freedom,* Joseph Raz provides an elegant defense of liberalism against these charges.[4] He thinks that liberalism is neither atomistic nor ignores community values. Although he denies the primacy of rights to freedom within liberalism he places great importance on the idea of individual freedom. Freedom requires, he says, the "autonomously led life" which, in turn, requires that the community has a duty to provide an "adequate" range of choices. If there is only an extremely limited range of choices ("options for living") then lives cannot be said to be lived with sufficient freedom ("autonomy"). He gives as an example a man who is kept in a pit and is given sufficient food to survive. Nevertheless, the man is free to do what he likes within the pit although he is not allowed to escape. This is not a liberal life; so, Raz says, liberalism must take account of the value in people's lives. What is value in a person's life? He believes it is characterized by a commitment to various forms of life such as the pursuit of projects and careers (in the widest sense of that word). Here the community plays an important part in providing, through its public institutions, the means by which adequate options can be provided. It follows that the community must have a serious and fundamental concern with various perfect ways of living. Nevertheless, it also must keep an arm's length from what people decide to do in taking up these options since doing otherwise would be to interfere with their freedom.

Raz's view is a comprehensive moral view because it endorses a way of living that can apply to all people's lives; it does so by declaring that the best way of living is the pursuit of personal ideals, goals and careers in the exercise of freedom. There are, however, some difficulties with the limits of toleration that are implied with such a view. What about ways of living that are incompatible with one another in the sense that it would not be possible to fulfill both ways of living freely? Raz sees this objection and gives the example of the life of the perfect nun, saying that it is, for example, incompatible with the life of the perfect mother: no one can be both a nun and a mother at the same time. Nevertheless, it is Raz's view that each form of life is compatible in the sense that from one single comprehensive ethical view, both the mother's and the nun's lives can be judged as perfect lives, provided we understand that each life was the result of a decision to act amongst a decent range of initial choices. Both lives can, therefore, be compatible in the sense that each is capable of being a perfect way of living within a political structure that has endorsed the principle of freedom that allows such lives to be led.

Raz's liberalism does not appear to allow for more extreme ways of living that many liberals think are fundamental to liberalism. These are lives of which most people might well thoroughly disapprove but which nevertheless require toleration. Raz is nevertheless consistent and he just rules out certain incompatible forms of life by saying that the community is not required to tolerate "repugnant" lives. This leaves his theory standing in need of something more if it is to account for strong intuitions many of us have about liberalism; briefly, that we should tolerate conduct that is repugnant to, or "discontinuous" with, our own personal ethical convictions. Why should we do so?

THE DISMISSAL OF DISCONTINUITY THEORIES

The subjectivist foundation, and the twin comprehensive foundations of the hippie and Raz, are unsatisfactory. What other possibilities are there? The major one, discussed in modern liberal theory, is that of contractarianism, according to which the rights of individuals to conduct their affairs derive from an arrangement of government by agreement. Important to the account is that there are independent reasons for the agreement so that the grounds for the rights, and the grounds for agreeing, are two different sorts of justification. Dworkin describes the contractarian theory as a *discontinuity* theory meaning that there is a break in the connection between a person's private moral convictions (Dworkin describes these as first person ethics, or well-being) and morality itself (third person ethics). The idea is that people have private reasons for entering a contract but once the contract has been formed morality itself governs the operation of the contract. Put in another way, if we think, as Dworkin does, that contractarian theory depends on something like the idea of an ordinary legal contract, our moral rights and duties follow from the contract and not from our private moral convictions about what should happen overall. Raz doesn't rely on the idea of a contract; his form of liberalism directly promotes the ethical life and so ethics and morality are continuous.

Dworkin says that John Rawls's theory that the basis of liberalism must be sought in an "overlapping consensus" among different comprehensive ethical views[5] is the "most sophisticated" discontinuity theory. Rawls's idea is that liberal principles can only be founded on a shared assumption that they were necessary for co-operation (that is, they require agreement) in a community in which there were markedly different ethical outlooks. Surprisingly, Rawls has been famously clear in stating that liberal principles are not, on this view, only a matter of self-interested expedience (he specifically denied they were a mere *modus vivendi*). Rather, he says they "connect" with each person's moral views but, clearly, in a way that is not continuous with them. Nevertheless, it is easy to imagine a contract being endorsed as much by self-interest, or self-preservation (as Hobbes thought) as by morality. Co-operation is not clearly neutral between self-interest and morality and Rawls's account appears weak because of this. On the other hand, it is clearly not antagonistic to personal morality and so Dworkin's interpretation (and Rawls's interpretation of his own position) cannot be ruled out. The overlapping consensus idea is nevertheless a discontinuous one since people's rights and duties arise from the different personal moral convictions of each person. That means that Rawls's liberalism must be endorsed for reasons independent of private ethics.

Dworkin's theory—both in the Tanner Lectures and in *Justice for Hedgehogs*—bridges personal ethics and political ethics; it is firmly non-contractarian. It is much more pronounced and refined in *Hedgehogs* but you can see the clear emergence of the idea so much earlier (the Tanner Lectures were in 1990). His view is that our personal moral convictions should provide the foundation principles of liberalism. The originality of the idea is striking, for most people think it is the other way around and that our ethical life is determined by our moral life. In particular, he acknowledges that the personal moral convictions we have will be fundamentally different from what principles of liberalism maintain. For example, while liberalism requires that the community take a stance of neutrality and impartiality towards its members, each person is, in his private ethical convictions, attached and committed to different views and actions (it would be ethically wrong *not* to favor one's wife and children, for example). This distinction casts light upon the weaker and stronger versions of confused liberalism I discussed. Take, for example, the confused argument for liberalism from the basis of the supposed subjectivity of moral judgments. Its attempt to derive neutral principles from the nature of moral argument conceals a proposition about mutual respect contained within each party's private moral convictions. Your views are equal to my views and should be respected since we cannot prove them to each other. That is a continuous strategy. It's not the same—it is considerably less subtle—than supposing liberalism derives from self-interest.

Strong hippie liberalism, according to which all actions are good, is clearly a continuous theory, however. It says that you should adopt as part of your personal ethics the personal ethics of everyone. It does not really make sense, although there are well-meaning people who try to practice it; if not contradictory it is extremely bland. Nevertheless it encourages us to be tolerant, to the extreme, by adopting everyone's personal ethics as continuous with our own.

DISCONTINUITY THEORIES AND CATEGORICAL FORCE

Dworkin attacks Rawls's contractarian account of justice; he thinks it is wrong because it is skeptical. Rawls describes his *A Theory of Justice* as a work of "Kantian constructivism." That, Dworkin says, means he has in his view "constructed" our moral judgments from an "intellectual device" to confront practical problems. Rawls's example of such a construct is Kant's categorical imperative—an intellectual device to help us formulate universal moral rules. Rawls's device of "the original position" is different. It helps him to produce two principles, first the prioritizing of specific individual liberties and second the famous "maximin" principle according to which inequalities are justified in the general political structure only when they work to improve the position of the worse-off. Dworkin asks why we should accept these principles. He had suggested egalitarian reasons in his earlier work, *Taking Rights Seriously*, but Rawls specifically rejected that interpretation.

Dworkin says that Rawls changed his view—to the "overlapping consensus" view—and that it is consistent with Dworkin's continuous and interpretive view. He says that the overlapping consensus does not deny the truth of a comprehensive view but only that Rawlsian constructivism consists of showing that political justice need not depend on moral truth. However, Dworkin politely doubts that this "marginalization" can work, pointing out that Rawls in his later writings relied increasingly on historical and political traditions. Obviously, given the Humean principle, Dworkin says that the sociological method couldn't yield what Rawls wanted, suggesting that Rawls was actually engaging in an "interpretive search," hoping to identify "conceptions and ideals" that would "provide the best account and justification of the liberal traditions." So, Dworkin claims, Rawls's project is not a "morally neutral" project because he would be bound to choose some interpretations to be superior to others. In support of this interpretation, of course, Rawls had already, in *A Theory of Justice*, clearly ruled out utilitarianism. Dworkin provides this account of Rawls's later political philosophy as an example of skepticism about morality that actually turns out, in Dworkin's terms, to be the acceptable sort of skepticism—the internal form. (Dworkin says, using his own terms, that Rawls believed he was engaged in a form of external skepticism).

This is all very polite to Rawls. I find it hard to accept that Rawls believed he was providing a skeptical account of justice; rather, Rawls was just searching for morality in the wrong place. When he gave his famous overlapping consensus lecture (the Hart Memorial Lecture in 1985) it was immediately apparent to many in the audience—I was there—that his view was mistaken for a simple, obvious Humean reason: you can't derive general principles of morality from empirically true political facts. This was an audience that could cope with new ideas and developments, not with outright mistakes.

Dworkin calls his own continuity version of liberalism "political equality."[6] He says that in order to succeed in establishing a liberalism of this kind he will have to show that it has a visionary appeal, the possibility that it will be able to attract support in the form of a consensus, and that it will be sufficiently well justified to provide what he calls "categorical force." All these problems arise from the central difficulty with liberalism that it appears both to allow and disapprove of ways of living. If continuous liberalism is to be derived from people having different moral convictions on what should constitute the correct ways of living, there are going to be great problems with both the vision of the community it encourages and the possibility of a consensus. The promise of political equality looks bleak since what will appeal to one person's moral convictions will not appeal to another's.[7] Since it assumes different ethical views, it is difficult to see what visionary force it can have. Its appeal is not supposed to lie in any person's particular personal ethical perspective. In what, then? The best will be in some idea, such as Rawls's, of "mutual respect and co-operation" but we have seen that there are problems with that idea which might lie in a non-moral, Hobbesian, basis of self-interest. It would seem to follow that if the vision is weak then the possibility of consensus is remote and Dworkin concedes that it is unrealistic to suppose that political liberalism can gain a consensus yet.

These matters would not be so important if categorical force can be found for this form of liberalism, since then, visionary appeal and consensus are at least a possibility. There is a difficulty here, too. How do we find moral justification? People's views are partial and involve commitments to quite differing forms of life and so the hope of finding independent moral force which has appeal within each person's convictions seems only a remote possibility. The discontinuity strategy assumes different ethical perspectives, so that categorical force can only arise from the contract. Here we can return to the paradigm of the ordinary commercial contract, in which the rights and duties flow from the contract and not the personal perspectives of the parties. Briefly, no one is going to accept as binding upon her a proposition which is not part of her personal ethical perspective.

Dworkin is straightforward. There never was any social contract matching the ordinary legal contract. Since there are no rights and duties under ordinary contracts before the contract comes into existence, it is impossible to use the idea of an independent contract as the source of the rights and duties that liberalism requires. This is an obvious argument against the discontinuous contractarian justifications for liberalism. He concludes that discontinuity theories therefore lack categorical force. Do discontinuity theories hold the promise of attracting a consensus about them? It could be argued, as perhaps is Rawls's intention, that both visionary appeal and categorical force arise from the promise, or prediction, that consensus may, in the future, collect around a political structure within the community that ensures "mutual respect and co-operation." Dworkin doubts this, however. Why, he asks, would you be bothered to argue for a consensus which was utterly contrary to what you believed to be right? You would also be caught up in an odd situation. You might find yourself arguing for a consensus that you did not believe in because you thought it was likely to succeed only marginally over the one you could fully endorse. By a margin you assign an entirely different categorical force to the political structure you now support. That, says Dworkin, would be an unconvincing assignment of categorical force because it would be too casual. The discontinuity theory fails in Dworkin's view just because it does not give an adequate answer to the three features of visionary appeal, consensus and categorical force. On the other hand, the continuity strategy copes much better with categorical force and hence visionary appeal. Both of these depend for their success on liberalism being seen from the personal moral perspective. It is easy to endorse a political structure that flows from your own moral convictions and it is not necessary to use some device like the legal contract.

One objection that people will make to this is the one that we saw in Chapter 7 over objectivity. How could objective status attach to a political ideal which was drawn from the necessarily subjective and personal ethical perspectives? People's moral views differ so greatly that it is too much to hope for that the continuity strategy would work (say, in a community where there in fact exists "strong pluralism" in Joseph Raz's sense). What does this objection really mean? We can deal with one (likely) interpretation of it. It is no objection to say that lack of demonstration or proof of the rightness of moral propositions shows that there is no such objective status to the political structure. A more complex interpretation might be that argument is not possible because the diversity and plurality of personal moral views are of a nature that not even modes of argument are shared. It is a more complex view because it allows for controversial true moral propositions. When people talk of irreconcilable conflict (in Dworkin's terms, a "contradiction" of principles, as opposed to "competition") between moral standpoints they mean, in this more complex sense, that the conflict is between different communities sharing different modes of argument. I doubt Dworkin would accept this sort of objection, given both his view on the "internal" skepticism of critical legal scholars, and the remarks he has made on objectivity,[8] that this position could not be accepted as a default position. Merely to point to the fact that people disagree is an insufficient argument for the no right answer position. It is, instead, just an uninteresting—because obvious—statement of the sociology of moral argument. Nevertheless, a problem remains as to how we can have these ideas of partiality and commitment, which are clearly part of our moral convictions, but still only require impartiality and non-commitment, or detachment, at the political level. This fundamental feature of liberalism was the one which sent the contractarians to the idea of the device of the social contract and, to preserve it, the idea of a contract, discontinuous with our personal moral lives, seemed to be a good one.

Dworkin thinks that there are two ways in which we might consider solving this problem. Using the idea familiar in political philosophy, we could say that in matters of state, the "right" takes priority over the "good" and so this would allow morality rather than ethics to govern politics, where, as Dworkin says, "the stakes are higher." This will not do in his view, however. Why should morality be sovereign in the political sphere? Why should it not also be sovereign in the personal sphere? In any case, our ideas of personal well-being and the moral requirements and permissions of the political sphere are not clearly separate. For example, fairness is a moral idea common to both spheres, and yet at the personal level it allows partiality towards friends and family. In fact, the right/good priority is not sensitive to the bridge that exists between the moral principles both at the personal level and at the political level.

THE INTERPRETATION OF JUSTICE

Dworkin suggests that another way of uniting the two perspectives would be to adopt the interpretive approach. Take Rawls's political conception of justice which supposedly gains its categorical force, as well as its consensual promise, from the overlapping consensus. We can see that in some sense the principles of this conception are thought by him to be "latent" within the community. An interpretive judgment extrapolates these principles by making best sense of the principles of justice that members of the community actually accept. This strategy aims to provide a single theory of justice from a number of different, overlapping ones and, for this reason, appears to be attractive. Dworkin does not think it would work, however, since he thinks that it is unlikely to be able to cope with the dimension of "fit." Imagine that, in the United States, there was significant degree of consensus on what the correct set of political principles are, but on some matter there were two possible and equally plausible interpretations of that consensus. For example, one is that the consensus is best understood in terms of fairness and the other is best understood as utilitarianism. How do we decide which is the correct interpretation? Obviously, the answer is not going to lie *in* the consensus since an independent judgment must be made about what that consensus means. That independent judgment must be provided for within a theory of justice which is more abstract than the theory that says that the principles lie within the consensus. That further theory of justice, Dworkin says, must be the one that supplies the categorical force:

> At some point we must rely on what (we believe) is *true* about matters of justice in order to decide which interpretation of our own traditions—which way of telling our story—is best.[9]

At times this argument seems to be a dressed-up version of the early utilitarian distinction between positive and critical morality, which relies in turn on Hume's principle. What people happen to believe, however many people there are and however few dissenting views there are, cannot be a final criterion of what is just. If this is the argument it is a good one (although more straightforward the way I put it) but in my experience it is incomprehensible to people who can't stomach propositions about justice being true. Dworkin wrote this before *Justice for Hedgehogs* and it was a little puzzling. What he had said suggested that interpreting justice is not like interpreting other social practices and that it is not possible to appeal to an ideal of justice when making judgments about what, in an actually existing community, constitutes a just political structure. Earlier, in *Law's Empire*, after stating that justice is the "most distinctly political" of the moral ideals, he says:

> Interpretations of justice cannot themselves appeal to justice, and this helps to explain the philosophical complexity and ambition of many theories of justice. For once justice is ruled out as the point of a fundamental and pervasive political practice; it is natural to turn for a justification to initially non-political ideas, like human nature or the theory of the self, rather than to other political ideas that seem no more important or fundamental than justice itself.[10]

Justice for Hedgehogs now makes it clear what he was getting at. I think it is that all evaluative judgments are interpretive, although he nowhere puts it like this. But his unity of value theory (Chapter 9) makes it clear that the concepts of morality are interpretive—we continually reinterpret our moral traditions and they expand, change, refine, and so on as a result. We must conclude that justice is interpretive and that this passage from *Law's Empire* means that when we come to assess values we must—and can only—assess them by nesting them within other values that we hold; in his examples these are value judgments about human nature and self-identity.

We need to refer back to the idea of measuring equality of resources by use of the envy test. Dworkin's view, you will remember, is that people should be made equal in their impersonal resources and that because, in the real world, people have different personal resources and have different luck, liberal equality requires compensation for the resulting inequalities of resource. He said that there should be redistributive tax which mimics a hypothetical insurance market, the purpose of which is to calculate the true cost to all other members of the community. Further, within the sphere of thus equalized impersonal resources, each person should be free; treating people as equals means that invasions of liberty are invasions of equality as well: crudely, equality of resources would be defeated by lack of freedom. In his terms, a *principle of abstraction* (maximum freedom) operates to maintain resource equilibrium through a *bridge principle* (we can always cross the bridge back to this fundamental principle). Naturally, constraints on freedom will be justified to protect this scheme since it is founded upon freedom, and equality requires that we are only free so far as not harming others; such constraints will include, for example, the protection of each person's personal security. But infringements of other sorts of exercise of freedom where overall principle of freedom is not being endorsed—no harm to others—are not justified as, for example, community intervention to prevent certain sorts of consensual sexual behavior.

CRITICAL WELL-BEING AND THE WORTHWHILE LIFE

What is important about one's life, according to Dworkin, is constituted not by what one wants, what he calls *volitional well-being*, but by one's *critical well-being*, which refers to a more sophisticated account of what you and I want. Critical well-being is what—in some senses—you should want as opposed to what you actually want, which is volitional well-being. Simple satisfaction of desires (for example, pleasure) is too basic and unstructured an idea to give a decent account of what it is that we think is good in life. We want what is good in life; however, we do not seriously think that what is good and worthwhile in life is obtained by simple volitional desires. Your and my lives are not better lives just because our desires, such as being able to lift weights better, or eat better food, are satisfied, nor are our lives worse merely because we suffered in the dentist's chair. Not that these things are irrelevant, but these sorts of want satisfactions and dissatisfactions can't be constitutive of good and bad lives. There are, however, desires which *do* matter, those that relate to what you think is of fundamental importance to your life, such as achieving a certain kind of life. Dworkin suggests, as an example, the desire to have a better relationship with your family.

I am not sure that the distinction amounts to much more than a distinction between what we regard as less or more important in our lives. He is keen to say that his distinction between the volitional and the critical does not involve him in asserting a distinction between subjective and objective wants. Given the general unease which he—I think rightly—feels about that distinction, that is not surprising. But I can employ those terms to express quite usefully the distinction in terms of what I subjectively want which is less important, and perhaps volitional, and what is more important and critical. We can use the distinction objectively, too. A person can wrongly judge what it is critically in his interest to do. He can be wrong, in other words, about what is important in his life, not from the perspective of his own personal ethics, but from an independent—objective—standpoint. Objective success theories of welfare were dismissed by Dworkin in "Equality of Welfare" because objectivist theories assumed a resources metric, like the subjectivist theories.[11] For Dworkin, I suspect that for the volitional-critical distinction, the subjective approach is the important one since that best brings out the liberal emphasis on personal freedom. To do otherwise is to endorse a paternal attitude to what people should want and what they should judge as critical in their lives. What at first sight appears as a judgment of the psychology of personal ethical judgments is actually a judgment about what is an ethical requirement: people's judgments about what is important in their lives is important for what constitutes their good life. These judgments must be ones that are personal to them.

Dworkin first draws some distinctions. He first distinguishes between the "product" value of a life, measured by what that life produces, and a life's "performance" value, measured by how a life is lived. To use his examples, a life of good product value would be something like Mozart's life, because he produced great works of music, or Alexander Fleming's life, because he discovered penicillin. A life of good performance value, on the other hand, would be one where a person responds to his circumstances in, as Dworkin says, an appropriate way. It is possible that a composer lives a life that has both performance and product value where we judge his life, lived as a performance, as achieving value from the way he lives it—what he calls in *Justice for Hedgehogs* its adverbial value—without making any judgment about what he produced and then make the independent judgment that what he produced is of value.

Dworkin says that what is of critical value about a person's life only makes sense in terms of the performance value of a life. Otherwise, he says, for most of us our lives would be, in his term, puny if compared to, say, Mozart or Fleming. If we judge lives according to their performance then, because our lives are "parametered" by our particular capacities, our performance relates to those capacities and the product of our lives is of secondary importance. Although the highly gifted person produces something of great value compared with what I produce, my performance in life could be better. There is a lot of sense in this (the sense of the idea that it is not whether you win or lose but how you play the game). He gives the example of Fleming's janitor who disobeys his instructions and omits to throw away the moldy culture dish from which Fleming discovered penicillin. That Fleming's janitor's life had product value makes no difference to the question whether Fleming's janitor lived a critically good life. Briefly, he still broke his duty even though the consequences turned out to be good. Dworkin uses a similar argument here to the one he used to derive the tax on talents: the appeal of the idea lies in our not wanting to praise people for doing what it is thoroughly easy for them to do. This attitude that desert should take a secondary place, if any place, in a liberal understanding of society, is a common strand to liberal attitudes.

Dworkin also argues that it is important for critical well-being that each person approves, or endorses, what he does, because it is confused to live a life which is good but which you yourself do not approve. For him, this feature of approval must not just be an "additive" to the good life you lead but must also be constitutive of it. Dworkin says the additive view fits the product value model much better. A person who values what he has produced has more value in his life, thereby, than someone who does not. The idea that one is sovereign in the judgment as to what is critically successful as a product of one's life would, in my view, be thoroughly odd. Dworkin does not go into this question because he prefers the performance model. Consider that Mozart's life is better for his having endorsed his products, as it were, than if he had merely produced the works for money. It does not make much sense to suppose that Mozart's symphonies are better than his quartets because he considered them better. It is not difficult to think of examples where we can say that we thought that composers, artists and so on were wrong in their judgments of what they thought was good.

MORE DISTINCTIONS

In order to provide an additional argument for rejecting the product value Dworkin also distinguishes between *transcendent* and *indexed* accounts of the good life. A transcendent account judges a person's life in a way that transcends a person's particular circumstances. One way of making that judgment would be by employing the idea of how much pleasure people experience in their lives. If two people are equal in their capacity for pleasure and they have equal means of fulfilling it, the person who lives longer has more pleasure in her life. Obviously, the transcendent account fits the product value of a person's life rather than the performance model. An *indexed* account of one's life, on the other hand, is a judgment about what is good about a person's life given the particular circumstances of that person. This idea is central for Dworkin, since it connects what a person achieves to the parameters which surround a person's actions. My failure to achieve through circumstances, he says, is not a limit to my well-being but a parameter. If what is valuable about our lives is what we transcendently achieve we shall always think that circumstances limit us. If we think that our achievements are fundamentally indexed to, or linked to, our personal circumstances then our judgments of value are markedly different. Thus he says:

> It seems irresistible that living well, judged as a performance, means among other things living in a way responsive and appropriate to one's culture and other circumstances. A life of chivalrous and courtly virtue might have been a very good one in twelfth-century Bohemia but not in Brooklyn now.[12]

It becomes clear where Dworkin is going. He dismisses transcendental judgments because he favors lives of critical performance. People's achievements are to be indexed to the parameters of their circumstances and these will include all those things which enter into the judgment about whether a life has been critically worthwhile. For example, they will include a person's character and his volitional interests. They will also include his critical interests, for they will provide the background against which he enacts his life. The parameters will also include the expected length of life. For example, the value in what a person does, in the only life for him to lead, will be parametered by some expectation about lifespan, say, the upper end of the average lifespan of the present generation. Only under this assumption, says Dworkin, can we make "critical" sense of saying that it was a misfortune for a person to die young. That expresses a judgment about that person's missing out on a life we would have expected. The resources we have available over our lifetime must also be a parameter. If they were not, says Dworkin, we would have to accept the absurd idea that the only critically good life would be an immortal life with limitless resources.

Under the transcendent or product views we would counter-intuitively conclude that had Mozart died when he was fourteen, since he had already produced a number of great pieces of music, there was no great value lost by his early death. That is not counter-intuitive because we would have hoped for more of value to have been produced by Mozart measured in product or transcendent terms. At the other end of the age spectrum, we feel that, for some people, there was more that they could have done which would have made their lives (critically) better. Nevertheless, I believe that we have a strong intuition that both product and transcendent values are important in making judgments about the value in people's lives. True, Mozart's critically good life ought to be judged from the point of view of his own convictions about what was important to him—one presumes his music—and his own understandings of the time he had to do what he wanted to do. On the other hand, there is some room for the product sense of what counts as value. Mozart undoubtedly aimed at producing what actually was to be good art on the product model. We can agree that Mozart's convictions about the worthwhile life constitute a significant parameter on the final judgment but it is difficult to ignore the fact that this would, too, include a significant judgment, by him, on his life judged upon a product model.

JUSTICE AND THE WORTHWHILE LIFE

We can now conclude the discussion. Dworkin included, reasonably enough, resources as a parameter of the critically good life. But it is difficult to say that a person's life is critically good when measured against the resources he actually has because it is an insight to say that a person's life was not a good one just because he had too few resources. This point is most important for Dworkin. The resources that parameter a person's critically good life are those which justice says he ought to have; the best life is one that he can lead with the resources that the best theory of distributive justice would give him. This is a major thesis and unites in Dworkin his theories of equality and of the good life. To those who say that equality is an empty and formal concept,[13] he can answer that respect requires that people have space to live a critically good life. Justice connects continuously with our personal ethics by limiting the amount of resources a person may have to live a critically good life. It achieves that connection by respecting others as equals since the measure of resources is its true cost to other people. Dworkin claims here that there is in this idea the appeal of Plato's claim that justice is always in a person's interests, saying that the critically ideal life is the best life we could lead if we had at our disposal the material and other resources that the best theory of justice entitles us to have.[14]

To sum up, the question whether I have lived a critically good life is indexed to what I am entitled to in justice. It follows that, for example,

I cannot have a *reasonable* regret that I did not succeed in political life if I could only have succeeded had I started with an unjust amount of resources. Conversely, I can have reasonable regrets about having lived well despite my having only a pauper's share of resources.[15] Justice affects my private space by setting major parameters around that space and the way I live is colored by the justice of the freedom that is distributed to me. Since I cannot escape the effect justice has on my own ethical life, justice and my personal ethics cannot be separated. The result is that justice is to be seen as an integral part of my ethical life and is inseparably connected with my (right) convictions. That means that a proper concern for my own personal ethical life must lead me to a proper concern for the just distribution of freedoms in the community. The continuity between personal ethics and the political structure is, in Dworkin's view, thereby established.

We now need to examine aspects of the ethical life over which governments often feel they have a right to employ their considerable powers of control. These aspects are often connected through religious awe; they are the problems of what constitutes the rights and wrongs of preventing people from coming into being, encouraging people to go out of being, and making decisions on behalf of all as to what constitutes answers to the deepest ethical questions of all, such as who we are and what our purposes are and how we connect with the cosmos. These are the questions of abortion and euthanasia, and the question concerning the extent to which the community has a right to enforce religious orthodoxy.

CHAPTER TWELVE

Religion and the Beginning and End of Life

Dworkin is sometimes thought to base his entire view of morality on the idea of rights. This is true in one important sense since he thinks, as we have seen, that each person has a right to dignity—to equality and to liberty. It is why I think equality is the most fundamental value in his theory of morality: a person's dignity is never in the balance except where another person's dignity, equally weighed, requires it; so in this sense, the right to dignity is fundamental. It does not follow, however, that Dworkin denies other ways of expressing ethical and moral value. For our own individual dignity depends on judgments we make that do not concern the rights of other people but that concern ways we view ourselves, our relations with others and our relationship with—there is no other way of putting it—the cosmos. There are two parts to Dworkin's work that bring this non-rights dimension out: his brief important remarks about the status of religion and religious experience in *Justice for Hedgehogs*, and his earlier and much more extensive treatment of abortion and euthanasia in *Life's Dominion*. Both parts concern what he calls "intrinsic" value and, at times, "secular sacredness." Briefly, such values are of a different category from those values, the protection of which is appropriately expressed as rights. They are of great importance.

"INTEGRATED EPISTEMOLOGY" AND RELIGION

Dworkin points out that our thoughts have to be about something and so naturally our thoughts are dependent on what that thing is. The reasons then multiply for everything we believe because they, too, must be supported by reasons we believe. It never ends. Thus Dworkin says, "There is no such thing as an entirely abstract condition on knowledge."[1] That our beliefs are caused by the existence of empirical facts is plausible in science, because these facts contribute to the truth of facts: they are evidence of facts. In the case of value, however, Dworkin says that the idea of the cause of our beliefs is senseless; it is argument other than argument from evidence. That distinction between evidence and argument is uncontroversially accepted, note, in all modern legal systems where there are separate principles that determine how facts are to be proved, from arguments about what the law is that applies to those facts. Unity of value requires that our system of beliefs forms an "integrated epistemology" in which we assume truths about, say, optics or biology even though we use scientific method to confirm those truths. The problem with such epistemology—Dworkin calls it *Archimedean*, after the Greek philosopher who said he could do all sorts of things if he could only stand outside the world—is that it assumes an abstract way of understanding all knowledge but excludes itself from that knowledge. Instead, Dworkin says, "Abstract epistemology and concrete belief must fit and support each other, and neither must be given a veto over the other."[2] It follows that we can't just believe something because "it would be nice to believe," because—as we saw in Chapter 9—our beliefs must integrate with a full epistemological account of our other beliefs.

Religious convictions therefore often offer a challenge to the unity of value thesis because many people hold strong convictions that are contrary to their general principles of "respectable belief." People believe in miracles, for example, which by definition are miraculous because what people claim to have occurred does so outside orthodox rational expectation. Such beliefs can be accounted for in two ways. First, religious philosophers might try to show that scientific method can explain religious claims, for example, by a theory such as that of intelligent design—that there is some super-intelligent and super-powerful intelligent being who has "designed" the occurrence of the miracle. Second, religious philosophers might go in the opposite direction and revise their "general epistemology" so that it can fit those of the religious beliefs in miracles that people are unwilling to give up, perhaps because they have a special sense of "heightened awe." Dworkin's view about theories such as intelligent design is that they are implausible science.[3] Contrary to many critics of intelligent design, Dworkin thinks that we can accept it as a possible scientific theory. This seems right, since it is a theory that purports to explain the whole field of empirical knowledge in terms of its being both coherent and rationally constructed. But it is a wildly implausible theory.

Dworkin says we should distinguish three claims often made in support of the theory of intelligent design: (i) that scientists have not fully established that Darwinian processes are at work; (ii) that there is good scientific evidence that certain features of the world are not amenable to Darwinian explanation; and (iii) that this evidence suggests that an intelligent designer created the processes of development that produced human beings. Dworkin says (i) is true. Although scientists overall accept the Darwinian explanation, there are pockets of controversy about the application of Darwin in particular instances. He says (ii) is false, however; it doesn't follow that because there is controversy about the application of any particular theory that it is thereby defective, any more than that would follow from, say, any historical or mathematical theory. More of an argument is needed and none has been forthcoming. Claim (iii), he says, would be false even if claim (ii) were true, for science depends on evidence and the mere absence of a scientific explanation can't be evidence. In any case, the unwritten hand behind the "theory of intelligent design" is that of the existence of a god. If it was controversial that smoking caused lung cancer, that fact would not be evidence that it was a god who caused lung cancer, or that global warming was all done by a god who raises and lowers temperature as he wishes. "Very few socially conservative Americans would vote for a school board that allowed teachers to explain anything they wished by citing a supernatural intelligence at work," he says.

It is important to see that Dworkin is not knocking religious belief here. Rather, he is keen to maintain the distinction between reason and faith:

> Science can provide no reason for restricting appeals to supernatural intelligence to those that confirm the claims of a particular religious tradition. Only faith can do that, and faiths differ dramatically. So once appeals to a supernatural intelligence are recognized as competitive with scientific explanations, the damage to reason cannot be limited or controlled.[4]

Why, for example, should we suppose that the intelligent being at the same time is identical to the "Abrahamic God"? he asks. It is not *just* implausible science, either. Our sense-perception in ordinary day-to-day thinking about things must integrate with theories of scientific method—those explanations that make us look for evidence to support our perceptions and abandon explanations falsified by evidence. But we have no method of integrating what we believe through a "sense of awe" with anything that explains it. Further, if religious belief depends on our sense-perception, how could we possibly explain the great diversity of religious belief? People have all sorts of religious beliefs that are incompatible.

Any "integrated epistemology," Dworkin says, should guard against "two tyrannies." The first is that of feeling one can stand outside matters—Archimedeanism—and be insensitive to the force of particular intellectual domains and so deny the force of religious belief altogether. The second tyranny is that of supposing we can have discrete convictions that require a special *ad hoc* exception to how we ordinarily form reasonable beliefs. Therefore, merely believing in that *ad hoc* way of creating something that completely contradicts all those other things that we believe through evidence of how we behave and talk will not be sufficient. He emphasizes that if we believe something deeply, we have to believe it, although he adds we should only do so because we also believe there is no "decisive refutation" of it.

THE RELIGIOUS TEMPERAMENT

For most people, living well requires, to use E. M. Forster's phrase, "connecting" appropriately to their circumstances—their culture, for example, or their locality, in accordance with the history or traditions they find themselves in. For many, there is such a thing as a "religious temperament" which seeks some connection with "the universe," that whole world in which human beings find themselves.[5] Even non-believers, Dworkin says, respond at different levels with an answer to the question of how our lives fit with "the universe," for example, by the story of our evolution, or more grandly as a part of a "vastly larger story" of the evolution of the universe itself. They may do so even by responding to the challenge of connection by showing that there is *no* connection and that our lives have value independent of the universe. Dworkin asks first why people should "find value" in these ways of thinking, and second how people should respond to this perceived value. His answer to the first question is that we want to live non-arbitrary lives, which is right, he says, because that adds to the "adverbial" value of our lives. It is not an arbitrary life if its value consists in how well it is lived. The answer to the second question is that people can live well in response to the view that there is "no point or purpose in the universe":

> Why must value depend on physics? From this perspective, it is the assumption that ethical value does depend on eternity, that it can be undermined by cosmology, that seems absurd. It is just another in the endless string of temptations to violate Hume's principle.[6]

Hume's principle, you will remember, states that we cannot derive matters of value from matters of fact; if Dworkin's arguments in support of it are right (see Chapter 9), then whatever we learn about science, however random the creation of the Universe appears to be, however chaotic are the movements of everything physical, our moral life is completely unaffected.

GOD AND HUMAN RIGHTS

A basic human right is a right to believe—the right to conscience in the First Amendment of the U.S. Constitution, mirrored in Article 18 of the Universal Declaration of Human Rights ("Everyone has the right to freedom of thought, conscience and religion"). It means we have a right to a religious belief, irrespective of our religion, and even if we don't have a religious belief. If we think religion justifies human rights it is therefore difficult to see how we are able to justify this basic human right of religious tolerance. If we tolerate someone's beliefs and behavior, that means that we disapprove of it but recognize it as in accordance with some right we believe that person to have. So certainly our own religion can't found that right; and so it follows that neither can any other. In short, no divine authority can provide the ground because, Dworkin says, human rights are "independent and logically prior" to accepting divine authority.

Dworkin says that this argument about human rights is perfectly consistent with accepting that there is a god who created the cosmos. Religions have two parts, a cosmological ("is") part ("God created the earth") and an evaluative ("ought") part ("God requires you to obey the Ten Commandments") although many people find this an illegitimate distinction. If we can't derive value from fact, you can believe a god exists, and that a god issued you commands; but not that you have a *moral* reason to obey a god's commands. You need an additional premise, just the same as for secular rulers. The difficulty here was expressed in an ancient theological controversy. Could gods be good because they obeyed moral laws, or were these laws moral because they had created them? This was often phrased as a dilemma. If the gods obeyed them then they were good but not omnipotent. If, on the other hand, the gods were omnipotent and had created morality then it was not interesting to say that they were good; it would just follow from the fact that they were able to create moral rules. Dworkin says this is not a true dilemma because no one can create morality without violating Hume's principle. It does not follow that no god can have moral authority; it is just not automatic that a god—by being a god—has moral authority.

The fact that gods are omnipotent, so powerful that they can punish people by bringing AIDS upon them or by rewarding suicide bombers, say, is irrelevant: threats and bribes don't create obligations. That a god created us doesn't mean he can impose obligations on us. A sculptor can't impose obligations on the sculpture he has created. The closest one could get would be where the parents "create" their child, although that is still an odd way of putting it, he says, and we might want to say that children's duties to their parents are created by their parents.[7] But duties can't be created in this way. The moral duties that children have arise independently from social practices that impose such duties upon, not just the natural parents but adoptive parents and, in some cultures, the community as a whole. Further, Dworkin says that faith alone can't invest a god with moral authority—an argument sometimes called the epistemic power of faith. The reason is that a god's moral authority could not be determined as a bare fact. We can't just expect moral authority to arise out of the identification of the unique nature of a god, even if a god could be identified by faith alone:

> If we claim that a god has moral authority over all peoples then we must suppose an equal divine concern and respect for all peoples.[8]

Dworkin says his arguments here are not intended to denigrate religion but that, rather, his aim has been to place the case for human rights "on a different plane."

GOD'S ATTITUDE TOWARDS US

It is useful to distinguish between two kinds of respect we have for people. One is basic and not variable or, we might say, non-negotiable: we must, as soon as we recognize that another person is a human being, accord to them the same equality of respect; that is, a human being has objective equal value to every other human being. The second—judgmental or appraisal respect—is variable; it means that we might respect people in varying degrees according to how we judge their character and behavior: a person may be equal as a human being and entitled to respect for that reason but live a worthless life for which no respect is due. Dworkin asks what sort of god wouldn't care about converting less worthy human beings to worshipping him. Imagine a religion that justified slaughter on the ground that its members have special importance. One would assume that any plausible god who valued human dignity would respect people as a matter of recognition as people, not on the ground that they are particular people who have achieved worthwhile lives. If God respects human dignity then God must also respect the personal responsibility of human beings.

Also He would not respect dignity if a human being was required only to go through the external motions of believing in Him. In any case, God will be aware of the internal disbelief. A person must, in exercise of his personal responsibility to make something of his life, endorse that religion. So God can't force a religion on us because we can only choose our religion freely if we are to believe in that religion properly, that is, with dignity.

Of course, people only have a right to independence in matters such as religious choice so far as it doesn't interfere with those same rights to independence possessed by others. Dworkin adds that torture is the "most profound outrage" on dignity because it consists of the complete subjugation of the human being; it denies both the right to be treated as of equal objective value to all other human beings and the right to act as the responsible author of one's own life. So the Inquisition—in which people were tortured because they were considered heretics—was not only a catastrophic affront to human dignity on both counts, it was a terrible contradiction of religion.

ABORTION

As with reverse discrimination, Dworkin's arguments for the moral rightness of abortion in wide circumstances and the moral rightness of euthanasia speak to the wide moral audience and not just to the U.S. Constitution. I shall deal with his arguments in turn although you should appreciate that his arguments for both derive from the same moral principles. Fundamental is his distinction between *derivative* and *detached* objections to the intentional ending of human life. A derivative objection derives from the view that a fetus has rights and interests which should be protected. A detached objection depends on no such view but declares, from a detached point of view, that human life, whether fetal or irreversibly comatose, has fundamental intrinsic value: it is not a matter of anyone having rights that need to be protected but that there is, instead, something of important value that should be preserved. The difference is brought out in the sort of case where people declare that something should (or should not) be done to a person because that is right, even though it would not be in that person's interests to be the object of that action or inaction. A good example is the U.S. case, well-known as the *Nancy Cruzan* case, in which the court declared that it was wrong to withdraw feeding tubes from a patient. The court said clearly that it was in the patient's interest to die but it said that she should, nevertheless, remain alive out of respect for sanctity of life.

It is people who have rights and interests, says Dworkin. Although pro-lifers say life begins at conception, Dworkin says few people, whatever they say, actually believe that a fetus is a person and that it could be murder to kill an early-term fetus, as it clearly would be if the early-term fetus were a person. Of course people think it is wrong, just not murder. At least in the criminal law, the offence has always been that of abortion rather than mur-der. Statistics support that view, since a significant number of people think abortion wrong but not quite murder. At least some explanation might be offered of why people's intuitions on these two sorts of killing differ.

What is the basis for saying that something has rights or interests? Merely being en route to becoming a human being is not sufficient in itself for rights and interests, he says. And it makes no sense to suppose that something has interests of its own—as distinct from it being important what happens to it—unless it has, or has had, some form of consciousness in the form of some mental and physical life. So, he concludes, on this hypothesis fetuses do not have interests at least before the cortex has formed (the absence of which means no consciousness) and therefore no interest in surviving. An important corollary to this argument is that because a living thing has interests now, such as Frankenstein's monster as soon as it was given life by Dr. Frankenstein, doesn't mean that it had them before. Dworkin gives the example of the pregnant woman who smokes. It is wrong for her to smoke because that will damage the interests of someone who will come into being. However, if she aborts, no person exists whose interests have been affected.

So how do we approach the question of when life begins? Is it a matter of reporting a biological fact, such as implantation in the womb, or earlier, at conception? No, says Dworkin, it is in large part a moral question, since the question of whether a fetus is a human, either at conception or at some later point in pregnancy, is simply "too ambiguous to be useful." These sorts of questions should be set aside since we do not have to consider when life begins, or whether fetuses are people, in order to consider whether they have interests which should be protected by rights, or whether the life of a fetus is sacred whether or not it has interests.

How do we explain the idea of an "intrinsically valuable life"? He says that we discover the idea of sacredness when we say, for example, that a lost life was "intrinsically regrettable." It means that it was wrong in itself in a way that is meant to be independent of whether it is instrumental to some-thing further (like money, which is clearly not intrinsically valuable) and also independent of whether it is subjectively valuable (single malt whiskies are valuable in a way that is not instrumental but nevertheless not independent, either). It is not too difficult an idea: we think Rembrandt's portraits are wonderful, for example, for these sorts of non-instrumental, subjective reasons. We look at them because they are independently good. Human life can be instrumentally, subjectively and independently good. ("He cooks for me, I enjoy his company and he's honest.") We do, of course, differ in our views of what counts as sacred but that does not matter since it only reflects our different conceptions of that idea. Our differences reflect our views as to what shows contempt or respect for the sacred and that is just another way of saying that we are united in valuing the sacred. These differences arise in all sorts of ways. We perceive degrees of sacredness, classifying works of art, for example, in terms of minor and major paintings and, further, we exercise a degree of selectivity in what we count as sacred, as when we consider the AIDS virus, or the meningitis bacterium—both forms of life—not to have sacred quality. There are two ideas, Dworkin thinks, in the idea that life itself is sacred. One is that life is sacred because it is uniquely created in nature. This idea is in Hamlet's remark "what a piece of work is Man." There is also the idea that human lives are intentionally created, in the sense in which we think of ourselves as our own creation. These two ideas correspond to a distinction the Greeks drew between *zoe,* which meant the biological life of a person, and that person's *bios,* meaning the life *as it is lived* by that person. "The horror we feel in the willful destruction of a human life," says Dworkin, "reflects our shared inarticulate sense of the intrinsic importance of each of these dimensions of investment."[9]

When we judge a life's intrinsic worth how do we make comparative judgments? What is the metric of respect that we use? For example, why does a later abortion seem more regrettable than an earlier one, and why is it worse that a young person die than an old person? That we can sensibly ask these questions shows that the metric of respect is not dependent on the idea of rights or interests. It is clear that if we take the position that fetuses have rights and interests, they still have those irrespective of their age, and so precisely the same argument applies to old people (who have as much right to live as young people). Further, what is, in any case, meant by "a waste of a life"? Dworkin thinks neither the length of the life, nor its quality, are the correct ideas here. Length of life does not work for abortion since an early abortion is better than a later one and death becomes less tragic the older you get once you are born. Quality-of-life arguments do not work, either, because life does not become qualitatively better by incremental steps of quality so that you can say: this early death is tragic because there were things of quality that could have been lived in the future since that, says

Dworkin, "ignores the crucial truth that waste of life is often greater and more tragic because of what has already happened in the past."[10] Dworkin thinks it is much better to see waste of life in terms of frustration rather than simple loss. The metric of that frustration of investments will depend on the stage of life, bearing in mind a natural life span. The explanation is much richer than the simple loss of life because it takes account of what has been put into a life in ambition, expectations, plans, projects, relationships and emotional involvements and measures the tragedy against these rather than against what might have been.

In Dworkin's view, the two crucial questions are (i) When are rights and interests acquired? and (ii) When does a life embody intrinsic value? In order to get into these questions, Dworkin looks in turn at the conservative and the liberal arguments. He says there are two kinds of conservative view. The first is that abortion is wrong and the state has a right to ban it; the second is that abortion is wrong but the decision to abort is entirely a private one. To both of these positions there are common exceptions. One is the well-known one that abortions are permitted in order to save the life of the mother. Dworkin says that this doesn't make sense, since there is no reason for supposing that the mother's life counts more than the fetus's, and the argument sometimes advanced that the mother is acting in self-defense does not work since the fetus is innocent and in any case it is the doctor and not the mother who most frequently carries out the abortion. The other well-known exception is rape. That is even more confused. Why should the wholly innocent party—the fetus—be killed because it was conceived as the result of rape? Dworkin then turns to the liberal arguments. Liberals mostly do not think of abortion as merely a "surgical procedure" and so share the conservative view that intentional killing of the fetus is wrong. The paradigmatic liberal position, he says, is that (i) the decision to have an abortion is a grave one; (ii) it is justified, nevertheless, for some reasons (but not to determine sex, or to make a European trip easier); (iii) the interests of the mother and family are an acceptable part of the reasons to abort; and (iv) the state has no business in at least the early stages.

Can we reconcile both conservative and liberal reservations about abortion at any level? Dworkin says that the conservatives and the liberals are united in thinking that it is not rights, nor interests, that determine what is wrong with abortion, for any of the defenses they permit for abortion would not otherwise make sense. What is it about abortion then that makes it wrong for both camps? Dworkin's answer is that it lies in the respect we have for sanctity of life—a feeling for its sacred and intrinsic quality—and this means that the correct view of abortion is the detached one. If he is right, then he has found a basis upon which conservatives and liberals can unite and he has succeeded in destroying the idea that the conservatives and liberals merely trade in moral absolutes.

Dworkin regards abortion as intrinsically wrong because it is the frustration of an investment in a unique human life. If it is true that both conservatives and liberals agree on this, then it is important to see why they nevertheless disagree. His answer is that conservatives place more weight on the divine nature of human life, that is, on the naturally created investment; liberals, on the other hand, place more weight on the human investment. Each side accepts sacredness of natural and deliberate investments and the difference is not one of non-arguable absolutes, but of different emphases. We can see this point in the fact that almost all conservatives accept that abortion is sometimes permissible, since most conservatives allow exceptions where the mother's life is at stake. This can only mean that almost all conservatives accept that sometimes the interests of the mother outweigh the intrinsic quality of life. There is, too, a common exception for rape and that can be explained, first, by the view that life beginning in rape is "an insult"—not a proper investment—which suggests a view about life's intrinsic worth that is distinct from the fetus's interests or rights; and second, by the idea that rape is a desecration of a woman's own investment in her own life, a view that is also consistent with sacredness. Liberals allow abortion when quality of life of the future child and/or the mother or family is at stake; the quality of life of the future child cannot be for them a judgment about the worth of a person's life, since that would imply—contrary to liberal principles—contempt for lives that lack quality. That is to say, liberals would not permit an abortion on the ground that inferior lives are not worth living. Rather, it is on the more straightforward ground that, once the child comes into existence, it is important that the child's life have quality. As far as the lives of the mother and family are concerned, the concern for the mother and family are based on endorsement of intrinsic value for human life.

Ethical independence requires religious freedom, says Dworkin. It used to be the case that tolerating it was the best way to civil peace and so religious freedom was granted for instrumental reasons, not reasons of principle. If we accept this justification then there is nothing *sui generis* about it: the same principle supports "other foundational ethical choices," for example, reproduction, marriage and sexual orientation. This is important in the case of abortion. The first principle is that "human life is of intrinsic importance," but if an early fetus is "no more than a flower," having no interests of its own, our duty to help the early fetus is different because it has no rights protecting any interests. There is an ethical issue, too: abortion might be disrespect-ful to human dignity—as Dworkin has argued, great paintings shouldn't be destroyed although they don't have interests. Then the moral question must be decided collectively, for example, whether to forbid murder. If it is not murder, then the question is an ethical one and the government cannot decide for the woman: "It must be left to women, as their dignity demands, each to take responsibility for her own ethical convictions."[11]

CONSTITUTIONAL ARGUMENTS ABOUT ABORTION

Dworkin has spent much effort in making sense of the constitutional wrangles on abortion in the United States that have arisen since *Roe* v. *Wade* which, in 1973, recognized a mother's rights to an abortion in both the first and second trimesters of pregnancy as part of the right to privacy.[12] He says that the judges took that right in different ways. Judge Blackmun, for example, thought that it was a strong right which required a "compelling reason" to overturn whereas Judge Rehnquist thought that it was a weak right which a state could overturn if the reasons given were merely rational. Dworkin thinks that the "weaker" approach is wrong since it is well established that there is a strong right to contraception as demonstrated in *Griswold* v. *Connecticut* and there is no principled distinction between the right not to beget and the right not to bear.[13]

The question remains, though, whether there is a compelling reason to restrict a woman's right to abortion. Maybe yes, says Dworkin, where life is at stake. Is the fetus a constitutional person? If so, then there would be the most compelling of reasons to prohibit even very early abortions for it would be murder intentionally to kill the fetus. "Person" is part of the Constitution because of the Fourteenth Amendment which states "No state shall deny any person equal protection of the laws." If the fetus were a constitutional person then states would be under a duty to protect it. Therefore, anyone who claims that states have a right to choose to prohibit abortion, has already accepted that fetuses are not constitutional persons. This a powerful point although, of course, the Constitution is always open to interpretations which might show this interpretation to be mistaken. Dworkin also considers whether the indi-vidual states could make a fetus a constitutional person, perhaps on the ground that permitting abortions would encourage a "killing culture." He doubts that protection of the fetus is within the national constitutional arrangements—which the states cannot override—and, in any case, there is no evidence of a relationship between "killing cultures," which the United States might be said to have already, and liberal laws on abortion. In European countries where there are more liberal rules on abortion there is no "killing culture."

Nevertheless, two questions remain. Would it follow from a fetus's not being a person that a woman's right to control her own role in procreation be defended? And do the states have a compelling detached reason for forbidding abortion? The opponents of *Roe* v. *Wade* argue that the constitution does not *mention* the right and, in any case, this was not the intention of those who created the constitution. As we have seen, Dworkin opposes that view of the constitution with the idea of the "constitution of principle" and, he says:

> The narrow, detailed conception of our Constitution is not even an option for contemporary America, and pretending to adopt it would provide no real check on judges' power to impose their own convictions on the law, but only the dangerous illusion of such a check.[14]

With a richer conception of the constitution in mind, Dworkin considers two competing traditions: that of personal freedom and that of governmental responsibility for "guarding the public moral space in which all citizens live."[15] He says that this second idea is ambiguous between the antagonistic ideas of aiming to make citizens responsible and making them conform to what the majority want. They are antagonistic because responsibility requires that people should act in accordance with their convictions, whereas conformity can mean forcing people to act contrary to their convictions. If there is no reason for prohibiting abortion that derives from the personhood of the fetus, the state can have only a detached interest in the maintenance of the sanctity of the fetus. It would follow that the reason for prohibiting abortion could only be that the mother is acting irresponsibly. That question depends on the highly controversial question of what counts as sanctity of life and so the convictions of a majority should not, in aiming at moral responsible citizens, override the conviction of the mother. In other words, the state cannot pursue both responsibility and conformity at the same time.

Of course, states should aim to make citizens treat decisions about life and death responsibly but, he says, the courts cannot allow a state to disguise what is actually a coercive rule as a rule merely encouraging responsibility. In *Casey*, which confirmed *Roe* v. *Wade*, the Supreme Court held that states could encourage responsibility in a woman's decision about whether to abort, provided the requirements did not place an "undue burden" on her. It took the view that requiring a woman to inform her husband about the proposed abortion would place such a burden on her but that it would be permissible to require a waiting period of twenty-four hours for personal deliberation, as a kind of "cooling off" period.[16] These sorts of restrictions need to be looked at carefully because the line between encouraging responsibility and coercion is very thin. The effects once it is crossed are particularly burdensome since it impinges on one person alone as opposed to "women as a whole" and so it is markedly different from placing coercion on people not to damage other things to which sanctity attaches, such as art, or historic buildings, or hunting endangered species. Further—and obviously—the decision to have an abortion is intimately connected with our moral personality and the conduct of our own life. This is, of course, the principle behind our right to "procreative autonomy." Dworkin thinks *Casey* open to challenge. A twenty-four-hour waiting period would be sensible for gun ownership, he says, but unnecessary for abortions; there are much better methods of encouraging responsibility such as providing financial aid to poor mothers so that financial necessity is not a ground, for example. Some women might be deterred by the waiting period. Perhaps they would have to make two expensive trips instead of one, or perhaps they would have to endure a gauntlet of protests.

Dworkin tries another argument. He says that there is a "textual home" for the idea of the protection of a woman's right to "procreative autonomy" in the First Amendment, which protects religious freedom. He says it is a possible defense of procreative autonomy because it has held that belief in God is not required in order for someone to have First Amendment protection. In *Seeger* a man who opposed all war on general ethical principles but did not believe in God was entitled to an exemption from military service under a statute limiting the grounds for claiming exemption to religious ones.[17] Thus, Dworkin believes that what the First Amendment requires is that the state has no business saying what people should think about the ultimate point and value of human life.

> I can think of no plausible account of the content that a belief must have in order to be deemed religious that would rule out convictions about why and how human life has intrinsic objective importance, except the abandoned notion that religious belief must presuppose a god.[18]

Certain beliefs people have are of great subjective importance to them; there are those who believe very strongly that taxation is an unjustifiable imposition. Dworkin, unsurprisingly, rejects the test of intrinsic value as what is of "subjective importance" to a person; he says that the test must be an objective one of *content*. And so, he says, someone could not refuse to pay taxes on the ground that they thought that taxes impaired one's faith in the intrinsic, sacred worth of the free market (say) because those taxes are not intended to support religious matters. Where there is an overlap, for example, as in the example of taxes used for war objected to by a pacifist, he says, a little weakly, that an "appropriate balancing" justifies the tax, given that the restriction of freedom is "limited" and the importance of uniform taxation is great.

EUTHANASIA

Dworkin applies the same principles to the justification of euthanasia. Note the differences. Euthanasia applies where there are living people with rights and interests and the principle of the intrinsic value of life is obviously relevant, and more significant in situations of the sort where a person becomes irreversibly comatose. There are three possible sorts of situation: where someone is both conscious and competent and wishes to die (and perhaps wants assistance to do so); where someone is unconscious, perhaps irreversibly so; and where someone is conscious but is incompetent to do anything, as where she suffers from advanced Alzheimer's disease. Dworkin considers in turn the ideas of a person's autonomy, their best interests and the sanctity of their lives.

How do we assess whether it is in a person's interests to die, or remain alive? It always seems particularly wrong—tragic—when young people kill themselves and we are usually quick to say that they are mistaken. That feeling of wrongness does not apply with the same strength to old people. On the other hand, why do we care about dying when there is nothing to live for? One reason for drawing the distinction between young and old age is the idea of investment; the young person's investment is continuing and results of that investment are yet to come, whereas the old person's investment is mostly spent. Compare "she was young and showed so much promise" with "she'd had a good and long life." They express sorrow in strikingly different ways. Dworkin considers the meaning of "dying with dignity," saying it "shows how important it is that life ends appropriately, that death keeps faith with the way we want to have lived."[19] There is a difference, he says (recall the arguments in the last chapter) between our merely *experiential* interests, such as watching football, working hard, or eating well and our *critical* interests which, while not necessarily being consciously aware of them, form the basis of our convictions. He says that we have the abstract ambition to lead a good life, one which is led with integrity and dignity, and it is because of this that we are led to fear or regret not having achieved much in our lives. Since our life is our own in that it is what we make of it, and that principle is of great importance, it must follow that the decision to die belongs to the person whose life it is:

> Whether it is in someone's best interests that his life end in one way rather than another depends on so much else that is special about him—about the shape and character of his life and his own sense of his integrity and critical interests—that no uniform collective decision can possibly hope to serve everyone even decently.[20]

What does it mean to respect someone's choice to die? It can be difficult to establish what a person wants, given mood changes or their emotional stability. How do you determine, for example, when a person is making a genuinely truthful and untroubled account of what she wants, free from duress, depression, impulse, and so on? Dworkin thinks that it is clearer and better to judge the person as a whole. Suggestion: ask yourself what that person really wants, given what that person says, and what you understand or know about the person's character, personality and so on. It is difficult, and sometimes will be impossible, to do with confidence but the important—crucial—principle is that it requires reference to that person's autonomy. You are not substituting what the person wants for what is in that person's interests although, in practice, that idea will be difficult to distinguish from interests. The respect for the person's choice appeals to "the idea that it is better for someone to live a life that is structured by a theme, even though at its end."[21] The difficulties of respecting autonomy arise most prominently in cases where there is a conscious but incompetent person suffering, say, from dementia, although many of the difficulties can be lessened by reference to a "living will."

Dworkin distinguishes between an *evidentiary* view of autonomy and an *integrity* view. The evidentiary view raises the question primarily whether each person knows what is in their best interests and so it cannot extend to the demented and it does not provide a satisfactory answer to the problem of weakness of will; for example, is a weak decision an autonomous decision? However, an "integrity" view of autonomy—what he also calls "precedent autonomy"—incorporates the idea of a structured, coherent life. That idea depends on the idea of the person's will being autonomous when competent and that supports making decisions on behalf of an incompetent. It is useful to see how this respect for autonomy applies to the Jehovah's Witness who says that on no account should there be a blood transfusion if he is hospitalized after a serious accident, but then at the time and in great pain pleads for it. Dworkin says that if the person was competent at the time of making the request, the present competence should govern the decision, but if he is not presently competent, then his earlier request should be respected. Why? The person who has the "fiduciary" right to care for the patient must act in the "best interests" of the patient. They must be the best critical interests and those support the idea of respecting the patient's precedent autonomy.[22]

Dworkin further considers the idea of the sanctity of life in someone who is living. What if the person genuinely does not want to live, and it is not in his interest to live, as when a person faces great pain in a terminal illness? One reason for resisting euthanasia, as Catholics have, for example, is that euthanasia is wrong despite a person's rights and interests and that shows a consistency on euthanasia and abortion which is based on the idea of the sanctity of life. Another conservative view, which links the wrongness of euthanasia with that of abortion, is that euthanasia "cheats nature." There clearly are difficulties with this idea, however. Euthanasia cannot cheat nature where a person is being kept artificially—unnaturally—alive. More important, though, are the different views people have over what sanctity of life means. If someone thinks that life loses its sanctity in an artificially prolonged irreversible comatose state, it cannot be clear that his thoughts are of no consequence. He has formed his critical interests based on a view about the sanctity of life. We cannot then sensibly argue, says Dworkin, that he must sacrifice his own interests out of respect for the inviolability of human life. It must be a matter for individual decision. People have critical interests in the kind of death that they should have and it would be doing harm to them to keep them alive against their wishes. To put it another way: it does not follow that killing people is always offensive to sanctity of life:

> A true appreciation of dignity argues decisively . . . for individual freedom, not coercion, for a regime of law and attitude that encourages each of us to make mortal decisions for himself. Freedom is the cardinal, absolute requirement of self-respect: no one treats his life as having any intrinsic, objective importance unless he insists on leading that life himself, not being ushered along it by others.[23]

TO SUM UP

I believe Dworkin places the value of human dignity—with its twin principles of equality and freedom—as the fundamental human value. All else follows. Although dignity must be protected by rights, it is also of intrinsic value because human life is capable of sustaining—and has sustained—worthwhile lives. Morality follows from the ethics of dignity. When we exercise our rights responsibly—when we treat others as of equal objective value and make something valuable of our own lives—only then will we live in a just and appealing community. We will understand our politics and laws as fundamentally about ways of enhancing human dignity. Our arguments of politics and law will become the business of the minutiae of making decisions that concern the much less abstract level of what dignity requires and permits in particular cases.

Reference Matter

Notes

INTRODUCTION

1. See "Objectivity and Truth: You'd Better Believe It," *Philosophy and Public Affairs* Spring 1996 Vol. 25 No. 2 pp. 87–139.

2. See "The Supreme Court Phalanx: An Exchange," *New York Review of Books*, Dec. 6, 2007 and see Dworkin's response. It is the complacency and confidence of the "self-satisfied chuckle" coupled with the utter banality of the remark that is so common. Are judges undemocratic only because they are unelected? The voter is unelected but he is crucial to democracy. See Chapter 6.

3. It is baffling, therefore, when the academic also says, "I can't honestly say I've ever read him providing these sorts of articles." Dworkin in reply gives the example of the well-known Supreme Court decision of *Lochner* which he criticised in *Law's Empire* because the wrong principle—unrestricted freedom of contract—was invoked by bakers concerning onerous hours of working. (See *Law's Empire*, p. 374.) I would just add: there are *many* articles on cases by Dworkin, many of them in the *New York Review of Books*!

4. See *Law, Pragmatism and Democracy* (Cambridge: Harvard UP 2005).

5. See *A Constitution of Many Minds: Why the Founding Document Doesn't Mean What It Meant Before*. Sunstein, C. (Princeton: Princeton UP 2009).

6. See Shiffrin, S. "Methodology in Free Speech Theory" in 97 *Virginia Law Review* (1995) 1557.

7. See Perry, S., "Responsibility for Outcomes, Risk, and the Law of Torts," in *Philosophy and the Law of Torts* ed. Postema, G. (Cambridge: Cambridge UP 2001) 72.

8. See Waldron, J. "The Core of the Case against Judicial Review," *Yale Law Journal* 115 (2006): 1346; his *Law and Disagreement* (Oxford: Oxford UP 1999) chs. 9, 12 and 13; and see, my remarks later, in Chapter 6.

9. See the New Zealand Mining Act 1886, ss. 125, 232–34. Also, see Chapter 6, where I mention Dworkin's lifeboat example, and see, for example, his *Law and Disagreement* (Oxford: Oxford UP 1999) particularly, pp. 203–4 and p. 213.

10. See my remarks in Chapters 1 and 10, and see Cohen, J. "Expensive Taste Rides Again," in Burley, J. *Dworkin and his Critics* (Oxford: Blackwell, 2004) p. 1.

11. See Chapter 1.

12. I'm glad I thought legal theories should "instruct" rather than describe.

13. People occasionally try to interpret Dworkin's characteristic grin. He has a small paralyzed facial muscle and apparently can't drink from a straw. The great lifeman, P. Wilkes of Stephen Potter's *Lifemanship* (London: Hart-Davis, 1950), had a similar asymmetrical facial expression but it was intentionally created turning on the bath taps with his mouth each morning. His purpose was to create a face with "lookability"(see pp. 60–61, esp. fig. 10). In Dworkin's case it is nothing so sinister, just paralysis.

CHAPTER 1: A SKETCH OF RONALD DWORKIN

1. BBC Books (1978).

2. "Judicial Discretion," *Journal of Philosophy* (1963), pp. 624–38.

3. See "Does Law Have a Function? A Comment on the Two-Level Theory of Decision," *Yale Law Journal* 74 (1965), pp. 640–51. This was previously printed under the title "Wasserstrom: The Judicial Decision," *Ethics* 75 (1964), p. 47; "Philosophy, Morality and Law—Observations Prompted by Professor Fuller's Novel Claim," *University of Pennsylvania Law Review* 113 (1965), pp. 668–90; and "The Elusive Morality of Law," *Vanderbilt Law Review* 10 (1965), pp. 631–39. (This last is a shortened form of "Philosophy, Morality and Law.")

4. *Philosophical Review* 64 (1955), pp. 3–32. Also in *Theories of Ethics*, Foot, P. (ed.), (Oxford, 1967), p. 144.

5. "The Model of Rules," *University of Chicago Law Review* 35 (1967), pp. 14–46. This article is reprinted as "Is Law a System of Rules?" in *Essays in Legal Philosophy*, Summers, R. (ed.), (Blackwell, 1968), p. 25 and as ch. 2, "The Model of Rules I," in *Taking Rights Seriously* (Duckworth, 1977), p. 14 and also appears in *The Philosophy of Law*, Dworkin, R. (ed.), (Oxford, 1977), p. 38.

6. It has amusing quiddities. For example, legal principles are "eroded" not "torpedoed" (like rules) just as "eroded" erodes "torpedoed"; the article also likens judicial discretion to a doughnut.

7. See MacCormick, N., *Hart* (Jurists in Profile Series, Edward Arnold, 1981), p. 19; now see the second revised edition: Stanford Law and Politics 2008.

8. Penguin.

9. *Oxford Essays in Jurisprudence*, Guest, A. G. (ed.), (Oxford UP, 1961).

10. See *The Common Law Tradition*, Llewellyn, K. (Boston, Toronto, Little, Brown, 1960).

11. See *Columbia Law Review* 19 (1929), p. 113; and 29 (1929), p. 285. Also "Legal Rules: Their Function in the Process of Decision," *University of Pennsylvania Law Review* 79 (1931), p. 833. See also his *Administrative Justice and the Supremacy of Law*, acknowledged by Hart in *The Concept of Law*, (Oxford: OUP, 1961), as "the most illuminating general discussion" of the character and relationships between different forms of legal control.

12. See their *The Legal Process* (1958).

13. See *Harvard Law Review* 71 (1958) at p. 598 for Hart's article, and at p. 630 for Fuller's reply.

14. He is thought by many to have solved the problems raised by what is known as the "causal" theory of knowledge. See *Collected Papers*, Evans, G. (Oxford: OUP, 1985).

15. In "No Right Answer?" in *Law, Morality and Society: Essays in Honour of H.L.A. Hart*, Hacker, P. & Raz, J. (eds.), (Oxford: OUP, 1977), Dworkin thanks Gareth Evans for his contribution in the seminars they held together on objectivity in 1975 in Oxford.

16. *The Independent*, Tuesday, June 22, 1993.

17. See, for example, Gardner, J. in Hershowitz, S. ed., *Exploring Law's Empire* (Oxford: OUP 2006), p. 207.

18. Jerry Cohen's intellectual relationship with Dworkin was interesting; Cohen certainly didn't seem to me to grasp either what Dworkin meant by interpretivism, nor what equality of resources was. It was lack of grasp, but how could that be? I felt that Dworkin thought that Cohen's method was all over the place ("Fifties linguistic philosophy," he said once). But it was good to hear them talk: it forced insights. The drawn-out wrangle—that Cohen kept up rather than Dworkin—over whether the state should compensate expensive tastes was entirely off Dworkin's radar. It seemed bizarre that someone of acknowledged egalitarian Marxist leanings was keen to compensate upper class twits (or was it that this was a "philosophical game"?), even odder that justice imposed no upper limit to that compensation. But Cohen was forthright, like Gareth Evans, and clearly contributed to Dworkin's intellectual plan; I note how neatly Cohen's excellent 2003 paper "Facts and Principles" dovetails with the unity of value thesis. After that paper, at one of our Colloquia in 2002, Dworkin said he "agreed with all of it." See *Philosophy & Public Affairs* 31:3 Summer 2003 1.

19. Betsy died not long after Dworkin joined us at UCL in 1998. It was immensely sad. She became very ill, with an aggressive cancer, almost exactly at the time of the first session. She could not travel to their London home from New York as they usually did in the early New Year. Dworkin nevertheless chaired three of the sessions, flying from New York the day before and returning early the following day (once immediately after a post-Colloquium dinner). He wrote long and detailed responses to the papers he could not attend, and we circulated them. He was very upset; I imagine he found solace in hard work. But no one really understood how he did this.

20. It was chiefly on questions concerning abortion and euthanasia and other topics in the late eighties in Oxford; it was known as "Star Wars"—Oxford's version of the celebrity culture.

21. See Lord Bingham in *The Susskind Interviews: Law Experts in Changing Times*, ed. Susskind, R. (London: Sweet & Maxwell 2005).

22. "Political Judges and the Rule of Law," *Maccabaean Lecture in Jurisprudence, Proceedings of the British Academy* 64 (1978). Reprinted in *A Matter of Principle*, ch. 1, p. 9.

23. It is common to say that Dworkin is "good at rhetoric" but short on "substance"; representative is Blackburn's review of *Justice for Hedgehogs* in the *Times Higher Ed. Supp.* January 27, 2011.

24. Here is a striking case. Imagine describing a particular scene of torture from every point of view but the view that it is unjustified. It is possible to do that. Someone might aim to discriminate between the different methods of torture used from century to century. But imagine teaching someone what torture *was* simply by handing them the book. It would just be a manual on torture. See *Natural Law and Natural Rights*, Finnis, J. (Oxford UP, 1980), who thinks that it is the question of justification that distinguishes Dworkin's theory from theories of "positivism" such

as Hart and Raz. Because of this, Dworkin's attack on their theories "miscarries." His theory is a "normative theory of law, offering guidance to the judge as to his judicial duty; theirs is a descriptive theory, offered to historians to enable a discriminating history of legal systems to be written," p. 21.

25. *Law's Empire* (Cambridge: Harvard UP, 1986), p. 413.

26. *Oxford Journal of Legal Studies*, vol. 24, no. 1 (2004) 1, 36–37. Also see ch. 6 of *Justice in Robes* (Cambridge: Harvard UP, 2004).

27. "They teach courses limited to 'legal philosophy' or analytic jurisprudence in which they distinguish and compare different contemporary versions of positivism, they attend conferences dedicated to those subjects, and they comment on each other's orthodoxies and heresies in the most minute detail in their own dedicated journals." See *Justice for Robes*, ch. 7, 212–13.

28. *Loc.cit.*, 213.

29. See *Essays in Jurisprudence and Philosophy*, H.L.A. Hart (Oxford: OUP, 1983), pp. 139–40: "If I may venture a prophecy, I think the chief criticism that it will attract will be of his insistence that, even if there is no way of demonstrating which of two conflicting solutions, both equally well warranted by the existing law, is correct, still there must always be a single correct answer awaiting discovery."

30. See *A Matter of Principle*, Dworkin, R. (Cambridge: Harvard UP, 1985), p. 411, n. 15.

31. See *Legal Right and Social Democracy*, MacCormick, N. (Oxford: OUP, 1982), ch. 7. Dworkin's reply to this article, in *Ronald Dworkin and Contemporary Jurisprudence*, Cohen, M. (ed.), (London: Duckworth, 1984), pp. 278–81 is helpful for a restatement of his views on the idea of constructive theorizing.

32. See later, Chapter 10.

33. See the Introduction to his *A Fragment of Government* where he "arranges" the legal institutions according to "Utility." Dworkin says in *Justice for Hedgehogs* that Bentham was a "closet interpretivist," p. 486 n. 6.

34. See later, Chapters 10 and 11.

35. See Plato's definition of justice in *The Republic*, ch. 14, as a virtue in the individual in which justice is an internal order of the soul that leads to right behavior. The connection with Plato's view of justice is one which Dworkin suggests in his Tanner Lectures on the foundations of liberalism but it is an indirect one, linked through Dworkin's idea of a person's living a "critical" life. See Chapter 11.

36. See Chapter 8.

37. And see Sen, A. "Dworkin on Ethics and Freewill: Comments and Questions," *Boston U.L.R.* 90 (2010) 2, p. 657.

CHAPTER 2: LAW AS PLAIN FACT

1. *Leviathan*, Hobbes, T. (1651), MacPherson, C. (ed.), (Penguin 2002).

2. But Kelsen thought his *Grundnorm* would make life easier for people by presenting them with coherent reasons for action: See chs. X and XIII of his *Essays in Legal Philosophy*, Weinberger, O. (ed.), (Dordrecht: Reidel, 1973).

3. *The Concept of Law*, 2nd ed., Hart, H. L. A. (Oxford: Oxford UP, 1994), Preface.

4. *Ibid.*, p. 210.

5. See Bentham's *An Introduction to the Principles of Morals and Legislation*, Hart, H. & Burns, J. (eds.), (London: Athlone Press, 1970), pp. 293–94.

6. See Austin's *The Province of Jurisprudence Determined*, Hart, H.L.A. (ed.), (1954), Lecture V, p. 184.

7. See Kelsen's *General Theory of Law and State*, Wedberg, A. (ed.), (1945): "In social and especially in legal science, there is still no influence to counteract the overwhelming interest that those residing in power, as well as those craving for power, have in a theory pleasing to their wishes, that is, in a political ideology. . . . The ideal of an objective science of law and State, free from all political ideologies, has a better chance for recognition in a period of social equilibrium" (at p. xvii).

8. See *Taking Rights Seriously* (London: Duckworth, 1977), p. 162. A revised edition with a "Reply to Critics" appeared in 1978.

9. *Loc.cit.* "The constructive model [of judicial reasoning] . . . demands that decisions taken in the name of justice must never outstrip an official's ability to account for these decisions in a theory of justice. . . . It demands that we act on principle rather than on faith. . . . It presupposes that articulated consistency, decisions in accordance with a program that can be made public and followed until changed, is essential to any conception of justice." The idea is an essential part, I think, of his idea of integrity. See, for example, *Law's Empire*, at p. 413, where he sums up his views about the argumentative nature of law. It is clear that legal argument must draw from a set of *public* principles: "Law's empire is defined by attitude. . . . It is an interpretive, self-reflective attitude addressed to politics in the broadest sense. It is a protestant attitude that makes each citizen responsible for imagining what his society's public commitments to principle are."

10. This form of liberalism we might call "political liberalism"; fundamentally, it stands against laws such as Article 386 of the Chinese Great Qing Code of 1646 — in effect until 1912 — which threatened forty blows of the lighter bamboo to anyone who just did "what ought not to be done."

11. Too numerous to name them all.

12. Neil MacCormick says that he thinks I am right that Dworkin thinks this, but that is why Dworkin's terminology is, as he says, "tendentious." It ignores the idea of the "internal view" that judges must have towards the rule of recognition and the role that view must play in the construction of complex legal arguments in hard cases. Dworkin should be defended here. Pivotal to Hart's project is the separation of law from morality. Hart achieves this by asserting the existence of the acceptance by officials of criteria of identification of the law. It must be one of his central concerns that the existence of that acceptance is a factual matter, in the end to be discovered in the "settled practices" (Hart's term) of judges. Hart, I think, has been consistent in his account. Take, for example, his reiteration of the positivist nature of his thesis in "Legal Duty and Obligation," first published in 1966, but substantially revised in 1982, with a section discussing Dworkin's and Raz's accounts of law, in his *Essays on Bentham* (Oxford: Oxford UP, 1982), p. 127: "I have only argued that when judges or others make committed statements of legal obligation it is not the case that they must necessarily believe or pretend to believe that they are referring to a species of moral obligation." And in the Introduction to his *Essays in Jurisprudence and Philosophy* (Oxford: Oxford UP, 1983), he confirms his view on the "detached"

nature of normative legal statements, saying: "Such detached statements constitute a third kind of statement to add to the two (internal and external statements) which I distinguish. To have made all this clear I should have emphasized that as well as the distinction between mere regularities of behavior and rule-governed behavior we need a distinction between the acceptance of rules and the recognition of their acceptance by others" (p. 14). If MacCormick's point is that the "facts of the matter" here are complex, or controversial, and not "plain," then his criticism is not of Dworkin's idea of "plain fact," but of Dworkin's view that conventionalism makes the "best sense" of positivism. MacCormick has to supply the sense of positivism, given that we are to interpret the factual "detached" statements of judges in a complex way.

13. See "Kelsen Visited," Hart, H.L.A., *Essays in Jurisprudence and Philosophy* (Oxford UP, 1983), p. 286; also see the Preface to this work, at pp. 14–15. Can we both have positivism *and* see legal argument in all the complex ways that seem at first sight much more easily explained in terms of moral argument? MacCormick thinks so. But that is where I see the virtue of legal positivism drain away. We do not have the "this is where the law stops" clarity and "certainty" (see Hart's justification of the rule of recognition). When I first read MacCormick's *Legal Reasoning and Legal Theory* (Oxford: Oxford UP, 1978), I thought that it was not very different from what I had been hearing Dworkin argue out at Oxford. Dworkin, naturally, coming from his background in American constitutional law, sees the complexity of legal argument as critical of positivism. Dworkin assumes that the complexity of moral argument is part of legal argument. MacCormick's argument comes from the opposite, more difficult direction, arguing towards the complexity from the point of view of positivism. To repeat, that journey, to my mind, is a retreat from the central virtue of positivism: not clarity about the question that law is distinct from morality but clarity in working out what the law demands. That is how I read Hart's comments in *The Concept of Law*, pp. 210–11.

14. See *The Concept of Law*, 2nd ed., Hart, H.L.A., pp. 185–86. Ch. 9, entitled "Laws and Morals," refines the arguments to support his definition and is a culmination of many of the arguments he advances in his "Positivism and the Separation of Law and Morals," originally published in *Harvard Law Review* 71 (1958) and now to be found in Hart's *Essays in Jurisprudence and Philosophy* (Oxford: Oxford UP, 1983) as ch. 2. It is salutary to see Hart's recognition of the over-complexity of legal positivism if extended to the hard cases. I think that much the best interpretation is that it is *because* of the over-complexity that he prefers to think of judges as law-makers rather than law-finders in hard cases.

15. *The Concept of Law*, 2nd ed., Hart, H.L.A. (Oxford: Oxford UP, 1994), p. 110.

16. *Ibid.*, p. 292. Frequently and in many important cases the law is not clearly settled and dictates no results either way. In such cases in my view, which is hotly challenged by Dworkin and others, the judges have an inescapable though restricted law-making function, which standardly they perform by promoting one or other of those moral values or principles which the existing law can be regarded as instantiating.

17. See s. 78 Police and Criminal Evidence Act 1984. Like the unfair prison sentence, the decision to exclude unfair evidence can be appealed only on the ground that the judge did not reasonably put his mind to what was fair, that direction being the only requirement of law.

18. *Law's Empire*, p. 429 n.3 and n.6. Also, see Dworkin's reply to Lyons in *Ronald Dworkin and Contemporary Jurisprudence*, Cohen, M. (London: Duckworth, 1984), pp. 254–60. Dworkin's remarks since are largely repeats of what he said much earlier, but see generally *Justice in Robes*, particularly chs. 6 and 7 for the detail of the arguments; *Justice for Hedgehogs* provides the most abstract account in ch. 19. Why are they "law-making" here? What is so significant about the fact that the law is not *settled* that it requires the invocation of some different function? In my view, it can only be that Hart regards plain rules (plain facts) as the central idea of his positivism. And that accords perfectly with the interpretive underpinnings he supplies and which I have already discussed at some length.

19. See Chapter 4 and also *Law's Empire*, ch. 1.

20. See *Justice for Hedgehogs*, ch. 19. Dworkin envisages a family situation where the father has to adjudicate on the rightness of a broken promise between two children. He says two distinct questions could emerge: (i) what keeping faith with family morality requires and (ii) what family morality *should* require. He says it is "crucial" to see that both questions are moral questions. See also *Law's Empire* ch. 11.

21. See "Positivism and the Separation of Law and Morals," in *Essays in Jurisprudence and Philosophy*, (Oxford: Oxford UP, 1983), ch. 2.

22. "I cannot understand how any person who has considered the subject can suppose that society could possibly have gone on if judges had not legislated," said Austin in Lecture 7, *The Province of Jurisprudence Determined*, Hart, H. (ed.), (London: Weidenfeld and Nicolson, 1954), p. 191. Despite these remarks, Austin was clear that judge-made law was law only by virtue *of what the sovereign had commanded*. The judge would, therefore, have only the weaker discretion to do what it was that the sovereign would have commanded had he been aware of the facts.

23. See *The General Theory of Law and State*, Kelsen, H., pp. 146–53. This is debated among Kelsenian scholars. See *Essays on Kelsen*, Tur, R. & Twining, W. (eds.), (Oxford: Oxford UP, 1986).

24. Dworkin says in his Introduction to *The Philosophy of Law*, Dworkin, R. (ed.), (Oxford: Oxford UP, 1977), p. 7, that the positivist theory of judicial discretion is a "consequence" of their theory of propositions of law.

25. I can't take what Hart says in his *Postscript* seriously; it was designed to answer Dworkin's criticisms and it is inconsistent with what he says in *The Concept of Law*. It was a pity in my view that it was ever published, and a tragedy that it is published in the same volume as *The Concept of Law*. It is not well written. It would have been simpler and better if Hart had just accepted that his theory was one of interpretive positivism, I believe.

26. "Judicial Discretion," *Journal of Philosophy* 60 (1963), pp. 624–38.

27. See *Taking Rights Seriously*, pp. 31–3.

28. *Ibid.*, p. 32.

29. Compare Bentham's approach, which was much more clearly motivated by his utilitarianism. See *Bentham and the Common Law Tradition*, Postema, G. (Oxford: Oxford UP, 1986), particularly ch. 9, entitled "Utilitarian Positivism."

30. See the Preface of Bentham's *A Fragment of Government* where he says that it is the principle of utility that should order the arrangement of the jurisprudential materials. In the last paragraph (para. 48) of ch. 1 of *Fragment*, Bentham says the

following: "Now this other principle that still recurs upon us, what other can it be than the principle of UTILITY? The principle which furnishes us with that reason, which alone depends upon any higher reason, but which is itself the sole and all-sufficient reason for every point of practice whatsoever."

31. *The Province of Jurisprudence Determined*, Hart, H.L.A. (ed.), lecture 5, p. 184.

32. See *The Concept of Law*, 2nd ed.

33. See, for example, section 4 of Hart's "Positivism and the Separation of Law and Morals," *Harvard Law Review* 71 (1958), p. 593. Rules of statutory construction are much less help than commonly realized. The so-called literal rule will be invoked by one counsel to counter the "mischief" or "golden" rule used by the other counsel. There is no rule formally recognized by the courts offering a reconciliation of the different rules, although Rupert Cross attempted to formulate such a rule. In Cross's *Statutory Interpretation* 2nd ed., Bell & Engle (eds.), (London: Butterworth, 1987), he argues towards a fusion of the three rules. He says the literal rule has been treated too literally; that it has been applied as though there were a "true," contextless, meaning. To introduce context, the mischief rule must be "insinuated into" the literal rule. Further, when the literal rule, so interpreted, leads to some absurdity or inconsistency, the words of the statute may be modified, in accordance with the golden rule, to avoid the absurdity or inconsistency, but no further.

34. *Riggs v. Palmer* 115 NE (1889) 188.

35. An exception here is the requirement that a court must disqualify from driving, for at least one year, any person convicted of drunken driving unless there are "special reasons" for not doing so. Road Traffic Act 1972 s. 93.

36. See *Lim v. Camden Health Authority* [1979] 2 All ER 910, at p. 914.

37. *Donoghue v. Stevenson* [1932] AC 562, at p. 580. Maybe we could try "Who, in law, *ought to be considered* my neighbor?" which doesn't sound odd.

38. [1975] A.C. 653, at pp. 700–701 (Lord Kilbrandon), and pp. 695–96 (Lord Simon).

CHAPTER 3: THE COMPLEXITY OF LEGAL ARGUMENT

1. Dworkin says positivism and interpretivism are both about *doctrinal law*, the law on some topic in some jurisdiction; other concepts of law are *sociological* (for example, law began in primitive societies) and *aspirational* (for example, celebration of the rule of law).

2. See Hart's *Postscript* to the second edition of *The Concept of Law*.

3. Kelsen's theory may be seen to raise a problem since, relying on the distinction between the "is" and the "ought," he declared that the law's normativity—its characteristic of directing action—was dependent on the law's existing within the world of "oughts." Laws existed in the world, not of "causality," but "imputation." But his theory still made the determination of law dependent on a master test, the basic norm, which could be described as a clear presupposition of validity. The significance of the basic norm in legal theory is that it marked the step towards understanding the relevance of acceptance of standards as the essential part of legal argument. Its obscurity lies only in Kelsen's non-specification of the reasons for the acceptance of those standards. There is no obscurity in the root-of-title conception of being able in all cases to identify law by reference to a clear master rule.

4. The position of what are known as "persuasive" precedents, where judgements of judges in other jurisdictions are *taken into account*, fits best with the way I have suggested principles may be captured by a rule of recognition. They are "persuasive" and not "binding."

5. This tactic against Dworkin's dismissal of the rule of recognition theory is one that Sartorius once attempted. See his "Social Policy and Judicial Legislation," *American Philosophical Quarterly* 8 (1971), p. 151.

6. See *Law's Empire*, pp. 127–28. Dworkin's criticism of Jules Coleman's thesis of "inclusive" positivism: "Thirty Years On," in *Justice in Robes*. See Coleman, J. *The Practice of Principle: In Defence of a Pragmatist Approach to Legal Theory*. (Oxford: Oxford UP 2001).

7. Hart's doctrine of "fair opportunity" is an important parallel here. See his *Punishment and Responsibility*, (Oxford: Oxford UP, 1968).

8. *Law's Empire*, p. 118. Should the ideal be served by requiring judges to engage their own convictions as little as possible and be as deferent as possible to the legislature? Dworkin says that the judge might still be mistaken, and even if correct about what the current legislature thinks, that decision will not have been announced in advance.

9. See *D & C Builders v. Rees* [1966] 2 QB 617.

10. See Postema, G., "Coordination and Convention at the Foundations of Law," *Journal of Legal Studies* 11 (1982) p. 165; Green, L., "Law, Co-ordination and the Common Good," *Oxford Journal of Legal Studies* 3 (1983) p. 299.

11. See Griffith, J., *The Politics of the Judiciary*, 5th ed. (London: Fontana, 1997).

12. Impartiality, not coming with preconceived judgments, being fair, are all much better ways of characterizing the judicial role; but they all require judgments of *value*, which means controversy, of course. For excellent discussions on the problems raised by the idea of neutrality, see the article by Montefiore in *Neutrality and Impartiality*, Montefiore, A. (ed.), (Cambridge UP, 1975), p. 1, and *The Morality of Freedom*, Raz, J. (Oxford: Oxford UP, 1986), ch. 5.

13. s. 54 of the Metropolitan Police Act 1839 states "A person is liable on summary conviction to a penalty if in any thoroughfare or public place in the Metropolitan Police District or in any street elsewhere in England and Wales to the annoyance of the inhabitants or passengers he . . . makes or repairs any trailer, cart or carriage except in cases of accident where repair on the spot is necessary."

14. Warren, S. & Brandeis, L., "The Right to Privacy," *Harvard Law Review* 4 (1890), p. 193.

15. At p. 214.

16. 171 NY 538 (1902).

17. *Ibid.*, p. 544.

18. *Loc.cit.* (emphasis added).

19. He also employed the familiar argument that recognition of the right would result in "a vast amount of litigation."

20. 22 Ga. 190 (1904).

21. See Bork, R., "Neutral Principles and Some First Amendment Problems," *Indiana Law Journal* 47 (1971), p. 1, at p. 17. See also Dworkin's responses: "The Bork Nomination," *New York Review of Books*, (1987), also in *Cardozo Law Review* 9 (1987), p. 101; "The Bork Nomination: An Exchange"; "The Bork Nomination"; and "From

Bork to Kennedy"; all in *New York Review of Books* (1987). Bork claims to have changed his views and so I describe those relevant to the time of the Senate hearings in 1987 of his nomination to the Supreme Court by President Reagan.

22. *Life's Dominion: An Argument About Abortion, Euthanasia & Individual Freedom*, Dworkin, R. (London: Knopf, 1993), p. 136.

23. See "Definition and Theory in Jurisprudence," in *Essays in Jurisprudence and Philosophy*, Hart, H.L.A. (Oxford: Oxford UP, 1983), p. 25.

24. See Shapiro, S. *Legality*. (Cambridge, Mass: Harvard UP, 2011). 312.

25. *Ibid.*, 307.

26. See *Justice for Hedgehogs*, Part II.

27. See *Stanford Encyclopaedia of Philosophy* entry by Green in 2003.

28. Gardner, J. "Law's Aims in *Law's Empire*," in *Exploring Law's Empire: The Jurisprudence of Ronald Dworkin*. Hershowitz, S. (Oxford: Oxford UP. 2006). 207.

29. See MacCormick, N., *Law and Values: Reflection on Method* (Oxford: Oxford UP 2008). 305.

30. See Schauer, F., "Institutions and the Concept of Law: A Reply to Ronald Dworkin (with some help from Neil MacCormick)," ch. 3 of *Law as Institutional Normative Order: Essays in Honour of Sir Neil MacCormick*, Del Mar, M. ed., (Ashgate, 2009).

31. Raz makes the same mistake of running a sociological sense of a legal system together with an account of legal reasoning. Lawyers don't debate about what the "essence" of law is but about what the law requires. It begs the question in favor of legal positivism to say that "the concept" of law includes what lawyers debate because it misses the point of the sort of thing the lawyers are debating *about*. See Raz, J. "Can There Be a Theory of Law?" in *The Blackwell Guide to the Philosophy of Law and Legal Theory* (Malden, Mass.: Blackwell, 2005), 324. Raz says there "I will use 'law', as it is often used, to refer sometimes to a legal system, and sometimes to a rule of law, or a statement of how the law is on a particular point. Sometimes I will use the word ambiguously to refer to one of the other of these, as it does not matter for the purposes of the discussion." (326). Hart, more or less, does the same thing. His sociological concept "the union of primary and secondary rules" identifies central cases of legal systems but includes within it the "secondary rules of adjudication and recognition" which are supposed to identify and adjudicate the "valid" rules of particular systems. Fixation on the sociological identification of law results in failure to give much significance to the kind of disputes lawyers have in identifying law. Saying merely that "they dispute," or worse, confining legal argument to what arises from agreement, would beg the question of what "a theory" of law is about.

CHAPTER 4: THE INTERPRETATION OF LAW

1. *Justice for Hedgehogs*, 131.

2. See references in *Justice in Robes* and *Justice for Hedgehogs* (see later in this chapter).

3. *Ibid.*, p. 73.

4. *Lynch v. D.P.P.* [1975] A.C. 653, pp. 695–696.

5. *Ibid.*, 700–701.

6. *Law's Empire*, p. 421, n.12. In *Justice for Hedgehogs*, Dworkin again says that feminist criticisms that bring out sexism are often directed towards the lack of

responsibility on the part of critics that ignore them. He calls such a lack of responsibility a "failure in an important and traditional critical responsibility." See p. 143.

7. See *Justice for Hedgehogs*, p. 23.

8. See *The Concept of Law*, 2nd ed., pp. 56–8, and pp. 82–91.

9. *Ibid.*, Chapter 5.

10. "Working on the Chain Gang: Interpretation in Law and Literature," Fish, S. *Texas Law Review* 60 (1982), p. 373; "Wrong Again," *Texas Law Review* 62 (1983), p. 299.

11. See *Natural Law and Natural Rights*, Finnis, J. (Oxford: Oxford UP, 1980), ch. 1.

12. See *Justice in Robes* (2006).

13. *The Concept of Law*, 2nd ed., pp. 94–9.

14. *Law's Empire*, p. 52.

15. *Ibid.*, p. 53. And see *Justice for Hedgehogs*, p. 130: "We seek value—point—in interpretations and have responsibility to 'promote that value.'"

16. *Ibid.*, p. 93. Emphasis added.

17. *Proceedings of the Aristotelian Society* 56 (1965), p. 167.

18. *Ibid.*, p. 167 and pp. 171–2.

19. *Loc.cit.*, and p. 180.

20. For example, he says, disagreements about baldness are "spurious"—or "verbal"—because we "use the same criteria in standard cases"; so we can have "vague criterial concepts."

21. Imagine if Hart's work had been called *A Conception of Law* or, U.S.-style, *A Theory of Law*.

22. See later, Chapter 6.

23. [1932] AC 562. For a detailed, and jurisprudentially friendly, discussion of this case, see *Legal Reasoning and Legal Theory*, MacCormick, N. (Oxford: Oxford UP, 1978).

24. See Dworkin, *Law's Empire*, pp. 108–9. See also Raz, J., "Authority, Law and Morality," *The Monist* 68 (1985), p. 295.

25. *Law's Empire*, p. 179.

26. *Ibid.*, p. 404.

27. *Law's Empire*, p. 184.

28. See Chapters 7 and 8.

29. *Law's Empire*, p. 134.

30. See MacCormick, N., "The Role of Coherence in Legal Justification," in Peszenick (ed.), *Theory of Legal Science*.

31. See *Essays in Jurisprudence and Philosophy*, Hart, H.L.A. (Oxford: Oxford UP, 1983), ch. 15.

32. *Law's Empire*, p. 407.

CHAPTER 5: THE EVALUATIVE COHERENCE OF LEGAL ARGUMENT

1. I suggest the answer is obvious!

2. The idea of "criterionlessness" was what Hart ascribed to Bentham's dislike of "natural rights" (see Hart, *Essays on Bentham*); this suggests to me that Dworkin's interpretation of positivism as providing a "criterial" account of law is in line with at least Bentham's interpretation of positivism and, dare I say, lends support to Hart's own understanding.

3. *Taking Rights Seriously*, p. 105.

4. See Shapiro, S., *Legality* (Cambridge, Mass: Harvard U.P. 2011). 326.

5. *Ibid.*, 33.

6. Even now, 18 years on from the first edition: see my "How to Criticize Ronald Dworkin's Theory of Law," *Analysis*, Vol. 69 No. 2 April 2009 1.

7. See Fish, S., "Working on the Chain Gang: Interpretation in Law and Literature," *Texas Law Review* 60 (1982), p. 551 and "Wrong Again," *Texas Law Review* 62 (1983), p. 299 (these are reprinted in his *Doing What Comes Naturally* (Oxford: Oxford UP 1989). See Dworkin's replies in *A Matter of Principle*, part 2.

8. See *Justice for Hedgehogs* 147–49. Dworkin considers the claim that translations which, he says, attribute meanings in a "large variety of very different packages" can have, as Quine has said, no "plausible sort of equivalence." Dworkin takes Quine's claim to be a skeptical claim. Rather, Dworkin says, translation may be understood as the interpretation of different speech acts. He says that Davidson's well-known "principle of charity"—the making of reasonable assumptions about a speaker's background—shows the point of translation. What if there are two "markedly different" translations? He asks why one can't be true and the other false (or "correct" and "incorrect") and emphasizes the importance of not confusing the psychological fact of our *uncertainty* with *indeterminacy*, that is, the conclusion that there is just no right answer.

9. *Law's Empire*, p. 235.

10. See *Judging Judges*, Lee, S. (London: Faber, 1988), p. 30.

11. Here is an example of such corruption, drawn from the U.K. Legal Services Institute in a recent paper written in 2010: "Law differs from [other] disciplines in important ways. New science is often created in universities. However, new law is created by legislatures. . . . New insights and interpretations in science, engineering and medicine will often result from university research. However, in law, new interpretations are the prerogative of the higher courts. . . . these limitations play a part in shaping the type of research that is carried out in university law departments." "The Education and Training of Solicitors: Time for Change," November 2010. Para. 2.33 "Research," p. 26.

12. See *The Authority of Law*, Raz, J. (Oxford: Oxford UP, 1979), p. 205, n. 19.

13. See *Legal Reasoning and Legal Theory*, MacCormick, N. (Oxford: Oxford UP, 1978), particularly ch. 7.

14. *The Authority of Law*, p. 204.

15. *Law's Empire*, p. 438, n. 30; *Justice for Hedgehogs*, pp. 327–31.

16. *Taking Rights Seriously*, p. 90.

17. *Ibid.*, p. 22.

18. *Justice for Hedgehogs*, p. 329.

19. *Ibid.*, p. 91.

20. *Ibid.*, p. 22.

21. See *Justice for Hedgehogs*, p. 329.

22. *Spartan Steel v. Martin & Co.* [1973] 1 QB 27 at p. 36.

23. *Ibid.*, pp. 37–8.

24. *Taking Rights Seriously*, p. xv.

25. See *R.(Garde) v. Strickland* [1921] 2 IR 317.

26. What is often referred to as a "side effects" argument for utilitarianism. See *Causing Death and Saving Lives*, Glover, J. (Penguin, 1977), pp. 40–1.

27. See also Dworkin's "What Is Equality? Part I: Equality of Welfare," *Philosophy and Public Affairs* 10 (1981), pp. 185–246, particularly towards the end. Further important discussions are to be found in *Taking Rights Seriously*, pp. 94–100 and 272–8; and in *A Matter of Principle*, pp. 359–72.

28. *Taking Rights Seriously*, p. 275.

29. *Ibid.*, p. 96.

30. See *A Matter of Principle*, p. 359.

31. Hart's article, entitled "Between Utility and Rights," which contains a brilliantly clear résumé of various of both Nozick and Dworkin's positions in political philosophy, is to be found in Hart's *Essays in Jurisprudence and Philosophy*, (Oxford: Oxford UP, 1983), p. 198, and esp. pp. 208–21. The article is also to be found in *Ronald Dworkin and Contemporary Jurisprudence*, Cohen, M. (ed.), (London: Duckworth, 1984), p. 214. Dworkin's reply to the article is in the Cohen volume, at p. 282. See also *A Matter of Principle*, pp. 353–72.

32. *A Matter of Principle*, p. 370.

33. *Justice for Hedgehogs*, p. 329.

34. *Loc.cit.*

35. *Taking Rights Seriously*, p. 13.

36. [1961] 1 QB 394, p. 400.

37. [1975] AC 653, pp. 695–6.

38. *Myers v. D.P.P* [1964] 2 All ER 881 per Lord Hodson at p. 893: "There is not in my opinion any justification for endeavoring to extend the rule. . . . Hedge the extension about with safeguards as you will, this surely would be judicial legislation with a vengeance in an attempt to introduce reform of the law of evidence which, if needed, can properly be dealt with only by the legislature." The history is that Parliament, very shortly after this judgment and in response to criticisms of its result, enacted the *Criminal Evidence Act* 1965, which made admissible those statements contained in business records of the type adduced in *Myers*.

39. [1983] AC 410, p. 431.

40. *Shaw v. D.P.P.* [1962] AC 200.

41. *National Provincial Bank, Ltd. v. Ainsworth* [1965] AC 1175, p. 1239. The situation was "rectified" by statute.

42. [1947] 1 K.B. 130.

43. [1979] 2 All E.R. 910.

44. *Ibid.*, 913–4.

45. See *Law's Empire*, pp. 238–50.

46. See *Marshall v. Lionel Enterprises Inc.* [1972] at 177; *Chadwick v. British Transport* [1967] 1 WLR 912.

47. See, for example, *Alcock v. Chief Constable* [1991] 3 WLR 1057.

48. The positivist would actually say—black-letterly—"the law says that you must be at the scene of the accident to obtain damages." If he taught at a law school he would demand that answer in his examination papers and his class marks would be high; for such a teacher, law would be a memory test—of hard law—and his examination scripts would not be required to display the ability to handle controversy.

49. *Law's Empire*, p. 243.

50. See *Taking Rights Seriously*, pp. 98–100.

51. *Law's Empire*, p. 413.

52. In the first and second editions of this book, I said the reason was that there was a "greater suspicion" of theory in England. In the fourteen years that has elapsed, things have changed. It is not that there is now a suspicion of theory; in fact there has been an exponential growth of theory. But I think much of it is unconfident, even pretentious. Much of it is only lip-service: it is now common to embellish fairly pedestrian legal research with titles that announce that the work is on some "theoretical aspect" of the law.

53. See my comments in the Introduction and *Justice for Hedgehogs*, p. 486, n.6.

CHAPTER 6: INTEGRITY AND COMMUNITY

1. See *Tesco Supermarkets Ltd v. Natrass* [1972] AC 170. *Mens rea* may in this way be attributed to the corporation.

2. These virtues were loyalty, honesty, obedience, hardness, decency, poverty and bravery. But, as Joachim Fest points out in his biography of Hitler (Penguin, 1982) "all these virtues were detached from any comprehensive frame of reference" (p. 377). In Dworkin's terms, their application required justifying them in other values. "Decency" didn't mean much in SS thought.

3. See "Law Respecting Reich Citizenship," *Reich Law Gazette* (September 15, 1935), p. 146.

4. See *The Holocaust: The Jewish Tragedy*, Gilbert, M. (Fontana, 1986), p. 50, where he describes a doctoral thesis, by a Hans Pavogel, in which it was argued that an individual's worth in the community "is measured by his or her racial personality. Only a racially valuable person has a right to exist in the community. A racially inferior or harmful individual must be eliminated."

5. See *Essays on Bentham*, Hart, H.L.A. (Oxford: Oxford UP, 1982), p. 151.

6. See *Ronald Dworkin and Contemporary Jurisprudence*, Cohen, M. (ed.), (London: Duckworth, 1984), p. 259. The asides to Hart are in a reply by Dworkin to an article in the same volume by Lyons, D., entitled "Moral Aspects of Legal Theory," p. 49.

7. *Ibid.*, p. 259.

8. See the debate between Wacks and Dugard on the position of the South African judges. Wacks, R., "Judges and Injustice," *South African Law Journal* 101 (1984), p. 266; Dugard, J., "Should Judges Resign? — A Reply to Professor Wacks," *South African Law Journal* 101 (1984), p. 286. These papers, and some additional ones, are usefully collected together in *Bulletin of the Australian Society of Legal Philosophy* 12 (1988) entitled "Should Judges Work in an Unjust Legal System? — A Debate Based on South Africa." An interesting approach lawyers might adopt to apartheid-type legal systems is in *Wicked Legal Systems*, Dyzenhaus, D. (Oxford: Oxford UP, 1993).

9. See *Justice for Hedgehogs*, pp. 410–12.

10. *Justice for Hedgehogs*, p. 323.

11. *California Law Review* 77 (1991), pp. 479–504; reprinted in *Sovereign Virtue*, pp. 211–36.

12. See also the section "The Morality Behind Conventions," pp. 171–73 in Chapter 9.

13. See, for example, Hart's article "Are There Any Natural Rights?" in *Political Philosophy*, Quinton, A. (ed.), (Oxford: Oxford UP, 1967), p. 53, where he justifies political obligation in these terms.

14. *Law's Empire*, p. 196.

15. *Justice for Hedgehogs*, 321.

16. And that also means, he says, that for conflicts between people's associative obligations and questions of justice, say, where the demands of "crude nationalism" are contrary to political obligations, justice must settle the argument: "The best interpretation of our own political practices disavows that feature. . . . When and where it is endorsed any conflict between militant nationalism and standards of justice must be resolved in favor of the latter" (*Law's Empire*, p. 206). In *Justice for Hedgehogs*, Dworkin describes tribal associations where there is no special structure to protect dignity as a "powerful source of evil."

17. The model of principle, he says, "makes the responsibilities of citizenship special: each citizen respects the principles of fairness and justice instinct in the standing political arrangement of his particular community, which may be different from those of other communities, whether or not he thinks these the best principles from a Utopian standpoint." *Law's Empire*, p. 213.

18. *Sovereign Virtue*, p. 215.

19. The idea that community plays an important role in the enhancement of a person's life, in particular his autonomy, by according to him an "adequate" range of options is, for example, to be found in *The Morality of Freedom*, Raz, J. (Oxford: Oxford UP, 1986), chs 8, 14 and 15.

20. See *Liberalism and the Limits of Justice*, Sandel, M. (Cambridge: Harvard UP, 1982).

21. See Jonathan Sumption's review of *Justice for Hedgehogs* in *The Spectator* March 21, 2011. It is a common comment and just as commonly never backed up (Sumption's review is a typical example). Why, is an interesting question.

22. Dworkin also considers another of the "need"-type arguments. It is Selznick's claim in "The Idea of a Communitarian Morality," *California Law Review* 75 (1987), p. 445, that a "background" of shared community convictions is needed to "anchor" morality by giving it "objectivity." It is obvious how Dworkin would deal with such a claim. It cannot be a reference to a psychological "feeling" of objectivity, because eccentric views are held by people who are characteristically convinced of their objectivity. So it must be the claim that moral objectivity is constituted by moral conventionalism. But, "paradoxically," as Dworkin says, one thing that people do not share is the idea that the objectivity of morality is constituted by shared views: "Moral judgments cannot be made true or false by consensus, that they have force across cultural boundaries, that they are not, in short, creatures of culture or community but rather judges of them." See Dworkin's remarks on Walzer's *Spheres of Influence*, in *A Matter of Principle*, p. 214, ch. 10, entitled "What Justice Isn't."

23. Dworkin, R., "Liberal Community," *California Law Review* 77 (1991), pp. 479, 492.

24. So, says Dworkin, integration rejects Mill, because it rejects the idea of individuality.

25. *Supra*, "Liberal Community" at p. 496.

26. *Justice for Hedgehogs*, p. 348.

27. *Justice for Hedgehogs* 349–50; he follows up by saying this method is "strikingly different" from the "historical" approach of Berlin and Williams and that the interpretive method depends on history but can't be driven by it: "interpretation engages history but history does not fix interpretation."

28. Dworkin placed some of the blame on the then recent Thatcher government for unwittingly running down what he describes as "the culture of liberty" in a democracy. The Tory government calls itself conservative, but it is wrecking the best part of Britain's legal heritage. Thatcher's people are not despots. But they have a more mundane and corrupting insensitivity to liberty. (*A Bill of Rights for Britain: Why British Liberty Needs Protecting* London: Chatto & Windus, 1990, pp. 9–10.)

29. *Democracy and Distrust: A Theory of Judicial Review*, Ely, J. (Cambridge: Harvard UP, 1980).

30. "Equality, Democracy, and Constitution: We the People in Court," *Alberta Law Review* 28 (1990), pp. 324–46.

31. See *Law's Empire*, p. 189: "Many of our political attitudes, collected in our instinct of group responsibility, assume that we are in some sense the authors of the political decisions made by our governors, or at least that we have reason to think of ourselves that way. Kant and Rousseau based their conceptions of freedom on this ideal of self-legislation. The idea needs integrity, however, for a citizen cannot treat himself as the author of a collection of laws that are inconsistent in principle, nor can he see that collection as sponsored by any Rousseaunian general will."

32. "Political Equality," in *Sovereign Virtue*, pp. 184–210.

33. *Ibid.*, n. 23 at p. 333.

34. See 558 U.S. 08-205 (2010) and Dworkin, "The 'Devastating' Decision," *New York Review of Books*, February 25, 2010.

35. See above "Liberal Community."

36. See "Equality, Democracy, and Constitution: We the People in Court," 28 *Alberta L.Rev.* 324 1989-90, p. 337.

37. See *A Theory of Law*, Soper, P. (Cambridge: Harvard UP, 1984). I discuss the sense of his claim in my review of the book in *Law Quarterly Review* (1986), pp. 332–35.

38. *Supra*, "Equality, Democracy, and Constitution: We the People in Court," p. 341.

39. *Loc.cit.*

40. See also *A Matter of Principle*, ch. 3.

41. *Supra*, n. 23.

42. See Waldron, J. "The Core of the Case Against Judicial Review," *Yale Law Journal* 115 (2006): 1346. And see his *Law and Disagreement* (Oxford: Oxford UP 1999) chs. 9, 12 and 13.

43. *Justice for Hedgehogs*, p. 391.

44. See Waldron, J. "A Right-Based Critique of Constitutional Rights," *Oxford Journal of Legal Studies* Vol. 13 (1993) 18, 33n.44.

CHAPTER 7: OBJECTIVITY IN LAW AND MORALITY

1. "The Enforcement of Morals." This is to be found in *The Enforcement of Morals*, Devlin, P. (Oxford: Oxford UP, 1965), a collection of essays by Lord Devlin mostly

on the same theme. Although there are refinements in later essays, none of these affect Dworkin's criticisms.

2. In later writings, Lord Devlin abandoned the measure of "the man in the Clapham omnibus" in favor of the jury. The difference is a pragmatic one. The first is "theoretical," the second "actual," but both point to the same test of conventional morality. At p. viii of the Preface of *The Enforcement of Morals*, he affirms that, despite criticisms of his phrase "intolerance, indignation and disgust," he was still unwilling to qualify it six years later.

3. He allows the case of not having a reason because of its being some major premise that it is just taken to be axiomatic or self-evident as being a reason of a special sort. See *Taking Rights Seriously*, p. 252: "The claim that a particular position is axiomatic, in other words, does supply a reason of a special sort. . . ."

4. *Taking Rights Seriously*, p. 255.

5. See Dworkin's remarks about the relationship between conventions and morality in connection with promising in Chapter 9; also his criticisms of conventionalism as a legal theory in Chapter 3.

6. See "Social Rules and Legal Theory," *Yale Law Journal* 81 (1972), pp. 855–90, which is reprinted in *Taking Rights Seriously* at p. 46. At p. 47, he says: "Positivism, with its doctrine of a fundamental and commonly-recognized test for law, mistakes part of the domain of that concept for the whole."

7. 40 *U. Chi. L. Rev.* 500 (1973), reprinted as "Justice and Rights" in *Taking Rights Seriously* as ch. 6, p. 150.

8. Notice how powerful this theory is in explaining the shifts and turns in our moral perceptions during our lives. I know some post-modernists who abhor the role of intuition in this methodology because it does not capture "*le reel.*" They have a strong intuition that this is so!

9. *Justice for Hedgehogs*, pp. 263–64.

10. See now *Justice for Hedgehogs* in which Dworkin allows for "internally skeptical" arguments in literary interpretation, for example, that there is no right answer—an ambiguity—in a poem (he cites Leavis's reading of *Sailing to Byzantium*), or film (citing Michael Haneke's films *Hidden* and *The White Ribbon* in which the right answer might be that there is no answer as to who the murderers are); p. 146.

11. See "Indeterminacy and Law," in Guest, S. (ed.), *Positivism Today* (Ashgate 1996), p. 1. Although Dworkin doesn't generally use musical examples, it is clear that "no right answer" applies to musical ambiguity, too. Blues derives its power from ambiguity. The technique lies in playing a minor scale against major chords (the well-known "12-bar chord progression," which on its own is consonant, even martial). The sound is suggestive of both pessimism and optimism. A skilful blues player constantly keeps tension by alternating between these two feelings. Augmenting the fourths and sevenths of the scale (bending) is one common way of achieving the effect. Blues lyrics are the same. Sometimes they're serious (minor)—"I really got the blues so bad I'm going to die"—then they are laughing (major): "Yeah, I got them so bad . . . I fell out of bed." That is why good blues always manages to mock—and explains why it has a teasing, menacing feel to it: "the devil's music." I understand that those who think that all value is subjective will think this is so much tosh. But they can't *disagree*.

12. *Justice for Hedgehogs*, p. 154.

13. It is also a significant characteristic of Kelsen's writings in legal theory since he viewed law as meaningful only from the point of view of a general presupposition about its normative force. Kelsen's basic norm is clearly intended to provide logical coherence to a person's full set of legal reasons for acting from either that person's "legal" point of view, or the point of view of the professional, non-committed "legal scientist." See *The Authority of Law*, Raz, J. (Oxford: Oxford UP, 1979), ch. 7 for an excellent discussion. Kelsen is closer to Dworkin than Hart on the internal point of view, although Dworkin does not, of course, share with Kelsen any idea of a morally neutral but "committed" point of view.

14. See *Justice for Hedgehogs*, "Law as Morality: A Tree Structure" 405–7. See Soper, P., *Philosophy and Public Affairs* 18 (1989), pp. 209–37. Soper thinks that a line can be drawn between the insider as far as the concept of law goes and the insider as far as adjudication goes. He appears to think that Dworkin is right on the first, but that it does not follow, as he says Dworkin assumes, that one must then be an insider on the second. I am at a loss to know why. Hart had a theory of adjudication as a prominent part of his account of the concept of law (the "rules of adjudication"); I can't see why the commitment that the judges (as officials) must have to the identifying rules should disappear as soon as adjudication begins. It would be question-begging to argue that positivism *requires* this change in commitment but I don't see what other argument Soper can employ. See also Dworkin's remark in his Introduction to his *The Philosophy of Law* (Oxford: Oxford UP, 1977), p. 7, that some theory of adjudication will be a "consequence" of the positivist theory of law.

15. What Dworkin calls the "Dependence Thesis."

16. *Law's Empire*, p. 81, his emphasis.

17. *Philosophy & Public Affairs*, vol. 25, Spring 1996, pp. 87–139.

18. *Justice for Hedgehogs*, p. 9.

19. William Shakespeare, *Richard III*, Act I scene 1: "since I cannot prove a lover, To entertain these fair well-spoken days, I am determined to prove a villain, And hate the idle pleasures of these days."

20. *Justice for Hedgehogs*, p. 9.

21. *Ibid.*, pp. 85–6.

CHAPTER 8: TREATING PEOPLE AS EQUALS

1. See Williams, B. "The Idea of Equality," in *Philosophy, Politics and Society*, 2nd series, Laslett, P. & Runciman, W. (eds.), (1962), p. 125.

2. See *Nonsense upon Stilts: Bentham, Burke and Marx on the Rights of Man*, Waldron, J. (ed.), (London: Methuen, 1987), p. 51. Williams says that because people's empirical differences so clearly affect their capacities Kant was wrong to assert a universal moral capacity derivable solely from the status of personhood. The Kantian principle, too, he says, is a secular analogue of the Christian conception of respect. It is empty to conclude, he says, that men are equal in their moral capacities. See *op.cit.*

3. See *The Morality of Freedom*, Raz, J. (Oxford UP, 1986), ch. 9. Also, *On Justice*, Lucas, J. (Oxford: Oxford UP, 1980), ch. 9.

4. Dworkin notes this feature obliquely in his article "Equality of Welfare," discussed later in Chapter 11. See also "What Is Equality? Part 1: Equality of Welfare," *Philosophy and Public Affairs* (1981), p. 185, at p. 245.

5. *Taking Rights Seriously*, p. 227.

6. *Ibid.*, p. 275.

7. See "Equality of Welfare," pp. 244–45.

8. *Loc. cit.*

9. *Taking Rights Seriously*, 277–78.

10. See *A Matter of Principle*, ch. 8.

11. Posner, R. *Hofstra Law Review* (1980) 487, 492.

12. See Calabresi, G., "About Law and Economics: A Letter to Ronald Dworkin," *Hofstra Law Review* 8 (1980), p. 553, where Calabresi answers Dworkin's article criticizing Posner, R., "Is Wealth a Value?" now in *A Matter of Principle*, p. 237.

13. *A Matter of Principle*, p. 283.

14. See "The Law of the Slave-Catchers," *Times Literary Supplement* (December 5, 1975), p. 1437 and "Justice Accused," *Times Literary Supplement* (January 9, 1976).

15. "The *Defunis* Case: The Right to Go to Law School," *New York Review of Books* (February 5, 1976); "The *Defunis* Case: An Exchange," *New York Review of Books* (1976); "Why Bakke Has No Case," *New York Review of Books* (November 10, 1977); "The *Bakke* Case: An Exchange," *New York Review of Books* (1978); "The *Bakke* Decision: Did It Decide Anything?" *New York Review of Books* (August 17, 1978); "How to Read the Civil Rights Act," *New York Review of Books* (December 20, 1979); "Let's Give Blacks a Head Start," *The Times* (December 12, 1981).

16. "Journalists' Right to a Fair Trial," *The Times* (November 30, 1976); "The Rights of Myron Farber," *New York Review of Books* (1978); "The Rights of Myron Farber: an Exchange" *New York Review of Books* (October 26, 1978); "Is the Press Losing the First Amendment?" *New York Review of Books* (December 4, 1980); "The Press on Trial," *New York Review of Books* (February 26, 1987); "Time's Settlement," *New York Review of Books* (1978); "Time's Rewrite," *New York Review of Books* (1987); "Reckless Disregard: An Exchange," *New York Review of Books* (September 24, 1987); "Devaluing Liberty," *Index on Censorship* (1988); "The Ragged Banner of Liberty," *The Independent* (September 8, 1988); "The Coming Battles Over Free Speech," *New York Review of Books* (November 7, 1991); "Liberty and Pornography," *New York Review of Books* (August 14, 1991); "A Harmful Precedent," *Index on Censorship* (1991); "Women and Pornography," *New York Review of Books* (October 21, 1993); "A New Map of Censorship," *Index on Censorship* (February, 1994); "Pornography: An Exchange," *New York Review of Books* (March 3, 1994); "The Unbearable Cost of Liberty," *Index on Censorship* (1995); "The Curse of Money," *New York Review of Books* (October 17, 1996).

17. "Principle, Policy, Procedure," in *Crime, Proof and Punishment: Essays in Memory of Sir Rupert Cross*, Tapper, C. (ed.), (London: Butterworth, 1981), p. 193.

18. "Reagan's Justice," *New York Review of Books* (November 8, 1984); "Reagan's Justice: an Exchange," *New York Review of Books* (1981); "The Bork Nomination," *New York Review of Books* (1981), p. 3; "The Bork Nomination: An Exchange," *New York Review of Books* (October 18, 1987); "The Bork Nomination," *New York Review of Books* (August 13, 1987); "The Great Abortion Case," *New York Review of Books* (June

29, 1989); "The Future of Abortion," *New York Review of Books* (September 28, 1989); "Bork's Jurisprudence," *University of Chicago Law Review* 57 (1990); "Taking Rights Seriously in the Abortion Case," *Ratio Juris* (1990), p. 68; "The Center Holds!" *New York Review of Books* (August 13, 1992); and "Unenumerated Rights: Whether and How *Roe* Should Be Overruled," *University of Chicago Law Review* 59 (1992), p. 381.

19. See the bibliography. The best account is to be found in his *Life's Dominion: an Argument About Abortion and Euthanasia* (New York: Knopf, 1993).

20. See Chapter 3 earlier on "original intention," and Dworkin's writings on the constitutional status (in the United States) of statutes prohibiting or restricting abortion. See *Life's Dominion*, especially chs. 4–6 ("Abortion in Court: Part I," "The Constitutional Drama," and "Abortion in Court: Part II"). Also generally see *Freedom's Law*.

21. *Sweatt v. Painter* 70 S. Ct. 848 (1949).

22. 347 U.S. 486 (1954).

23. *Report of the Committee on Obscenity and Film Censorship* Cmd. 7772 (HMSO, 1979). Dworkin thinks that what he calls "the Williams strategy" is wrongly based on the idea that what is important, or unimportant, about the banning of pornography revolves entirely round the question of whether community goals are enhanced. Although he is in favor of a number of conclusions of the Report, he does not think the goal-based strategy is sufficient to support them. Goal-based justification, he says, "has the weakness of providing contingent reasons for convictions that we do not hold contingently." (*A Matter of Principle*, p. 352).

24. See *The Morality of Freedom*, Raz, J. (Oxford: Oxford UP, 1986), chs. 14 and 15.

25. *Law's Empire*, p. 395.

26. *Ibid.*, p. 394.

27. Note Dworkin's discussion of the case of *Regents of the University of California v. Bakke* 438 U.S. 265 (1978). Dworkin says a possible line Bakke (who was a majority, white applicant) might have taken was that the Davis medical program did not consider the impact of the quota system upon his group in assessing the contribution to the general welfare by having a greater number of qualified black doctors. But, he says, "Hercules would decide (I believe) that this claim is confused: a quota system gives the same consideration to the full class of applicants as any other system that relies, as all must, on general classifications." See *Law's Empire*, p. 397.

CHAPTER 9: JUSTICE FOR HEDGEHOGS

1. *Justice for Hedgehogs*, p. 7.

2. *Ibid.*, p. 4.

3. *Op.cit.*, p. 78.

4. *Justice for Hedgehogs*, p. 193. For a moving account, see Rae Langton's "Maria von Herbert's Challenge to Kant," *Ethics (Oxford Reader)*, ed. Singer, P. New York: OUP (1994) 281.

5. See later Chapter 11.

6. *Justice for Hedgehogs*, p. 195.

7. *Ibid.*, p. 198.

8. And see Chapter 11.

9. See *The Morality of Freedom* (Oxford: OUP, 1987).

10. *Justice for Hedgehogs*, p. 212.

11. See Hare's *Freedom and Reason* (Oxford: OUP, 1963), pp. 171–173.

12. See Darwall, S. "Two Kinds of Respect," (1977) *Ethics* 88, pp. 36–49; reprinted in *Dignity, Character, and Self-Respect*, Dillon, R. (ed.), (New York: Routledge, 1995).

13. *Justice for Hedgehogs*, p. 258. Dworkin has an interesting aside on Nietzsche here. Nietzsche, he says, thought only a few (e.g., himself) had distinguished lives. But it was not clear that he thought those who didn't have such lives were unimportant. But some interpreters think he thought that people should live well (Nietzsche thought, for example, that it was wrong that priests had imposed a "slave mentality" that made living virtually impossible). For Nietzsche, living well was different from living a good life; living well required sacrifice and suffering. It is a further question in Nietzsche whether only some could "live well." Zarathustra thought that his insights were for "the species." In Dworkin's view Nietzsche was contemptuous of the "servile morality" of equality and democracy but only because he thought it was a bad account of how people should live. Nietzsche had special contempt for utilitarians, for example ("Anglo-angelic shopkeeperdom"). He thought happiness/ pleasure almost pointless. He also had contempt for Kantians who thought living well was constituted by fulfilling duties to others. And so Dworkin concludes that Nietzsche *did* think it important how people lived: it was just that Nietzsche thought current moralities didn't support it.

14. *Ibid.*, p. 260.

15. *Ibid.*, pp. 262–63.

16. *Ibid.*, p. 272.

17. *Ibid.*, pp. 278–79.

18. *Ibid.*, p. 281.

19. *Ibid.*, p. 282.

20. *Ibid.*, p. 283.

21. See Dworkin's remarks in reply to Goldberg in the *Justice for Hedgehogs* Symposium: *Boston University Law Review*, (2010) 2, vol. 90, at pp. 1072–73: "many of the lives people lead are failures and . . . this is a matter of regret not just for them but for everyone. But I try to make clear that these ethical judgments have not moral or political consequence. We do not owe less by way of equal treatment or respect, either as individuals or in politics, to those who have lived badly."

22. *Justice for Hedgehogs*, p. 289. Presumably there are limits to what one may consent to. One's dignity must also encompass the intrinsic value of the human body (see later, Chapter 12); it would be a moral affront to that value, perhaps, to consent to someone sawing one's leg off and eating it. It is common for legal systems to disallow consent to serious bodily injury as a defense.

23. See *U.S. v. Carroll Towing Co.*, 159 F.2d 169, 173 (2d Cir.1947), referred to in *Taking Rights Seriously*, p. 98.

24. *Justice for Hedgehogs*, p. 291.

25. "The Trolley Problem," (1985) *Yale Law Journal* vol. 94, p. 1395.

26. See John Harris "The Survival Lottery," (1974) *Philosophy* 49, p. 81.

27. *Justice for Hedgehogs*, p. 296.

28. *Ibid.*, p. 298.

29. *Loc.cit.*
30. *Conventions*, (Cambridge: Harvard UP, 1969).
31. *Justice for Hedgehogs*, p. 309.
32. *Loc.cit.*
33. *Ibid.*, p. 310.
34. *Ibid.*, p. 334.
35. See his "Two Concepts of Liberty," in Berlin, I. *The Proper Study of Mankind*, Hardy and Hausheer (eds.), (London: Chatto & Windus, 1997) 191, at pp. 234–35.
36. *Justice for Hedgehogs*, pp. 369–70.
37. *Ibid.*, p. 371.
38. See further "Principle, Policy, Procedure," in *A Matter of Principle*, (Cambridge: Harvard UP, 1985), ch. 3.

39. He says there are two kinds of "incompatibilist": *optimistic*, who think sometimes our actions are not determined, so sometimes we have responsibility; and *pessimistic*, who think our actions are always determined and so we never have responsibility.
40. *Justice for Hedgehogs*, p. 229.
41. *Ibid.*, p. 422.

CHAPTER 10: EQUALITY OF WHAT?

1. "What Is Equality? Part I: Equality of Welfare," *Philosophy and Public Affairs* 10 (1981), p. 185; "What Is Equality? Part II: Equality of Resources," *Philosophy and Public Affairs* 10 (1981), p. 283.
2. "What Is Equality? Part III: The Place of Liberty," *Iowa Law Review* 73 (1987), p. 1.
3. *Justice for Hedgehogs*, p. 356.
4. "Equality of Welfare," p. 210.
5. *Sovereign Virtue*, p. 38.
6. *Ibid.*, p. 219.
7. See "The Place of Liberty," p. 41: "Equality of resources leaves no basis for interpersonal comparison of liberty deficits rising from the same constraint."
8. "The distributive norm that I favor takes part of its inspiration from the socialist slogan, 'To each according to their needs—according, that is, to what they need for fulfilment in life,' which is an antimarket slogan." Jerry Cohen, "Expensive Tastes Rides Again" in Justine Burley, ed. *Dworkin and his Critics* (Oxford: Blackwell, 2004) 3, 17.
9. See Dworkin: "Justice is relational: it is a matter of how people should treat one another, not of how the world should otherwise be." In "Reply to Cohen" in Burley, above, 339, 344.
10. See my "Ronald Dworkin and the Question of Political Stability and Legitimacy," ch. 4 in Gough & Stables, (eds.). *Sustainability and Security Within Liberal Societies: Learning to Live with the Future*, Routledge Studies in Social and Political Thought series, (London: Routledge, 2008) 49.
11. In Dworkin's language, "the stipulated function of the stipulated conception of welfare is something good in itself that ought to be produced for its own sake." "Equality of Welfare," p. 244.
12. This is Derek Parfit's "repugnant conclusion." Dworkin also says that egalitarian utilitarianism cannot explain what is wrong with a natural disaster which kills thousands but improves the situation of a few.

13. "Our interest," he says, "is primarily in the design of an ideal, and of a device to picture that ideal and test its coherence, completeness, and appeal." In "Equality of Resources," p. 292.

14. "Equality of Resources," p. 288.

15. *Ibid.*, p. 285.

16. See Chapter 8.

17. See "Equality of Resources," p. 295: "resources gained through a successful gamble should be represented by the opportunity to take the gamble at the odds in force."

18. *Ibid.*, p. 299.

19. *Ibid.*, p. 323.

20. *Ibid.*, p. 331.

21. *Ibid.*, p. 330.

22. The arguments in this section are largely drawn from his "What Is Equality? Part III: The Place of Liberty," *Iowa Law Review* 73 (1987), p. 1. (Reprinted in *Sovereign Virtue* as ch. 3).

23. "Equality of Resources," p. 303.

24. Consistently with that principle, of course. A person cannot use his freedom to limit another's, obviously.

25. "Foundations of a Liberal Equality," *The Tanner Lectures on Human Values XI*, (University of Utah Press, 1990), p. 1.

26. I add "genuine" to rule out someone claiming compensation for "not looking good," say. Human beings have to be fairly robust (there are genuine cases of sensitivity of course) or they lose dignity.

27. "Equality of Resources," p. 25.

28. See *Justice for Hedgehogs*, p. 357: "A free market is not equality's enemy, as is often supposed, but indispensible to genuine equality. An egalitarian economy is a basically capitalist economy."

29. Magee, in his dialogue with Dworkin in *Men of Ideas*, makes the same sort of objection to the idea of Rawls's "original position," at p. 216.

30. Note, incidentally, that Dworkin thinks that any attempt to improve the lot of the worst off is egalitarian. He also thinks that about giving priority to the worst off. It's arithmetic, really. There will always be a worst-off group in any non-egalitarian distribution. Such theories stand or fall on their substantive and not these procedural merits in my view. Magee: "But all this [theory], it seems to me, bears excessively little relation to the historical realities out of which actual societies emerge, and which therefore shape them, and the social realities in which actual individuals find themselves—and therefore the real factors to which political philosophies need to relate."

31. *Ibid.*, p. 42. Dworkin: "We're not concerned with the historical question here. We're concerned about which principles *are just* . . . "

32. Federal Election Campaign Elections Act Amendments of 1974, 88 Stat. 1263 (1974). In other words, the riposte to the argument that Dworkin or Rawls are utopian is to say, of course they are. *That* is their point, to set up a model by which we can test and criticize the practices of the real world.

33. 424 U.S. 1 (1976).

34. *Lochner v. New York* 198 U.S. 45 (1905).

CHAPTER 11: THE BASIS OF LIBERALISM

1. See the Introduction to *Contemporary Political Philosophy*, Kymlicka, W. Oxford UP, (1990), ch. 6, and the essays in *Communitarianism and Individualism*, Avineri, S. & de-Shalit, A. (eds.), Oxford UP, (1992). A good liberal response is the article by Gutmann, A., and entitled "The Communitarian Critics of Liberalism," in that volume.

2. Note Thatcher's infamous statement that "there is no such thing as society, only individuals and families." She asserted this as central to conservative thinking, when the communitarians in the United States, who would share many of Thatcher's convictions, urge the opposite view, that individuals cannot be separated from the society in which they live.

3. See Gutmann, A., *op.cit.*

4. See *The Morality of Freedom*, Raz, J. Oxford UP, (1986). See also my review of his book in *Law Quarterly Review* 103 (1987), p. 642.

5. See *A Theory of Justice*, Rawls, J. (Oxford: Oxford UP, 1972), pp. 197–98 and pp. 221–24. Also his "Kantian Constructivism in Moral Theory," *Journal of Philosophy* 77 (1980), p. 515; "Justice as Fairness: Political Not Metaphysical," *Philosophy and Public Affairs* 14 (1985), p. 223; "The Idea of an Overlapping Consensus," *Oxford Journal of Legal Studies* (1987), p. 1; "The Priority of Right and Ideas of the Good," *Philosophy and Public Affairs* 17 (1988), p. 251; "The Laws of Peoples," in *Human Rights*, Shute & Hurley (eds.), (Basic Books, 1993). In general, see his *Political Liberalism* (Columbia UP, 1993).

6. See, in general, his "Foundation of Liberal Equality," *The Tanner Lectures on Human Values XII* (University of Utah Press, 1990).

7. Dworkin thinks that it may be that Rawls's appeal to his overlapping consensus as being more than a *modus vivendi*, by his appeal to something in the personal ethics of everyone participating in such a consensus gives visionary appeal. Dworkin says that there is "plain nobility" in the goal of mutual respect and co-operation.

8. See earlier, Chapter 7, and his "Objectivity and Truth: You'd Better Believe It," *Philosophy & Public Affairs* (1996), p. 87.

9. "Foundation of Liberal Equality," *op.cit.*, p. 34.

10. *Law's Empire*, p. 425, n. 20.

11. See "Equality of Welfare," p. 225.

12. "Foundation of Liberal Equality," *op.cit.*, p. 63. And see, *Justice for Hedgehogs*, 211, where Dworkin uses this example to illustrate the justifiable constraints on authenticity.

13. See Chapter 8.

14. "Foundation of Liberal Equality," *op.cit.*, pp. 74–75. In ch. 14 of *The Republic*, Socrates defines justice as an individual virtue. Justice is an internal order of the soul which will bring about right behavior: "The just man does not allow the several elements in his soul to usurp one another's functions; he is indeed one who set his house in order, by self-mastery and discipline coming to be at peace with himself. . . . Only when he has linked these parts together in well-tempered harmony and has made himself one man instead of many, will he be ready to go about whatever he may have to do, whether it be making money and satisfying bodily wants, or business transactions, or the affairs of state." *The Republic of Plato*, Cornford (trans.), (Oxford: Oxford UP, 1941) pp. 138–39.

15. This example is not so intuitively obvious. I suppose that one's pleasure in that is the perverse one of having borne up well in unjust circumstances. Is that so

different from someone from a poor country, but one where resources are justly distributed, saying "I made the best of a bad lot?" Dworkin is aware of this point: see "Foundation of Liberal Equality," *op.cit.*, p. 75.

CHAPTER 12: RELIGION AND THE BEGINNING AND END OF LIFE

1. *Justice for Hedgehogs*, p. 82.
2. *Ibid.*
3. See *New York Review of Books*, Vol. 53, No. 14 (2006), "Three Questions for America," Part I: "Should Alternatives to Evolution be Taught in Schools?"
4. *Loc.cit.*
5. "Religious temperament" is a phrase Nagel uses to describe this way of being. See his *Secular Philosophy and the Religious Temperament: Essays 2002–2008*, (New York: Oxford UP 2010).
6. *Justice for Hedgehogs*, p. 218.
7. Although it is, too, an odd way of putting it to talk of the human "investment" that parents put into their children in raising them. See *Life's Dominion*, ch. 2.
8. *Justice for Hedgehogs*, p. 388.
9. *Life's Dominion*, p. 84.
10. *Ibid.*, p. 87.
11. *Justice for Hedgehogs*, p. 378. There will be occasions where abortion is—in Dworkin's terms—"an act of self-contempt" because the woman "betrays her own dignity" by not showing "the respect for human life that her dignity demands."
12. 410 U.S. 113 (1973). The right was unconditional for the first trimester, conditional for the second.
13. 85 S. Ct. 1678 (1965).
14. *Life's Dominion*, p. 124.
15. See "Unenumerated Rights: Whether and How *Roe* Should Be Overruled," *Chicago Law Review*, vol. 59 (1992) at 464. This article is reprinted as ch. 3 of *Freedom's Law*.
16. *Planned Parenthood of Southeastern Pennsylvania v. Casey* 112 S. Ct. 2791 (1992).
17. *United States v. Seeger* 380 U.S. 163 (1965).
18. *Life's Dominion*, p. 163.
19. *Ibid.*, p. 199.
20. *Ibid.*, p. 213.
21. *Ibid.*, p. 192.
22. See Dworkin's remarks on free will and responsibility in Chapter 9.
23. *Ibid.*, p. 239.

Bibliography of Ronald Dworkin's Works

BOOKS AND ARTICLES

2012

"Why the Mandate Is Constitutional: The Real Argument," *New York Review of Books*, May 10, 2012, (http://www.nybooks.com/articles/archives/2012/may/10/why-mandate-constitutional-real-argument/).

2011

"The Court's Embarrassingly Bad Decisions," *New York Review of Books*, May 26, 2011, (http://www.nybooks.com/articles/archives/2011/may/26/courts-embarrassingly-bad-decisions/).

"More Bad Arguments: The Roberts Court & Money in Politics," *NYRB Blog*, April 27, 2011, (http://www.nybooks.com/blogs/nyrblog/2011/apr/27/more-bad-arguments-roberts-court-money-politics/).

"Bad Arguments: The Roberts Court & Religious Schools," *NYRB Blog*, April 26, 2011, (http://www.nybooks.com/blogs/nyrblog/2011/apr/26/bad-arguments-roberts-court-religious-schools/).

"What Is a Good Life?" *New York Review of Books*, February 10, 2011, (http://www.nybooks.com/articles/archives/2011/feb/10/what-good-life/).

Justice for Hedgehogs (Cambridge, MA: Belknap Press, 2011).

2010

(with Mark Lilla, David Bromwich, and Jonathan Raban) "The Historic Election: Four Views," *New York Review of Books*, December 9, 2010, (http://www.nybooks.com/articles/archives/2010/dec/09/historic-election-four-views/).

"Americans Against Themselves," *NYRB Blog*, November 5, 2010, (http://www.nybooks.com/blogs/nyrblog/2010/nov/05/americans-against-themselves/).

Paper presented at the NYU Colloquium in Legal, Political and Social Philosophy on October 14, 2010, entitled: "Human Rights and International Law" (not for

quotation), (http://www.law.nyu.edu/ecm_dlv4/groups/public/@nyu_law_website__
academics__colloquia__legal_political_and_social_philosophy/documents/documents/
ecm_pro_067009.pdf).

"The Temptation of Elena Kagan," *New York Review of Books*, August 19, 2010,
(http://www.nybooks.com/articles/archives/2010/aug/19/temptation-elena-kagan/).

"The Decision That Threatens Democracy," *New York Review of Books*, May 13,
2010, (http://www.nybooks.com/articles/archives/2010/may/13/decision-threatens
-democracy/).

"'The "Devastating" Decision': An Exchange," *New York Review of Books*, April 29,
2010, (http://www.nybooks.com/articles/archives/2010/apr/08/devastating-decision
-exchange/).

"The 'Devastating' Decision," *New York Review of Books*, February 25, 2010, (http://
www.nybooks.com/articles/archives/2010/feb/25/the-devastating-decision/).

2009

"Keep Corporations Out of Televised Politics," *NYRB Blog*, October 5, 2009,
(http://www.nybooks.com/blogs/nyrblog/2009/oct/05/keep-corporations-out-of
-televised-politics/).

"Justice Sotomayor: The Unjust Hearings," *New York Review of Books*, September
24, 2009, (http://www.nybooks.com/articles/archives/2009/sep/24/justice-sotomayor
-the-unjust-hearings/).

Contribution to "Questions to Judge Sotomayor: The Unjust Hearings," *New
York Times*, July 13, 2009.

"Looking for Cass Sunstein," Review of *A Constitution of Many Minds: Why the
Founding Document Doesn't Mean What It Meant Before* by Cass R. Sunstein, *New York
Review of Books*, April 30, 2009, (http://www.nybooks.com/articles/archives/2009/
apr/30/looking-for-cass-sunstein/).

2008

"A Fateful Election," *New York Review of Books*, November 6, 2008, (http://www
.nybooks.com/articles/archives/2008/nov/06/a-fateful-election/).

"Why It Was a Great Victory," *New York Review of Books*, August 14, 2008, (http://
www.nybooks.com/articles/archives/2008/aug/14/why-it-was-a-great-victory/).

2007

"'The Supreme Court Phalanx': An Exchange," *New York Review of Books*, December
6, 2007, (http://www.nybooks.com/articles/archives/2007/dec/06/the-supreme-court
-phalanx-an-exchange/).

"Lotto for Learning?" (letter) *New York Review of Books*, October 25, 2007, (http://
www.nybooks.com/articles/archives/2007/oct/25/lotto-for-learning/).

"The Supreme Court Phalanx," *New York Review of Books*, September 27, 2007,
(http://www.nybooks.com/articles/archives/2007/sep/27/the-supreme-court-phalanx/).

"The Court & Abortion: Worse Than You Think," *New York Review of Books*, May
31, 2007, (http://www.nybooks.com/articles/archives/2007/may/31/the-court-abortion
-worse-than-you-think/).

"So You Think You Live in a Democracy?" *The Guardian*, March 12, 2007, (http://
www.guardian.co.uk/commentisfree/2007/mar/12/isdemocracypossiblehere).

2006

Justice in Robes (Harvard University Press, 2006).
Is Democracy Possible Here? (Princeton University Press, 2006).
"Darwin and Spirituality: An Exchange," *New York Review of Books*, November 2, 2006, (http://www.nybooks.com/articles/archives/2006/nov/02/darwin-and-spirituality-an-exchange/).
"Do not sacrifice principle to the new tyrannies," *Financial Times*, October 9, 2006.
"Three Questions for America," *New York Review of Books*, September 21, 2006, (http://www.nybooks.com/articles/archives/2006/sep/21/three-questions-for-america/).
"It Is Absurd to Calculate Human Rights According to a Cost-Benefit Analysis," *The Guardian*, May 24, 2006, (http://www.guardian.co.uk/commentisfree/2006/may/24/comment.politics).
"What Lincoln Said," (letter) *New York Review of Books*, May 11, 2006, (http://www.nybooks.com/articles/archives/2006/may/11/what-lincoln-said/).
"'The Strange Case of Justice Alito': An Exchange," *New York Review of Books*, April 6, 2006, (http://www.nybooks.com/articles/archives/2006/apr/06/the-strange-case-of-justice-alito-an-exchange/).
"The Right to Ridicule," *New York Review of Books*, March 23, 2006, (http://www.nybooks.com/articles/archives/2006/mar/23/the-right-to-ridicule/).
"The Strange Case of Judge Alito," *New York Review of Books*, February 23, 2006, (http://www.nybooks.com/articles/archives/2006/feb/23/the-strange-case-of-judge-alito/).
"On NSA Spying: A Letter to Congress," (letter), *New York Review of Books*, February 9, 2006, (http://www.nybooks.com/articles/archives/2006/feb/09/on-nsa-spying-a-letter-to-congress/).

2005

"Judge Roberts on Trial," *New York Review of Books*, October 20, 2005, (http://www.nybooks.com/articles/archives/2005/oct/20/judge-roberts-on-trial/).
"Reponse aux articles de Ronald Dworkin," *Revue Internationale de Philosophie*, 2005/3 (n° 233).

2004

From Liberal Values to Democratic Transition: Essays in Honor of Janos Kis, Dworkin and others (eds.), (Central European University Press, 2004).
"Hart's Postscript and the Character of Political Philosophy," *Oxford Journal of Legal Studies*, vol. 24, 1, 2004, pp. 1–37; reprinted in *Justice in Robes*, pp. 140–86.
"The Election and America's Future," *New York Review of Books*, November 4, 2004, (http://www.nybooks.com/articles/archives/2004/nov/04/the-election-and-americas-future/).
"What the Court Really Said," *New York Review of Books*, August 12, 2004, (http://www.nybooks.com/articles/archives/2004/aug/12/what-the-court-really-said/).

2003

"Equality, Luck and Hierarchy," *Philosophy and Public Affairs*, vol. 31, Spring 2003, pp. 190–8.

"Terror and the Attack on Civil Liberties," *New York Review of Books*, November 6, 2003, (http://www.nybooks.com/articles/archives/2003/nov/06/terror-the-attack -on-civil-liberties/).

"The Court and the University: An Exchange," *New York Review of Books*, August 14, 2003, (http://www.nybooks.com/articles/archives/2003/aug/14/the-court-the -university-an-exchange/).

"The Court and the University," *New York Review of Books*, May 15, 2003, (http:// www.nybooks.com/articles/archives/2003/may/15/the-court-and-the-university/).

2002

A Badly Flawed Election: Debating Bush v. Gore, The Supreme Court, and American Democracy (New York Press; distributed by Norton, 2002).

"Sovereign Virtue Revisited," *Ethics: Symposium on Ronald Dworkin's "Sovereign Virtue,"* vol. 113, 2002, pp. 106–43.

"Taking Rights Seriously in Beijing," *New York Review of Books*, September 26, 2002, (http://www.nybooks.com/articles/archives/2002/sep/26/taking-rights-seriously-in -beijing/).

"The Trouble with the Tribunals," *New York Review of Books*, April 25, 2002, (http:// www.nybooks.com/articles/archives/2002/apr/25/the-trouble-with-the-tribunals/).

"The Threat to Patriotism," *New York Review of Books*, February 28, 2002, (http:// www.nybooks.com/articles/archives/2002/feb/28/the-threat-to-patriotism/).

"Thirty Years On," *Harvard Law Review*, vol. 115, 2002, pp. 1655–87; republished in *Justice in Robes*, pp. 187–222.

2001

(co-edited with Mark Lilla and Robert B. Silvers) *The Legacy of Isaiah Berlin* (New York: New York Review of Books, 2001).

"'A Badly Flawed Election': An Exchange," *New York Review of Books*, February 22, 2001, (http://www.nybooks.com/articles/archives/2001/feb/22/a-badly-flawed -election-an-exchange/).

"A Badly Flawed Election," *New York Review of Books*, January 11, 2001, (http:// www.nybooks.com/articles/archives/2001/jan/11/a-badly-flawed-election/).

"Do Values Conflict: A Hedgehog's Approach" (New York University Law School Isaac Marks Memorial Lecture) published in *Arizona Law Review*, vol. 43, p. 251.

2000

Sovereign Virtue: The Theory and Practice of Equality (Cambridge, MA: Harvard University Press, 2000).

"The Phantom Poll Booth," *New York Review of Books*, December 21, 2000, (http:// www.nybooks.com/articles/archives/2000/dec/21/the-phantom-poll-booth/)

"A Question of Ethics," *New York Review of Books*, May 25, 2000, (http://www .nybooks.com/articles/archives/2000/may/25/a-question-of-ethics/).

"'An Affair of State': An Exchange" (reply by Dworkin to an article by Richard Posner), *New York Review of Books*, April 27, 2000, (http://www.nybooks.com/articles/ archives/2000/apr/27/affair-state-exchange/).

"Philosophy and Monica Lewinsky," Review of *An Affair of State: The Investigation, Impeachment, and Trial of President Clinton* by Richard A. Posner and *The Problematics of Moral and Legal Theory* by Richard A. Posner, *New York Review of Books*, March

9, 2000, (http://www.nybooks.com/articles/archives/2000/mar/09/philosophy
-monica-lewinsky/).

1999

"Do Liberty and Equality Conflict?" in Paul Barker (ed.), *Living As Equals* (Oxford: Oxford University Press, 1996), pp. 39–58.

"Free Speech, Politics, and the Dimensions of Democracy," in E. Joshua Rosencrantz (ed.), *If Buckly Fell* (New York: Century Foundation, 1999); reprinted in *Sovereign Virtue*, pp. 351–85.

"Playing God: Genes, Clones and Luck," *Prospect Magazine*, 1999; reprinted in *Sovereign Virtue*, pp. 427–52.

"THE LAW; The Court's Impatience to Execute," *Los Angeles Times*, July 11, 1999.

"The Wounded Constitution," *New York Review of Books*, March 18, 1999, (http://www.nybooks.com/articles/archives/1999/mar/18/the-wounded-constitution/).

"A Kind of Coup," *New York Review of Books*, January 14, 1999, (http://www.nybooks.com/articles/archives/1999/jan/14/a-kind-of-coup/).

1998

"Affirming Affirmative Action," Review of *The Shape of the River: Long-Term Consequences of Considering Race in College and University Admissions* by William G. Bowen and Derek Bok, *New York Review of Books*, October 22, 1998, (http://www.nybooks.com/articles/archives/1998/oct/22/affirming-affirmative-action/); reprinted under the title "Affirmative Action: Does It Work?" in *Sovereign Virtue*, pp. 386–408.

"Darwin's New Bulldog," *Harvard Law Review*, vol. 111, 1998, reprinted in *Justice in Robes*, pp. 75–94.

"Is Affirmative Action Doomed?" *New York Review of Books*, November 5, 1998, (http://www.nybooks.com/articles/archives/1998/nov/05/is-affirmative-action
-doomed/); reprinted under the title "Affirmative Action: Is it Fair?" in *Sovereign Virtue*, pp. 409–52.

1997

"In Praise of Theory," *Arizona State Law Journal*, vol. 29, p. 353.

"Reply," *Arizona State Law Journal*, vol. 29, p. 431.

"Assisted Suicide and Euthanasia: An Exchange," *New York Review of Books*, November 6, 1997, (http://www.nybooks.com/articles/archives/1997/nov/06/assisted
-suicide-and-euthanasia-an-exchange/).

"Assisted Suicide: What the Court Really Said," *New York Review of Books*, September 25, 1997, (http://www.nybooks.com/articles/archives/1997/sep/25/assisted-suicide
-what-the-court-really-said/); revised and published under the title "Sex, Death and the Courts," in *Sovereign Virtue*, pp. 453–74.

"'The Philosophers' Brief': An Exchange," *New York Review of Books*, May 29, 1997, (http://www.nybooks.com/articles/archives/1997/may/29/the-philosophers
-brief-an-exchange/).

(with Thomas Nagel, Robert Nozick, John Rawls, Thomas Scanlon and Judith Jarvis Thomson) "Assisted Suicide: The Philosophers' Brief," *New York Review of Books*, vol. 44, March 27, 1997, (http://www.nybooks.com/articles/archives/1997/mar/27/
assisted-suicide-the-philosophers-brief/).

"Reply by Ronald Dworkin," in Symposium on "Objectivity and Truth: You'd Better Believe It," *BEARS in Moral and Political Philosophy*, posted on 4/9/97, (http://www.brown.edu/Departments/Philosophy/bears/9704dwor.html).

1996

(with Thomas Nagel, Robert Nozick, John Rawls, Thomas Scanlon and Judith Jarvis Thomson) "Brief of Amicus Curiae in Support of Respondents: *Washington v. Glucksberg*, No. 96-110, and *Vacco v. Quill*, No. 95-1858," filed in the United States Supreme Court, Washington, DC, December 10, 1996.

Freedom's Law: The Moral Reading of the American Constitution (Cambridge, MA: Harvard University Press, 1996); (Oxford: Oxford University Press, 1996); (Bridgewater, NJ: Replica Books, 1997).

"Indeterminacy and Law," in Stephen Guest (ed.), *Positivism Today* (Ashgate Publishing Ltd, July 1996), p. 1.

"Objectivity and Truth: You'd Better Believe It," *Philosophy & Public Affairs*, vol. 25, Spring 1996, pp. 87–139.

"Politics, Death, and Nature," *Health Matrix*, vol. 6, pp. 201–18, 1996.

"We Need a New Interpretation of Academic Freedom," in Louis Menand (ed.), *Academic Freedom and Its Future* (Chicago: University of Chicago Press, 1996), published under the title "Why Academic Freedom?" in *Freedom's Law*, pp. 244–60.

"The Curse of American Politics," *New York Review of Books*, October 17, 1996, (http://www.nybooks.com/articles/archives/1996/oct/17/the-curse-of-american-politics/).

"Sex, Death and the Courts," Review of the judicial decisions: *Compassion in Dying v. State of Washington, 79 F. 3d 790, United States Court of Appeals, Ninth Circuit (1996); Quill v. Vacco, 80 F 3d 716, United States Court of Appeals, Second Circuit (1996); Romer v. Evans, 116 S. Ct. 1620, United States Supreme Court (1996)*; published in *New York Review of Books*, August 8, 1996; revised and reprinted in *Sovereign Virtue*, pp. 453–74.

"The Moral Reading of the Constitution," *New York Review of Books*, March 21, 1996, (http://www.nybooks.com/articles/archives/1996/mar/21/the-moral-reading-of-the-constitution/).

1995

Etica Privada e Igualitarismo Politico (Barcelona: Paidos Iberica, 1995).

"Death, Politics and the Sacred," *Case Western Law Review*, 1995.

"The Unbearable Cost of Liberty," *Index on Censorship*, vol. 24, May–June 1995, pp. 43–46.

1994

"Constitutionalism and Democracy," *European Journal of Philosophy: Colloquium on Law and Morality*, vol. 3, 1994.

"Ethik und Pragmatik des zivilen Ungehorsams," in *Widerstands Recht in der Demokratie* (Germany, 1994).

"Gleichheit, Demokratie und die Verfassung," in *Zum Begriff der Verfassung* (Frankfurt am Main: Fisher, 1994).

"A New Map of Censorship," *Index on Censorship*, vol. 23, 1994.

"Mr. Liberty," Review of *Learned Hand: The Man and the Judge* by Gerald Gunther, *New York Review of Books*, August 11, 1994, (http://www.nybooks.com/

articles/archives/1994/aug/11/mr-liberty/); reprinted under the title "Learned Hand," in *Freedom's Law*, pp. 332–47.

"Reply to Paul Ricoeur," *Ratio Juris*, vol. 7, 1994, p. 287.

"Tyranny at the Two Edges of Life: A Liberal View," *New Perspectives Quarterly*, Winter 1994.

"When Is It Right to Die? Doctor-Assisted Suicide for the Terminally Ill," *New York Times*, May 17, 1994; reprinted as Addendum to "Do We Have a Right to Die?" in *Freedom's Law*, pp. 143–6.

"Would Clinton's Plan Be Fair? An Exchange," *New York Review of Books*, May 26, 1994, (http://www.nybooks.com/articles/archives/1994/may/26/would-clintons-plan-be-fair-an-exchange/).

"Pornography: An Exchange," *New York Review of Books*, March 3, 1994, (http://www.nybooks.com/articles/archives/1994/mar/03/pornography-an-exchange/); Dworkin's letter reprinted as Addendum to "MacKinnon's Words," in *Freedom's Law*, pp. 239–43.

"Will Clinton's Plan Be Fair?" *Health Security Act* 103d Congress, 1st Session, *New York Review of Books*, January 13, 1994, (http://www.nybooks.com/articles/archives/1994/jan/13/will-clintons-plan-be-fair/); reprinted under the title "Justice and the High Cost of Health" in *Sovereign Virtue*, pp. 307–19.

1993

Life's Dominion: An Argument About Abortion, Euthanasia and Individual Freedom (New York: Alfred Knopf, 1993).

"Justice in the Distribution of Health Care," *McGill Law Journal*, vol. 38, 1993, pp. 883–98.

"Svobada, Rovnost, a Politost," in *Liberalni Spolecnost* (Prague, 1993).

"Unenumerated Rights: Whether and How *Roe v Wade* Should be Overruled," *University of Chicago Law Review*, vol. 59, 1992, pp. 381–432; reprinted under the title "What the Constitution Says," in *Freedom's Law*, pp. 72–116.

"Women and Pornography," Review of *Only Words* by Catharine A. MacKinnon, *New York Review of Books*, October 21, 1993, (http://www.nybooks.com/articles/archives/1993/oct/21/women-and-pornography/); reprinted under the title "MacKinnon's Words," in *Freedom's Law*, pp. 227–43.

"The Price of Life," *Los Angeles Times*, August 29, 1993.

"THE PRICE OF LIFE; How High the Cost Before It Becomes Too High?" *Los Angeles Times*, August 29, 1993.

"Feminism and Abortion," *New York Review of Books*, June 10, 1993, (http://www.nybooks.com/articles/archives/1993/jun/10/feminism-and-abortion/).

"Life Is Sacred, That's the Easy Part," *New York Times Magazine*, May 16, 1993.

"Not on the Right," *New York Review of Books*, April 8, 1993, (http://www.nybooks.com/articles/archives/1993/apr/08/not-on-the-right/).

1992

"Court of Appeal: The Black Community Speaks Out on the Racial and Sexual Politics of Clarence Thomas *vs* Anita Hill," *New York Times*, October 25, 1992.

"'Free Speech and Its Limits,' by George Brunn, Reply by Ronald Dworkin," *New York Review of Books*, November 19, 1992.

"One Year Later the Debate Goes On," *New York Review of Books*, October 25, 1992, reprinted under the title "Anita Hill and Clarence Thomas," in *Freedom's Law*, pp. 321–31.

"The Center Holds!" *New York Review of Books*, August 13, 1992, (http://www.nybooks.com/articles/archives/1992/aug/13/the-center-holds/); reprinted under the title "Roe Was Saved," in *Freedom's Law*, pp. 117–46.

"The Coming Battles over Free Speech," Review of *Make No Law: The Sullivan Case and the First Amendment* by Anthony Lewis, *New York Review of Books*, June 11, 1992, (http://www.nybooks.com/articles/archives/1992/jun/11/the-coming-battles-over-free-speech/); reprinted under the title "Why Must Speech Be Free?" in *Freedom's Law*, pp. 195–213.

1991

"A Harmful Precedent," *Index on Censorship*, 1991; reprinted under the title "No News Is Bad News for Democracy," in *The Times*, 27 March, 1991, and under the title "A Compelling Case for Censorship?" in the Addendum to "Pornography and Hate," in *Freedom's Law*, pp. 223–26.

"Jurisprudence and Constitutional Law," in Leonard Williams Levy, Kenneth L. Karst and Adam Winkler (eds.), *Encyclopedia of the American Constitution* (New York: Macmillan, 1991).

"La Cour Supreme," *Pouvoirs*, 1991.

"Pragmatism, Right Answers, and True Banality," in Michael Brint and W. Weaver (eds.), *Pragmatism in Law and Society* (Boulder, CO: Westview Press, 1991), p. 359.

"On Gaps in the Law," in P. Amselek and N. MacCormick (eds.), *Controversies About Law's Ontology* (Edinburgh: Edinburgh University Press, 1991).

"Justice for Clarence Thomas," *New York Review of Books*, November 7, 1991, (http://www.nybooks.com/articles/archives/1991/nov/07/justice-for-clarence-thomas/); reprinted under the title "The Thomas Nomination," in *Freedom's Law*, pp. 306–20.

"Liberty and Pornography," *New York Review of Books*, August 15, 1991, (http://www.nybooks.com/articles/archives/1991/aug/15/liberty-and-pornography/); based on "Two Concepts of Liberty," in Edna Ullman-Margalit (ed.), *Isaiah Berlin: A Celebration* (Chicago: University of Chicago Press, 1991).

"Revolution in the Court," *New York Review of Books*, August 15, 1991, (http://www.nybooks.com/articles/archives/1991/aug/15/revolution-in-the-court/).

"The Reagan Revolution and the Supreme Court," Review of *Order and Law: Arguing the Reagan Revolution—A Firsthand Account*, by Charles Fried, *New York Review of Books*, July 18, 1991, (http://www.nybooks.com/articles/archives/1991/jul/18/the-reagan-revolution-and-the-supreme-court/); reprinted under the title "Gag Rule and Affirmative Action," in *Freedom's Law*, pp. 147–62.

"The Right to Death," *New York Review of Books*, March 28, 1991, (http://www.nybooks.com/articles/archives/1991/mar/28/the-right-to-death/).

(with Anthony Smith, Gerald Cohen, Alan Montefiore, Michael Walzer) "The Detention of Sari Nussiebeh," *New York Review of Books*, March 7, 1991, (http://www.nybooks.com/articles/archives/1991/mar/07/the-detention-of-sari-nussiebeh/).

"The Right to Death," *New York Review of Books*, January 31, 1991, (http://www.nybooks.com/articles/archives/1991/jan/31/the-right-to-death/); reprinted under the title "Do We Have a Right to Die?" in *Freedom's Law*, pp. 130–46, Addendum originally published under the title "When Is It Right to Die?" *New York Times*, May 17, 1994.

1990

A Bill of Rights for Britain: Why British Liberty Needs Protecting (London: Chatto & Windus, 1990), the basis of "Does Britain Need a Bill of Rights," in *Freedom's Law*, pp. 352–72.

"Bork's Jurisprudence," *University of Chicago Law Review*, vol. 57, 1990; reprinted under the title "Bork's Own Postmortem," in *Freedom's Law*, pp. 287–305.

"Equality, Democracy, and Constitution: We the People in Court," *Alberta Law Review*, vol. 28, 1990, p. 324.

"Foundations of Liberal Equality," in G. B. Petersen (ed.), *The Tanner Lectures on Human Values*, vol. XI (Salt Lake City: University of Utah Press, 1990); reprinted in S. Darwall (ed.), *Equal Freedom* (Ann Arbor: University of Michigan Press, 1995), pp. 190–206; revised and reprinted in *Sovereign Virtue*, pp. 237–84.

"Posner's Charges: What I Actually Said," (http://article.chinalawinfo.com/ArticleHtml/Article_19649.asp), 1990.

"Taking Rights Seriously in the Abortion Case," *Ratio Juris*, 1990, p. 68.

"The Tempting of America: The Political Seduction of the Law," *University of Chicago Law Review*, vol. 57, 1990, p. 479.

1989

"The Future of Abortion," *New York Review of Books*, September 28, 1989, (http://www.nybooks.com/articles/archives/1989/sep/28/the-future-of-abortion/); reprinted under the title "Verdict Postponed," in *Freedom's Law*, pp. 60–71.

"The Great Abortion Case," *New York Review of Books*, June 29, 1989, (http://www.nybooks.com/articles/archives/1989/jun/29/the-great-abortion-case/); reprinted under the title "*Roe* in Danger," in *Freedom's Law*, pp. 44–59.

"Liberal Community," *California Law Review*, vol. 77, 1989, pp. 479–504; reprinted in *Sovereign Virtue*, pp. 211–36.

1988

"Devaluing Liberty," *Index on Censorship*, vol. 17, 1988.

"Ethical Theory: Character and Virtue," *Midwest Studies in Philosophy: Special Issue*, vol. 12, 1988.

"What Is Equality?—Part 3: The Place of Liberty," *Iowa Law Review*, vol. 73, 1988, pp. 1–54; reprinted in *Sovereign Virtue*, pp. 120–83.

"The New England," October 27, 1988, *New York Review of Books*, (http://www.nybooks.com/articles/archives/1988/oct/27/the-new-england/).

1987

"Legal Theory and the Problem of Sense," in R. Gavison (ed.), *Issues in Contemporary Legal Philosophy: The Influence of HLA Hart* (Oxford: Oxford University Press, 1987).

"Philosophical issues concerning the rights of patients suffering serious permanent dementia," prepared for the Office of Technology Assessment, Congress of the United States (Washington, DC: Government Printing Office, 1987).

"From Bork to Kennedy," *New York Review of Books*, December 17, 1987, (http://www.nybooks.com/articles/archives/1987/dec/17/from-bork-to-kennedy/); reprinted under the title "What Bork's Defeat Meant," in *Freedom's Law*, pp. 276–86.

"'Reckless Disregard': An Exchange," *New York Review of Books*, September 24, 1987, (http://www.nybooks.com/articles/archives/1987/sep/24/reckless-disregard -an-exchange/).

"'The Bork Nomination' by Nathan P. Glazer, Reply by Ronald Dworkin," *New York Review of Books*, November 5, 1987, (http://www.nybooks.com/articles/archives/1987/ nov/05/the-bork-nomination/).

"'The Bork Nomination': An Exchange," *New York Review of Books*, October 8, 1987, (http://www.nybooks.com/articles/archives/1987/oct/08/the-bork-nomination -an-exchange/).

"'Reckless Disregard': An Exchange," *New York Review of Books*, September 24, 1987, (http://www.nybooks.com/articles/archives/1987/sep/24/reckless-disregard -an-exchange/).

"The Bork Nomination," *New York Review of Books*, August 13, 1987, (http://www .nybooks.com/articles/archives/1987/aug/13/the-bork-nomination/); reprinted in the *Cardozo Law Review*, vol. 9, 1987, p. 101; and appears under the title "Bork: The Senate's Responsibility," in *Freedom's Law*, pp. 265–75.

"Time's Rewrite," *New York Review of Books*, April 9, 1987, (http://www.nybooks. com/articles/archives/1987/apr/09/times-rewrite/).

"Time's Settlement," *New York Review of Books*, March 12, 1987, (http://www .nybooks.com/articles/archives/1987/mar/12/times-settlement/).

"The Press on Trial," Review of *Reckless Disregard: Westmoreland v. CBS et al.; Sharon v Time* by Renata Adler, *New York Review of Books*, February 26, 1987, (http:// www.nybooks.com/articles/archives/1987/feb/26/the-press-on-trial/); reprinted in *Freedom's Law*, pp. 167–94.

"What Is Equality?—Part 4: Political Equality," *University of San Francisco Law Review*, vol. 22, 1987, pp. 1–30; reprinted in *Sovereign Virtue*, pp. 184–210.

1986

Introduction to *Nunca Más: The Report of the Argentine National Commission on the Disappeared* (by Elias Canetti), (New York: Farrar, Strauss, and Giroux, 1986).

"A New Link in the Chain," *University of California Law Review*, vol. 74, 1986, p. 103.

Law's Empire (Cambridge, MA: Belknap Press, 1986).

"Report from Hell," *New York Review of Books*, July 17, 1986, (http://www.nybooks .com/articles/archives/1986/jul/17/report-from-hell/).

1985

A Matter of Principle (Cambridge, MA: Harvard University Press, 1985).

"Art as Public Good," *Art and the Law*, vol. 9, 1985, p. 143.

"Law's Ambition for Itself," *Vanderbilt Law Review*, vol. 71, 1985, p. 173.

"The High Cost of Virtue," Review of *Morality and Conflict* by Stuart Hampshire, *New York Review of Books*, October 24, 1985, (http://www.nybooks.com/articles/ archives/1985/oct/24/the-high-cost-of-virtue/).

"Reagan's Justice: An Exchange," *New York Review of Books*, February 14, 1985, (http://www.nybooks.com/articles/archives/1985/feb/14/reagans-justice-an-exchange/).

1984

"A Reply to Critics," in Marshall Cohen (ed.), *Ronald Dworkin and Contemporary Jurisprudence* (Totowa, NJ: Rowman and Allanheld, 1984; London: Duckworth).

"Reagan's Justice," *New York Review of Books*, November 8, 1984, (http://www
.nybooks.com/articles/archives/1984/nov/08/reagans-justice/).

1983

"Civil Disobedience and Nuclear Protests," talk delivered in Bonn, September
1983; adapted and published in *A Matter of Principle*, pp. 104–16.

"In Defence of Equality," *Social Philosophy and Policy*, 1983, pp. 24–40.

"'Spheres of Justice': An Exchange," *New York Review of Books*, July 21, 1983, (http://
www.nybooks.com/articles/archives/1983/jul/21/spheres-of-justice-an-exchange/).

"Equality First," *New York Review of Books*, May 12, 1983, (http://www.nybooks.com/
articles/archives/1983/may/12/equality-first/).

"To Each His Own," Review of *Spheres of Justice: A Defence of Pluralism and Equality*
by Michael Walzer, *New York Review of Books*, April 14, 1983, (http://www.nybooks
.com/articles/archives/1983/apr/14/to-each-his-own/); reprinted under the title "What
Justice Isn't," in *A Matter of Principle*, pp. 214–20.

"Why Liberals Should Believe in Equality," *New York Review of Books*, February 3,
1983, (http://www.nybooks.com/articles/archives/1983/feb/03/why-liberals-should
-believe-in-equality/); reprinted under the title "Why Liberals Should Care About
Equality," in *A Matter of Principle*, pp. 205–13.

"What Liberalism Isn't," Review of *Social Justice in the Liberal State* by Bruce A.
Ackerman, *New York Review of Books*, January 20, 1983, (http://www.nybooks.com/
articles/archives/1983/jan/20/what-liberalism-isnt/).

1982

"Law as Interpretation," *Texas Law Review*, vol. 60, March 1982; revised under the
title "Natural Law Revisited," *University of Florida Law Review*, vol. 34, 1982, p. 165.

"Please Don't Talk About Objectivity Any More," *Critical Inquiry*, vol. 9, 1982,
pp. 179–200; published by W. J. T. Mitchell (ed.), in *The Politics of Interpretation* (Chicago
and London: University of Chicago Press, 1983); forms the basis of "Interpretation
and Objectivity," in *A Matter of Principle*, pp. 72–103.

1981

"Do We Have a Right to Pornography?" *Oxford Journal of Legal Studies*, vol. 1,
Summer 1981, pp. 177–212; reprinted in *A Matter of Principle*, pp. 335–72; and under
the title "Rights as Trumps," in J. Waldron (ed.), *Theories of Rights* (Oxford: Oxford
University Press, 1984), pp. 153–67.

"Principle, Policy, Procedure," in *Crime, Proof and Punishment: Essays in Memory
of Sir Rupert Cross* (London and Boston: Butterworths, 1981), p. 193; reprinted in *A
Matter of Principle*, pp. 72–103.

"The Forum of Principle," *New York University Law Review*, vol. 56, May–June
1981; reprinted in *A Matter of Principle*, pp. 33–71.

"What Is Equality?—Part 2: Equality of Resources," *Philosophy and Public Affairs*,
vol. 10, 1981, pp. 283–345; reprinted in *Sovereign Virtue*, pp. 65–119.

"What Is Equality?—Part 1: Equality of Welfare," *Philosophy and Public Affairs*,
vol. 10, 1981, pp. 185–246; reprinted in *Sovereign Virtue*, pp. 11–64.

"An Exchange on William O. Douglas," *New York Review of Books*, May 28, 1981,
(http://www.nybooks.com/articles/archives/1981/may/28/an-exchange-on-william
-o-douglas/).

"Dissent on Douglas," Review of *Independent Journey: The Life of William O. Douglas* by James F. Simon and *The Court Years, 1939 to 1975: The Autobiography of William O. Douglas* by William O. Douglas, *New York Review of Books*, February 19, 1981, (http://www.nybooks.com/articles/archives/1981/feb/19/dissent-on-douglas/).

1980

"Is Wealth a Value?" *Journal of Legal Studies*, vol. 9, 1980, pp. 191–226; reprinted in *A Matter of Principle*, pp. 237–66.

"Why Efficiency?" *Hofstra Law Review*, vol. 8, 1980, pp. 563–90; reprinted in *A Matter of Principle*, pp. 267–92.

"Is the Press Losing the First Amendment?" *New York Review of Books*, December 4, 1980; reprinted in *A Matter of Principle*, pp. 381–97, (http://www.nybooks.com/articles/archives/1980/dec/04/is-the-press-losing-the-first-amendment/).

"How to Read the Civil Rights Act: An Exchange," *New York Review of Books*, May 15, 1980, (http://www.nybooks.com/articles/archives/1980/may/15/how-to-read-the-civil-rights-act-an-exchange/).

1979

"How to Read the Civil Rights Act," December 20, 1979, (http://www.nybooks.com/articles/archives/1979/dec/20/how-to-read-the-civil-rights-act/); reprinted in *A Matter of Principle*, pp. 316–34.

"Some Views of Mrs. Thatcher's Victory," *New York Review of Books*, June 28, 1979, (http://www.nybooks.com/articles/archives/1979/jun/28/some-views-of-mrs-thatchers-victory/).

"Three Concepts of Liberalism," *New Republic*, April 14, 1979, pp. 41–49.

1978

"Is Law a System of Rules?" in R. Dworkin (ed.), *The Philosophy of Law*; also appears as chs. 2 and 4 of *Taking Rights Seriously*, pp. 1–13.

"Liberalism," in S. Hampshire (ed.), *Public, Private Morality* (Cambridge, U.K.: Cambridge University Press, 1978), pp. 113–43; reprinted in *A Matter of Principle*, pp. 181–204.

"Political Judges and the Rule of Law," *Proceedings of the British Academy*, vol. 64, 1978; reprinted in *A Matter of Principle*, pp. 9–32.

"The Rights of M. A. Farber: An Exchange," *New York Review of Books*, December 7, 1978, (http://www.nybooks.com/articles/archives/1978/dec/07/the-rights-of-ma-farber-an-exchange/).

"The Rights of Myron Farber," *New York Review of Books*, October 26, 1978, (http://www.nybooks.com/articles/archives/1978/oct/26/the-rights-of-myron-farber/); reprinted under the title "The Farber Case: Reporters and Informers," in *A Matter of Principle*, pp. 373–80.

"Soulcraft," Review of *The Pursuit of Happiness, and Other Sobering Thoughts* by George F. Will, *New York Review of Books*, October 12, 1978, (http://www.nybooks.com/articles/archives/1978/oct/12/soulcraft/).

"Begging the Bakke Question," *New York Review of Books*, September 28, 1978, Reply to Paul Vogt (http://www.nybooks.com/articles/archives/1978/sep/28/begging-the-bakke-question-2/).

"The Bakke Decision: Did It Decide Anything?" *New York Review of Books*, August 17, 1978, (http://www.nybooks.com/articles/archives/1978/aug/17/the-bakke-decision -did-it-decide-anything/); reprinted under the title "What Did Bakke Really Decide?" in *A Matter of Principle*, pp. 304–315.

"The Bakke Case: An Exchange," *New York Review of Books*, January 26, 1978, (http://www.nybooks.com/articles/archives/1978/jan/26/the-bakke-case-an-exchange/).

1977

Taking Rights Seriously (London: Duckworth, 1977); rev. ed. includes "Reply to Critics" (Cambridge, MA: Harvard University Press, 1978; Duckworth, 1981).

(ed. with Introduction) *The Philosophy of Law* (London and New York: OUP paperback series, 1977).

"No Right Answer?" in P. M. S. Hacker and J. Raz (eds.), *Law, Morality and Society: Essays in Honour of H. L. A. Hart* (Oxford: Oxford University Press, 1977), pp. 58–84; revised and reprinted in *New York University Law Review*, vol. 53, 1978; reprinted under the title "Is There Really No Right Answer in Hard Cases?" in *A Matter of Principle*, pp. 119–45.

"DeFunis v. Sweatt," in Marshall Cohen, Thomas Nagel, and Thomas Scanlon (eds.), *Equality and Preferential Treatment* (Princeton, NJ: Princeton University Press, 1977).

"Seven Critics," *University of Georgia Law Review*, vol. 11, 1977, p. 1201.

"Social Sciences and Constitutional Rights," *Educational Forum*, vol. XLI, 1977, p. 271

"Why Bakke Has No Case," *New York Review of Books*, November 10, 1977, (http://www.nybooks.com/articles/archives/1977/nov/10/why-bakke-has-no-case/); reprinted under the title "Bakke's Case: Are Quotas Unfair?" in *A Matter of Principle*, pp. 293–30.

1976

"The DeFunis Case: An Exchange," *New York Review of Books*, July 15, 1976, (http://www.nybooks.com/articles/archives/1976/jul/15/the-defunis-case-an-exchange/).

"The DeFunis Case: The Right to Go to Law School," Review of *DeFunis versus Odegaard and the University of Washington: The University Admissions Case, The Record*, edited by Ann Fagan Ginger, published in *New York Review of Books*, vol. 23, February 5, 1976, (http://www.nybooks.com/articles/archives/1976/feb/05/the-defunis-case-the -right-to-go-to-law-school/); review revised and reprinted under the title "Reverse Discrimination," in *Taking Rights Seriously*, pp. 223–39.

1975

"Hard Cases," *Harvard Law Review*, vol. 88, 1975; revised and reprinted in *Taking Rights Seriously*, pp. 81–130.

1974

"Did Mill Go Too Far?" Review of *On Liberty and Liberalism: The Case of John Stuart Mill* by Gertrude Himmelfarb, *New York Review of Books*, October 31, 1974, (http://www.nybooks.com/articles/archives/1974/oct/31/did-mill-go-too-far/); revised and reprinted under the title "Liberty and Liberalism," in *Taking Rights Seriously*, pp. 259-65.

1973

"The Original Position" 40 *U. Chi. L. Rev.* 500 (1973), reprinted under the title "Justice and Rights," in *Taking Rights Seriously*, pp. 150–83.

1972

"A Special Supplement: The Jurisprudence of Richard Nixon," *New York Review of Books*, May 4, 1972, (http://www.nybooks.com/articles/archives/1972/may/04/a-special-supplement-the-jurisprudence-of-richard-/); reprinted under the title "Constitutional Cases," in *Taking Rights Seriously*, pp. 131–49.

"Social Rules and Legal Theory," *Yale Law Journal*, vol. 81, 1972, p. 855; reprinted under the title "The Model of Rules II," in *Taking Rights Seriously*, pp. 46–80.

1971

"Rights and Interests," *New York Review of Books*, March 11, 1971, (http://www.nybooks.com/articles/archives/1971/mar/11/rights-and-interests/).

1970

"A Special Supplement: Taking Rights Seriously," *New York Review of Books*, December 17, 1970, (http://www.nybooks.com/articles/archives/1970/dec/17/a-special-supplement-taking-rights-seriously/); reprinted as ch. 7 of *Taking Rights Seriously*, pp. 184–205.

"Comments on the Unity of Law Doctrine (A Response)," in *Ethics and Social Justice*, Howard E. Kiefer and Milton K. Munitz (eds.), (Albany, State University of New York Press, 1970), p. 171 (available on Google Books at http://books.google.com/books?printsec=frontcover&vid=ISBN873950542#v=onepage&q&f).

"A Theory of Civil Disobedience," in *Ethics and Social Justice*, Howard E. Kiefer and Milton K. Munitz (eds.), (Albany, State University of New York Press, 1970), p. 225 (available on Google Books at http://books.google.com/books?printsec=frontcover&vid=ISBN873950542#v=onepage&q&f).

1969

"Morality and the Law," Review of *Punishment and Responsibility: Essays in the Philosophy of Law* by H. L. A. Hart, *New York Review of Books*, May 22, 1969, (http://www.nybooks.com/articles/archives/1969/may/22/morality-and-the-law/); reprinted under the title "Jurisprudence" in *Taking Rights Seriously*, pp. 1–13.

1968

"On Not Prosecuting Civil Disobedience," *New York Review of Books*, June 6, 1968, (http://www.nybooks.com/articles/archives/1968/jun/06/on-not-prosecuting-civil-disobedience/); revised and reprinted under the title "Civil Disobedience," in *Taking Rights Seriously*, pp. 206–22.

"There Oughta Be a Law," Review of *The Lawyers*, by Martin Mayer, *New York Review of Books*, March 14, 1968, (http://www.nybooks.com/articles/archives/1968/mar/14/there-oughta-be-a-law/).

1967

"The Case for Law—A Critique," *Valparaiso Law Review*, vol. 1, 1967, p. 215.

"The Model of Rules," *University of Chicago Law Review*, vol. 35, 1967, p. 14; reprinted under the title "Is Law a System of Rules?" in R. Summers (ed.), *Essays in Legal Philosophy* (Oxford: Blackwell, 1968), p. 25; and as "The Model of Rules I," in *Taking Rights Seriously*, pp. 14–46; and in R. Dworkin (ed.), *The Philosophy of Law*, p. 38.

1966

"Lord Devlin and the Enforcement of Morals," *Yale Law Journal*, vol. 75, 1966, p. 986; reprinted under the title "Liberty and Moralism," in *Taking Rights Seriously*, pp. 240–58; and in R. Wasserstrom (ed.), *Morality and the Law* (Belmont, CA: Wadsworth, 1971), p. 55.

1963–1965

"Does Law Have a Function? A Comment on the Two-Level Theory of Decision," *Yale Law Journal*, vol. 74, 1965, p. 640; retitled from "Wasserstrom, 'The Judicial Decision'," *Ethics*, vol. 75, 1964, p. 47.

"Judicial Discretion," *Journal of Philosophy*, vol. 60, 1963.

"Philosophy, Morality and Law—Observations Prompted by Professor Fuller's Novel Claim," *Ethics*, vol. 13, 1965, p. 47.

"The Elusive Morality of Law," *Vanderbilt Law Review*, vol. 10, 1965, p. 631; shortened version of "Philosophy, Morality and Law—Observations Prompted by Professor Fuller's Novel Claim."

VIDEOS

Dworkin's two-minute summary of the central focus of *Justice for Hedgehogs*, http://www.law.nyu.edu/faculty/facultyvideos/index.htm (2011).

Presentation held at the Central European University "Ronald Dworkin in Budapest," available at: http://vimeo.com/19803304 (January 27, 2011).

Lecture at Harvard University on "Truth in Interpretation" (with T. M. Scanlon and Martha Minow), available at: http://www.ovguide.com/video/dworkin-at-harvard -922ca39ce10036ba0e11a2a204f9e06d (December 2010).

Inaugural Frederic R. and Molly S. Kellogg Biennial Lecture on Jurisprudence in the Coolidge Auditorium of the Library of Congress, available at: http://www .youtube.com/watch?v=742JyiqLhuk (December 17, 2009).

"*Justice for Hedgehogs*: A Conference on Ronald Dworkin's Forthcoming Book," many links available at: http://www.bu.edu/law/events/audio-video/hedgehogs. shtml (September 25–26 2009).

E. N. Thompson Forum on World History, "Democracy and Religion: America and Israel," http://www.youtube.com/watch?v=AU9kUlY-xUY (September 14, 2009).

The Tenth Lecture of "A Series of Special Lectures by Distinguished Scholars," *Human Rights, Justice and Equality—The Unity of Value*, Lecture 2. "Do People Have a Human Right to Equality?" hosted by Korea Academic Research Council, available at: http://www.youtube.com/watch?v=5sVCgUDzbho (November 21, 2008).

"Can We Disagree About Law or Morals?" New York Institute of Philosophy (NYU), available at: http://www.thirteen.org/forum/topics/can-we-disagree-about -law-or-morals/14/ (November 13, 2007).

Holberg International Memorial Prize award ceremony speech, available at: http://video.google.com/videoplay?docid=5578670885909370583# (2007).

Holberg Prize Symposium, Dworkin's talk "Law and Political Morality," available at: http://video.google.com/videoplay?docid=5473594255273113558#docid=-8182465071522193147 (2007).t

PODCASTS

Laurie discusses *Justice for Hedgehogs* with Ronald Dworkin and A. C. Grayling, BBC, "Thinking Allowed" Radio 4 Programme, available online at: http://www.bbc.co.uk/programmes/b00xw157 and http://www.bbc.co.uk/iplayer/console/b00xw15726 (January 2011).

New York Review of Books, "The Consequences to Come" on the 2008 U.S. presidential elections, available at: http://www.nybooks.com/podcasts/events/2008/sep/24/consequences-come/ (14 September 2008).

Jurists: Profiles in Legal Theory

GENERAL EDITOR

William Twining

Martin Krygier, *Philip Selznick: Ideals in the World*

Hugh Baxter, *Habermas: The Discourse Theory of Law and Democracy*

Thomas Garden Barnes, edited and with an introduction by Allen D. Boyer, *Shaping the Common Law: From Glanvill to Hale, 1188–1688*

William E. Conklin, *Hegel's Laws: The Legitimacy of a Modern Legal Order*

Neil MacCormick, *H.L.A. Hart*, Second Edition

Wouter de Been, *Legal Realism Regained: Saving Realism from Critical Acclaim*

John Dinwiddy, edited by William Twining, *Bentham: Selected Writings of John Dinwiddy*

Allen D. Boyer, *Sir Edward Coke and the Elizabethan Age*

Colin Imber, *Ebu's-su'ud: The Islamic Legal Tradition*

Robert W. Gordon, ed., *The Legacy of Oliver Wendell Holmes, Jr.*